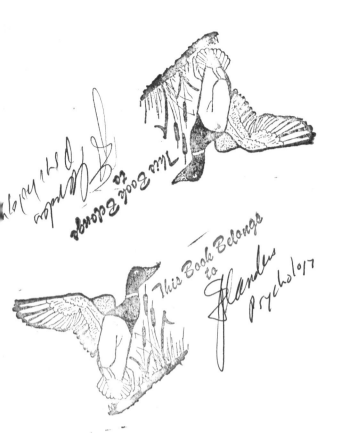

This Book Belongs
to
Flanders
Psychol/17

Y0-BRA-958

The

99

Best
Residential

Recreational
Communities
in America

The
99
Best
Residential

&

Recreational
Communities
in America

For

Vacation,
Retirement

&

Investment
Planning

Lester J. Giese, PCAM
L. Anne Thornton
William Kinnaman

John Wiley & Sons, Inc.
New York • Chichester • Brisbane
Toronto • Singapore

In recognition of the importance of preserving what has
been written, it is a policy of John Wiley & Sons, Inc.
to have books of enduring value published in the United
States printed on acid-free paper, and we exert our best
efforts to that end.

Copyright © 1992 by John Wiley & Sons, Inc.
All rights reserved. Published simultaneously in Canada.

Reproduction or translation of any part of this work
beyond that permitted by Section 107 or 108 of the
1976 United States Copyright Act without the permission
of the copyright owner is unlawful. Requests for
permission or further information should be addressed to
the Permissions Department, John Wiley & Sons, Inc.

This publication is designed to provide accurate and
authoritative information in regard to the subject
matter covered. It is sold with the understanding that
the publisher is not engaged in rendering legal, accounting,
or other professional service. If legal advice or other
expert assistance is required, the services of a competent
professional person should be sought. *From a Declaration
of Principles jointly adopted by a Committee of the
American Bar Association and a Committee of Publishers.*

Library of Congress Cataloging-in-Publication Data

Giese, Lester J., 1947–
    The 99 best residential & recreational communities in
  America: for vacation, retirement, and investment planning/by
  Lester J. Giese, L. Anne Thornton, William Kinnaman.
    p. cm.
    Includes bibliographical references.
    ISBN 0-471-54577-5 (cloth) – ISBN 0-471-54578-3 (paper)
    1. Planned communities–United States–Directories.
  2. Condominiums–United States–Directories. 3. Resorts–United
  States–Directories. 4. Retirement communities–United States-
  -Directories. 5. Life care communities–United States–Directories.
  6. Vacation homes–United States–Directories. I. Thornton, L.
  Anne, 1953–   . II. Kinnaman, William, 1922–   . III. Title.
  IV. Title: Ninety-nine best residential & recreational
  communities in America. V. Title: 99 best residential and
  recreational communities in America.
  MT169.57.U6G54   1991
  307.76'8–dc20   91-4756

Printed in the United States of America

10 9 8 7 6 5 4 3 2 1

We dedicate this book to all seekers of the "good life."
May you find your own heaven on earth . . .
We know you can find it in a planned community . . .

Acknowledgments

Our thanks go to the many people and organizations who helped make this book possible. Special thanks to the entire staff at Condo Management Maintenance Corp. for their support and their willingness to take over so many of the day-to-day duties of running the company while we wrote page after page after page.

Special thanks to Ken Nakari, Professional Community Association Manager of Evergreen, Colorado. Ken, you are a dedicated professional in the field of community association management, and you helped us tremendously with your insights and knowledge.

We would also like to thank the Community Associations Institute, a group of 10,000 professionals and volunteers who help to make living in a planned community a rewarding and stimulating experience.

Finally, and most importantly, thanks to Audra, T. J., and Ginny. We missed being with you so much during the entire writing process of this book...but we're proud of what we accomplished and hope you are, too. The many hours you spent without us will not be forgotten.

LESTER J. GIESE, PCAM
L. ANNE THORNTON
WILLIAM KINNAMAN

Preface

It's a good bet that you or a member of your close family will buy into or live in a private planned community within the next five years. Recent research conducted by the Community Associations Institute (CAI), an industry professional association, revealed that one out of every eight Americans was living in a planned community in 1988. That proportion is growing. Approximately one-fifth of the total housing units sold each year are condominiums; some predict that this proportion will reach 50 percent by the turn of the century.

All planned communities are private, by definition, because the homes, common grounds, and recreational facilities are for the exclusive use and enjoyment of the owners and guests. However, the extent of the privacy varies, as you will see in the descriptions of our "99 best."

Planned communities come in all shapes, sizes, names, legal entities, lifestyles, privacy levels, personalities, and physical appearances. The communities that have made our "99 best" list are large (generally over 500 homes) master planned communities that offer a variety of social activities, recreational opportunities, housing options, and maybe even commercial and retail centers. Our "99 best" represent 263,916 units/homes sold as of January 31, 1991, spread across 26 states and every region of the country. At final build-out for all of the 99 communities listed here, there will be a total of 474,743 units/homes.

Remember, though, that large is not always better—some communities of less than 100 homes made the "99 best" list; they did so because of their uniqueness.

There are many social and lifestyle benefits that make these private communities feel like an extended family—a pleasant situation for those who wish and need these ties. Beyond the tangible values, private planned community living often provides more time for family, business, friends, travel, neighbors, or recreation. Best of all, you are usually surrounded by a compatible group of like-minded people. Planned communities, taken together, have something for everybody. However, just as with a marriage, you, the prospective buyer, must make sure the planned community is compatible with your lifestyle and expectations before the marriage vows (signatures on the contract) are exchanged. This book lists 99 of the most eligible "companions" and provides assistance to help you make your best selection.

The first-time buyer often finds that condominiums are the only units that are affordable. The busy professional, with less concern about cost, appreciates the time saved by the yard and maintenance services and the convenience of nearby recreational facilities. The vacation planner finds a way to continue visiting a favorite area without spending a fortune on hotel and restaurant costs. The mature professional finds a second home with potential as either a rental property or a place to play and work. Empty-nesters scaling down their bedroom, storage, and garage needs gravitate toward a home with lower taxes and less maintenance expense. The retiree appreciates an economical place to spend more time with peers in recreation and social activities. Those having concerns about care in their old age look for places that can provide for both active living and medical needs.

Beyond special buying interests, almost everyone benefits from the special attributes of a private planned community. These include increased safety because of a planned, separated location; increased accessibility of most planned locations; better services and amenities; generally better "curb appeal" resulting from uniform architecture and attention to maintenance; rules and regulations that match lifestyles; opportunities for social interaction; and a positive environmental impact on land use by virtue of being a private planned community.

Contents

Chapter 1

Defining Planned Communities

Like the elephant described by blind men, planned communities can be contemplated from many different vantage points. They have a variety of legal, lifestyle, recreational, and social characteristics. There are no fast and firm boundaries separating "planned" communities from all the rest. Planning, for the purposes of the kinds of communities we're talking about, generally involves architecture, construction, service, rules about sharing and using common areas, community government, use of amenities, and social interactions that are available to members; in other words, planning extends beyond just physical layout.

In general, planned communities are part of a larger universe called *community associations*. A community association consists of two separate parts: (1) a purchase of real estate and (2) mandatory membership in the association. Upon sale of the real estate, membership in the association is terminated.

Community associations offer condominium, cooperative, and single-family home ownership options. Community associations can also be many things: converted apartment buildings, subdivisions, multi-family attached houses, high-rise buildings, small (as few as two housing units), large (over 30,000 housing units), tiered (master association with a number of neighborhood associations), and master planned communities (including commercial and retail buildings).

We will provide you with a general view of community associations, and, in particular, how they apply to our 99 best planned communities. You may choose to live in one of our "best," but then again you may find your own *best*. In any case, you will be a knowledgeable consumer.

LEGAL CHARACTERISTICS

Most, but not all, of the planned communities offer condominium ownership. The buyer obtains two bundles in his or her purchase package—the exclusive ownership of a housing *unit* (home) and an *undivided* interest in the *common* areas. *Undivided* means that the interest cannot be used or sold separately. It must be shared with other owners.

The legal documents that created the association define the boundaries of the unit and the boundaries of the common areas. Each owner enjoys the exclusive use of his or her unit in fee simple ownership and shares in the common property as defined in the community documents. In fact, each owner owns a percentage of the entire complex. The community documents define ownership percentages that the owner of each specific unit is entitled to and responsible for. The sum of all ownership percentages is 100 percent. The association generally does not hold title to any property. Figure 1.1 shows who owns title to what in a community association.

Ownership type \ Property type	Unit (home)	Common areas
Condominium	Home owner	Home owner
HOA or POA	Home owner	Association

Figure 1.1
Who Holds Title to What?

Homeowners' associations (HOA) and property owners' associations (POA) are other legal variations of community associations. They are a bit more conventional in that owners own the house and/or lot exclusively. The community association owns the common areas, and each lot/house owner is a mandatory member of the community association. Maintenance and landscape services of the individual home units may or may not be provided by the association. Owners of lots and homes enjoy the common areas of the development as defined in the association documents.

Many of the communities described in this book offer a combination of ownerships and are usually referred to as *master planned communities*. The driving force behind these types of communities lies in their master plan. Land use has been extensively and carefully planned. Percentages for residential, commercial, retail, green space, and recreational uses are all identified in the initial planning stages. This approach to land use usually ensures that property values are maintained and that a balanced community is achieved.

A good example of thoughtful planning is the Foothills at South Mountain Park in Phoenix, Arizona. Colors, styles, landscaping, and lighting are coordinated to blend with the desert environment. The developers have paid special attention to water use—the most valuable resource in a desert environment. All landscaping utilizes native and drought-tolerant vegetation to help reduce the demand of water. They even use run-off water to help irrigate the golf course.

Master planned communities are usually quite large and have separate neighborhood community associations throughout the overall community. These smaller *neighborhood associations* govern and maintain their particular area within the entire community. The *master,* or *umbrella, association* oversees operations of all areas common to all neighborhoods, such as main roads, recreational facilities, and perimeter access gates.

When you buy into a master planned community, your purchase actually makes you a mandatory member of two associations: the neighborhood association (where your home is located) and the master association. Indigo Lakes in Daytona Beach is an example of a neighborhood and master association structure. Figure 1.2 gives a visual interpretation of Indigo Lakes. Each neighborhood (Pebble Creek, Eastpointe, Muirfield Estate, and so on) is a separate community association and is responsible for the common areas within its own boundaries. A master association oversees the common areas that are common to all neighborhoods.

Every planned community has its own set of documents that define the responsibilities and benefits of the owner and the responsibilities of the community as a whole. These documents are usually written for the developers by attorneys and are quite different for each community, but they generally cover the same areas of concern. The documents can be very confusing and contain a lot of legalese; however, they are very important to your pleasure and your pocketbook. It will pay to understand them.

Both master and neighborhood associations are governed according to their charter documents:

- Covenants, conditions, and restrictions (CC&R)
- Master deed
- Bylaws
- Articles of incorporation
- Public offering statement (POS)

The documents have six purposes:

1. To provide a *description* defining who owns what
2. To establish a set of *restrictions* that binds all owners
3. To establish protective covenants or *standards* for all owners to abide by
4. To create *administrative* procedures to operate the daily affairs of the community
5. To provide *financial* means to allow funding of community responsibilities
6. To establish a *transition* process by which the developer transfers control of the community to the owners

All documents contain a process whereby a community may amend its documents to match the desires and expectations of its members. This can happen often, especially in a mature community. Once a community becomes fully populated, the residents may have a different vision than the original developer of what their community should be. It is not unusual for a community to change, add, or delete regulations. In effect, living in a planned community adds another layer of government below the local municipality.

A GUIDE TO INDIGO LAKES

1 GOLF COURSE VILLAS
A Augusta Circle
B Sea Island Circle
C Pinehurst Circle
D Dunes Circle
E Meadowbrook Circle
F Spyglass Circle

3 SINGLE FAMILY HOMES
A Peachtree Circle
B Fernwood Circle
C Cedarcrest Circle
D Pine Needle Circle
E Point-O' Woods Drive
F Sweetwater Oak Lane

4 INDIGO PINES
COURTYARD PATIO HOMES
A Crooked Stick Drive
B Bob O'Link Circle
C Fiddlesticks Circle
D Wing Foot Circle
E Firestone Court
F Bardmoor Circle
G Shoal Creek Circle
H Innisbrook Circle

2 EGRET'S LANDING
A Fox Fire Circle
B Sawgrass Circle
C Sea Pines Circle

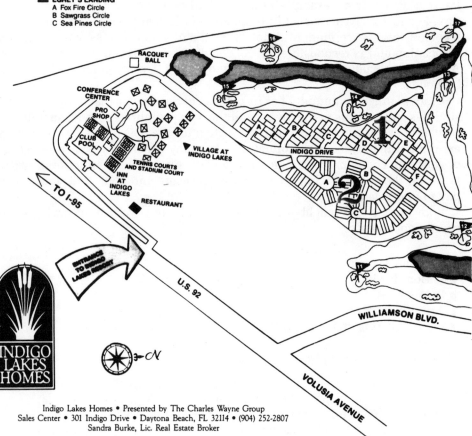

Indigo Lakes Homes • Presented by The Charles Wayne Group
Sales Center • 301 Indigo Drive • Daytona Beach, FL 32114 • (904) 252-2807
Sandra Burke, Lic. Real Estate Broker

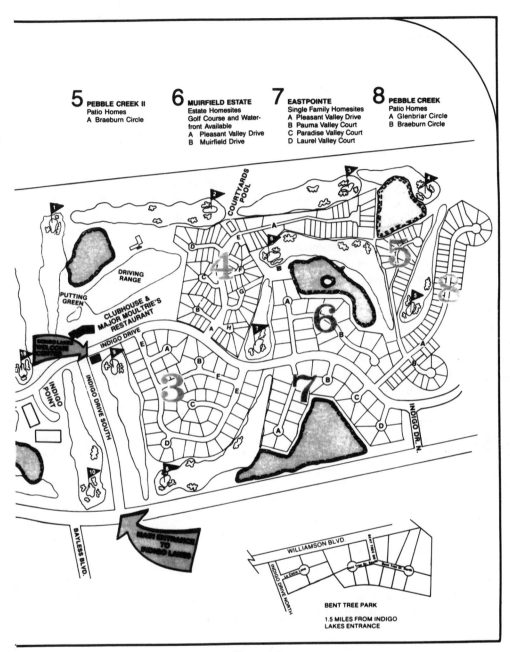

5 **PEBBLE CREEK II**
Patio Homes
A Braeburn Circle

6 **MUIRFIELD ESTATE**
Estate Homesites
Golf Course and Water-
front Available
A Pleasant Valley Drive
B Muirfield Drive

7 **EASTPOINTE**
Single Family Homesites
A Pleasant Valley Drive
B Pauma Valley Court
C Paradise Valley Court
D Laurel Valley Court

8 **PEBBLE CREEK**
Patio Homes
A Glenbriar Circle
B Braeburn Circle

Figure 1.2
Layout of Indigo Lakes

DON'T BE NERVOUS ABOUT THE SERVICE

Service is one of the hallmarks of a planned community. A few of the services duplicate those offered by most municipalities, but most of the services save the residents time and money. Services don't come free; the expenses are covered by the monthly community association fee or assessment. However, the economy of scale invariably results in a lower unit price than the owner could negotiate for a stand-alone single-family home. From another angle, the association generally raises the overall quality of the property; no one property owner is allowed to be a laggard who drags down the appearance of the neighborhood.

For openers, the association generally services all of the common area, taking responsibility for landscaping, snow removal, cleaning, painting, repairs, seasonal plantings or decorations, street and parking lot maintenance, garage upkeep, and the like. Generally, all of the amenities are in the common area and are covered by association-managed services: The pool is chemically treated and cleaned, the tennis courts are cleaned, the golf course is manicured and operated, the health club is tended, and so on.

There can be some variation in building maintenance when separate single-family structures are involved. Landscaping, snow removal, and maintenance service to the house and lot are often optional, in which case the quality standards are determined by the association and monitored to keep the curb appeal of the entire community at the desired level. Joint-use buildings rarely have an option with service. The association maintains the common areas in all mid-rise or high-rise buildings. Maintenance service for connected townhouses might be optional depending upon the governing association documents.

There can be some variation in the types of municipal services, such as water, sewer, street lights, main thoroughfare maintenance, and so on. For instance, many associations include the water/sewer charge in the homeowner assessments. When comparing planned communities you should obtain this information. Without this knowledge it is difficult to fully evaluate the value received from property taxes or the community assessments that each property owner must pay.

A sideline to the municipal services issue deals with double taxation, a question that some state and local legislators are presently dealing with. For example, your community association might provide snow removal which you would pay for in your monthly assessment. But you would also be paying local municipal taxes (just like all the other single-family non-association homeowners in your town). Therefore, you are actually subsidizing service for non-association home owners while also paying for the services you receive in your association. This issue will continue to be important in years to come.

There is literally no end to other services offered by many of the specialized communities (retirement, continuing-care retirement, vacation, resort, and recreation), and these services will be covered as each type of community is discussed.

IF YOU DISLIKE RULES, WATCH OUT

The adage "your home is your castle" doesn't necessarily extend to a planned community. All associations have rules that are superimposed on existing municipal regulations. The sharing of amenities and the close proximity of neighbors make these extra rules necessary. Ninety-five percent of the residents will view these rules as common courtesy and will have no problem accepting them. Unfortunately, some people don't share the same regard for courtesy, have different standards, or are rugged individualists who insist on going their own way. There are always a few fitting the description attributed to Groucho Marx: "Any club that would accept me as a member, I wouldn't want to join."

Actually, the rules are rarely oppressive. For one thing, they cannot violate any of your constitutional rights. Next, they have to relate to the purpose of the community. The rules cannot be capricious or single out a particular group. They must be made known to everyone, especially new or prospective purchasers. It is incumbent on both the salesperson and the buyer to give and get all the necessary facts.

In each of our 99 community descriptions there is a section outlining rules within that particular community. The rules that we have described within each of our 99 communities are only a few of the more important rules; you must check all of the rules and regulations of any association before making the purchase decision.

AMENITIES ARE THE CROWN JEWELS

Amenity, the attractiveness and value of real estate, is the term used for those recreation facilities in the common areas that make planned community living unique. The amenities, by virtue of being shared, give every resident the playground of a millionaire. For example, the expense of a swimming pool and the trouble and expense of keeping it clean are borne by several hundred people instead of just one. These super-economies have their price—shared use means no midnight skinny dipping—but most residents find sharing to be no problem.

The beauty of sharing is that very few users expect to spend much time with any one amenity. Even the devoted jacuzzi user would rarely spend more than an hour a day in the jacuzzi. The most avid entertainer would rarely be using a barbecue area more than once a day. Most people find that they don't need exclusive use of an amenity, so the system is built to serve the expected traffic. In those high traffic situations, reservation systems and time limitations for each use of an amenity generally provide a suitable solution.

The amenities are not only cost-effective but also they are time effective. The facilities are often located in a central convenient spot that doesn't require driving. Users need not face holiday traffic or crowds to reach their recreation sites.

Who pays for the cost of maintenance and operation of these amenities? In most situations the answer is all of the members of the community. However, there usually are two-tiered cost allocations in place. One source of income is a mandatory annual fee (often payable in monthly or quarterly assessments) that all members are required to pay whether they use the facilities or not. The second source of income consists of various user fees that spread the cost directly to those who use or wish to use the facilities. This can be accomplished by optional season passes or a pay-as-you-use fee.

Some amenities, such as a golf course or ski run, are so costly to maintain that fees have to be assessed for each usage. Most users accept these use charges, just as users accept electric, gas, or water meters, which charge each user according to individual use. One might also expect fees for guests at pools and other attractive recreation spots. However, most of the amenities (tennis courts, racketball courts, jacuzzis, barbecue pits, putting greens, shuffleboard courts) normally do not have user fees attached.

A SOCIAL SMORGASBORD

Planned communities offer a wide assortment of social opportunities. Some, particularly the adult age-restricted communities, feature the "good life" as their most important asset. By virtue of the shared common areas, all communities provide more points for social contact than most other living arrangements. The social life is there for the taking; it is not, however, mandatory. Those residents who have no need or desire for further social contacts can live and play without having any unwanted social interplay with other members.

Most communities have communication channels that feature events and activities in the community purview. Most prevalent is the newsletter, which is usually published monthly and even weekly in larger communities. Some communities have their own closed circuit television; others may have a dedicated channel on the local cable service. Most have clubhouses with rooms available for special activities, hobbies, parties, and just visiting. Many of the larger communities also have social/recreation directors who organize planned entertainment, trips, and activities. Almost all of the communities have a social committee to plan events. Many communities are also very active in social causes, civic affairs, and educational endeavors. It's not unusual, particularly in larger communities, to find that the local community college holds classes right in your very own clubhouse or that the local rescue squad teaches CPR or lifesaving at the pool house.

Whatever your inclination, social opportunity is potentially available as a central part of your life, as an opportunity for volunteer work, as an occasional diversion, or as something in the background to be participated in when needed. As an anonymous sage put it, "Happiness is not something you get, it's something you do."

Bedroom Planned Communities

The bedroom planned community is usually where the first-time or busy professional buyer purchases. These communities are located close to major metropolitan areas to allow for easier commutes. They can be large in size (1,000 units or more), but they tend to be smaller. They may have limited recreation amenities, but these amenities are not used extensively. We have not listed any bedroom communities in this book, not because no first-class ones exist, but because we want to concentrate on communities that provide exceptional social, recreational, and quality-of-life features.

High-Rise Planned Communities

High-rise planned communities generally consist of a single building, but they may be a development where several high-rise buildings constitute the community, part of a larger master planned community, or established as condominium or cooperative ownership forms. What sets high-rise communities apart is that they are almost always located in a city or by an ocean shore. They usually have a high level of security and a self-sustained lifestyle. Commercial enterprises are either a part of the building or within walking distance. You do not have to leave the shadow of the building to enjoy the recreation aspects, buy groceries, dine out, or visit the dry cleaners.

Residential-Recreational Communities

The residential-recreational planned community attracts a greater quantity and a wider spectrum of buyers than any other. This community consists of the primary residence of its occupants, who may be in any walk of life or at any stage of their career. Here you would find a few first-time buyers and a number of professionals who want to save time in yardwork, who travel for recreation, and who are flexible on where they live. The second-home buyer often purchases here, living here part of the year and at another home other times of the year. There would also be semi-retired or retired people who desire the recreational facilities or social climate the community offers.

The residential-recreational community might be anywhere, even in some areas that are considered resorts such as Hawaii, Arizona, or Florida. This community might have a plethora of recreational facilities, but the chief characteristic is that it combines all the qualities many people are looking for in a good place to live, whether for work, for play, or for retirement. The majority of our most elgible list consists of residential-recreational communities.

Resort-Recreational Communities

The resort-recreational community, by definition, is located in a resort or vacation area. It is a second home for the majority of the residents. Although there will be a smattering of permanent residents, the basic orientation is for vacation living in larger, less expensive quarters than is available in hotels.

In this type of community there might be some sections that offer various time-share plans and other sections or individual units that are fully furnished rentals on a daily, weekly, or monthly basis.

Age-Restricted Communities

Our anonymous sage says, "Retirement means twice as much spare time on half as much money." This situation means that many couples seek cost-effective ways of enjoying their retirement years. Age-restricted communities have been around for over 30 years; they presently offer so many activities that "good life, extended-family villages" would be a more appropriate name.

Physically, the living units in age-restricted communities are similar to other communities but have a tendency toward more single-family homes. The common areas resemble those in other communities, but invariably the clubhouse is big and active. Most important is what you cannot see: the emphasis on social activity, arts and crafts, field trips, and other favorite pastimes of people in the golden years. The age-restricted communities radiate a magnetism that draws a high proportion of active residents. Even though age-restricted for residency, most of these communities will allow grandchildren to visit for an established period of time. Each community determines its own visitation rules; however, the average community allows young people to visit about three months a year. A number of age-restricted communities are listed in our "99 Best."

Most of the age-restricted communities also offer extensive maintenance programs. Even in single-family home neighborhoods, it is not uncommon for the association to offer additional maintenance services to the residents. In attached housing units, the association almost always takes care of every outdoor maintenance item.

Continuing-Care Communities

A subset of the age-restricted community is the continuing-care retirement community (CCRC), which is growing more popular all over the country. Communities sponsored by churches or fraternal groups have long been on the scene, but now there are hundreds of for-profit businesses that offer residential areas and health care, usually for lifetime. These projects generally do not offer property ownership as in other planned communities but contract to furnish a living space and health care services. The average age of entering residents is 78 years, but keep in mind that you shouldn't wait too long, because most places expect new residents to be able to take care of themselves. While there are a number of very fine continuing-care communities, none made our "99 Best" list because they do not tend to offer the vast array of recreational and social activities we were searching for.

Campground Communities

There are not very many campground communities that offer real estate ownership, but some do, and the large ones certainly offer lots of seasonal recreation opportunities. Of course, almost all do not allow year-round residency and usually require nonpermanent, mobile-housing units. Only recreational vehicles, park model trailers, campers, and tents are acceptable. However, they do offer the "good life" to those hardy souls who love to live in a traveling house or rough it in a tent. The campground communities that offer the benefits of real estate ownership are quite unique; a few made our "99 Best" list. One of them, Woodhaven Lakes in Illinois, is billed as the largest campground community in the world with 6,156 lots.

"Almost A City" Planned Community

While still a planned master community, many of these communities are very large, even larger than some small towns. Part of the developer's initial planning includes schools, fire stations, churches, shopping centers, office buildings, and so on. There are twelve communities included in our "99 Best" list that, when completed, will each exceed 10,000 homes. Mission Viejo in California will have 30,783 homes upon completion, and in 1987 the residents actually voted to incorporate themselves as a real city. We chose to still include them in our "99 Best" because they have retained the community association restrictions, responsibilities, recreation, and social characteristics. Two of the neighborhoods within Mission Viejo have retained their age-restriction status as well.

Other Types of Communities

There are many other types of community associations: Commercial or industrial condominium buildings, grain elevators, parking garages, and boat docks are just a few of the other types of condominium associations that have been formed. In New York, there have been combinations of cooperative and condominium forms of ownership in a single building, called condo-operative. The imagination is the only limitation.

For the purpose of this book we have chosen to concentrate on private planned communities that will offer you a high quality of life on a personal basis: recreation, fun, social activities—the all-around "good life."

WHAT THE FUTURE HOLDS

There are many trends evident in planned communities, most of them positive. It's a safe bet that planned community growth will continue to outpace single-family or apartment housing because of its economic, lifestyle, and environmental advantages. These planned communities are already ahead of their counterparts in their spatial arrangements and their environmental considerations. At one end of the spectrum, condominiums will offer the best value for the first-time home buyer. At the other end, there will be more specialized communities that cater to special recreation or living interests: university alumni, military retirees, and boating or sailing fans, to name a few.

Community management, satisfactory now, will become more professional. Florida, for example, has enacted legislation for the licensing of all community association managers; others states are expected to follow suit. As trade associations grow to service the industry, more educational opportunities will be made available to professionals and homeowners alike. At present, Community Associations Institute offers a broad range of educational opportunities for professionals and homeowner board of directors members. These classes, especially the ones for homeowner board members, will continue to be invaluable as association living progresses.

These private planned communities, which generally fund capital improvements and replacements in advance, will be financially better off than their counterparts (most local towns and cities). It's nice to know that your association is required to set aside money to replace roofs, repave roads, or paint all the buildings.

These communities will attract people who like a planned and orderly life and who will become involved in the management activity. Because they are large enough to create an impact but small enough to retain a small town atmosphere, these communitities will be leaders in recycling, day care, children's activities, crime prevention, and involved citizenry. When neighbors share and share alike and when the elected officials (board of directors/trustees) are your neighbors, a true democracy is born.

Private planned communities, maturing in a period of great growth, are well positioned to make the "good life" even better as the future unfolds. Everyday, six thousand people are turning 60 years of age. Even in uncertain economic times, this group of people will have disposable income from pensions, social security, and prior investments. They will be looking for the "good life." Some are calling the 1990s the *fun* decade because of this large group of people who will have free time and disposable income. For those who want to decrease their cost of living and increase their quality of life, we offer you 99 planned communities to consider.

Chapter 2

How This Book Is Organized

Applying personal preference to a critical and complex home-buying decision is the goal of this book's approach. Stand-alone single-family home buying is complex enough. Add the extra level of community association and shared ownership concepts and the choice becomes even more confusing. With this in mind, we have organized this book, its information, and its "99 best" communities in a manner that will help you find your perfect home.

WHERE TO LOOK

Chapter 1 has already led you through the anatomy of planned communities— their purpose, characteristics, legal basis, benefits, advantages, and some of their pitfalls. By now you should be able to recognize the field of play, the entrants, and some of their common characteristics.

Chapter 2 provides you with an overview that allows you to get the best use out of the information in each chapter. You'll be given the background of how the participants were nominated, and how each community description is organized.

Chapter 3, "How Were the Best Selected," discusses how the authors evaluated the communities that were selected for your consideration in this book.

Chapter 4, "Your Personal Selection Criteria," gives you the tools you need to make an informed decision. You will be able to evaluate those qualities representing intrinsic value and those representing your own personal preferences.

Chapter 5 provides a cross-reference for ease in finding communities with certain characteristics or amenities.

Chapters 6 through 12 list our "99 best" planned communities by state and provide individual descriptions of each. Each planned community description is divided into the following sub-headings: Introduction; Recreation and Social Activities; Homeowner Assessments, Taxes, and Utilities; and Restrictions in the Community.

Also, at the beginning of each planned community you will see two numbers describing how many units or homes are at the development (example: 2,176/3,450 Garden-style Condos and Single-family Homes). The first number is how many homes or lots have been sold as of January 31, 1991. The second number is the final build-out of the community.

As you will see, each of our "99 best" has all the characteristics of planned communities as described in Chapter 4, but now these more detailed descriptions will help bring their personality and lifestyle to life.

HOW WE FOUND THE BEST

The authors have developed a multiple-source approach in seeking nominations for the most eligible communities among the over 130,000 that exist today. Because there is no single directory that lists planned communities in the United

States, the authors chose to use six major sources to obtain nominees for evaluation.

The first source is an industrywide organization that operates in the United States and abroad: the Community Associations Institute (CAI). CAI is a broad-based organization of over 10,000 members representing not only the communities but the homeowners, public officials, developers, and those who serve the associations (managers, management companies, landscapers, engineers, accountants, attorneys, and so on). For our second source, we queried the top 160 builders (as listed in *Builder's Magazine*) for nominees, feeling that each builder would be rightfully proud of his or her handiwork. The 36 most relevant trade associations were chosen for our third source. Through information and press releases, we asked the members of these organizations to nominate communities. We also searched the directories of specialized community associations for listed communities that appeared from brief descriptions to be potential qualifiers. These comunities selected from our fourth source were sent questionnaires. For our fifth source, we sent information and nomination forms to the state agencies that govern condominiums. The authors' personal visits and knowledge of the planned communities across the United States served as the sixth source.

Questionnaires were obtained from all participating communities. Some also chose to send extensive detailed information about themselves that helped further. As this effort was a volunteer affair, we cannot guarantee that every planned community participated, but it wasn't for the lack of a diligent and thorough effort.

Chapter 3

How Were the Best Selected?

The selection of the most eligible planned communities employed a key factor rating system based on the most important factors that affect the desirability of a community. The result is an ordered, professional evaluation that enables you to apply your personal preferences to make the right choice for you. At the end of this chapter, the key factors are listed in a checklist that will allow you to make your own independent evaluation. Armed with these tools, you will be able to make a solid decision. Your final product will be a clear picture of the ingredients necessary for enjoying the "good life."

To bring organization into the appraisal process, we selected the five categories that most determine the selection of a planned community.

1. *Area and availability*—the location of the planned community with respect to basic municipal infrastructures and important services
2. *Bricks and mortar*—the factors affecting the price and future value of the living units
3. *Rules and restrictions*—those bylaws and local rules that are meant to optimize contentment and reduce the potential for friction inherent in community living
4. *Amenities*—those recreational facilities that, by virtue of being shared, bring a multi-millionaire's playground within the reach of the members of a planned community
5. *Social programs*—those activities that homeowners and retirees pursue in order to increase their personal fulfillment

We have given each of the five categories equal weight in the selection process. However, you should make your own evaluation based on those factors that are most important to you.

These key factors provide a comprehensive picture of the overall merit of each planned community. However, this listing does not contain judgments about the quality of any given factor. There are good reasons why such a judgment would be misleading. First, beauty is often in the eye of the beholder. In addition, the passage of time can alter the quality of many factors; the appearance of the outside paint, the landscaping, and the upkeep of the parking lot can change from season to season, depending on the diligence of the management and the contractors. Some qualities—for example, the capability of the property manager, the finesse or heavy-handedness with which the rules are applied, the capability of the social director—are difficult to measure objectively. Accordingly, each prospective buyer must establish a personal judgment of the quality of each element.

Even though personal preference should play a leading role, there can be exceptions. For instance, a nongolfer might not give much weight to the presence of a championship course, but with so many golfers in the market and the huge increase in golf participation, a superior course increases the resale value for golfers and nongolfers alike. In the same manner, the proximity of a lake or ocean for water sports raises the market value of all properties, regardless of the owner's own interest in water sports.

Finally, we left some room for extra benefit points to cover particular factors in which a community might excel. You also might discover some extra factors that might be of special interest to you.

AUTHORS' BEST FACTORS FOR
CHOOSING A PLANNED COMMUNITY

Local Area Factors

Yes___	No___	Within one hour drive of 50 most populated metropolitan areas?
Yes___	No___	Within 15 minutes from hospital with emergency care?
Yes___	No___	Has local police protection?
Yes___	No___	Within 15 minutes to lake/ocean?
Yes___	No___	Within 5 minutes to retail establishments?
Yes___	No___	Within 5 minutes to interstate highway?
Yes___	No___	All utilities under ground?

Bricks and Mortar Factors

Yes___	No___	Water/sewer provided by local municipality?
Yes___	No___	What is the percent of homes sold in the community?
Yes___	No___	Are most of the units/homes two or more bedrooms?
Yes___	No___	Is there restricted access to the community?
Yes___	No___	Are extra storage areas provided on site?
Yes___	No___	Is there a variety of maintenance plans?
Yes___	No___	Is there a variety of unit/home floor plans?

Rules and Regulations Factors

Yes___	No___	Is there an active community association?
Yes___	No___	Is membership in the association mandatory?
Yes___	No___	Are there any resale restrictions?
Yes___	No___	Are the pet restrictions reasonable?
Yes___	No___	Are there restrictions on how many people can occupy a unit?
Yes___	No___	Are the guest restrictions reasonable?
Yes___	No___	Are there any age restrictions for ownership?

Social Factors

Yes___	No___	Recreation/social director
Yes___	No___	Valet/concierge service
Yes___	No___	Monthly newsletter
Yes___	No___	Organized trips
Yes___	No___	Organized on-site entertainment
Yes___	No___	Internal bus service
Yes___	No___	Food catering service
Yes___	No___	Visiting nurse/caregiver
Yes___	No___	Organized on-site crafts
Yes___	No___	Maid service
Yes___	No___	Daycare for children
Yes___	No___	Activities for teens
Yes___	No___	24-hour security
Yes___	No___	Patrol within community
Yes___	No___	Perimeter restrictions
Yes___	No___	Guard
Yes___	No___	Electronic

Amenities Factors

Yes___	No___	9-hole golf
Yes___	No___	18-hole golf
Yes___	No___	USGA-rated golf course
Yes___	No___	Indoor pool: number?___
Yes___	No___	Outdoor pool: number?___
Yes___	No___	Kiddie pool: number?___
Yes___	No___	Lake: number?___
		Miles of shoreline___
Yes___	No___	Ocean
		distance___
Yes___	No___	Boating
Yes___	No___	Private boat slip: size___ft.
		Number of boat slips___
Yes___	No___	Downhill skiing
		Number of trails___
		Types of lifts___
Yes___	No___	Cross country skiing
		Number of trails___
Yes___	No___	Snow-making capabilities
Yes___	No___	Open space land *within* the community
		Less than 10 acres___
		10–50 acres___
		50–100 acres___
		over 100 acres___
Yes___	No___	Hiking trails: number?___
Yes___	No___	Picnic areas: number?___
Yes___	No___	Ball playing fields: number?___

Yes___   No___   Tennis
                              Number of outdoor courts___
                              Number with lights___
                              Number of indoor courts___
Yes___   No___   Handball/racquetball/squash
Yes___   No___   Stables
                              Number of bridle paths___
Yes___   No___   Private air strip
Yes___   No___   Clubhouse (check approp. response)
                              ___   less than 5,000 square feet
                              ___   5,000 to 15,000 square feet
                              ___   over 15,000 square feet
                              ___   Gymnasium
                              ___   Exercise room
                              ___   Steam/sauna

Extra Benefit Factors

___ _____

___ _____

___ _____

Chapter 4

Your Personal Selection Criteria

It's evaluation time. You've decided that a planned community is the right answer to your current needs. You're ready to take those steps leading to the "good life." The checklists in this chapter are designed to help you reduce the risk in both your buying process and your final choice. Before you start, though, there are other important points to remember.

Contrary to many salespersons' claims, your home in a private planned community is not maintenance free. Although the community association may perform maintenance on the common property or provide recreational or utility type services, you do own your property in fee simple and you are responsible for that property. In addition, as a member of the association you are responsible for a portion of the common maintenance charges that are required to fund the association's responsibilities. As a member of the association you also have a duty to voice your opinion, vote on various issues, and volunteer to assist your community in your areas of interest.

All condo ownership is divided into three parts: your own living unit (which you own outright), the common element (those areas and facilities you share with other members), and the limited common element (such as a patio or terrace that is for your exclusive use but remains part of the common property). Your rights and options will vary with each of the three parts.

In the condominium form of ownership, you will own your individual unit outright. More specifically, you own the air space within that unit. The physical limits of your ownership may extend to either the inside or outside of your walls, doors, and windows, depending how the boundaries are defined in your association's documents. The boundary difference comes into play when maintenance or repair is necessary. On the building exterior, with some exceptions, the maintenance and repair will be the responsibility of the association. You will find little need to visit your local hardware store. But even if you wish to be a handyperson or painter, you probably won't be allowed to touch the outside. The reason is perfectly sound: The project must keep a uniform appearance and cannot rely on do-it-yourselfers to achieve this goal. You will find that property insurance carried by the association may have boundary differences as well. Some policies will cover the restoration of your inside walls, ceilings, cabinets, major appliances, and plumbing fixtures in case of a casualty loss. The insurance may or may not cover upgraded decoration. Other policies might cover only the bare walls, making everything within the unit your responsibility for insurance purposes. The community association's insurance agent must be consulted for these details.

In the single-family/lot form of ownership, you will own the single-family residence and the lot on which it is located. Like the condominium form of ownership, though, all common property is shared with others. Even with single-family ownership, the maintenance or property insurance features may be similar to the condominium form of ownership. More likely, though, what you own individually in a single-family home within a community association is similar to what you own in a stand-alone single-family home.

The major difference between participation in a planned community and the stand-alone single-family residence situation lies in what you share with others. You will have an undivided interest in a fraction of the common element, which is normally the outside areas. Everything the association owns is included: amenities, clubhouses, streets, garages, parking areas, and the like. You cannot claim as your own any one part of this area. Whether you use it or not, you own a shared fraction of this property outside your home. Your share in the common element not only involves the use of these spaces, but also the expenses and/or the proceeds. Your percentage will be your share of the expenses, usually called a maintenance fee or an assessment. Your percentage will also determine your vote for directors or changes to the by-laws that require membership vote. If your percentage is one percent, that would be your share of the expenses, votes, and proceeds. However, your percentage does not affect your use of the common element or your eligibility in becoming a volunteer for elected or appointed positions within the governing bodies.

UNIVERSAL HOME-BUYING GUIDELINES

The basic guidelines for buying into a planned community are the same as those for buying anywhere, except there are new considerations arising from the sharing concept. It's a matter of superimposing the planned community conditions on the normal home-buying considerations. Thus, to the usual bricks and mortar and location factors, we add the planned community factors of amenities, rules, social programs, special services, and community association administration.

PLANNED COMMUNITY FACTORS

Location, the primary criterion for real estate selection, applies as much to the planned community as to others. A planned community buyer receives an extra benefit because the development itself is often the best location in the area. In addition, most developers position their projects to make them easy to reach via interstate highways.

Location within the planned community can be just as important. In high-rise units, being opposite the elevator door or the trash chute can be disturbing; normally the top floors are valued more than the lower ones; the end units command a higher price; the relation of the balcony or lanai to the sun can be critical. In garden-style developments, being next to the refuse dumpsters or clubhouse can create a noise problem; being close to the open spaces (especially the golf course) is a big plus; being in a low traffic area is often better than being close to the entrance or the main road.

Planned communities have another criterion you must consider: compatibility. Before choosing a community, the first look you take should be inward. What bothers you? If there is any place that your cage will be rattled, it is in an association. Most of the problems start with something small that somehow escalates into impasse and confrontation. The issue of rules cuts two ways. For the most part, your concern will be whether you are the type that can live happily within the rules. On the other hand, some people tend to be sticklers for a rigorous rule enforcement. You need to examine the rules of a community carefully to decide if they are compatible with your needs and personality.

After you have filled out the checklists that we have provided, you can face the closing with the knowledge that you have made a personalized choice that will provide you with the passport to the "good life" made possible by the better private planned communities in the United States.

Why Am I Buying?
Personalized Checklist

Give each factor a 1 (very important), 2 (somewhat important), or 3 (not important).

Factor	Personal Importance
1. Recreation	____
2. Hobbies	____
3. Travel more/less	____
4. Medical facilities	____
5. Medical climate	____
6. Social interaction	____
7. Property values	____
8. Investment	____
9. Vacation home	____
10. Decrease cost of living	____
11. Moving up	____
12. Down-sizing	____
13. Second home	____
14. Close to work	____
15. Close to recreation	____
16. Retirement	____
17. Semi-retirement	____
18. Entertainment	____
19. Raise family	____
20. Less exterior maintenance	____
21. More yard	____
22. Less yard	____
23. Security	____
24. Closer to family	____
25. Golf	____
26. Tennis	____
27. Boating	____
28. Fishing	____
29. Indoor swimming	____
30. Outdoor swimming	____
31. Close to ocean	____
32. Stables	____
33. _____	____
34. _____	____

Bricks and Mortar Personalized Checklist

Give each factor a 1 (very important), 2 (somewhat important), or 3 (not important). We've added the rating for resale value.

Factor	Personal Importance		Importance for resale		Overall rating
1. Living space, square feet					
Above 2,000 square feet	____	×	1	=	____
Above 1,500 square feet	____	×	1	=	____
Above 1,000 square feet	____	×	2	=	____
2. Two baths	____	×	1	=	____
3. Three or more bedrooms	____	×	1	=	____
Two bedrooms	____	×	2	=	____
4. Two-car garage	____	×	1	=	____
One-car garage	____	×	2	=	____
No garage	____	×	3	=	____
5. Attic or other storage	____	×	2	=	____
6. Fireplace	____	×	2	=	____
7. Separate dining area	____	×	2	=	____
8. Patio, porch, or balcony	____	×	1	=	____
9. Air-conditioning	____	×	1	=	____
10. Gas heat	____	×	1	=	____
11. Jacuzzi	____	×	2	=	____
12. One or more showers	____	×	2	=	____
13. Refrigerator over 15 CF	____	×	2	=	____
14. Electric range and oven	____	×	2	=	____
15. Microwave oven	____	×	1	=	____
16. Automatic garbage disposal	____	×	2	=	____
17. Washer	____	×	1	=	____
18. Dryer	____	×	1	=	____
19. Screens and storm windows	____	×	1	=	____
20. Hot water heater > 40 gallons	____	×	2	=	____
21. 100 watt fuse box	____	×	1	=	____
22. Electrical outlets per room > 4	____	×	2	=	____
23. Hardwood floors	____	×	2	=	____
24. No living unit above	____	×	2	=	____
25. No steps or stairs	____	×	1	=	____
26. Low property taxes	____	×	1	=	____
27. Low community association assessments	____	×	1	=	____
28. _____	____	×	____	=	____
29. _____	____	×	____	=	____
30. _____	____	×	____	=	____

Multiply your personal rating by the resale rating. If the product is 3 or below, ascertain whether you are ready to accept a home that falls short in this factor.

Amenities and Social Programs Personalized Checklist

Give each factor a 1 (very important), 2 (somewhat important), or 3 (not important). We have added the rating for resale value.

Factor	Personal importance		Importance for resale		Overall rating
1. Golf course, par 3	_____	×	2	=	_____
2. Golf course, 9 holes	_____	×	2	=	_____
3. Golf course, 18 holes	_____	×	1	=	_____
4. Golf course, USGA Rating	_____	×	1	=	_____
5. Outdoor pool(s)	_____	×	1	=	_____
6. Indoor pool	_____	×	1	=	_____
7. Downhill skiing	_____	×	1	=	_____
8. Cross-country skiing	_____	×	2	=	_____
9. Ice skating rink(s)	_____	×	2	=	_____
10. Snow-making machines	_____	×	1	=	_____
11. Open spaces (50+ acres)	_____	×	1	=	_____
12. Picnic areas	_____	×	2	=	_____
13. Hiking trails	_____	×	2	=	_____
14. Ball-playing fields	_____	×	2	=	_____
15. Tennis courts	_____	×	1	=	_____
16. Lighted tennis courts	_____	×	1	=	_____
17. Racquetball	_____	×	2	=	_____
18. Exercise room	_____	×	2	=	_____
19. Sauna	_____	×	2	=	_____
20. Jacuzzi	_____	×	2	=	_____
21. Pool tables	_____	×	3	=	_____
22. Table tennis	_____	×	3	=	_____
23. Putting green	_____	×	2	=	_____
24. Marina	_____	×	1	=	_____
25. Fishing pier or shore	_____	×	1	=	_____
26. Clubhouse	_____	×	1	=	_____
27. Meeting rooms	_____	×	1	=	_____
28. Recreation director	_____	×	1	=	_____
29. Organized trips	_____	×	1	=	_____
30. On-site entertainment	_____	×	1	=	_____
31. Daycare, children	_____	×	2	=	_____
32. Daycare, elderly	_____	×	2	=	_____
33. Teen activities	_____	×	2	=	_____
34. Valet services	_____	×	2	=	_____
35. Internal transportation	_____	×	2	=	_____
36. Monthly newsletter	_____	×	1	=	_____
37. Bridge	_____	×	2	=	_____
38. Hobby shop	_____	×	2	=	_____
39. Ocean	_____	×	1	=	_____
40. Lakes	_____	×	1	=	_____
41. Stables	_____	×	1	=	_____

Multiply your personal rating by the resale rating. If the product is 3 or below, ascertain whether you can tolerate the absence of this amenity or social program.

Services and Location Personalized Checklist

Give each factor a 1 (very important), 2 (somewhat important), or 3 (not important). We have added the rating for resale value.

Factor	Personal importance		Importance for resale		Overall rating
1. Hospital nearby	_____	×	1	=	_____
2. Fire station nearby	_____	×	1	=	_____
3. Local police force	_____	×	1	=	_____
4. Limited access gates	_____	×	1	=	_____
5. Security patrols	_____	×	1	=	_____
6. High school nearby	_____	×	2	=	_____
7. Middle school nearby	_____	×	2	=	_____
8. Elementary school nearby	_____	×	1	=	_____
9. Interstate highway nearby	_____	×	1	=	_____
10. Grocery nearby	_____	×	1	=	_____
11. Liquor nearby	_____	×	1	=	_____
12. Pharmacy nearby	_____	×	1	=	_____
13. Shopping mall nearby	_____	×	1	=	_____
14. Discount store nearby	_____	×	2	=	_____
15. Underground utilities	_____	×	1	=	_____
16. Trash dumpster site	_____	×	2	=	_____
17. Parking lot location	_____	×	2	=	_____
18. Window washing service	_____	×	3	=	_____
19. Housecleaning service	_____	×	2	=	_____
20. Landscaping service	_____	×	1	=	_____
21. Snow removal service	_____	×	1	=	_____
22. Home maintenance service	_____	×	2	=	_____
23. Trash collection service	_____	×	1	=	_____
24. Christmas decorations	_____	×	2	=	_____
25. Community barbeques	_____	×	3	=	_____
26. Volunteer opportunities	_____	×	2	=	_____
27. Cable TV	_____	×	1	=	_____
28. Closed circuit TV	_____	×	2	=	_____
29. City water	_____	×	1	=	_____
30. City sewer	_____	×	1	=	_____
31. _____	_____	×	_____	=	_____
32. _____	_____	×	_____	=	_____
33. _____	_____	×	_____	=	_____
34. _____	_____	×	_____	=	_____
35. _____	_____	×	_____	=	_____
36. _____	_____	×	_____	=	_____

Multiply your rating by the resale rating. If the product is 3 or less, determine whether any deficiency in this factor would be a cause for rejection.

Association Documents, Rules, and Bylaws Checklist

Factor	Item checked	Results ok
1. Obtain copy of basic documents Is there more than one association that I would belong to? If so, do I have documents from each association?	——	——
2. Obtain copy of bylaws	——	——
3. Obtain copy of house rules	——	——
4. Obtain copy of minutes from annual meeting	——	——
5. Obtain copy of minutes from last two or three board meetings	——	——
6. Speak with manager	——	——
7. Meet social director	——	——
8. Is association in litigation?	——	——
9. Resale restrictions	——	——
10. Rental restrictions	——	——
11. Guest restrictions	——	——
12. Household occupant restrictions	——	——
13. Architectural restrictions	——	——
14. Parking restrictions	——	——
15. Vehicle restrictions	——	——
16. Age restrictions	——	——
17. Flag pole restrictions	——	——
18. Antenna restrictions	——	——
19. Patio restrictions	——	——
20. Noise problems	——	——
21. Traffic problems	——	——
22. Parking problems	——	——
23. Pet problems	——	——
24. Children problems	——	——
25. _____	——	——
26. _____	——	——
27. _____	——	——
28. _____	——	——
29. _____	——	——
30. _____	——	——

Personal Document Checklist

Factor	Item checked	Results ok
1. Warranties on common area	——	——
2. Warranties on appliances	——	——

Have you read all the documents and understood them? If not, discuss your concerns with your attorney and real estate agent. Get answers to your concerns in writing.

Association Finances Checklist

Factor	Item checked	Results ok
1. Percentage of project completed	____	____
2. History of assessment increases	____	____
3. Does developer subsidize association?	____	____
4. Copies of last two audits	____	____
5. Copy of current year budget	____	____
6. Does association provide any common utilities?	____	____
Water	____	____
Sewer	____	____
Refuse removal	____	____
Electricity	____	____
HVAC	____	____
Cable TV	____	____
Other	____	____
If not, then who does?		
7. Annual reserve allocation	____	____
8. Total of reserve fund	____	____
9. Association receivables	____	____
10. Insurance—property	____	____
11. Insurance—liability	____	____
12. Insurance—workmen's compensation	____	____
13. Insurance—Directors and Officers Liability	____	____
14. Insurance—fidelity bond	____	____
15. Is flood insurance required?	____	____
16. Percentage of rentals in project	____	____
17. Does any investor own more than ten homes?	____	____
18. Litigation in process?	____	____
19. Was there an architect/engineer's study? If so, obtain copy and review conclusions	____	____
20. Are all facilities complete?	____	____
21. Can project be expanded?	____	____
22. Has association been notified of any government land use violations?	____	____
23. Is association a party to a land lease?	____	____
24. Does the association have a loan to repay?	____	____

Have you read all the documents and understood them? If not, discuss them with your attorney, insurance agent, real estate agent, or accountant. Get answers to your concerns in writing.

Personalized Finances Checklist

Factor	Item checked	Results ok
1. When is the first association assessment due?	____	____
2. Do I pay a single association assessment or several?	____	____
3. Any transfer fees?	____	____
4. Any future capital or special assessment?	____	____
5. Is the home I am purchasing current on its assessments?	____	____
6. Annual property taxes	____	____
7. User fees on amenities	____	____
8. Private or regular telephone service? Fees?	____	____
9. How are utilities hooked up? Deposits?		
Water	____	____
Sewer	____	____
Refuse removal	____	____
Electricity	____	____
HVAC	____	____
Cable TV	____	____
10. Monthly fuel bill	____	____
11. Monthly electrical bill	____	____
12. What kind of insurance do I need?		
Personal property	____	____
Real (fixtures) property	____	____
Real (structure) property	____	____
Liability	____	____
13. Who were the contractors and suppliers for my		
HVAC	_____	
Kitchen cabinets	_____	
Major appliances	_____	
Window/doors	_____	
Bath fixtures	_____	
Other		
_____	_____	
_____	_____	
_____	_____	

In addition, you will need to prepare your checklist for the normal home-buying closing and moving tasks.

Developer/Builder Considerations Checklist

Factor	*Item checked*	*Results ok*
1. Has the developer built other communities? (If so, visit them or call them)	_____	_____
2. Who are the principals of the developer?	_____	_____
3. Check local municipal officials		
Building inspector	_____	_____
Tax collector	_____	_____
Planning/zoning clerk	_____	_____
4. Has the developer:		
Obtained all municipal approvals?	_____	_____
Posted any bonds?	_____	_____
Paid all fees?	_____	_____
Paid real estate taxes?	_____	_____
5. Check with local trade organizations		
Better Business Bureau	_____	_____
Chamber of Commerce	_____	_____
Local builder organization	_____	_____
6. Check with applicable state agencies		
Is the developer properly licensed?	_____	_____
Are there any actions against the developer?	_____	_____
7. Check with local contractors/suppliers		
Has the developer paid bills on time?	_____	_____
Any disputes?	_____	_____
8. What is the quality of the home?	_____	_____
9. Is the price comparable to the quality?	_____	_____
10. Are all amenities completed?	_____	_____
11. Are all roads completed?	_____	_____
12. Are all site improvements completed?		
Retention/detention areas	_____	_____
Landscape	_____	_____
Signs	_____	_____
13. Does the developer have control or interest in the management company?	_____	_____
14. Are the association people employees of the developer?	_____	_____
15. Is the developer in litigation?	_____	_____
16. Is the developer subsidizing the community association?	_____	_____
17. Does the developer owe the association any money?	_____	_____
18. Does the association owe the developer any money?	_____	_____
19. Does the developer pay any amounts to the association?	_____	_____
20. Check with previous buyer	_____	_____
21. Verify warranties	_____	_____
22. Verify customer service procedures	_____	_____
23. Verify boundaries of responsibilities	_____	_____

Chapter 5

Cross Reference of 99 Best Communities

For your ease in evaluating our 99 best communities, we have included lists and a cross-reference.

1. List of all 99 communities by state showing how many homes are currently sold (as of January 31, 1991) and how many homes will ultimately be built.
2. List of age-restricted communities detailing their specific age-related regulations.
3. Cross-reference list of the 99 communities detailing the availability of the following amenities: golf courses (with number of holes), lakes within the boundaries of the community, oceanfront property, snow-skiing on site, equestrian centers, and electronic or manned gates.

99 Best Communities Sorted by State with Number of Current and Ultimate Homes

	Number of homes		
	Currently	Ultimately	Page
Bella Vista Village Bella Vista, AR	5,300	13,000	81
Hot Springs Village Hot Springs Village, AR	3,100	9,000	84
Sun City West Sun City West, AZ	10,200	13,000	166
Leisure World Mesa, AZ	2,537	2,656	164
Gainey Ranch Scottsdale, AZ	467	962	162
Sunland Village East Mesa, AZ	900	2,500	169
The Foothills at South Mountain Park Phoenix, AZ	600	7,000	159
The Dobson Ranch Mesa, AZ	4,950	4,950	157
Rossmoor at Walnut Creek Walnut Creek, CA	6,300	7,600	203
Palm Desert Greens Palm Desert, CA	1,850	1,922	201
Oakmont Santa Rosa, CA	2,700	2,855	199
Sunrise Country Club Rancho Mirage, CA	746	746	207

99 Best Communities Sorted by State with Number of Current and Ultimate Homes

	Number of homes		
	Currently	Ultimately	Page
Leisure Village Camarillo, CA	2,136	2,136	187
Leisure World of Laguna Hills Laguna Hills, CA	12,736	12,736	192
The Villages Golf and Country Club San Jose, CA	1,994	2,700	212
Lake Forest Lake Forest, CA	1,702	1,702	183
Canyon Lake Canyon Lake, CA	4,802	4,802	181
Silver Lakes Helendale, CA	1,804	5,000	205
Leisure Village Ocean Hills Oceanside, CA	1,375	1,640	189
Mission Viejo Mission Viejo, CA	25,400	30,783	194
Woodbridge Village Irvine, CA	9,292	9,292	214
Aliso Viejo Mission Viejo, CA	5,100	20,000	179
Lake Shastina Weed, CA	563	4,071	185
Tahoe Donner Truckee, CA	3,000	6,170	209
Northstar Truckee, CA	1,153	1,252	197
Heather Gardens Aurora, CO	2,426	2,426	233
Pagosa Lakes Pagosa Lakes, CO	1,600	12,000	241
Ken-Caryl Ranch Littleton, CO	2,839	5,800	238
Highlands Ranch Highlands Ranch, CO	5,707	35,900	235
The Highlands Winter Springs, FL	1,125	1,647	140
Tops'l Beach and Racquet Club Destin, FL	186	700	154
The Hemispheres Hallandale, FL	1,295	1,295	138
Bluewater Bay Niceville, FL	1,800	3,600	132
Riverwood Plantation Port Orange, FL	300	450	149

99 Best Communities Sorted by State with
Number of Current and Ultimate Homes

	Number of homes		
	Currently	Ultimately	Page
The Meadows Sarasota, FL	3,300	3,700	145
Indigo Lakes Daytona Beach, FL	300	450	142
Greenlefe Resort and Conference Center Haines City, FL	1,188	1,324	136
Edgewater Beach Resort Panama City Beach, FL	691	973	134
Seaside Seaside, FL	180	300	151
Oak Run Country Club Ocala, FL	1,371	4,926	147
Black Diamond Ranch Lecanto, FL	75	599	130
Amelia Island Plantation Amelia Island, FL	1,100	2,200	127
Reynolds Plantation Reynolds Plantation, GA	185	3,000	89
The Landings on Skidaway Island Savannah, GA	2,416	4,250	87
Mililani Town Association Mililani Town, HI	9,312	16,000	216
Wailea Resort Kihei, HI	1,400	1,400	218
Apple Canyon Lake Apple River, IL	452	2,727	249
Woodhaven Lakes Sublette, IL	6,000	6,156	253
Lake Barrington Shores Barrington, IL	1,152	1,360	251
Tipton Lakes Columbus, IN	407	2,000	255
Avenel Potomac, MD	414	823	47
Ocean Pines Berlin, MD	3,654	7,057	51
Montgomery Village Montgomery Village, MD	10,212	12,000	49
Samoset Village Rockport, ME	26	111	37
Woodbridge Hills Portage, MI	480	1,200	258
Communities of Four Seasons Four Seasons, MO	843	4,100	259

**99 Best Communities Sorted by State with
Number of Current and Ultimate Homes**

	Number of homes		
	Currently	Ultimately	Page
Lake Sherwood Estates Lake Sherwood, MO	225	1,300	262
Sea Trail Plantation Sunset Beach, NC	200	2,000	94
Fairfield Mountains Lake Lure, NC	467	1,800	91
The Village at Nags Head Nags Head, NC	200	750	96
Waterville Valley Waterville Valley, NH	1,270	1,500	41
Eastman Grantham, NH	1,008	2,140	39
Smithville Smithville, NJ	1,426	4,860	60
Leisure Village West Lakehurst, NJ	2,620	2,725	56
Rossmoor Jamesburg, NJ	2,223	2,246	58
Galaxy Towers Guttenberg, NJ	1,075	1,075	53
Desert Shores Las Vegas, NV	1,500	2,800	243
Spanish Trail Las Vegas, NV	1,020	1,300	245
Sunriver Sunriver, OR	2,800	4,100	227
Little Whale Cove Depoe Bay, OR	150	312	223
Black Butte Ranch Black Butte Ranch, OR	1,203	1,255	221
Mountain Park Lake Oswego, OR	3,500	3,800	225
The Hideout Lake Ariel, PA	2,490	4,100	71
Hidden Valley Resort Hidden Valley, PA	900	3,000	69
Lake Adventure Milford, PA	1,760	1,794	73
Hemlock Farms Hawley, PA	2,375	4,240	66
Shawnee Village Shawnee-on-Delaware, PA	776	1,016	78
Eagle Lake Gouldsboro, PA	2,862	3,933	64

99 Best Communities Sorted by State with
Number of Current and Ultimate Homes

	Number of homes		
	Currently	Ultimately	Page
Buck Hill Falls Buck Hill Falls, PA	278	500	62
Lake Naomi and Timber Trails Pocono Pines, PA	1,700	2,200	75
Harbison Columbia, SC	2,209	6,900	100
Wild Dunes Charleston, SC	1,357	2,334	105
Kingston Plantation North Myrtle Beach, SC	1,018	2,000	102
Chickasaw Point Fairplay, SC	208	700	98
Fairfield Glade Community Club Fairfield Glade, TN	2,442	14,837	107
Great Northwest San Antonio, TX	4,330	4,750	171
Kingwood Kingwood, TX	12,725	18,000	173
The Woodlands The Woodlands, TX	9,550	25,000	176
Brandermill Midlothian, VA	3,850	4,000	111
Little Rocky Run Clifton, VA	2,091	2,364	120
Aquia Harbour Stafford, VA	1,865	2,814	109
River Walk on the Elizabeth Chesapeake, VA	500	1,350	123
Lake of the Woods Locust Grove, VA	1,800	4,250	116
Ford's Colony at Williamsburg Williamsburg, VA	487	3,250	114
Lake Ridge Parks and Recreation Association Lake Ridge, VA	6,550	7,500	118
Woodlake Midlothian, VA	1,850	2,600	125
Stratton Resort Stratton Mountain, VT	1,000	1,647	44
Sudden Valley Bellingham, WA	2,500	4,000	230
Jackson Hole Racquet Club Jackson, WY	473	473	247

13 Best Age-restricted Communities

	Age	Page
Heather Gardens Aurora, CO	39	233
Leisure Village Camarillo, CA	55	187
Leisure Village Ocean Hills Oceanside, CA	55	189
Leisure Village West Lakehurst, NJ	55	56
Leisure World Mesa, AZ	55	164
Leisure World of Laguna Hills Laguna Hills, CA	55	192
Oak Run Country Club Ocala, FL	55	147
Oakmont Santa Rosa, CA	55	199
Rossmoor Jamesburg, NJ	55	58
Rossmoor at Walnut Creek Walnut Creek, CA	55	203
Sun City West Sun City West, AZ	55	166
Sunland Village East Mesa, AZ	55	169
The Villages Golf and Country Club San Jose, CA	55	212

99 Best Planned Communities, Sorted Alphabetically

Name of community	City	State	Number of golf holes	Lakes Y/N	Ocean Y/N	Snow skiing Y/N	Equestrian center Y/N	Electronic gate or manned gatehouse
Aliso Viejo	Mission Viejo	CA	54	Y	N	N	N	N
Amelia Island Plantation	Amelia Island	FL	45	N	Y	N	Y	Y
Apple Canyon Lake	Apple River	IL	9	Y	N	Y	N	N
Aquia Harbour	Stafford	VA	9	N	Y	N	Y	Y
Avenel	Potomac	MD	18	N	N	N	Y	N
Bella Vista Village	Bella Vista	AR	117	Y	N	N	N	N
Black Butte Ranch	Black Butte Ranch	OR	36	Y	N	Y	Y	Y
Black Diamond Ranch	Lecanto	FL	18	N	N	N	N	N
Bluewater Bay	Niceville	FL	45	Y	N	N	N	N
Brandermill	Midlothian	VA	18	Y	N	N	N	N
Buck Hill Falls	Buck Hill Falls	PA	27	N	N	N	Y	N
Canyon Lake	Canyon Lake	CA	18	Y	N	N	Y	Y
Chickasaw Point	Fairplay	SC	18	Y	N	N	N	N
Communities of Four Seasons	Four Seasons	MO	45	Y	N	N	Y	Y
Desert Shores	Las Vegas	NV	0	Y	N	N	N	N

99 Best Planned Communities, Sorted Alphabetically

Name of community	City	State	Number of golf holes	Lakes Y/N	Ocean Y/N	Snow skiing Y/N	Equestrian center Y/N	Electronic gate or manned gatehouse
The Dobson Ranch	Mesa	AZ	18	Y	N	N	N	N
Eagle Lake	Gouldsboro	PA	0	Y	N	N	N	Y
Eastman	Grantham	NH	18	Y	N	Y	N	N
Edgewater Beach Resort	Panama City Beach	FL	28	Y	Y	N	N	Y
Fairfield Glade Community Club	Fairfield Glade	TN	81	Y	N	N	Y	N
Fairfield Mountains	Lake Lure	NC	36	Y	N	N	Y	Y
The Foothills at South Mountain Park	Phoenix	AZ	18	Y	N	N	N	Y
Ford's Colony at Williamsburg	Williamsburg	VA	27	Y	N	N	Y	Y
Gainey Ranch	Scottsdale	AZ	27	Y	N	N	N	Y
Galaxy Towers	Guttenberg	NJ	0	N	N	N	N	Y
Great Northwest	San Antonio	TX	0	N	N	N	N	N
Greenlefe Resort and Conference Center	Haines City	FL	54	Y	N	N	N	N
Harbison	Columbia	SC	0	Y	N	N	N	N
Heather Gardens	Aurora	CO	9	N	N	N	N	N
The Hemispheres	Hallandale	FL	18	N	Y	N	N	Y
Hemlock Farms	Hawley	PA	18	Y	N	N	N	Y
Hidden Valley Resort	Hidden Valley	PA	18	Y	N	Y	N	N
The Hideout	Lake Ariel	PA	9	Y	N	Y	N	Y
The Highlands	Winter Springs	FL	18	Y	N	N	N	N
Highlands Ranch	Highlands Ranch	CO	18	N	N	N	N	N
Hot Springs Village	Hot Springs Village	AR	72	Y	N	N	N	Y
Indigo Lakes	Daytona Beach	FL	18	Y	N	N	N	Y
Jackson Hole Racquet Club	Jackson	WY	18	N	N	Y	N	N
Ken-Caryl Ranch	Littleton	CO	0	N	N	Y	Y	N
Kingston Plantation	North Myrtle Beach	SC	0	Y	Y	N	N	Y
Kingwood	Kingwood	TX	72	Y	N	N	Y	N
Lake Adventure	Milford	PA	0	Y	N	N	N	Y
Lake Barrington Shores	Barrington	IL	18	Y	N	Y	N	Y
Lake Forest	Lake Forest	CA	0	Y	N	N	N	N
Lake Naomi and Timber Trails	Pocono Pines	PA	18	Y	N	Y	N	N
Lake of the Woods	Locust Grove	VA	18	Y	N	N	Y	N
Lake Ridge Parks and Recreation Association	Lake Ridge	VA	0	Y	N	N	N	N
Lake Shastina	Weed	CA	27	Y	N	Y	N	N
Lake Sherwood Estates	Lake Sherwood	MO	0	Y	N	N	N	Y
The Landings on Skidaway Island	Savannah	GA	90	N	Y	N	N	Y
Leisure Village	Camarillo	CA	18	N	N	N	N	N
Leisure Village Ocean Hills	Oceanside	CA	18	N	N	N	N	Y
Leisure Village West	Lakehurst	NJ	18	Y	N	N	N	Y
Leisure World	Mesa	AZ	36	N	N	N	N	Y
Leisure World Laguna Hills	Laguna Hills	CA	27	N	N	N	Y	Y
Little Rocky Run	Clifton	VA	18	N	N	N	N	N
Little Whale Cove	Depoe Bay	OR	0	N	Y	N	N	N
The Meadows	Sarasota	FL	54	Y	N	N	N	N
Mililani Town Association	Mililani Town	HI	18	N	N	N	N	N
Mission Viejo	Mission Viejo	CA	36	Y	N	N	N	N
Montgomery Village	Montgomery Village	MD	18	Y	N	N	N	N
Mountain Park	Lake Oswego	OR	0	N	N	N	N	N
Northstar	Truckee	CA	18	N	N	Y	Y	N
Oak Run Country Club	Ocala	FL	9	N	N	N	N	Y
Oakmont	Santa Rosa	CA	36	Y	N	N	N	N
Ocean Pines	Berlin	MD	18	Y	N	N	N	N
Pagosa Lakes	Pagosa Lakes	CO	27	Y	N	Y	Y	N
Palm Desert Greens	Palm Desert	CA	18	Y	N	N	N	Y

99 Best Planned Communities, sorted alphabetically

Name of community	City	State	Number of golf holes	Lakes Y/N	Ocean Y/N	Snow skiing Y/N	Equestrian center Y/N	Electronic gate or manned gatehouse
Reynolds Plantation	Reynolds Plantation	GA	18	Y	N	N	N	Y
River Walk on the Elizabeth	Chesapeake	VA	0	Y	N	N	N	N
Riverwood Plantation	Port Orange	FL	0	Y	N	N	N	Y
Rossmoor	Jamesburg	NJ	18	N	N	N	N	Y
Rossmoor at Walnut Creek	Walnut Creek	CA	27	N	N	N	Y	Y
Samoset Village	Rockport	ME	18	N	Y	Y	N	N
Sea Trail Plantation	Sunset Beach	NC	54	Y	Y	N	N	N
Seaside	Seaside	FL	0	N	Y	N	N	N
Shawnee Village	Shawnee-on-Delaware	PA	27	N	N	Y	Y	N
Silver Lakes	Helendale	CA	27	Y	N	N	Y	N
Smithville	Smithville	NJ	0	Y	N	N	N	N
Spanish Trail	Las Vegas	NV	27	N	N	N	N	Y
Stratton Resort	Stratton Mountain	VT	18	Y	N	Y	Y	N
Sudden Valley	Bellingham	WA	18	Y	N	N	N	N
Sun City West	Sun City West	AZ	126	Y	N	N	N	Y
Sunland Village East	Mesa	AZ	18	Y	N	N	N	N
Sunrise Country Club	Rancho Mirage	CA	18	Y	N	N	N	Y
Sunriver	Sunriver	OR	36	Y	N	Y	Y	N
Tahoe Donner	Truckee	CA	18	Y	N	Y	Y	N
Tipton Lakes	Columbus	IN	0	Y	N	N	N	N
Tops'l Beach and Racquet Club	Destin	FL	45	Y	Y	N	N	Y
The Village at Nags Head	Nags Head	NC	18	Y	Y	N	N	N
The Villages Golf and Country Club	San Jose	CA	27	Y	N	N	Y	N
Wailea Resort	Kihei	HI	36	N	Y	N	N	Y
Waterville Valley	Waterville Valley	NH	9	Y	N	Y	Y	N
Wild Dunes	Charleston	SC	36	N	Y	N	N	Y
Woodbridge Hills	Portage	MI	18	Y	N	Y	N	N
Woodbridge Village	Irvine	CA	0	Y	N	N	N	N
Woodhaven Lakes	Sublette	IL	0	Y	N	Y	N	Y
Woodlake	Midlothian	VA	0	Y	N	N	N	N
The Woodlands	Woodlands	TX	54	Y	N	N	N	N

Chapter 6

New England
Maine
New Hampshire
Vermont

SAMOSET VILLAGE

Warrenton St.
Rockport, Maine 04856
207-594-2511

$278,000 to $305,000
26/111 Townhomes
Victorian Architecture

18-hole USGA-rated golf course
2 outdoor pools
2 cross-country ski trails
2 lighted outdoor tennis courts
Exercise room

1 indoor pool
½ mile to ocean
2 picnic areas
1 indoor tennis court
Steam/sauna

INTRODUCTION

The luxury townhomes at Samoset Village are nestled between the golf course called the "Pebble Beach of the East" and the beautiful Penobscot Bay. The community is 88 miles north of Portland, Maine. The drive from Boston is approximately 182 miles. Flights are available into Portland (88 miles), Bangor (61 miles), and Augusta (42 miles). All three airports have 4 to 12 flights per day to the area. Helicopter and airline charters are available out of Boston's Logan Airport and the Portland jetport. Chartered buses are also available.

Samoset Village is a new development; the first unit was built in 1988. Even though the community is small (total build-out is 111 townhomes), it is quite a special place. The Samoset has been Maine's premier coastal resort for a century. In the mid-1850s "summer folk" began coming to the area for its spectacular views of the bay, the offshore islands, and the rolling Camden Hills. In 1889 the luxurious Bay Point Resort opened for business, catering to well-to-do vacationers from all over the East Coast. Later renamed the Samoset, today it is a four-season destination community that wins high praise. It merits the much coveted four-diamond rating from the American Automobile Association. The moderating breezes off Penobscot Bay stretch the golfing season from mid-April to late November. You can enjoy such natural pleasures as a schooner ride across the bay, a walk into the hills, or a ferry ride to an island artists' colony that hasn't changed much in a hundred years.

Area attractions include the Farnsworth Art Museum (keepers of one of the nation's largest Wyeth collections) and contemporary works at the Maine Coast Artists Gallery. You can see the planes, trains, and cars of the Owl's Head Transportation Museum, shop for antiques, listen to live musical performances at the famous Bay Chamber Concerts, and watch the Camden Shakespeare Company in an outdoor amphitheater.

Police protection is provided by local authorities, and the fire department is staffed by professionals. The Pen Bay Medical Center is within two miles of the community. A gourmet restaurant is located on site, and all other services (pharmacy, medical clinic, hair salon, grocery and liquor store, retail shops, and movie theaters) are within one mile.

RECREATION AND SOCIAL ACTIVITIES

The joys of summer at Samoset Village include golf (on the 18-hole USGA-rated golf course), racquet sports, strolls along the breakwater to the lighthouse, sailing, and other water activities. The Samoset Golf Club course has seven holes bordering the ocean and thirteen holes with ocean vistas. The golf course includes a golf practice range, trap, and putting green. A pro shop and daily golf clinics and lessons round out the golf offerings.

In autumn, swimmers move from the outdoor pools to the expansive indoor swimming area, which is lined with tropical foliage. Samoset has tennis courts both indoors and out. Indoor exercise begins at the fitness center, complete with Nautilus™, rowing machines, Lifecycle™ Exercise bikes, treadmill, StairMaster™, sauna, and two racquetball courts.

In winter, cross-country ski trails lead you along the ocean's edge, and downhill skiing awaits at nearby Ragged Mountain. Located next to the on-site hotel is a breakwater where homeowners and guests can fish for striped bass and blues.

Samoset provides a full-time activities director and staff. The resort also offers catering, on-site entertainment, activities for teens, and 24-hour security by patrol. Homeownership does not automatically include membership in the club and recreation facilities; however, there is a 15 percent discount for Samoset owners. Golf charges are about $625 per year for a family (two cards).

HOMEOWNER ASSESSMENTS, TAXES, AND UTILITIES

Twenty-six homes have been sold since the community opened in 1988. Ultimately there will be 111 townhomes. Samoset Village offers four models to choose from: Sebago, Kennebec, Monhegan, and Pemaquid. Some of the homes stand along the fairways of the golf course; others have windows facing the sea. The homes were designed by the award-winning architectural firm of Sasaki Associates from Watertown, Massachusetts.

Current monthly homeowner assessments are $270 ($3,240 per year). Yearly property/municipal taxes run about $3,000. Cable television is available; however, there are no community channels. The site is heated by electricity, and the local municipality provides both water and sewer services. All utilities are below ground.

RESTRICTIONS IN THE COMMUNITY

Membership is mandatory in the community association at Samoset Village. Since all of the living units at the site are attached townhomes, the community association handles all exterior buildings/grounds maintenance for the development. Exterior modifications must be approved by the community association. It is against regulations to install additional landscaping in the common areas.

There are no restrictions on age or length-of-stay for visitors. Small domestic pets are allowed. There are restrictions on how many people can occupy a unit (four for a one-bedroom unit; six in a two-bedroom unit; eight in a three-bedroom home). There is a one-week minimum stay for renters of units. Operating a business from a home is prohibited. There are no restrictions on resales. Large campers, recreational vehicles, boats, and the like cannot be parked on site. However, there are extra parking areas available for these vehicles.

EASTMAN

P.O. Box 53
Grantham, New Hampshire
03753
603-863-4240

$110,000 to $500,000
1,008/2,140 Garden-style
Condos and Single-family
Homes
Mixed Architecture

18-hole golf course
2 lakes with 8 miles of shore
15 boat slips (18 feet)
1 double chair lift
40 km of hiking trails
1 ball-playing field
2 lighted tennis courts

1 indoor pool
70 miles to Atlantic Ocean
Downhill skiing, 3 trails
30 km of cross-country skiing
8 picnic areas
13 outdoor tennis courts
Clubhouse, steam/sauna

INTRODUCTION

Eastman is a private, 3,600 acre, four-season recreation community located in central New Hampshire. Concord, the state capital, is conveniently located 42 miles from Eastman. Access is easy with Interstate 89 right at the entrance of the community. The nearest major airport is located in Manchester, 60 miles away. Police coverage is provided by local, county, and state organizations, and a volunteer fire department is nearby. The New London hospital, with emergency facilities, is 8 miles from Eastman. Dartmouth College is 18 miles from the site, and there are numerous ski areas within an hour's drive.

There is a restaurant onsite, and within one mile of the homes you will find medical clinics, dry cleaners, hair salons, grocery stores, and retail shops. About 8 miles away are a pharmacy and a liquor store. A movie theater is 12 miles from the community.

The community is heterogeneous, primarily because of the absence of any requirements for price or minimum square footage of house size. The preponderance of full-time residents (approximately 30 percent of the 1,000 homes) are retirees. There has been a gradual increase of full-time working-age families that is expected to continue. The construction of the new Dartmouth/Hitchcock Medical Center only 18 miles from Eastman will probably cause a large increase in full-time residents.

The first unit at Eastman was built in 1972 by Controlled Environment Corporation of Grantham, New Hampshire. Control of the community has now passed to the community association, which, with a few minor exceptions, owns and maintains all common properties and amenities.

RECREATION AND SOCIAL ACTIVITIES

The community is laid out around Eastman Pond, two smaller ponds, and an 18-hole golf course. The golf course has been consistently ranked among the top five in the state of New Hampshire and currently holds the number one ranking in the state as reported by *Golf Digest*. The golf and ski center was recently expanded and now has a 100-seat restaurant that is operated by a concessionaire. The pro shop is also located in the center. This building converts to a cross-country ski center in the winter. There are 30 km of cross-country ski trails that are groomed and tracked when there is sufficient snow. Alpine skiing is offered on a small ski area with three trails and a 30-chair double lift.

There are 13 tennis courts, including three recently added soft surface courts. Recreation programs for both adults and children are planned throughout the year. During the summer months, the children's programs include baseball, soccer, basketball, lacrosse, swimming, tennis, and sailing. There are youth swimming and tennis teams that compete with other community and camp teams throughout the area.

The association employs a recreation director and publishes a bimonthly newsletter. Organized trips and on-site entertainment are provided. There is a 24-hour patrol throughout the community. Homeownership automatically entitles you to all recreation/club facilities; however, most recreation amenities require a nominal user fee. Golfing costs around $700 per year per couple.

HOMEOWNER ASSESSMENTS, TAXES, AND UTILITIES

Homes at Eastman range between $110,000 and $500,000. The 326 condominium owners pay a monthly association assessment of $125 plus a $668 annual fee to the master association. Their yearly property/municipal taxes run about $1,900. The 682 single-family homes also average about $1,900 in property taxes. All undeveloped-lot owners pay $541 annually in association assessments.

The association is financially sound and has no long-term debt. The annual assessment has three different categories: A home or condominium owner pays the highest rate; a vacant-lot owner pays a lower rate; and a homeowner who purchases a lot adjacent to the home pays the lowest rate. Annual adjustments in the association assessment are restricted to changes in the consumer price index. Therefore, any increase that may be established by the board of directors may be no more than the CPI.

Special assessments are provided for in the Declaration of Covenants and Restrictions. There have been only two such special assessments in the history of the development. One was in 1981, when the golf course was purchased from the developer and each homeowner was required to pay an additional $245. The second special assessment was in 1989, when the golf and ski center was expanded, requiring that each homeowner pay an additional $250.

Both cable and community television channels are available. There is a variety of home heating sources including gas, electricity, oil, solar power, and wood. Water is furnished to all homes by the village district of Eastman, which is a separate municipality formed for this purpose. All of the condominium homes and approximately 200 of the single-family homes are connected to a private sewer system that is still owned by the developer. Even though the sewer system is privately owned, it is regulated by the state. All other individual homes have on-site sewage disposal systems. All utilities are above ground. There are no extra storage facilities within the community.

RESTRICTIONS IN THE COMMUNITY

Membership in the community association is mandatory. There are nine condominium associations that provide their own exterior maintenance. Individual single-family homeowners provide exterior buildings/grounds maintenance for their homes. All exterior modifications or building must be approved by the community association. There are no restrictions for single-family homes regarding landscaping.

At Eastman there are no restrictions regarding age, length-of-stay for visitors, and pets. Operating a business from a home is limited to professionals only. Registered vehicles (with sticker) may be parked in association-owned parking areas, but there are no special lots for recreational vehicles, boats, and the like. There are no restrictions on how many people can occupy a unit.

WATERVILLE VALLEY

Waterville Company
Town Square Offices
Waterville Valley, New
Hampshire 03215
603-236-8311

$50,000 to $850,000
1,270/1,500 Mid-rise and
Garden-style Condos, Townhomes, Single-family Homes,
Condo Hotel, and Quarter-
shares

9-hole golf course
1 kiddie pool
Boating
Over 105 km (70 km groomed) cross-
   country trails
Over 100 km in hiking trails
1 ball-playing field
2 indoor tennis courts

4 indoor pools, 5 outdoor pools
6-acre lake
53 downhill ski trails, 13 lifts
Snowmaking capabilities
Picnic areas
18 outdoor tennis courts
Handball/racquetball

Horse stables with bridle paths
Gymnasium, exercise room
Concert pavilion
Indoor sports center
Covered hockey-sized
ice-skating pavilion

Helicopter landing area
Steam/sauna facilities
40 km of mountain bike trails
2-mile fitness trail

INTRODUCTION

For over a hundred years, those searching for the freshness of mountain air and the exhilaration of outdoor recreation have come to Waterville Valley. This private recreational and residential community is a 500-acre, self-contained village surrounded by 700,000 acres of national forest land. At its core are inns of natural wood and fieldstone fireplaces, the new town square with its white clapboard New England architecture, and tall green-gabled roofs housing luxury hotel suites, convenient condominiums, and single-family homes. Above it all towers 4,000-foot Mt. Tecumseh, just a short shuttle bus ride away.

Geology and nature have been especially generous to Waterville Valley. The 10-mile entrance road off Interstate 93 rises gradually through evergreen forests to the valley floor. The vast woodlands and 4,000-foot peaks of the White Mountain National Forest form a majestic panorama for all to see. Air transportation to Waterville Valley is provided in Manchester, New Hampshire, just 75 miles away. However, there is a helicopter landing site within the community for even easier access. Police protection is provided by local authorities, along with limited private security within the community. Both a volunteer and a staffed fire department are nearby. The nearest hospital with emergency facilities is 19 miles from the site.

Within the community you will find a grocery store, six restaurants, and retail shops. During the winter months, a daytime medical clinic is also operational within Waterville Valley. All other services (pharmacy, dry cleaners, hair salon, liquor store, and movie theaters) are within 20 miles of the community.

The community is being developed by the Waterville Company, which acquired the 500 acres and started residential building in 1967. Founder and president Tom Corcoran was a member of the U.S. Olympic ski teams in 1956 and 1960 and has just celebrated 25 years of "community spirit" at Waterville in 1990. To top it all off, Waterville Valley was host to the 1991 World Cup Alpine Skiing Finals in men's and women's slalom and giant slalom, marking the eleventh time that the World Cup events have been held at this New Hampshire resort. No other North American ski center can match that record.

RECREATION AND SOCIAL ACTIVITIES

Skiing at Waterville ranges from easy to exciting; 60 percent of the trails are in the mid-range of difficulty. There are 53 alpine ski trails and 105 km of cross-country trails within the community. The longest run is three miles. Named in honor of Robert F. Kennedy, whose last ski outing was at Waterville Valley, "Bobby's Run" is one of the more popular black diamond trails. Waterville also sponsors two skiing events every year in February. The Christa McAuliffe Ski Invitational honors the New Hampshire school teacher who perished in the Challenger shuttle accident, and the Jack Williams Race for Wednesday's Child raises funds and attention for an adoption program sponsored by a Boston TV station.

The 9-hole golf course challenges all who try it, and the community has recently acquired and received all approvals on land seven miles from the Valley for a future 18-hole course (expected completion in 1995). Waterville Valley's 18 outdoor clay courts, two indoor courts, and full pro shop will satisfy any tennis lover's needs. You can sign up for private lessons, clinics, and partner match-ups with the pro staff, or just play with a friend.

Riding stables and mountain bikes are available; over forty kilometers of trails and routes are maintained throughout the community. Waterville Valley's fitness path begins at the sports center and meanders for three miles in and around the community. Over 50 miles of marked trails are suitable for hikes, ranging from easy walks to day-long climbs up 4,000-foot mountain peaks.

The Waterville sports center houses both an indoor and outdoor 25-meter pool, a weight room, indoor tennis, racquetball, and squash courts, an indoor jogging track, a sauna, a steam room, and a massage and tanning room. A charter membership in the sports center costs a one-time fee of $4,750 plus $295 per year. The Golden Eagle Lodge is also available for swimming, sunning, and boating.

Waterville Valley also has extensive conference facilities with over 17,000 square feet of meeting and exhibit space and can accommodate groups up to 500. There are 11 conference rooms as well as private banquet and lounge areas.

HOMEOWNER ASSESSMENTS, TAXES, AND UTILITIES

Building at Waterville Valley is limited by its master plan to about 1,500 units, primarily because of geographic limitations. Currently there are 1,270 homes at the community. The 246 mid-rise condominiums range in price from $69,900 to over $200,000; owners pay an average monthly community association assessment of $150 and average property/municipal taxes of $1,200 per year. The 640 garden-style condos will cost anywhere from $55,000 to over $260,000, and owners pay an average of $110 per month in assessments and $1,300 per year in property/municipal taxes. The 260 townhomes range from $100,000 to over $400,000 and pay $125 per month in assessments, with about $1,500 per year in taxes. The 72 single-family homes start at $265,000 and surpass $850,000. They are exempt from association fees; however, their taxes run about $2,000 per year. There are also 80 condo hotel units at Waterville Valley that cost between $50,000 and $90,000, with a monthly average of $75 in association assessments and a yearly average of $500 in taxes. There are 56 quartershares that range in price from $45,000 to $62,000. For $280 per month, all expenses are included; yearly property taxes are about $350.

Both cable and community television channels are in service at Waterville Valley. Electricity provides the primary heating source, and the local municipality provides sewer waste and water services to the community. All utilities are below ground. There are extra storage facilities within the development for homeowner use.

RESTRICTIONS IN THE COMMUNITY

Membership is mandatory in the community association for all condo owners. Single-family homeowners are exempt. The association handles all the exterior buildings/grounds maintenance for condo owners; single-family homeowners handle their own. Owners of condominiums cannot alter exterior common areas without specific approval from the board of directors, which is generally not given. Landscaping additions for condominium owners must also be approved by the board of directors.

There are no age or length-of-stay restrictions at Waterville Valley. There are pet restrictions in three of the 25 neighborhood associations. No pets are allowed in condo lodges or quartershares. Renters are also prohibited from having pets.

Owners who rent their units when the units are not in personal use are subject to certain maximum occupancies based on unit size/bed set-up. Condominium owners and village members living in residentially zoned areas may not operate a business from a unit. There is a right of first refusal for resale of certain properties within the development. There is no assigned parking, but parking is restricted to owners of individual condominium projects and their guests. Although there are no designated areas for RV or boat parking, arrangements for limited stays can be made with the town of Waterville Valley or with individual condo complexes.

STRATTON RESORT

The Stratton Corporation
Stratton Mountain, Vermont
05155
802-297-2200

$200,000 to $1,200,000
1,000/1,647 Mid-rise and
Garden-style Condos,
Townhomes, and Single-family
Homes
Contemporary Architecture

18-hole golf course
1 small lake (1 mile of shore)
20 km cross-country ski trails
Over 100 acres of open space
25 outdoor tennis courts
Handball/racquetball
Clubhouse, gymnasium

1 indoor pool, 5 outdoor pools
92 downhill ski trails, 10 lifts
Snowmaking capabilities
10 hiking trails
4 indoor tennis courts
Horse stables and 10 bridle paths
Exercise room, steam/sauna

INTRODUCTION

You'll catch the spirit of the Stratton Resort community association from the moment you set off on your first run down one of 92 exhilarating downhill trails on southern Vermont's highest peak. This East Coast ski treasure is located 90 miles from Albany, New York and Hartford, Connecticut. Building began in 1961; the community is being developed by the Stratton Corporation of Vermont. Over 1,000 homes have been completed out of a planned total of 1,647.

If shopping is one of your favorite pastimes, there is plenty of opportunity here. The Alpine Clock Tower in the village square looks down upon the browsers and shoppers as they visit the thirty specialty shops including restaurants, Vermont crafts, men's and women's sportswear, art prints, books, fine leather, photography, deli, and a complete interior design store. There is even a branch of the Vermont National Bank.

A medical clinic is on site at the community along with a hair salon, a grocery store, and a movie theater. Other needed services, such as a pharmacy, a dry cleaners, and a liquor store, are located about ten miles away. Access by car is from Interstate 91, which is 30 miles away. Police protection is provided by the town of Winhall, the Windham county sheriff's department, and the Vermont state police. There is a volunteer fire department nearby for fire and rescue services.

RECREATION AND SOCIAL ACTIVITIES

Stratton Resort is the skier's paradise. With over 2,000 vertical feet on southern Vermont's highest mountain and 400 acres of ski terrain, Stratton offers a huge variety of gourmet skiing for every skier's taste and ability. There are over 90 downhill trails and a myriad of lifts (1 gondola, 4 quad chairs, 4 double chairs, and 1 triple chair). The new 7,200-foot Starship XII Gondola will deliver you to the summit in under eight minutes.

Because Stratton Resort is located in Vermont's famed snowbelt, it gets plenty of natural snow each winter (an average of 14 feet each year). Just in case nature doesn't contribute its fair share, though, the community has a sophisticated snowmaking system and snow-grooming operations.

Stratton hosts a variety of special events each year: the Volvo International Tennis Tournament in the summer, the International Ski Classic, the Bavarian Festival, and the Stratton Arts Festival. The Stratton Arts Festival is the region's oldest and largest art exhibition and performance series. The festival began in 1964 and now represents the work of more than 300 professional Vermont painters, sculptors, photographers, and craftspeople. Twelve hundred area school children participate in educational programs offered by the Festival.

Stratton Resort has five outdoor pools and one indoor pool as well as an 18-hole golf course. Greens fees are $30. Downhill skiing is $38 per day; cross-country skiing is $10 per day. The association publishes a monthly newsletter and provides organized on-site entertainment, internal bus service, and catering services. Maid service is also available, as well as daycare for children and activities for teens, including daily ski school instruction. The teen center/arcade provides chaperoned service for the kids during entertainment times. Stratton Resort provides a golf school, riding lessons, and a sporting shotgun course set in natural terrain (instructors are available). Homeownership automatically entitles you to the sports center membership. There is a 24-hour patrol within the community.

Future amenities include new ski lifts, trails, and more snowmaking capabilities. An additional 18-hole golf course will be completed in 1997. The community expects all construction to cease around the year 2000.

HOMEOWNER ASSESSMENTS, TAXES, AND UTILITIES

There are currently 300+ mid-rise condominiums, 160+ garden-style condos, 190+ townhomes, and over 350 single-family homes at Stratton Resort. The condominiums range in price from $200,000 to $400,000 with community association monthly assessments of $200 and yearly property/municipal taxes between $750 and $1,200. The townhomes cost between $250,000 and $1 million with community association assessments of $200 per month and yearly property/municipal taxes between $900 and $3,700. Single-family homes range in price from $400,000 to $1.2 million, with a current monthly cost of $75 in community association assessments and yearly property/municipal taxes ranging from $1,200 to $4,500. Single-family homeowners are responsible for their own exterior buildings/ grounds maintenance. The association handles maintenance for the condominiums and townhomes.

Upon completion of the Stratton Resort, there will be 120 one-bedroom homes, 110 two-bedroom homes, 950 three-bedroom homes, 300 four-bedroom homes, and 125 homes with more than four bedrooms. Cable and community television channels are available. The community is heated by gas, electricity, and oil. The local municipality provides water and sewer waste disposal services. Telephone and electric utilities are both above and below ground. There are no extra storage facilities on site.

RESTRICTIONS IN THE COMMUNITY

Stratton Resort has a community association and membership is mandatory. Any exterior modifications to homes must be presented in advance to the architectural review board, and all modifications must be based upon established design criteria. There are no restrictions regarding landscaping designs for your home.

There are no restrictions regarding age or length-of-stay for visitors. There are also no restrictions on how many people can occupy a unit, nor do any rental restrictions exist. Operating a business from a home is prohibited by the association. For resales, there is a right of first refusal restriction imposed by the association. There are no special areas to park recreational vehicles. Pet restrictions state that all dogs must be on a leash when outside.

Chapter 7

Mid-Atlantic
Maryland
New Jersey
Pennsylvania

AVENEL

Avenel Information Center
9501 Beman Woods Way
Potomac, Maryland 20854
301-299-5916

$498,000 to $1,000,000+
414/823 Townhomes, Single-
family Homes, Patio, and
Cluster Homes
Traditional Architecture

18-hole USGA-rated golf course
Picnic areas
3 outdoor tennis courts
Equestrian Center

Hiking trails
3 soccer fields, 1 baseball field
Horse stables
Tot lots

INTRODUCTION

The private community of Avenel was created by Potomac Investment Associates (PIA), a limited partnership founded in 1978 by Anthony M. Natelli, Ronald E. Holloway, and Dennis I. Meyer. PIA established Avenel as its flagship project and, within a few short years, Avenel has become a standard against which other planned luxury residential communities can be measured.

Located in Potomac, Maryland, Avenel is just 13 miles from Washington, D.C. Building began at the site in 1986. To date, 414 homes have been completed. The total build-out is expected to be 823 homes. The Capital Beltway (I-495) is only two miles from Avenel, and air travel is easy with Washington National Airport 15 miles from the site. Police protection is provided by local authorities, the county sheriff's department, and state police. There is a local volunteer fire department nearby. Suburban Hospital, the nearest hospital with emergency facilities, is five miles away.

Avenel is in the middle of a vibrant area of our country with many local attractions, including the historical buildings, monuments, museums, and cultural and arts centers of Washington D.C. No services are provided within the community; however, everything you need is within one mile of Avenel: a pharmacy, a medical clinic, a dry cleaners, a hair salon, a grocery and liquor store, a restaurant, retail stores, and movie theaters.

RECREATION AND SOCIAL ACTIVITIES

Every year the Avenel golf course plays host to the world-class PGA-Tour Kemper Open, which attracts hundreds of golf fans and some of the country's best golfers. The golf course was constructed and is owned and operated by the Tournament Players Club at Avenel, Inc., a subsidiary of the PGA Tour, Inc. Membership is composed of non-residents and some residents of Avenel. The Kemper Open is sponsored by the Kemper Group and operated by Kemper Sports Management, Inc.

Along with the excellent golfing facilities at Avenel, there is an equestrian center housed in what is said to be the largest one-story barn in Maryland (55 × 275 feet). The Avenel equestrian center provides access to miles of bridle paths and a multi-purpose ring for dressage, shows, and training. The equestrian center is owned by the Washington Suburban Sanitary Commission (WSSC), which leases the property to the Avenel Equestrian Center Corporation. They, in turn, sub-lease to an operator who deals directly with the boarders.

Avenel has 50 acres of stream valley parkland and a 30-acre public recreational park including soccer fields, tennis courts, multi-purpose courts, a baseball diamond, jogging trails, and children's playground areas. A variety of trails have also been constructed for bikers and pedestrians. The Avenel Community Park and the Stream Valley Park, located within the community, are owned and operated by the Maryland National Capital Park and Planning Commission.

HOMEOWNER ASSESSMENTS, TAXES AND UTILITIES

Even though the first home was only built in this community in 1986, 414 out of 823 total homes have already been completed. There are 67 townhomes ranging in price from $498,000 to $925,000+. Each of the townhome owners pay a monthly community association assessment of $173. There are 347 patio, cluster and single-family homes which range in price from $498,000 to over $1 million. The monthly assessments for these homes are as follows: single-family homes, $211; patio and cluster homes, $177; and single-family (2-acre) homes, $116. The Montgomery County property tax rate is approximately 1 percent of purchase price.

The developer of this community, Potomac Investment Associates, allows only seven designated builders to construct homes within this development. Within the community there are 10 separate villages with various traditionally styled homes constructed of brick or stone with cedar or slate roofs. All new home construction plans must be submitted to the community association for approval. There is a $2,500 plan review charge associated with new home construction.

Cable television channels are available; two television channels have been reserved for the community but are not currently in use. The primary heat source is gas; electric heat is secondary. The local municipality provides both sewer waste disposal and water services. All utilities are below ground. There are no extra storage facilities for homeowner use.

RESTRICTIONS IN THE COMMUNITY

There is a community association at Avenel; membership is mandatory. The association provides all exterior building/grounds maintenance for the common areas. Individual homeowners provide their own exterior maintenance for private dwellings. Any exterior modifications must be approved. There is a fee for this process payable to the association. No lots may be sub-divided.

The association enforces a strict minimum square footage requirement. Two-acre detached two-story homes must be at least 3,500 square feet. Two-acre one-story homes are required to have a minimum of 2,500 square feet. Homeowners of detached homes on one half acre to 2 acres can build no less than 3,000 square feet for a two-story home and 2,500 square feet for a one-story home. Cluster homes, patio homes, and townhomes must be between 2,200 and 2,800 square feet, depending on style.

There are no restrictions on how many people can occupy a single home and no rental restrictions within the community. There are certain landscaping requirements put forth by the association. Motorized equipment (such as lawn mowers, tractors, and grass trimmers) is not to be used before 10:00 A.M. or after 5:00 P.M. on Saturdays and not at all on Sundays. Vegetable gardens may only be grown in the rear portion of a lot. Children's play equipment is not allowed to remain overnight within any front yard, and large equipment such as swing sets must be screened from view by landscaping or a wall approved by the control committee. Fences must also be approved by the control committee. The construction of private tennis courts and pools must have prior association approval.

Operating a business from a home is prohibited. Restrictions also exist regarding resales of homes, particularly concerning the types of signs used to advertise home sales. No commercial vehicles are allowed. All homes have garages and there is ample off-street parking. On some streets, there are some designated "no parking" areas. There are no special lots for recreational vehicles, boats and the like.

MONTGOMERY VILLAGE

Montgomery Village Foundation
10120 Apple Ridge Road
Montgomery Village, Maryland
20879
301-948-0110

$60,000 to $300,000
10,212/12,000 Condos,
Townhouses, and Single-
family Homes
Mixed Architecture

18-hole golf course	11 outdoor pools
Lake for sailboats	Over 100 acres of open space
8 picnic areas	26 tennis courts
14 ball fields	4 community centers

INTRODUCTION

Montgomery Village is about 20 miles northwest of Washington, D.C., less than a quarter of a mile from Interstate 270, and equidistant from Washington National, Dulles, and Baltimore's Friendship Airports. Colonial Annapolis and the water activity of Chesapeake Bay are less than one hour's drive away. The rolling hills of the Maryland and Pennsylvania countryside extend to the west. Civil War buffs can visit a plethora of battlefields. Truly, Montgomery Village offers an ideal working, playing, and leisure location.

Montgomery Village is a private planned community that was started in 1966; it was over 80 percent complete at the end of 1990. The village covers over 2,500 acres and has a current population of about 32,000 people. The community is governed by the Montgomery Village Foundation. The foundation is managed by a nine-member board of directors with operations coming under an executive vice-president and a full-time staff of 50 people.

As the community celebrates its twenty-fifth anniversary, it has already formed a Village 2000 committee to develop long-range plans for services, communication, governance, development, and protection of the environment.

RECREATION AND SOCIAL ACTIVITIES

The foundation's recreational department, headed by a full-time director, ensures that residents don't have to travel to have fun. Residents can picnic, jog, fish, or bike in any of the seven parks. North Creek Park has a seven-acre lake and is the perfect place for a nature hike. Lake Whetstone Park maintains a fleet of canoes and rowboats available for rental. South Valley Park sports several playing fields. In the winter there is ice-skating when the ice is safe.

In the summer there are shows and concerts at the outdoor lawn theater. William Hurley Park features basketball courts, swings, monkey bars, and a swimming pool, one of eleven pools in the community. There are a total of 14 playing fields and picnic areas. Including courts at schools and in the residential neighborhoods of Montgomery Village, there are 26 outdoor tennis courts, six with lights.

A privately run golf course and the village center are located in the center of several clusters of residences. Four community centers scattered throughout the development provide additional recreational opportunities.

The association's community newsletter is published every other Friday and covers events, issues, transportation schedules, legislation, and news from each neighborhood association. Organized trips and on-site entertainment are also provided for residents; daycare for children and activities for teens are available. There are no perimeter restrictions for access to the community.

Through their association membership, all owners are allowed unlimited use of parks, lakes, open space, tennis courts, picnic areas, and other facilities. Owners in some communities pay a mandatory fee to use swimming pools and community centers owned by the foundation. Through their monthly assessments, condo owners pay for usage of pools owned by the condo association. Future amenities include completion in 1991 of a softball field and two more tennis courts and completion in 1993 of a basketball court and another softball/baseball field.

HOMEOWNER ASSESSMENTS, TAXES, AND UTILITIES

Living units vary in type, size, and architecture. Montgomery Village has about 350 mid-rise condos and about 2,400 garden-style condos, with current prices between $60,000 and $100,000. The 5,800 townhouses range from $90,000 to $200,000, and the 1,700 single-family homes vary from $170,000 to $300,000. The current monthly assessment costs between $45 and $62. Neighborhood association assessments, if any, are separate.

Cable television is available in most neighborhoods. The primary heating fuel for 70 percent of the units is electricity; about 20 percent of the units are served by gas and 10 percent by oil. All wires are underground. Municipal systems provide water and sewer service.

RESTRICTIONS IN THE COMMUNITY

All resident owners are members of the Montgomery Village Foundation, which manages and maintains the common facilities. Covenant control is an important responsibility of the foundation: Although various neighborhoods have different covenants, many have common rules.

No commercial vehicles, trucks, trailers, campers, or boats are allowed unless they are kept in garages. Outside antennas are not allowed. There are designated hours for the use of outdoor clotheslines and special rules for storage. The foundation exercises strict architectural control on any exterior change except minor plantings. Any exterior change requires advance plans which are reviewed by a nine-member board that meets twice a month.

County restrictions govern pets; only household pets are allowed, and leash laws apply. There are no age restrictions nor any restrictions on the length-of-stay of visitors. Operating a business from a unit is restricted in some of the neighborhoods. There are no restrictions on the resale of units. Most of the neighborhoods ban overnight parking of commercial vehicles, trucks, boats, and campers. The community does not provide oversize vehicle parking areas.

OCEAN PINES

2700 Ocean Pines
Berlin, Maryland 28111
301-641-7717

$89,000 to $1,200,000
3,654/7,057 Condos,
Townhomes, and
Single-family Homes
Mixed Architecture

18 hole USGA-rated golf course
4 outdoor pools, 1 kiddie pool
102 boat slips
1 hiking trail
2 ball-playing fields

4 ponds, numerous canals, a bay, and
a river
Over 100 acres of open space
14 tennis courts
5 picnic areas

INTRODUCTION

Ocean Pines is a private recreational community of unparalleled distinction. Nestled in a lovely natural setting, Ocean Pines is conveniently located just minutes from the Atlantic Ocean and Ocean City, one of the East Coast's finest resorts. Ocean City is filled with activities for vacationers and residents. The community lies between Philadelphia and Washington, D.C. (about 150 miles either way). The nearest interstate highway (I-95) is 120 miles from the community.

Building began at the site in 1968; there are now 3,654 homes built on the 7,057 original lots. All lots have water and sewer services available. There is a wide selection of existing homes and an excellent choice of attractive home sites. You may choose a magnificent wooded lot or a beautiful waterfront lot overlooking the river or canal.

A restaurant is located within the development, and many other services (pharmacy, dry cleaners, hair salon, grocery store, liquor store, and retail stores) are located within one mile of Ocean Pines. A movie theater is located eight miles away. The nearest hospital with emergency facilities is 30 miles away in Salisbury, Maryland. However, there is a medical clinic about eight miles from the community. Salisbury also offers a state college, a zoo, museums, and a civic center.

RECREATION AND SOCIAL ACTIVITIES

The clubs of Ocean Pines are an outstanding benefit of this community. All of these clubs charge a membership fee separate from the community association assessment.

The Ocean Pines Golf and Country Club has an 18-hole championship course designed by Robert Trent Jones. The club hosts many tournaments and special events for its members and guests. Facilities here include an enlarged and remodeled pro shop, locker rooms, a 19th-hole snack bar on the lower level, and a bar, lounge, and restaurant on the upper level.

The Ocean Pines Yacht Club overlooks the Isle of Wight Bay. The complex includes a three-level clubhouse with a spectacular view of the Ocean City skyline. The club includes a restaurant, snack bar, bar, lounge, and pool bar. A swimming pool surrounded by spacious sundecks is served by an outdoor bar and is limited to adults only. A marina adjacent to the yacht club provides docking facilities for boats up to 50 feet.

The Swim and Racquet Club, located on the St. Martin's River, contains four hard-surface tennis courts, a family swimming pool, a tots' wading pool, locker rooms, and slips for small boats (up to 18 feet long).

The Sports Core provides a heatable 36 × 75 foot swimming pool, locker rooms, and a sauna. During the summer, a popular aquacize program (aerobic exercise in the water) for adults is held at this facility, and swimming lessons are offered for both children and adults.

The Manklin Meadows Tennis Complex is a new facility that includes six composition tennis courts, four hard-surface tennis courts, a pro shop, benches, bleachers, water fountains, and plenty of parking.

The Ocean Pines Beach Club occupies a block of oceanfront in Ocean City. This club boasts a private parking lot for members, locker rooms, a family swimming pool with wind screens and sun lounges, a snack bar on the lower level, and, on the upper level, a bar/lounge and dining area overlooking the ocean. Spacious decking surrounds the club.

There are many community parks within the boundaries of Ocean Pines, as well as a modern community center complete with meeting hall, kitchen, and conference room. The recreation department, with a full-time director, features a summer day camp for children and weekly summer activities for all ages, in addition to year-round classes, activities, and special events. Homeownership automatically provides you with access to all activities in the recreation department.

HOMEOWNER ASSESSMENTS, TAXES, AND UTILITIES

The 3,654 homes built at Ocean Pines are a mix of contemporary, victorian, and colonial architecture. Ultimately, there will be over 7,000 homes in this community. The breakdown currently consists of 54 garden-style condominiums, 12 townhomes, and 3,588 single-family homes. Annual property/municipal taxes are $1.59 per $100 of assessed value. Homeowner association fees range from $370 to $770 per year.

Cable and community television channels are available. A myriad of fuel is used to provide heat: gas, electricity, oil, solar cells, and wood-burning stoves. A county sanitary district handles water service and sewer waste disposal. All telephone and electrical utilities are underground. There are no extra storage facilities within the community.

RESTRICTIONS IN THE COMMUNITY

Membership in the community association at Ocean Pines is mandatory for all homeowners. Exterior building/grounds maintenance is handled by individual homeowners. The association is responsible for all maintenance for common roads and amenities. Ocean Pines has an environmental control committee which publishes guidelines for all construction and improvements to existing structures. Homeowners must obtain this committee's approval for all new construction or modifications within the community.

A family of any size can occupy a home; however, no more than five unrelated people may occupy a home. There are restrictions regarding operating a business from a home; for example, owners must obtain a home occupation permit from the association, and only family members may be involved in the business. Homeowners to the right and left of a property retain a right of first refusal for resales. Vehicles one ton or over are prohibited from parking overnight. Boats and recreation vehicles may only be parked on private property and must be screened from view. Pets must be under an owner's control at all times; stray animals are impounded.

GALAXY TOWERS

7000 Boulevard East
Guttenberg, New Jersey 07093
201-861-7400

$140,000 to $400,000
1,075/1,075 High-rise
Condominiums
Contemporary Architecture

1 indoor pool, 1 outdoor pool
4 tennis courts with lights
Exercise room, gymnasium
Private bus service to
New York City

2 kiddie pools
Clubhouse
Steam/sauna
Manhattan skyline view

INTRODUCTION

The Galaxy Towers condominium association provides the ultimate in a gracious, comfortable, and covenient lifestyle; it combines the amenities, safety, and services of an ultra-luxury apartment complex with all the advantages of city life while eliminating the stress, insecurities, and turmoil of actually living in the city. It is no exaggeration to say that the Galaxy is not just a place to live but actually a way of life.

The Galaxy is situated atop the Palisade Cliffs in Guttenberg, New Jersey. It is directly opposite Manhattan's 79th street yacht basin, 2 $1/2$ miles north of the Lincoln Tunnel, and 5 miles south of the George Washington Bridge. The community consists of three octagonal skyscrapers (the "towers") rising 50 stories above the Hudson River, two apartment buildings, an 11-story garage, and an affiliated two-level shopping and convenience mall, all completely interconnected. Each of the tower floors has only two short halls off the elevator vestibule (on average, there are only eight or ten units per floor), thus avoiding the long, institutional hallways in most large high-rise buildings.

Interstate 95 is just three miles from the complex, and air travel is convenient with Newark International Airport located 14 miles from the Galaxy and LaGuardia just 12 miles away. Local police provide protection, and there is a local fire department.

All necessary services are located in the mall which was built into the complex: a pharmacy, a medical clinic, a dry cleaners, a hair salon, a grocery store, a liquor store, a restaurant, retail shops, a bank, a video store, a law office, a dentist's office, a florist, a shoe repair, and even a movie theater. The Palisades Hospital is one mile from the community.

RECREATION AND SOCIAL ACTIVITIES

For most of the Galaxy's residents, the skyscrapers are the hub of their social life. In addition to free movies every Friday night, residents also enjoy periodic televised sports events, socializing in the spa lounge, or participating in many activities: ski weekends, the annual New Year's Eve party and holiday bazaar, outdoor picnics, cabaret evenings, weekend bike trips, sing-alongs, photography exhibitions, singles' dinners, and so on. Social clubs offer owners many areas to explore their interests: bible study, business roundtables, dance, drama, golf, gourmet cooking, seniors, singles, and sports leagues.

One of the Galaxy's best-kept secrets from the outside world is the existence of its jewel of a park located on top of the mall building. This park affords the most magnificent unobscured river and cityscape views imaginable, from the George Washington Bridge to the Statue of Liberty and Verrazano Bridge.

At no additional charge to residents, the Galaxy provides one of the most comprehensive health and sports centers available to high-rise dwellers anywhere in the United States. The center contains a physical fitness room with a full line of equipment, an indoor heated pool (75 feet long with four lap lanes and a skylight roof), a heated kids' pool, a whirlpool, saunas, steam rooms, tanning rooms, and locker rooms. Also available by private appointment are massages, facials, tennis and swimming instruction, and special classes such as scuba diving. For children there are outdoor playgrounds, an indoor playroom, special movies, story hours, piano classes, art instruction, family sing-alongs, and holiday parties.

There is a recreation director, and the association publishes a monthly newsletter. Valet/concierge services include greeting and announcing guests, accepting mail and packages, calling for limos and taxis, and overseeing all move-ins and move-outs. Each of the three lobbies is staffed 24 hours a day. In the lobbies you can find shopping and luggage carts, assistance with loading or unloading, and deposit boxes for outgoing U.S. mail and the intra-complex mail system.

Security is very tight at the Galaxy. Access to the residential portion of the complex can be attained only through the lobbies, which are manned 24 hours a day. Each unit has an intercom connection to the concierge desk and an intrusion alarm system. Once the system is activated, any unauthorized entry results in the emission of a loud alarm in the unit and sends a signal to the concierge, who then immediately contacts security.

HOMEOWNER ASSESSMENTS, TAXES, AND UTILITIES

There are 1,075 homes at the Galaxy, ranging in price from $140,000 to $400,000. Monthly association assessments cost between $300 and $650. The current yearly property/municipal taxes range from $3,000 to $6,500. There are approximately 300 one-bedroom units, 500 two-bedroom units, and 275 three-bedroom units. There has never been a special assessment, and there are monies reserved for future replacements, new equipment, or other maintenance in excess of $3 million.

The community has both cable television service and community television channels. Electricity provides the primary heating source, and the local municipality provides both sewer waste disposal and water services. All utilities are below ground, and there are extra storage facilities within the community.

An in-house staff of 140 employees provides management of the facility. Counting the board of directors and committee volunteers, there are 250 people who oversee life at the Galaxy.

The community has an excellent working relationship with local municipal officials. In fact, a new district was created especially for the Galaxy; voting booths for all federal, state, and municipal elections are in the mall. Galaxy residents are members of every major municipal board and agency, including the board of education.

RESTRICTIONS IN THE COMMUNITY

There is a community association and membership is mandatory. The association handles all exterior building/grounds maintenance. Because the Galaxy is a high-rise association, exterior modifications to buildings and the grounds are strictly prohibited. The architectural control committee even governs window shades, balconies, and the like. The association also offers an in-unit service department that can provide interior repairs, installations, painting, and assistance in moving heavy objects.

There are no restrictions on the age of guests or their length-of-stay. Only two pets per unit are allowed. There are no restrictions on how many people can occupy a single unit. If a unit is to be leased, the lease must be for a minimum of six months. Only certain occupations are allowed in the units; for example, no traffic-generating businesses are permitted. The 11-story parking garage is open to all tenants; however, there are no special parking areas for recreational vehicles, boats, and other large vehicles.

LEISURE VILLAGE WEST

3C Buckingham Drive
Lakehurst, New Jersey 08733
908-363-9000

$80,000 to $179,990
2,620/2,725 Garden-style
Condominiums
Contemporary Architecture

2 9-hole par 3 golf courses	2 outdoor pools
6-acre lake and 3 ponds	14 miles to Atlantic Ocean
250 acres of open space	2 picnic areas
2 lighted outdoor tennis courts	Handball/racquetball
14 lighted shuffleboard courts	3 bocci courts
2 large clubhouses	Exercise room

INTRODUCTION

Leisure Village West, an age-restricted community in southern New Jersey, is comparable to a full-time summer camp for adults. Most of the buyers are early retirees from northern New Jersey and the New York metropolitan area. They move here for the low-maintenance living and high-energy activities.

Developed by Leisure Technology, which has been listed on the New York Stock Exchange since 1969, the first home in Leisure Village West was built in 1971. Over its 30-year history, Leisure Technology has built homes for more than 30,000 people in New Jersey, Florida, Illinois, California, and New York; it is one of our nation's largest and most successful builders of adult communities.

Just six miles from the Garden State Parkway Exit 88, Leisure Village West is located near beaches, shops, and entertainment. Both Newark and Philadelphia are 55 miles from the site; New York City is 65 miles away. The nearest air transportation is Newark's International Airport, but LaGuardia and JFK Airports are within a reasonable distance.

The local police department, with its 57 officers, provides police protection. The community is completely secured by a six-foot chain link fence surrounding the entire development, regular patrols, and a 24-hour guarded gate. Leisure Village West is also serviced by a 75-member volunteer fire department. The Community Medical Center, the nearest facility with emergency care, is seven miles from Leisure Village West.

The community is entirely residential with no commercial services on site; however, all necessary services are quite close. Within a quarter mile you will find a pharmacy, a dry cleaners and a hair salon. A grocery and liquor store and a movie theater are within two miles. The Ocean County Mall, just eight miles from the development, features Macy, Sears, Stern, and Penney stores as well as many smaller boutiques and shops. The nearest medical clinic is seven miles away.

This area of New Jersey offers an abundance of activities. Ocean beaches are 14 miles away from Leisure Village West, and there are several river and lake beaches within ten miles. Several public and private golf courses are within 15 miles, and the Atlantic City nightlife and casinos are 55 miles away. The Garden State Arts Center, known for its outstanding concerts, is 35 miles from Leisure Village. Of course, New York and Philadelphia are within a few hours' drive.

RECREATION AND SOCIAL ACTIVITIES

You could never possibly be bored at Leisure Village West. Two 9-hole par 3 golf courses, a putting green, and over 50 clubs can keep you busy for days on end. The community's two performing arts centers, with a combined seating capacity of 900, are available for dinners, dances, parties, meetings, lectures, movies, musicals, and shows.

Other recreational amenities include two large pools with patios, a jacuzzi, 14 lighted shuffleboard courts, three bocci courts, a stocked six-acre lake with rowboats, two ponds, cookout areas near the lake, two illuminated tennis courts, two paddle tennis courts, an outdoor exercise course, a volleyball court, and five nautilus machines.

The many interesting clubs are the heart of social interaction at Leisure Village West. Facilities for hobbies and club activities include two ceramic studios equipped with molds and kilns; two billiard rooms with a total of seven tables; a woodworking shop equipped with machines and tools; two sewing rooms with nine machines and accessories; two library rooms; a chamber music studio with a baby grand piano; a completely equipped color photography darkroom; and fully equipped art and lapidary rooms.

The community employs a full-time recreational staff and publishes a monthly newsletter. Leisure Village's private community television channels keep all owners abreast of activities and events in the development. A 44-passenger courtesy bus makes excursions for shopping, organized trips, and religious services. Visiting nurse services are also available.

HOMEOWNER ASSESSMENTS, TAXES, AND UTILITIES

All of the homes at Leisure Village West are one-story garden-style condominiums arranged in styles from duplex to sixplex and ranging in price from $80,000 to $179,990. Owners pay between $100 and $176 per month to the community association. These assessments cover operations and staffing costs; use of all recreation centers and amenities; 24-hour security; all water and sewer charges for common facilities; twice-weekly refuse pickup; master TV/FM cable system; exterior home maintenance; landscaping of all common areas and golf courses; street maintenance; use of the courtesy bus; property, fire, and liability insurance on all common areas; maintenance of all original G.E. appliances, heating and air conditioning equipment; reserves for replacement and repair of common facilities; designated parking areas for recreational vehicles and boats; and snow removal.

Homes built prior to 1985 are heated by electricity; homes built after 1985 are heated by gas. The local municipality provides both sewer and water systems. Irrigation for landscaping is handled by well water sources. All utilities are below ground. There are no extra storage facilities within the community.

RESTRICTIONS IN THE COMMUNITY

Age is the major restriction at Leisure Village West. You must be at least 55 years old to purchase here. Children are not allowed but may visit for up to three months.

Community association membership is mandatory at Leisure Village West, and the association handles all maintenance for homes and common areas. Any exterior changes must adhere to the community's approved list of modifications. Residents maintain a three-foot area at the front of each home; all other landscaping is handled by the association.

Pets are allowed but must be leashed when outside a unit, and they are not allowed in recreation areas. Only three full-time residents are allowed to live in each unit. Any renters must meet age requirements. Homes are strictly residential; no businesses may be operated from them. The association has a right of first refusal on resales. Parking is only allowed in driveways, garages, and designated areas. The association provides two parking lots for recreation vehicles.

ROSSMOOR

Rossmoor Community
Association
2 Rossmoor Drive
Jamesburg, New Jersey 08831
609-655-1400

$125,900 to $289,900
2,223/2,246 Condos and
Townhomes
New England Colonial
Architecture

18-hole golf course	Outdoor pool
2 outdoor tennis courts	4 shuffleboard courts
Clubhouse	Exercise room
Billiards room	Photography darkroom
Internal bus service	Woodworking shop

INTRODUCTION

Founded in 1967, Rossmoor was one of the first age-restricted communities in the country. Located about an hour's drive from New York City and just slightly farther from Philadelphia, Rossmoor gives retirees a rural location that is close to urban cultural opportunities. Princeton is next door, providing historical sites, cultural activities, and first-class medical facilities. If you take the New Jersey Turnpike (just one mile from Rossmoor), the drive to Newark's International Airport is less than one hour.

Rossmoor is one of the few planned communities that is 99 percent complete, leaving absolutely no question about future development. What you see is what you get. Age restrictions apply, but would probably not affect many retirees and even some still in the working world. One resident must be at least 55 years old; any housemates must be 48 years of age or older. Obviously, children do not qualify; there are strict rules for the length of stay of visitors. If renting is part of your plans, remember that the age restrictions also apply to the renters.

RECREATION AND SOCIAL ACTIVITIES

Rossmoor provides activities for everybody, so many that the problem is cramming the opportunities into a 24-hour day. Start with the golf course (a professional is on the premises) and the golf shop. Use the olympic-size outdoor pool, the tennis courts, and shuffleboard courts. Check out the 30,000 square foot clubhouse, which includes a large lounge, three party rooms, an art studio, a ceramic studio, a woodworking shop, a billiards room, a sewing room, a card room, a reading room, and a library. Keep up-to-date with the community newspaper and keep in shape with the hair salon and barber shop. All of the association's recreational facilities are free for homeowner use (except the golf course, which requires extra fees).

The social activities are organized by a full-time social director who supplements the on-site activities with theater parties in New York, gaming at the casinos in Atlantic City, world travel clubs, and education on a variety of subjects. A variety of clubs are available, and, as the association words it, there are "over 3,000 nice neighbors." Residents can be as busy as they want to be.

For retirees in the New York, Connecticut, Pennsylvania, and New Jersey area, Rossmoor offers an active life in an age-restricted community that is still within a few hours of friends and relatives. The senior citizen communities of New Jersey attract more residents than those in every state except Florida and Arizona. Residents of Rossmoor find that they can be active in both summer and winter and still stay close to familiar environments. For example, the golf course remains open all year, the indoor tennis groups are organized for different skill levels, and bowling, bocci, and billiards continue unabated throughout the year.

The association calendar of events for January 1991 listed up to six regularly scheduled events each day and about 80 other events that did not occur on a weekly basis. With all of these possible activities, there is no question that "Rossmoor is where the good life begins."

HOMEOWNER ASSESSMENTS, TAXES, AND UTILITIES

Rossmoor living units feature prices ranging from $125,900 to $289,900. Current monthly maintenance charges for all units varies from $183 to $202. Real estate taxes for the lower-priced units are about $200 monthly, while the higher-priced units can cost up to $438 in taxes. All building and grounds maintenance, trash collection, snow removal, and landscaping service are done by the association.

Cable television is available. Heat is provided by electricity, allowing individual control of the heat in each room. Water and sewage systems are municipally operated. All utility wires are underground. Extra storage facilities are available within the community. An internal bus service, operating from 8 A.M. to 4 P.M. every day except Sunday, makes every facility readily available. With prior reservation, shopping buses are available on both mornings and afternoons for grocery shopping at local supermarkets. Religious service buses go to Catholic, Episcopalian, and Community churches and a Jewish synagogue.

The association provides for perimeter restrictions and a 24-hour security guard with regular patrols. A medical clinic on community grounds is open for 24 hours daily; a registered nurse is on duty at all times, and there are three fully equipped examination rooms with EKG equipment and portable resuscitators. The cost of operating the clinic is covered by the regular monthly assessments, but medication and doctor's fees are not covered and will cost extra. A visiting nurse service is also available to Rossmoor residents.

RESTRICTIONS IN THE COMMUNITY

Rossmoor association exercises strict control over all exterior additions or changes, including plantings and gardens. The association handles all exterior buildings and grounds maintenance.

There are restrictions against using residences for business purposes if the business would involve nonresidents and vehicles coming in and out of the community. There are some parking restrictions, but separate space for recreational vehicles is provided. There are no restrictions on how many people may occupy a single unit. Pet restrictions conform with the township requirements. The association also maintains the right of first refusal on the sale of any unit and all sales are subject to age restrictions as well as certain income restrictions.

SMITHVILLE

One North New York Road
Smithville, New Jersey 08201
609-652-3311

$59,000 to $250,000
1,426/4,860 Garden-style
Condos, Townhomes, and
Single-family Homes
Contemporary/Colonial
Architecture

1 outdoor pool, 1 kiddie pool
10 miles to Atlantic Ocean
6 hiking trails, picnic areas
2 lighted outdoor tennis courts
Large clubhouse

3 non-swimming lakes
50 acres of open space
4 ball-playing fields
Private air strip
Exercise room, steam/sauna

INTRODUCTION

The Smithville community association, located within a few miles of New Jersey's shore resorts, offers a private master planned community for all walks of life. The developer, Smithville Development Company, has created a permanent buffer of undeveloped land in the community through a unique agreement with environmental agencies in south New Jersey. Smithville's tracts will not exceed 2,500 acres and 4,860 homes. To date, 1,426 homes have been sold.

Smithville Development Company is actively involved in the growth of the community. The company has built a daycare center and has established a $1,000 scholarship for the community's most outstanding high school scholar-athlete.

Atlantic City, the nearest large town, has a population of 35,000 and is ten miles from Smithville. The Garden State Parkway, only two miles from Smithville, eases access by car. Air transportation is available at the Atlantic City airport. Police protection is provided by Galloway Township, the Atlantic County sheriff's department, and the New Jersey state police. The Oceanville volunteer fire department provides emergency services to the community. The Atlantic City Medical Center, the nearest facility with emergency care, is three miles away.

Smithville is virtually a self-contained community. Within the development are restaurants, a pharmacy, a dry cleaners, a hair salon, a grocery and liquor store, retail shops and a video rental store. The nearest medical clinic is about two miles away; the nearest movie theater is ten miles from the site.

South Jersey provides many other local attractions. Atlantic City's casinos, convention center, and boardwalk are only ten miles away. The Jersey shore offers an incredible array of beach activity from Brigantine to Ocean City.

RECREATION AND SOCIAL ACTIVITIES

Smithville provides recreation centers, an in-ground swimming pool and a children's pool, a bath house, a universal gym, a dance studio, a library, tennis courts, bike paths, playgrounds, basketball courts, ball fields, and trails. Smithville is also home to a polo club where residents can cheer on their own polo team. In addition, a wealth of open space and two small lakes are set aside for exercise and fun.

The community employs a recreation director and organizes trips and on-site entertainment for homeowner enjoyment. For example, the January 1991 calendar of events had activities for everyone: Miss Smithville pageant for girls (ages 12 to 16); adult game night; afternoon shuffleboard; ski trip to Vernon Valley; wellness program for seniors; and a fireside evening of entertainment. Activities for the kids within the community include Cub Scouts, teen fitness, Brownies, a bookmobile, and pee wee flag football.

After a total of 1,800 homes have been sold, an additional recreation center with indoor pool facilities will be built at the complex.

HOMEOWNER ASSESSMENTS, TAXES, AND UTILITIES

Smithville offers a variety of distinct neighborhoods; you can choose your preferred lifestyle and environment at the price you can afford. All of the homes are a mix of contemporary and colonial architecture.

The 650 garden-style condominiums each cost $59,000+. Within the development there are 315 townhome style units, starting at $79,000. The condominium and townhome owners pay between $38 and $72 in monthly community association assessments, depending on the individual neighborhood. In addition, the owners pay $46.90 every month to Smithville's master association. Property taxes for these homes average about $1,500 per year.

The 450 single-family homes only belong to the master association, which makes their monthly community association assessment $46.90. These homes range in price from $110,000 to $250,000, their annual property taxes range between $2,000 and $3,000.

Both cable and community television channels are available to homeowners. Homes are heated primarily by gas or electricity. The local municipality provides both sewer and water services to Smithville. All utilities are underground.

RESTRICTIONS IN THE COMMUNITY

Community association membership is mandatory at Smithville. The association handles building and grounds maintenance for the condominiums and townhomes as well as all amenities and the infrastructure. Single-family homeowners provide their own building and grounds maintenance. All exterior and landscap-

ing changes must have architectural review committee approval. Guidelines have
been established for everything from exterior house color to fences.

Local ordinances govern how many people may occupy a single unit. There are
no rental restrictions within the community. Operating a business from a home is
prohibited. The association does not restrict resales in any way. Certain areas of
the development have assigned parking. The association does not provide an area
for oversized vehicle parking; however, there are private self-storage lots within
Smithville.

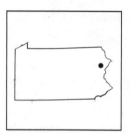

BUCK HILL FALLS

Box D-2
Buck Hill Falls, Pennsylvania
18323
717-595-7511

$160,000 to $1,400,000
278/500 Townhomes and
Single-family Homes
Contemporary Architecture

27-hole USGA-rated golf course
Ski area 5 miles away
10 miles of hiking trails
10 outdoor tennis courts

Outdoor pool, kiddie pool
4 cross-country ski trails
1 picnic area
Privately operated
horse stables

INTRODUCTION

Nestled on 5,000 acres in Pennsylvania's Pocono mountains, Buck Hill Falls is
a classic private country club resort community. Buck Hill Falls is just 90 miles
from New York City. Route 80 and Route 84 are both about 10 to 15 miles away.
Air transportation is provided by the Allentown-Bethlehem-Easton Airport which
is 52 miles from the site.

Buck Hill Falls is an interesting planned community that dates back to the
early 1900s. In the late 1890s, Samuel Griscom, a Philadelphia Quaker, held
title to the Falls area and a small parcel of adjacent land. Griscom envisioned
this setting as an ideal location for a Quaker summer meeting place. The first
parcels of land at Buck Hills were sold in 1901, and the first home was built in
1903. Although some land owners enjoyed camping out on their property, many
opted to build cottages. At that time the price for unimproved land was two
dollars per acre. The total cost, including painting and plumbing, for a cottage at
Buck Hill Falls was less than $600, a far cry from what it costs to build a home
today.

A restaurant is located within the community; however, all other services
(pharmacy, medical clinic, dry cleaners, hair salon, grocery and liquor store and
retail shops) are about one mile away. The nearest movie theater is seven miles
from the site. The nearest hospital with emergency facilities is the Pocono Hospital, about 18 miles away. Police coverage for the area is provided by local, county,
and state police authorities. A volunteer fire department and an ambulance corps
are about one mile away from the community.

The Buck Hill Falls community is surrounded by fine restaurants, excellent antique stores, and a myriad of country shops. The Pocono Playhouse is just minutes from the stone bridge entry into the community. There are also several downhill ski areas, including Camelback, Alpine Mountain, and Jack Frost, which are just a short drive away. Lake Walenpaupack, the largest lake in Pennsylvania, is also located just 17 miles from Buck Hill Falls.

RECREATION AND SOCIAL ACTIVITIES

The 27-hole vintage championship golf course is in the best shape it has ever been. With the irrigation of 20 of the 27 holes now complete, the golf course is ready for the 90s and beyond, quite different from the layout that had its beginning in 1907. The olympic-size outdoor swimming pool, along with the diving well and wading pool, offers many hours of fun and excitement. The community sponsors lawn-bowling and provides manicured and groomed croquet greens. There are trout streams, nature trails, and waterfalls for you to enjoy. Ten miles of hiking trails and four cross-country ski trails provide activities for the most energetic enthusiasts. There are picnic areas, ten outdoor tennis courts, a privately operated horse stable, and a bridle path that winds through the community.

Buck Hill offers a wealth of cultural, social, and community activities, including art and craft classes, seminars, concerts, sports tournaments, and seasonal festivities. Although the community does not have a recreation director, it does publish a monthly newsletter and organizes trips for homeowners. Food catering services and local visiting caregiver services are available. There is a 24-hour patrol within the community.

All club and recreational activities at Buck Hill Falls require additional membership fees. The fee to join the country club ranges from $900 (single) to $1700 (corporate). Golfers pay $28 for green fees and $12 for cart rental. Tennis fees are eight dollars per single and six dollars per double. Pool usage costs $275 per family for a seasonal ticket or an eight dollar daily charge.

HOMEOWNER ASSESSMENTS, TAXES, AND UTILITIES

Currently, at Buck Hill Falls there are 278 completed homes out of a planned 500 homes. There are 57 townhomes ranging in price from $160,000 to $250,000. Each of the townhome owners pay between $350 and $375 per month in community association dues and exterior maintenance fees. The townhome property/municipal taxes fall between $1,400 and $3,000 per year. The 221 single-family homes at Buck Hill Falls range in price from $125,000 to $1.4 million, with monthly association dues and exterior maintenance fees of between $240 and $375. Their yearly property/municipal taxes run between $1,200 and $12,000. Currently there are eight two-bedroom units, 90 three-bedroom units, 75 four-bedroom units and 105 homes with more than four bedrooms.

Cable television is available, but there are no community television channels. Heat is provided by both electric and oil sources. Sewer waste services are handled either by septic systems or community systems. Water is provided either by well water or community water sources. Telephone and electrical wires and poles can be either above or below ground, depending upon the home's location. There are no extra storage facilities within the community; however, there are private facilities within one mile.

RESTRICTIONS IN THE COMMUNITY

Buck Hill Falls has a community association and membership is mandatory. Any plans for exterior modifications to your home must be approved by the architectural review committee and must comply with the covenants of the association. Any exterior landscaping you wish to do must also be approved by this committee.

There are no restrictions on the age of visitors or length-of-stay. Any pets must be leashed. The restrictions on maximum occupation state that there can be no more people than the number of beds within a house. If you choose to rent your unit, the renters may not have pets and the lease must be for a minimum of one month.

The operation of a business from a home is prohibited. There are restrictions on the resale of units, including a required stock purchase and the right of first refusal. Parking and vehicle restrictions are determined according to the size of garages and driveways. The association provides a special area to park recreational vehicles and boats.

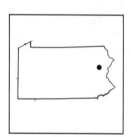

EAGLE LAKE

P.O. Box 305, Rt. 435
Gouldsboro, Pennsylvania
18424
717-842-4541

$25,000 and up
2,862/3,933 Fee Simple Lots
for RVs and Park Model Homes
Park Model Homes/Full-size
Travel Trailers

1 outdoor olympic-size pool
Boating, 400 boat slips
1 hiking trail
1 ball-playing field

70-acre lake with one mile of shore
Over 100 acres of open space
3 picnic areas
6 outdoor tennis courts

INTRODUCTION

The Eagle Lake community association is one of the largest and best-maintained RV resorts in the northeast. The builders of the community, The Larsen Family doing business as the Eagle Lake Corporation, calls it "Your Affordable Pocono Resort Community." It is truly an affordable alternative to a high-priced vacation home.

Eagle Lake has been carefully planned because the developer has recognized the need to preserve the surrounding environment, not only for the immediate needs of owners, but also for long-term environmental reasons. Four generations of the Larsen family have been planning and designing recreational communities, starting in 1892. They have developed nine communities throughout New York, New Jersey, and Pennsylvania. Eagle Lake's first lot was sold in 1981.

Located just nine miles from Scranton, Eagle Lake offers park model homes, individual lots, or a combination of both lot and home. The community comprises many acres of prime Pocono resort land including a 70-acre lake. Residents may utilize the community year-round, but all homes must retain their mobile qualities.

Even though the property is quite isolated, Routes 380, 80, 81, and 84 are all within two miles. The Wilkes-Barre/Scranton International Airport, 15 miles away, provides the nearest air transportation. With a population of 180,000, Scranton is eight miles from the site. Police coverage is provided by local, county, and state police authorities. Entrance to the community is through a guarded gatehouse. A nearby volunteer fire department provides emergency services to residents. The Community Medical Center, eight miles away, offers emergency care when needed.

Within Eagle Lake property there is a country retail store, a snack bar, and service shops. Just half a mile from the site you will find a pharmacy, a medical clinic, a dry cleaners, a hair salon, and a liquor store. The nearest movie theater is eight miles from Eagle Lake.

Outdoor activities abound in this Pocono Resort region. The Montage Water Park, the Everhart Museum, the Masonic Temple Theater, Steamtown USA, and McDade Park are just a few of the sites to see. There are excellent snow-skiing opportunities throughout the region.

RECREATION AND SOCIAL ACTIVITIES

The community's 70-acre pristine alpine lake offers residents the chance to experience nature at its best. There are 400 boat slips for owners' convenience, and fishing is a favorite pastime. Eagle Lake also has a 10,000-square-foot outdoor pool that kids love, six outdoor tennis courts, hiking trails, picnic areas, and ball-playing fields; the children will never be bored.

The multi-purpose lakefront clubhouse is the center of the community's social activities. Eagle Lake's recreation program is professionally directed by MLA Management Associates, Inc. Planned trips, on-site classes in crafts, activities for teens, and daycare for children (in the summer months) are a few of the offerings. The association publishes a quarterly newsletter, provides an internal bus service, and even provides food catering from the community's snack bar.

All amenities are included in the owner's monthly community association assessment. Some activities might require nominal user fees.

HOMEOWNER ASSESSMENTS, TAXES, AND UTILITIES

Currently, 2,432 of the 3,933 lots at Eagle Lake have been sold. The association's 1991 budget is $2.65 million.

You may either place a park model RV or drive your own recreational vehicle to your lot. Regardless, all units must maintain their mobility. Lots are owned on a fee simple basis and generally cost about $25,000. The new home unit averages $20,000 for a total minimum investment of $45,000. Each lot owner pays $70 per month in community association assessments and about $350 per year in property taxes.

There is a community-owned and -operated cable television service with community channels. Both gas and electricity provide the primary heat source for homes. Eagle Lake also owns its own sewer, electric, and water systems. All utilities are underground. There are extra storage facilities within the community for homeowner use.

RESTRICTIONS IN THE COMMUNITY

Membership in the Eagle Lake community association is mandatory. Individual lot owners provide their own exterior building and grounds maintenance. The association maintains common areas, recreational amenities, and infrastructure. Owners are prohibited from making any exterior alterations that would prevent the mobility of a unit. There are no restrictions regarding landscaping.

Age and length-of-stay restrictions do not exist at Eagle Lake as long as the property is not utilized for permanent residency. Pets are allowed but must be leashed when outside a unit and are restricted from all common areas. There are no restrictions on how many people may occupy a unit, nor are there any rental or resale restrictions. Operating a commercial activity from a home is strictly prohibited. All vehicles must be parked on the owner's designated lot. The association does provide extra parking space for oversized vehicles.

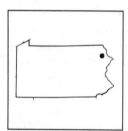

HEMLOCK FARMS

Box 1007 Hemlock Farms
Hemlock Farms Road
Hawley, Pennsylvania 18428
717-775-7377

$85,000 to $300,000
2,375/4,240 Single-family
Homes
Modern and Rustic Architecture

18-hole golf course
4 lakes
Boating
66 boat slips (16 to 20 feet)
10 outdoor tennis courts
5 picnic areas
Handball/racquetball/squash
Exercise room

1 indoor pool, 2 outdoor pools
1 kiddie pool
Teen center, library
Cross-country ski trails
1 hiking trail
2 ball-playing fields
Clubhouse
Sauna

INTRODUCTION

Hemlock Farms is a 4,500-acre private community located in Pike County, Pennsylvania, adjacent to Peck's Pond between Routes 402 and 739. Begun in 1963 by Home, Smith International, Hemlock Farms consists of 4,240 building lots of which 92 percent are located in Blooming Grove Township. About 7 percent of the lots are located in Porter Township and 1 percent in Dingman Township. The community is about 16 miles from Milford, 20 miles from Hawley, 25 miles from Port Jervis, New York, and about 30 miles from Stroudsburg, Pennsylvania.

Individual property owners now own ninety-five percent of the lots. Thus far, 2,375 homes have been constructed. About 800 of these homes are occupied by permanent residents, the rest by weekend or summer residents. Deed restrictions, which will be in effect until the year 2003, allow only single-family residences to be constructed. The nearest interstate is I-84, located one mile from the community. The Wilkes-Barre/Scranton International Airport, located 51 miles away, provides air transportation.

There are volunteer fire and ambulance services on the property, and the area is covered by state police patrol. The nearest hospital with emergency facilities is in Stroudsburg, 25 miles away. There are no services provided within the community; however, most services (including pharmacy, medical clinic, hair salon, restaurant, and retail shops) are within one mile of Hemlock Farms. About 18 miles away, you will find a dry cleaners, a grocery and liquor store, and movie theaters. Other local attractions include the many Pocono Mountains' resort ski areas and the Delaware Water Gap National Recreation Area.

RECREATION AND SOCIAL ACTIVITIES

The Hemlock Farm community association maintains three lakes with four beach areas; bath houses are available. Docks and boat racks can be found at five locations and are rented to members. There are two swimming pools with bath houses, 10 tennis courts, a baseball field, a basketball court, a volleyball court, an adult center, and a teen center. A library is operated on a volunteer basis by the Hemlock Farms women's club in a building provided by the association.

Also on the property is a private country club with an 18-hole golf course, a swimming pool, a tennis court, a restaurant, and other facilities. Membership is limited to 380 families.

Hemlock Farms has hiking trails and picnic areas for homeowner use. Currently, an indoor pool is under construction. The clubhouse contains an exercise room and a steam and sauna room. There is a recreation director, and the association publishes a monthly newsletter. The association sponsors organized trips and provides on-site entertainment and on-site crafts; the teen center also sponsors many activities. Security is tight at Hemlock Farms. There is a 24-hour patrol within the community, and perimeter restrictions include both guarded and electronic gates.

Future amenities include a 40-acre park; phase I is scheduled for completion in July 1991. There will also be a 10,000-square-foot addition to the recreation center, which will house an indoor pool, an arts and crafts center, locker facilities, and a snack bar. This addition is scheduled for completion in January 1992.

All facilities are free for homeowners except for the private country club facilities and the golf course.

HOMEOWNER ASSESSMENTS, TAXES, AND UTILITIES

Almost all of the lots at Hemlock Farms have been sold. There are currently 2,375 single-family homes at the site. These homes range in price from $85,000 to $300,000. Community association assessments vary, depending on the type of lot. Annually, type A lot owners pay $334, type U lot owners pay $516, and type I lot owners pay $853. The 1990 budget for the association was $3,260,000.

During the summer the recreation staff includes an adult center supervisor, a sports director, an aquatics director, a tennis director, a day camp director, and over 70 other personnel including lifeguards, tennis instructors, sports assistants, camp counselors, and instructors of arts and crafts. Approximately 80 other individuals are employed on a part-time or seasonal basis in the areas of clerical assistance, public works, snow removal, and security. Most of the homes are built in a modern or rustic architectural style. The association does require that homes meet a 1,500-square-foot minimum.

Both cable and community television channels are available to homeowners. Heating is provided by either electricity or oil. A septic system disposes of sewer waste; water is provided through the association-owned water company. Utilities are both above and below ground. There are no extra storage facilities within the community.

RESTRICTIONS IN THE COMMUNITY

There is a community association at Hemlock Farms and membership is mandatory. The community association owns all the common amenities, roads, buildings, and water system; community association assessments maintain all of these facilities. Individual homeowners are responsible for their own exterior building/grounds maintenance. Any modifications or building done at the site must be approved by the homeowners association, but the association does not govern landscaping of individual lots.

There are no restrictions regarding age or length-of-stay for visitors, no pet restrictions, no restrictions on maximum occupation of a single unit, and no rental restrictions. A deed restriction prohibits operating a business from a home. There are no restrictions on the resale of units at Hemlock Farms. All parking of vehicles must be on the owner's lot and not on berms or roads. Any trucks, recreational vehicles, or boats must be screened from public view when parked on private property. The association does not provide special parking areas for recreational vehicles.

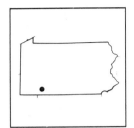

HIDDEN VALLEY RESORT

1900 South Ridge Drive
Hidden Valley, Pennsylvania
15502
814-443-3001

$80,000 to $500,000
900/3,000 Garden-style and
Mid-rise Condos,
Townhomes, and Single-family
Homes
Contemporary Architecture

18-hole USGA-rated golf
3 outdoor pools
21 downhill ski trails
Over 100 acres of open space
30 miles of hiking trails
2 ball-playing fields
6 lighted tennis courts
Clubhouse

1 Indoor pool, 1 kiddie pool
1 lake with 2 miles of shore
30 miles cross-country skiing
Snowmaking capabilities
2 picnic areas
14 outdoor tennis courts
Handball courts
Mountain bike trails

INTRODUCTION

Nestled in 2,000 private acres in the Laurel Mountains of southwestern Pennsylvania, Hidden Valley is a residential resort for moms, dads, and kids, with all the activities families enjoy. Springtime at Hidden Valley is a sight to behold: Budding trees and blooming wildflowers greet you daily. Spring is a time for exploring the full magic of Hidden Valley, a time for biking, hiking, flying kites, and watching fascinating wildlife. Summer brings with it the lush green fairways and long days to enjoy an outdoor picnic. In the summer, Hidden Valley is filled with the music of visiting orchestras and the fun of mountain festivals. In the autumn oak, elm, and maple leaves turn to brilliant golds, purples, and reds, providing a magnificent backdrop for a morning of golf or tennis. Winter is the magic season. You can ski all day and well into the night on 17 well-lit slopes.

Hidden Valley is located just 48 miles from Pittsburgh. Air transportation is provided by Greater Pittsburgh International Airport, about 70 miles from Hidden Valley. Route 31 is near the entrance to this community, allowing easy access. There is local police protection, and a volunteer fire department is nearby. The site is located 12 miles from the Somerset Hospital, the nearest facility with emergency medical care. Within the community there is also a first aid clinic as well as a grocery store, a restaurant, retail stores, and a movie theater. Other services are located within 12 miles of the development.

The Jennerstown Speedway is nearby, providing entertainment for the auto-racing fan. Falling Water, Idlewilde Park, and Seven Springs attract many visitors each year. Hidden Valley is being developed by the Kettler Brothers of Pennsylvania; the first home was built in 1983.

RECREATION AND SOCIAL ACTIVITIES

Hidden Valley is the ultimate four-season private resort community. You can play golf on a spectacular mountaintop course or take a caravan of mountain bikes on a scenic adventure. Thirty miles of hiking trails offer flowering woodlands, lazy streams, and rushing waterfalls. There are swimming pools (both indoor and outdoor), racquet sports, and seven beautiful lakes for family fishing and sailing. For both adults and children, Hidden Valley offers the ultimate in skiing with 17 well-lit slopes, 30 miles of cross-country ski trails, and state-of-the-art snowmaking capabilities. There are rope, double, triple, and quad lifts.

The community employs a recreation director, publishes a monthly newsletter, and provides on-site entertainment and crafts classes. An internal bus service can take you anywhere you need to be; food catering services can make your party just right. There are also facilities for child daycare.

Future amenities to be built at Hidden Valley include an indoor tennis area, a new spa facility, and additional pools. There is a 24-hour patrol within the community.

HOMEOWNER ASSESSMENTS, TAXES, AND UTILITIES

Hidden Valley currently has sold 900 homes; the ultimate build-out is expected to be around 3,000 homes. The developer currently has 25 completed homes for sale. The 900 homes (all contemporary architecture) are made up of 30 mid-rise condos, 304 garden-style condos, 516 townhomes, and 50 single-family homes.

The 304 garden-style condos range in price from $89,000 to $189,000. Condo owners pay $82 per month in community association assessments. Their property/municipal taxes run from $900 to $1,900 per year. The mid-rise units cost between $169,000 and $249,000, with $155 per month in association assessments. The mid-rise condos range between $1,700 and $2,500 per year in property/municipal taxes. The 516 townhomes can cost anywhere from $119,000 to $179,000; the monthly assessment is approximately $100. A townhome's yearly property/ municipal taxes cost between $1,200 and $1,800. The 50 single-family homes range from $200,000 to $500,000, with a monthly assessment of $80 and yearly property/municipal taxes of between $2,000 and $5,000. Health club membership costs $250 per year; golf costs $400 per year.

Cable television channels are available. Electricity provides the primary heat; the sewer waste system and the water service are private. All utilities are under ground.

RESTRICTIONS IN THE COMMUNITY

There is a community association and membership is mandatory. The association handles all exterior building/grounds maintenance for the community. All exterior modifications to a home must have the prior approval of the architectural control committee. Any additional landscaping must also have architectural control committee approval.

There are no restrictions regarding age or length-of-stay for visitors, no pet restrictions, no restrictions on maximum occupation of a unit, and no rental restrictions. Operating a business from a home is prohibited. Parking restrictions prohibit business vehicles, boats, or camping trailers from being parked near a unit. The association, however, does provide special areas to park such vehicles.

THE HIDEOUT

P.O. Box 6
Lake Ariel, Pennsylvania 18436
717-698-5682

$90,000 to $400,000
2,490/4,100 Single-family
Homes
Mixed Architecture

9-hole USG A-rated golf course
6 lakes, 80 boat slips
Double chair and rope tow lifts
Over 100 acres of open space
1 ball-playing field
6 tennis courts w/lights
Handball/racquetball/squash

2 outdoor pools, 1 kiddie pool
Downhill skiing
1 ½ miles of cross-country ski
4 picnic areas
8 outdoor tennis courts
2 indoor tennis courts

INTRODUCTION

The Hideout is a 2,700-acre private planned leisure community surrounded by six lakes. There is an abundance of outdoor activities for homeowners who own one of the 4,100 residential lots at the Hideout. Lake Ariel, located 18 miles from Scranton, is home to the Hideout. Scranton has a population of 180,000.

I-84 is just five miles from the community. Air transportation is provided by the Wilkes-Barre/Scranton International Airport, 22 miles from the site. Police protection is provided by the county sheriff and the Pennsylvania state police. There is a volunteer fire department nearby. The nearest hospital with emergency facilities is located ten miles from the development.

The Hideout was originally developed by the Boise Cascade Company; the first home was built in 1973. The only service located within the community is a restaurant. Within four miles of the Hideout, you will find other services: a pharmacy, a medical clinic, a dry cleaners, a hair salon, a grocery and liquor store, and retail shops. The closest movie theater is 18 miles away. Other local attractions include museums, concert halls, flea markets, and theme parks. Lake Wallenpaupack, one of Pennsylvania's largest lakes, is within four miles of the Hideout. The Hideout is located in the Pocono Mountains, which offers some of the best snow-skiing on the east coast.

RECREATION AND SOCIAL ACTIVITIES

Life outdoors is standard protocol for the Hideout homeowners. A comprehensive year-round amenity system is available. You can enjoy a day of golf at the community's 9-hole, 3,430-yard golf course. There are motorized golf carts, a pro shop, and a complete program of clinics, lessons, and tournaments. A golf pro is on site.

If you want a tan, try one of the community's two outdoor pools (both are heated). The kids will enjoy the kiddie pool, too. Around the lake there are also two large white sand beaches with shower and changing facilities. There are 80 boat slips (17-foot, 85 horsepower maximum) at Lake Roamingwood. There are six lakes at the Hideout: Roamingwood (225 acres); Deerfield (16 acres); Brooks (8 acres); Windemere (1 acre); Hidden Lake (1 acre); and Big Spring Pond (3 acres).

When the weather turns cold and you want some exhilarating outdoor activities, try the Hideout's downhill and cross-country skiing trails. There are three downhill trails and a double chair and rope tow lift. If nature doesn't provide enough snow, the community has its own snowmaking capabilities. If you desire a slower pace, try the two miles of cross-country trails, or relax at the ski lodge and snack bar.

The community has four picnic areas as well as campgrounds with 150 campsites, including a dump station and hookups for electricity and water.

There are two indoor and eight outdoor tennis courts. Six of the outdoor courts are lighted. The resident pro offers a complete program of clinics, lessons, and tournaments. The community owns a large clubhouse with outdoor facilities for handball and racquetball.

The association employs a recreation director, publishes a monthly newsletter, sponsors organized trips, and provides on-site entertainment. In 1990, a newly completed arts center added a new dimension to the site, providing space for arts, crafts, ceramics, and the like. The association sponsors activities for teens; local daycare is available for young children. To ensure security and privacy, the Hideout has a 24-hour patrol within the community and both guarded and electronic access gates. In 1991–92, the association plans to add a new kiddie pool and a new clubhouse/community center. Homeownership automatically qualifies you for participation in all recreational facilities.

HOMEOWNER ASSESSMENTS, TAXES, AND UTILITIES

The Hideout is property owner's association with 2,490 completed homes built and 4,100 lots. The homes range in price from $90,000 to $400,000. Each lot owner pays an annual assessment of $482. In addition, the association charges a $100 special assessment per year to fund its long-term reserve and replacements' accounts. Improved properties have an $85 central trash fee. The association's yearly budget is about $4 million. Current yearly municipal/property taxes for homes run between $600 and $1,500.

There is a mixed variety of architectural styles within the development. Cable television is available but there are no community channels. Both electricity and oil provide the primary heating source for homeowners. The community owns its own central sewer and water system; sewer and water fees are separate. All utilities are above ground. There is no extra storage on site; however, there are storage facilities within half a mile of the Hideout.

RESTRICTIONS IN THE COMMUNITY

There is a community association at the Hideout and membership is mandatory. Individual homeowners provide their own exterior building/grounds maintenance. The association provides all maintenance for recreational facilities and common areas (there are 40 miles of paved, private roads in the community). Any exterior modifications must follow the local building codes. Any landscaping done around a home must be approved by the environmental control committee.

There are no restrictions regarding age or length-of-stay for visitors. Pets are permitted; there is a leash law and a restriction forbidding excessive barking. All homes are limited to single-family occupation. If you rent your home, rental registration fees are required. Operating a business from your home is prohibited by the association covenants. There are no restrictions on resales of homes. Parking is not allowed on the streets. The community provides a special area to park recreational vehicles and boats.

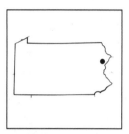

LAKE ADVENTURE

Route 739, Rural Route 3, Box 5000

Milford, Pennsylvania 18337

717-686-2800

$7,000 to $20,000

1,760/1,794 Campground Lots

Recreational Vehicles, Mobile Homes, and Tents

1 outdoor pool
Boating
100 acres of open space
1 ball-playing field
Clubhouse
Full-court basketball

26-acre lake
100 private boat slips/16-foot maximum
2 picnic areas
2 outdoor tennis courts
Bocci ball court

INTRODUCTION

Lake Adventure, a campground community, is situated in the midst of 76,000 acres of Pennsylvania gamelands and forest preserves. Since 1892 four generations of the Larsen family have been developing communities for thousands of families. In 1976, the Larsen family developed Lake Adventure. Ownership of Lake Adventure was transferred from the developer to the association in 1981. The community has assets of $6 million.

Your own recreational vehicle, park model home, or tent is your residence; no need to build or rent. You just drive your movable second home to your private wooded site and setup. As you enjoy the beauty of nature, you still have the conveniences of modern life, such as central water, sewer facilities, underground electricity, refuse collection, and comfort stations. For families who do not own a recreational vehicle, Lake Adventure's camping experts can suggest the vehicle that will best suit your family's lifestyle. Models are on display at the community center.

Lake Adventure is eight miles away from Milford, Pennsylvania, which has a population of 10,000. Route 84 is four miles from the entrance to this community. The Wilkes-Barre/Scranton International Airport is 40 miles from the site. Police protection is provided by local, county, and state police authorities. There is a volunteer fire department nearby. The nearest hospital with emergency facilities is 20 miles from the community.

The only service in Lake Adventure is a restaurant. Within two miles of the community you will find a pharmacy, a medical clinic, a hair salon, a grocery store, a liquor store, and retail shops. The nearest dry cleaners and movie theaters are eight miles away.

Throughout the Poconos you will find fabulous facilities for skiing, golf, horseback riding, glider and plane rides, snowmobiling, water sports (nearby Lake Wallenpaupak is Pennsylvania's largest lake), horse racing, auto racing, hunting, trout fishing, and much more, all within a 30-mile radius of Lake Adventure.

RECREATION AND SOCIAL ACTIVITIES

At Lake Adventure the possibilities are endless. You and your children can enjoy such activities as a lake stocked with sports fish, a supervised swimming beach, picnic areas, a children's playground, tennis courts, a heated and supervised outdoor pool, a family gamefield, and the community clubhouse with a teen center.

The lake can accommodate boats up to sixteen feet in length. There are 100 boat slips within the community. Lake Adventure employs a recreation director and publishes a monthly newsletter. The association organizes trips and provides on-site entertainment as well as on-site crafts. There is daycare for children and activities for teens. Lake Adventure is a highly secured community. Perimeter access is only by guard or electronic gate, and there is a 24-hour patrol within the campground.

Future amenities include a new state-of-the-art playground and a centralized laundry facility. Homeownership automatically includes membership in all of the club/recreation facilities at this community; however, certain special recreation functions do require a small fee to cover overhead.

HOMEOWNER ASSESSMENTS, TAXES, AND UTILITIES

Lake Adventure is almost full. Currently 1,760 campsites out of a possible 1,794 have been sold; 34 campsites remain. The individual campsites range in price from $7,000 to $20,000. Each campsite owner pays $65 per month in community association assessments. Property taxes average about $200 per year. All recreational vehicles must retain their mobile quality while parked at Lake Adventure. The recreational vehicles can cost anywhere from $10,000 to $200,000. If you would prefer to rough it, you may pitch a tent.

Cable television is available for homeowner use; however, there are no community television channels. The primary heat source is gas. The community owns its own central sewer system and its own water system. Telephone wires and poles are above ground. Electric wires and poles are below ground. There are extra storage facilities within the community.

RESTRICTIONS IN THE COMMUNITY

There is a community association at Lake Adventure and membership is mandatory. The community association provides all the grounds maintenance for the campsites and all maintenance for association-owned facilities and amenities. Exterior modifications to the site or the mobile home unit are governed by bylaws, restrictive covenants, and rules and regulations of the association. There are no restrictions regarding the installation of landscaping.

Sheds can be contructed but are to be used only for storage purposes. Decks may not exceed 300 square feet in total area. Screen houses and gazebos must be removed from the home from December 1 to April 1. Clotheslines are not permitted. Owners of lakefront lots are prohibited from installing their own dock or pier. Painting must be in earth tones and natural colors. No trees over three inches in diameter can be removed from the campsite without approval of the board of directors.

Swimming at Lake Adventure is only permitted in designated beach and pool areas and only when lifeguards are on duty. No dogs or other domestic animals are permitted in the lake water or pool area at any time. All boats must be removed from the lake after use and neatly stored in a designated area. All boats must be registered with the association and marked with authorized tags. Only electric motors (¼ horsepower or less) are permitted. All children under 12 years of age must be accompanied in boats by an adult and must wear a flotation device. Fishing is only permitted during state authorized seasons. A Pennsylvania fishing license is required.

There are no restrictions on age or length-of-stay for visitors. Pets are allowed but must be attended to at all times. There are no restrictions on how many people may occupy a single unit. Operating a business from your campsite is prohibited. If you decide to sell your campground lot, "for sale" signs are not allowed; however, the association does furnish a list of prospective buyers. Parking is restricted to individual driveways. The association provides a special area to park boats and other recreational vehicles.

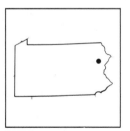

LAKE NAOMI AND TIMBER TRAILS

Route 423
P.O. Box T
Pocono Pines, Pennsylvania
18350
717-646-9191

$100,000 to $700,000
1,700/2,200 Single-family
Homes and Lots
Contemporary Architecture

9-Hole USGA-rated golf course
2 clubhouses
Boating for nonpowered boats
Cross-country skiing
24 outdoor tennis courts
5 picnic areas
2 clubhouses

2 outdoor pools, 1 kiddie pool
3 lakes with 7 miles of shore
800 boat slips
3,000 total acres
Hiking trails
1 ball-playing field

INTRODUCTION

In the early 1890s, Lake Naomi was created by damming Tunkhannock Creek near West Beach. The work was done with strong backs, horses, and pure determination; the builders envisioned a thriving ice business and a summer resort that would attract folks from the cities. The ice business did not survive the advent of refrigeration, but the lake remained for future generations to use for recreation. In 1963 the 3,000 acres surrounding Lake Naomi were purchased from the heirs of the ice company's founders, and the rebirth of Lake Naomi began. All of the 2,200 lots within Lake Naomi and Timber Trails have been sold. Because the community is surrounded by states forests, no further lots can be added. Thus, an active resale market has evolved.

Wilkes-Barre, with a population of 49,000, is the nearest large city to Lake Naomi and Timber Trails and is approximately 30 miles from the site. Route 380, four miles away, provides vehicle access to the community. The nearest airport is located at Wilkes-Barre/Scranton, approximately 35 miles from the community. The Pocono Medical Center, the nearest hospital with emergency facilities, is 25 miles away.

The only service within Lake Naomi and Timber Trails is a restaurant. All other needed services are outside the community: A pharmacy, a dry cleaners, retail stores, and a movie theater are five miles away; a medical clinic is three miles away; a hair salon and a grocery store are one mile from the site; a liquor store is seven miles away.

Other area attractions include whitewater rafting, Pocono Mountain snow-skiing, excellent antique stores, historical museums, outlet shopping, and amusement parks.

RECREATION AND SOCIAL ACTIVITIES

Your community association fees do not cover recreation facilities, but property ownership in Lake Naomi and Timber Trails gives you the opportunity to join the Lake Naomi club and thus utilize all of the recreation and social activities within the community. The country club's family membership will cost $2,000 for one year; golf is included in this fee. Lower cost options are also available.

The private Lake Naomi clubhouse on the lake shore is the center for many activities. Weekly dancing (with live music), card parties, fashion and craft shows, and similar events are part of the social scene at Lake Naomi clubhouse.

From May through September, sailing on Lake Naomi is a great sport. The Lake Naomi sailing association provides competent sailing instruction for the novice and organizes competitive races for young people and adults. Rowing, canoeing, and fishing are also permitted from early spring to late autumn.

There are 18 tennis courts at the Lake Naomi tennis club. Tennis club members also have the use of the four courts at the Timber Trails Clubhouse complex. The tennis clubhouse includes dressing rooms, lockers, showers, a snack bar, and an observation deck. Expert pro instruction is available for tennis clinics or individual lessons. A well-stocked pro shop provides needed equipment.

The recreation center in Timber Trails has a well-manicured and completely irrigated 9-hole executive golf course, a clubhouse, a heated swimming pool, and Har-Tru™ tennis courts.

In the winter, you will find excellent cross-country skiing at Lake Naomi and Timber Trails. There are multiple trails, and during the winter, the golf course is used for cross-country skiing. Bordered by over 25,000 acres of state forest, the community has several hiking trails, five picnic areas and one ball-playing field.

The Lake Naomi pool complex includes a regulation 50-meter heated olympic pool with a diving well 13 feet deep, a children's wading pool, and a poolside pavillion with a sun deck. The professionally organized aquatics program holds classes from beginner swimming to advanced lifesaving and includes a full schedule of competitive swimming.

HOMEOWNER ASSESSMENTS, TAXES, AND UTILITIES

As noted before, all of the 2,200 single-family lots within the community have been sold. Currently about 1,700 single-family homes have been built. The community expects between 1,800 and 1,900 single-family homes at total build-out. (Some residents purchase lots next to their property in order to expand their land, so the association expects to have fewer homes than the 2,200 lots could accommodate.) These homes range in price from $100,000 to $700,000. Property taxes vary greatly. Owners of improved lots pay $620 per year to the Timber Trails community association. Owners of unimproved lots pay $470 per year.

Cable television is available in the community, but there are no private community television channels. Homes are primarily heated by electricity. Private septic systems provide sewer waste disposal, and private wells provide water. All utilities are above ground. There are no extra storage facilities within the community.

RESTRICTIONS IN THE COMMUNITY

There is a community association at Timber Trails and membership is mandatory. Individual homeowners provide their own exterior building/grounds maintenance for their single-family homes. The community association handles exterior maintenance for common areas. There are strict architectural and landscaping regulations for both communities.

The community does not have any pet restrictions. Age or length-of-stay restrictions for visitors do not exist here. There are no restrictions on how many people may occupy a single home, nor are there any rental restrictions. Permission to operate a business is controlled by municipal zoning. There are no restrictions on the resale of homes. Parking is not allowed on the street. At this time, there is no parking for recreational vehicles or boats, although the association has taken the issue under consideration.

SHAWNEE VILLAGE

Shawnee-on-Delaware,
Pennsylvania 18356
717-421-1500

$97,500 to $175,000
776/1,016 Townhouses and
Single-family Homes
Contemporary Architecture

18-hole golf course
1 indoor pool, 4 outdoor pools
23 downhill skiing trails
Cross-country skiing
Hiking trails
Stables, four miles of paths
Racquetball courts

9-hole golf course
Picnic areas
7 double chair lifts
Over 100 acres of open space
8 outdoor tennis courts
3 indoor tennis courts
Exercise rooms

INTRODUCTION

Shawnee Village is only a 90 minute drive from both New York City and Philadelphia, yet residents feel miles away from the hectic pace of everyday living. In this resort for all seasons, the only pressure is deciding what to do. The bulletin of weekly activities lists 15 to 20 special activities each day; for example, the list may start with an adult morning swim at 9:30 A.M. and end with kids' movies at 8:00 P.M..

Founded in 1975, Shawnee Village features townhouse condos, some of which are wholly owned and some of which are time shared. Shawnee Development, Inc. develops and sells the homes and homesites. Interval Management, Inc. manages time-share villages and is responsible for day-to-day operations of all villages. There are ten separate owners' associations, each with a board of directors that sets assessment fees and approves expenditures. There are also two independently owned trading organizations, Interval International and Resort Condominiums International, that facilitate owner exchange and travel with other time-share operations all over the world.

Shawnee has received numerous national awards for the excellence of its service to the owners and guests and for the highest quality standards of facilities and units. Shawnee is adjacent to the Delaware Water Gap National Recreation Area, which guarantees 70,000 unspoiled acres for the foreseeable future. For vacationers and for residents who enjoy the outdoors, Shawnee provides a paradise.

RECREATION AND SOCIAL ACTIVITIES

A director and three assistants supervise the limitless activity. The Delaware River provides canoeing and rafting from spring through autumn and tubing during the summer. Hot air balloons at the autumn balloon festival allow the ultimate view of the rolling country scenery. The Shawnee Inn offers exceptional dining and a nightclub.

Regular activities range from scenic horseback rides and childrens' pony rides to indoor tennis and racquetball. Four of the eight outdoor tennis courts are illuminated for nighttime play; there are three indoor courts. An indoor pool, an exercise room, a sauna, and massages are all available. Ski activities in the Shawnee Mountain ski area abound from December through March, and for those who overdo, a medical group operates within the community. As Shawnee management says, "There's something here for every member of your family to enjoy every season of the year."

The championship golf course, built by millionaire C.C. Worthington in the early 1900s, was designed by the famous A.W. Tillinghaust, who located all but five holes on an island in the Delaware River. The island location provides a level area in the middle of the Pocono Mountains. A bridge that connects the island to the mainland is taken down every October to protect it from the ice in the river and is not reconstructed until April, thus eliminating winter golf. Nationally famous instruction schools are held annually, and individual classes are available from the same instructors.

The ten homeowner associations employ a recreation director, publish a quarterly newsletter, provide on-site entertainment, and organize trips for homeowners. An internal bus service operates daily. Daycare for children and activities for teens are also available. There are no perimeter restrictions for access but there is a 24-hour patrol.

Homeownership automatically entitles you to use of the indoor and outdoor pools, the tennis courts, and several other facilities. For skiing and golf, the private clubs offer 33-50 percent discounts to homeowners at Shawnee Village.

HOMEOWNER ASSESSMENTS, TAXES, AND UTILITIES

To date, the 250 townhouses have been sold at prices from $97,500 to $175,000. The 36 single-family homes average about $125,000. The current monthly community association assessment is $133 for the townhouses and $200 for the single-family homes. Townhome owners also pay $800 per year for use of utilities.

The 490 time-share units range from a low price of $7,500 per week in the off-season to over $13,000 per week during the height of summer season. The time-share deed is fee simple, meaning that there is no time or lease limitation to the owner's rights. The time-share unit's current assessment varies between $245 and $290 per year per week of use.

Management provides many special services for the time-share resident. A week before their arrival, Shawnee owners receive a confirmation call, information about ski conditions, and answers to any questions they might have. Before the resident's arrival, the units are thoroughly cleaned, the inventory is checked, and activity calendars are prepared.

Both cable and community television stations are available. Primary heat is provided by electricity. The community uses municipal water and sewer systems. All utility wires are below ground. There are no extra storage facilities within the commmunity.

RESTRICTIONS IN THE COMMUNITY

Shawnee has active community associations and membership is mandatory. Exterior modifications or additional landscaping for units is prohibited except if done by the association. The association handles all exterior buildings and grounds maintenance for homes and common areas.

There are some restrictions on rental and resale. For resale, all outstanding fees must be paid and, on wholly owned units, the developer retains the right of first refusal until the year 2000. Rentals require a security deposit, and the renter must be at least 21 years of age.

No pets are permitted. Depending on the size of the villa, six to ten people are allowed for maximum occupancy. Businesses in units are not permitted. Parking is limited to a maximum of two vehicles per villa. There are no extra parking areas for recreational vehicles, boats, and the like.

Chapter 8

South

Arkansas
Georgia
North Carolina
South Carolina
Tennessee
Virginia

BELLA VISTA VILLAGE

Bella Vista POA
Bella Vista, Arkansas 72714
501-855-7614

$70,000 to $300,000
5,300/13,000 Townhomes and
Single-family Homes
Mixed Architecture

6 18-hole USGA-rated golf courses
1 indoor pool
8 lakes with 40 miles of shore
4,000 acres of open space
12 lighted outdoor tennis courts
Exercise room, handball

1 9-hole golf course
3 outdoor pools, 2 kiddie pools
Boating with private boat slips
9 picnic areas
5 clubhouses
Sauna/steam facilities

INTRODUCTION

Bella Vista Village is the kind of community most people dream about; for 20 years it has offered an active lifestyle in the serene, wooded foothills of the Ozark Mountains. Bella Vista Village provides the perfect climate for relaxation and fun. Its 35,000 acres offer excellent land for building a home, for vacationing, or for retirement. Bella Vista is a vital community of 7,000 residents and over 30,000 property owners from all fifty states.

In 1965 John A. Cooper, Bella Vista's developer, chose northwest Arkansas to build his community. A popular tourist haven since the late 1800s, the area offered unique scenic and recreational resources. He felt it would be the perfect setting for his second and most extensive community, which would have carefully planned neighborhoods, recreational facilities, shopping areas, and—most importantly—a respect for natural surroundings.

Bella Vista was one of the first private master planned communities in the nation. Conveniently located in the extreme northwest corner of Arkansas, it is within driving distance of Kansas City, Tulsa, St. Louis, Oklahoma City, Wichita, Omaha, and Des Moines. There are airports in Fayetteville (38 miles away) and Tulsa, Oklahoma (150 miles away). Northwest Arkansas is one of the most dynamic parts of the country, with the University of Arkansas and some of America's top industries, such as Tyson Foods, Wal-Mart, Cargill, and Daisy Air Rifles.

According to the 1987 edition of *Retirement Places Rated,* a national survey by Rand McNally, northwest Arkansas is recognized as one of the most prized retirement centers in the nation. This area's average housing cost is only 70 percent of the nation's average. According to *U.S. News & World Report,* Arkansas has the lowest state and local per capita tax rates in the nation—less than 65 percent of the U.S. average. Health care costs are 17 percent lower than in the country as a whole, and the crime rate is very low.

Interstate 44 is 42 miles from Bella Vista. Police coverage includes local, county, and state police. There is a staffed fire department on site. The nearest hospital is eight miles from the development.

Just 17 miles from the community, Beaver Lake is a pristine waterway with 500 miles of shoreline. Eureka Springs (known as the "Little Switzerland of the Ozarks") is 48 miles away; this unique little artists' colony is visited by over two million people each year.

Within Bella Vista, the conveniently located Town Center contains restaurants, a supermarket, clothing stores, and a bakery. A liquor store is located within one mile, and the nearest movie theater is 12 miles away. Bella Vista's newest commercial center, Cunningham Corner, includes retail stores, fast food establishments, automatic teller machines (ATM), and other services. Also within the Village are five financial institutions and an office of the A. G. Edwards & Son brokerage firm, New York Stock Exchange and American Stock Exchange listed, which offers complete brokerage and discount brokerage services. The Bella Vista medical clinic includes physicians' and dentists' offices, an optometrist and an opthamologist, and ambulance service provided by an on-site team of professionals.

RECREATION AND SOCIAL ACTIVITIES

With over 35,000 acres, Bella Vista has ample space for all kinds of recreational endeavors. Twenty-five percent of Bella Vista's 35,000 acres is set aside as forested green belts, and every homesite adjoins one of these natural sites.

There are six immaculately maintained courses, many designed by the renowned golf course architect, Edmund Ault. The par 72 Country Club course is host to numerous tournaments throughout the year. The Kingswood par 72 course, complete with driving range, covers 6,928 yards. The 18-hole Berksdale course covers 7,032 rolling yards. Metfield is a shorter, 18-hole, par 63 executive course. The Branchwood Course is a 9-hole walking course. The newest course, the 18-hole Scotsdale Course, was designed to resemble the rugged course at St. Andrews in Scotland.

There are 12 lighted, pro-surfaced tennis courts at the community as well as pro shops and experts to help you improve your game. Northwest Arkansas is famous for its water sports, and Bella Vista Village has its own eight sparkling lakes, stocked with bass, crappie, catfish, and bream.

There are five major recreational centers and parks throughout Bella Vista Village, ranging in size from 7,200 to 30,000 square feet. These areas provide miniature golf, five different pools, softball, basketball, volleyball, and badminton. There are also picnic areas, playgrounds, a marina, and a yacht club.

Bella Vista Village employs a social director for the community, publishes a monthly newsletter, and provides on-site entertainment, catering service, visiting nurse services, on-site crafts, daycare for children, activities for teens, and 24-hour security patrols within the community. Use of all facilities is included in ownership. Bella Vista is also home to over 100 civic and social organizations, from bridge clubs to boating enthusiasts.

HOMEOWNER ASSESSMENTS, TAXES, AND UTILITIES

Bella Vista Village was designed and built by Cooper Communities, Inc. Currently there are 500 townhomes and 4,800 single-family homes at Bella Vista Village. The homes range from $70,000 to over $300,000, with a $14 monthly fee to the property owners' association; municipal taxes range from $500 to $2,200 per year. Neighborhood association assessments, if any, are separate.

Electricity provides the primary heat source. Both cable and community television stations are available. Single-family homes utilize a septic system for waste disposal; townhomes are serviced by city systems. Both townhomes and single-family homes utilize city water. Utilities are located both below and above ground. There is extra storage at the site.

RESTRICTIONS IN THE COMMUNITY

There is a community association within Bella Vista Village and membership is mandatory. The property owners' association provides all maintenance for common property; individuals are responsible for their private lots and homes. Any exterior modifications must conform with the surrounding architecture. White paint may only be used on trim work; it is not allowed on any other part of the house.

There are no pet restrictions within the complex, nor are there are restrictions on age or length-of-stay for visitors. Only one family may occupy a home. Rental or resale restrictions do not exist. Operating a business from a home is prohibited. Parking on the streets is prohibited. The association provides a special parking area for recreational vehicles.

HOT SPRINGS VILLAGE

Highway 7 and De Soto Blvd.
Hot Springs Village, Arkansas
71909
501-922-0250

$75,000 to $300,000
3,100/9,000 Townhomes and
Single-family Homes
Mixed Architecture

4 18-hole USGA-rated golf courses
2 outdoor pools, 1 kiddie pool
Boating
6 picnic areas
10 lighted outdoor tennis courts
2 clubhouses

1 indoor pool
7 lakes, 51 miles of shoreline
14 miles of hiking trails
1 ball-playing field
Exercise room, steam/sauna
Handball/racquetball/squash

INTRODUCTION

Hot Springs Village, located 21 miles from Hot Springs, Arkansas, is a private recreational community nestled in the Ouachita Mountains in central Arkansas. This planned community of 25,000 acres is home to 6,000 residents and an annual vacation spot for thousands. Hot Springs Village is being developed by Cooper Communities of Bella Vista, Arkansas. The first home was built in 1970. Hot Springs Village is truly a green community with 25 percent of the development's land dedicated to green space.

With six recreational lakes covering 1,842 surface acres, Hot Springs Village has been described as "a community of lakes surrounded by land." Lake Segovia, the smallest lake, has a surface area of 11 acres and a depth of 29 feet. Fishing and boating are allowed, although there is a 7½-horsepower motor limit. Lake Pineda has a surface area of 62 acres and is 41 feet deep. Fishing and boating are allowed; there is a three-horsepower motor limit. Lake DeSoto covers 200 acres with a depth of 74 feet: Waterskiing, fishing, and boating are allowed. Lake Cortez, located in the north central part of the Village, covers 245 acres with a depth of 65 feet. Waterskiing, fishing, and boating are permitted. Lake Coronado covers 380 acres with a depth of 73 feet: Waterskiiing, fishing, and boating are allowed. Lake Balboa is the Village's newest lake; at 944 surface acres, it is also the largest. Waterskiing, fishing, and boating are allowed.

The Arkansas Game and Fish Commission stocks these lakes and monitors their progress. The results are fish so big you don't have to lie about them. Lake Lago, the seventh lake, is the Village's water reservoir. For this reason it is closed to all residential development and recreational use.

Little Rock, the capital of Arkansas, is located 52 miles from the development. Interstate 30 is within 30 miles of the Village. The area is protected by local, county, and state police, and a staffed fire department is on site. The nearest hospital with emergency facilities is 24 miles away; however, six physicians and three dentists maintain offices in Hot Springs Village.

Two of the major attractions of the area are the nationally known thermal baths and the Oaklawn thoroughbred racetrack. The Hot Springs National Park, where the thermal springs and baths are located, was established in 1906. Over 1½ million people visit the park annually. There are statuesque hotels, built in the early years of this century, and elegant and ornate bathhouses. The Oaklawn Park thoroughbred racetrack operates 68 days per year and handled $168 million in 1987. During the past six seasons, more than 30 horses that have raced at Oaklawn have qualified for the Kentucky Derby, a record unbeaten by any other track in the nation.

Hot Springs Village has a vibrant business community sectioned into three different shopping centers. The Cordoba Center provides a bank, a grocery store, a hardware store, an attorney's office, a beauty salon, a diagnostic center and a pharmacy. The DeSoto Center offers restaurants, a bakery, a service station, a stockbroker's office, a newspaper office, dress shops, a laundry, and a gift shop. The Carmona Center is home to a watch repair shop and museum, medical offices, an eye clinic, a hearing aid shop, and a bookstore. A dry cleaners and a liquor store are just two miles away. The closest movie theater is 23 miles from the site.

RECREATION AND SOCIAL ACTIVITIES

Hot Springs Village has recreational offerings for everyone. The four community golf courses offer many hours of challenging golf. The Balboa Course is the newest course at the community and, at 6,782 yards, also the longest. This par 72 course is complemented by a driving range, a putting green, and a clubhouse. The Cortez Course, a 6,555-yard, par 72 championship course, is noted for its water hazards; golfers must contend with water on 10 of the holes. A driving range and a putting green are also available. The Coronado Course is a par 62 executive course. At 3,946 yards, this course demands a mastery of medium and short irons. Coronado also provides a pro shop, the Casa Coronado Restaurant, and a putting green. The DeSoto Course, a 6,613-yard, par 72 course, is the first golf course many visitors see when entering the Village. At the entrance to the course is the DeSoto Clubhouse, a pro shop, and the 19th Hole restaurant. A putting green and driving range are also available.

The indoor swimming pool is open 51 weeks per year; the outdoor facilities feature a trio of pools for swimming, diving, and wading. You can fish for bass, crappie or catfish on one of the six lakes or perfect a backhand on one of the 11 lighted, pro-surfaced tennis courts. A full-time tennis pro and staff are available.

At the Coronado Natatorium and Fitness Center you will find weight-lifting equipment, saunas, whirlpool baths, and water aerobics classes. In warm weather, when the Fitness Center's glass partition walls and part of the roof are rolled back, patrons are treated to a breathtaking view of Lake Coronado. A full-time swim instructor and a full-time fitness instructor work with the patrons to develop individual programs.

Softball, miniature golf, frisbee golf, basketball, and lawn bowling are available. The 18,200-square-foot Coronado Community Center hosts activities ranging from the weekly meetings of more than 40 social and civic clubs to the monthly meeting of the property owners' association. An arts and crafts room, a photographic darkroom and a library also draw visitors on a daily basis. A steady stream of plays, movies, concerts, and speakers appears at the 500-seat auditorium.

There is a recreation director, and the association publishes its own newspaper. Colorful features, editorials, updates on amenities, and news on the Village social scene are published weekly in the *LaVilla News*. The community also provides visiting nurse and caregiver programs. There are activities for teens. Patrol and perimeter guards provide 24-hour security.

HOMEOWNER ASSESSMENTS, TAXES, AND UTILITIES

The Hot Springs Village property owners' association is composed of 27,000 property owners. An elected board of directors meets once a month and sets policy for the community. The POA is funded by a monthly assessment fee, plus nominal user fees for recreational amenities. The community association assessment is set by a vote of the property owners and is currently $23 per month. The POA provides the usual city services such as police and fire protection, ambulance services, trash collection, and street maintenance. The amenities at this private community are owned by the property owners, not the developer, and therefore the owners have complete control over improvements, changes, maintenance, and fees.

Hot Springs Village currently has 300 townhomes which range in price from $75,000 to $120,000. Their property/municipal taxes average $580 per year. There are 2,800 single-family homes ranging in price from $75,000 to $300,000, with yearly property taxes of about $620.

Cable television is available, but there are no community television channels. Electricity provides the primary heating source, and the local municipality provides both sewer waste disposal and water services. All utilities are underground. There are extra storage facilities within the community.

RESTRICTIONS IN THE COMMUNITY

There is a community association and membership is mandatory. The association provides exterior maintenance for all recreational and public buildings and grounds. Individual single-family homeowners provide their own building and grounds maintenance. The association prohibits the use of white paint on any home exteriors.

There are no restrictions on age or length-of-stay for visitors. There are no pet restrictions, rental restrictions, or restrictions concerning how many people can occupy a unit. Operating a business from a home is prohibited. Resales may occur without association restrictions. Recreational vehicles are not allowed to park in the neighborhoods; however, there are special parking areas for these types of vehicles within the community's property.

THE LANDINGS ON SKIDAWAY ISLAND

One Landings Way
P.O. Box 13727
Savannah, Georgia 31411
912-598-0500

$150,000 to $500,000
2,416/4,250 Townhomes and Single-family Homes
Mixed Architecture

5 18-hole USGA-rated golf courses
Boating (slips up to 50 feet)
30 miles of hiking trails
2 ball-playing fields
6 lighted outdoor tennis courts
2 clubhouses (both over 15,000 square feet)

2 outdoor pools, 2 kiddie pools
50 percent of community is open space
2 picnic areas
30 outdoor tennis courts

INTRODUCTION

Skidaway Island has a colorful past: Confederate soldiers defended the island during the War Between the States, Benedictine priests established a monastery and school on the island to educate freedmen, and rum runners and moonshiners occupied the island during prohibition. The island remained sparsely inhabited until the late 1960s when the Union Camp Corporation began to develop it. The first homesites were available in 1972.

The master plan for the Landings limits the number of homes that can be built and specifies that almost half of the community must be preserved as nature conservancies, parks, golf fairways, greenbelts, and trail systems. In fact, Skidaway Island won the coveted Urban Land Institute's Award for Excellence in 1986.

The Landings on Skidaway Island, a private residential community, is just 12 miles from Savannah, Georgia. The community is easily accessible by I-95, which is 17 miles from the site. The Savannah International Airport is 24 miles away. Savannah, a community of 250,000 people, is also served by Amtrak. Chatham County provides police protection; the Skidaway Island volunteer branch of the Southside fire department provides fire-fighting and rescue services. Chandler General Hospital, the nearest facility with emergency services, is nine miles from the Landings.

Within the Village on Skidaway Island, just outside the Landings' main gate, you will find a pharmacy, a dry cleaners, a hair salon, a grocery and liquor store, and restaurants. Retail shops, movie theaters, and a medical clinic are seven miles away.

Savannah provides countless hours of entertainment for residents of the Landings. The Savannah Symphony Orchestra performs regularly at the civic center, which also hosts Broadway road shows, concerts, sporting events, and art exhibits sponsored by the Telfair Academy.

RECREATION AND SOCIAL ACTIVITIES

The Landings is a private residential community, not a resort. Only membership in the Landings club (subject to approval, availability, payment of established fees and dues, and other conditions) allows you and your guests to enjoy all of the recreational amenities the community has to offer. Equity golf memberships cost $30,000 plus a monthly fee of $180. Equity tennis membership costs $12,000 plus $95 per month, and a social membership costs $7,000 plus a monthly fee of $64.

Five 18-hole golf courses have been fashioned from Skidaway's richly wooded land. Each has its own character: Marshwood is mainly an inland course with strong par 3 holes; Magnolia has narrow fairways and parallel water; Plantation has spectacular holes on the marsh and dramatic views of Ossabaw Sound; Palmetto's contoured greens are surrounded by deep traps and high embankments; and Oakridge is a scenic course and a shotmaker's delight. There are three practice areas and three fully stocked pro shops.

With a boat from one of the Landings' two marinas, sailing, exploring the islands, fishing, shrimping, and crab fishing are easy. Within a five-mile radius of these two marinas lie the Intracoastal Waterway, the Atlantic Ocean, and a number of uninhabited islands. Both marinas have ships' stores that stock the essentials for boating enthusiasts and staffs that are familiar with the surrounding waterways. The Skidaway Island boat club organizes overnight jaunts to nearby islands and cities of interest. Annual events include fishing and crab fishing tournaments.

Nestled among oaks and pines, the Marshwood tennis complex offers eight Har-Tru™and two all-weather courts. Fourteen additional courts, including a center court and stadium that seats 500 people, are available at the Franklin Creek tennis center. Three USPTA pros conduct weekly clinics, teach group and private lessons, manage two pro shops, and coach the Landings' tennis teams.

Like the tennis centers, the club's swimming pools are located at Marshwood and Franklin Creek. At both pools you will enjoy ample sun decks and shaded areas cooled by ceiling fans. The Franklin Creek facility also has an in-pool jacuzzi.

The Landings offers a choice of clubs and restaurants for your dining and entertaining pleasure. Marshwood and Plantation are available for private parties. Both clubs have dance floors and regularly provide live entertainment by the area's finest musicians. The numerous social organizations at the Landings sponsor a host of activities ranging from theme parties and ethnic nights to art shows and dinner theaters.

The Landings employs a recreation director and publishes a monthly newsletter. This private community is very secure; there is a 24-hour patrol within the development, and access to the community is through guarded gates.

HOMEOWNER ASSESSMENTS, TAXES, AND UTILITIES

Homes at the Landings are built to suit individual tastes and the architects and builders can be chosen by the property owners. Therefore, you will find a wide variety of architectural styles at the Landings, predominantly island, traditional and contemporary. However, all new home building must be approved by the architectural review committee to ensure quality and consistency. Homes can be built on marshfront, golf, lagoon, and interior properties ranging from a third to a full acre.

Currently 3,478 homesites (out of a total 4,250) have been sold. Homesites range in price from $50,000 to $250,000. Undeveloped lot owners pay $380 per year in community association assessments. There are 2,292 single-family homes which average from $150,000 to $500,000. The owners pay $475 per year in community association assessments. There are also 124 townhomes at the Landings which range in price from $157,500 to $199,000; assessments range from $150 to $160 per month. Property/municipal taxes are approximately 1.2 percent of the purchase price of the homesite or of the single-family home or townhome.

Cable and community television channels are both available to homeowners. Gas and electricity provide the primary heat sources. The community is served by a central sewer and water system. All utilities are underground.

RESTRICTIONS IN THE COMMUNITY

Community association membership is mandatory. Three townhome/condominium projects within the Landings have their own neighborhood associations which are responsible for all exterior building/grounds maintenance. The association also handles the maintenance of streets, right-of-ways, and common areas. Single-family homeowners maintain their own buildings and lots.

The architectural review committee approves all exterior plans and modifications as per the covenants and restrictions and architectural guidelines of the Landings. Individuals may handle their own landscaping but must not install plants that can harbor or breed diseases or noxious insects.

There are no restrictions on age or length-of-stay for visitors. Any household pets must be domestic pets and under the owner's control at all times. The county leash law is enforced. Each homesite is only allowed to construct one single dwelling designed for occupancy of a single family. There are no rental restrictions within the community nor are there restrictions on the resale of homes. No occupation or profession may be conducted in any living unit or accessory building. Recreational vehicles, trailers, and boats, may not be parked outside homes for more than 24 hours. An RV storage area provides storage space for lease on a yearly basis.

REYNOLDS PLANTATION

100 Linger Longer Road
Reynolds Plantation, Georgia
30642
404-467-3151

$150,000 to $500,000
185/3,000 Garden-style
Condos, Townhomes, and
Single-family Homes
Georgia Traditional
Architecture

18-hole championship golf course
26 miles of lake shoreline
2 picnic areas

1 outdoor pool, 1 kiddie pool
Boating, dry boat storage
4 outdoor tennis courts
1 outdoor jacuzzi

INTRODUCTION

Reynolds Plantation is a picturesque reminder of the past. Once home to the Creek Indians, this land was purchased by the Reynolds family in the early 1900s.

They named the plantation "Linger Longer" and made it their hunting and fishing retreat. Today, Reynolds Plantation is a 4,000-acre community located in the woodlands along Georgia's Antebellum Trail, overlooking the expansive waters of Lake Oconee.

Madison and Milledgeville, both rich in antebellum architecture, are each only 26 miles away from Reynolds Plantation. The University of Georgia at Athens, offering collegiate sports and educational opportunities, is just 14 miles further. Augusta (80 miles) and Macon (50 miles) offer more shopping, dining, and entertainment. The mountains and the ocean are only a half day's drive away. Only 75 miles west of Reynolds Plantation, Atlanta has been chosen to host the upcoming 1996 Summer Olympics and the 1994 Super Bowl.

Interstate 20 is 8 miles from the site; Atlanta's Hartsfield International Airport provides air transportation. The community receives police protection from local, county, and state police authorities; both a volunteer and a staffed fire department are nearby. Oconee Medical and Surgical Associates, 13 miles from the community, is the nearest facility with emergency care.

The Plantation is fairly isolated and only provides a restaurant on site. However, several restaurants are located only minutes from the community. A pharmacy is within three miles. Five miles away are a hair salon and liquor store. The nearest dry cleaners, grocery store, and retail shops are 14 miles from the site. Numerous convenience stores are within a five-mile radius.

RECREATION AND SOCIAL ACTIVITIES

The 19,000-acre Lake Oconee is the focal point; of its 364 miles of shoreline, 26 miles lie along Reynolds Plantation. The lake offers residents a wonderful variety of water sports such as boating, swimming, fishing, and waterskiing. The community's marina provides complete dry dock facilities and rental fishing and pontoon boats.

One award-winning championship 18-hole golf course is already in play at the Plantation, and another is in the making. The completed course was designed by U.S. Open champions Fuzzy Zoeller and Hubert Green and noted architect Bob Cupp. In 1989, *Golf Magazine* rated the course as one of the "top ten new resort courses in the world." The second golf course is being designed by Jack Nicklaus and will be ready for play in the spring of 1992.

Membership in the club costs extra and includes use of the golf course, putting green, driving range, swimming and tennis complex, recreation building, snack bar, locker rooms, exercise facilities, and pro shop. The developer, Linger Longer Development Company, owns and operates the club facilities.

The community employs a recreation director and publishes a monthly newsletter. Throughout the year activities are planned for adults and teens. Some of the recent special events included a tea party for the children, the Linger Longer walk race, a teens' tennis weekend, a polar bear swim, and a murder mystery dinner. Reynolds Plantation is highly secure; entrance is made through a guarded gate, and there is 24-hour patrol within.

A second marina and boat storage area and an equestrian center are scheduled for completion in 1993. Other future amenities include hiking and fitness trails, a second clubhouse, a lodge, a fitness room, and bike paths.

HOMEOWNER ASSESSMENTS, TAXES, AND UTILITIES

Reynolds Plantation offers an exceptional selection of scenic homesites, beautiful custom-made homes, and luxurious villas. Interior features include hardwood floors, formal dining rooms, breakfast counters, cathedral ceilings, separate party sink and buffet cabinet, corner fireplaces, large screened porches, pull-down stairs for attic storage, and, in two story homes, separate heating and air conditioning systems for the second story.

Reynolds Plantation will be fairly large at completion: 3,000 homes, all with traditional Georgia architecture. One hundred eighty-five homes have been sold since building first began in 1987. There are 20 condominiums and 35 attached units which have sold from $175,000 to $240,000 and 30 cottages which range in price from $185,000 to $350,000. Owners of these units pay $100 to $125 per month to the community association. The 141 single-family homes sell from $150,000 to over $500,000 and pay community association fees of $30 to $100 per month. Property taxes run 1 percent of the property value.

Both cable and community television channels are available. Homes are heated by electric sources. A septic system provides sewer waste disposal, and a central water system is also provided. All utilities are below ground.

RESTRICTIONS IN THE COMMUNITY

Community association membership is mandatory at Reynolds Plantation. The association handles exterior maintenance for common areas, condominiums, and townhomes. Single-family homeowners provide their own maintenance services. Reynolds Plantation has an architectural control committee that reviews all new homes, site improvements, and exterior renovations to existing homes.

There are no age or length-of-stay restrictions for visitors. Household pets are allowed but may not be kept in excessive numbers. All renters are required to adhere to association covenants and restrictions. Businesses are not allowed to operate from a residence. There are no resale restrictions within the community. All parking must be on site, but parking boats, trailers, and RVs on site is not allowed. All-terrain vehicles are prohibited.

FAIRFIELD MOUNTAINS

Route 1
Lake Lure, North Carolina
28746
704-625-9111

$80,000 to $200,000
467/1,800 Garden-style
Condos, Townhomes,
Single-family Homes, and Lots
Mixed Architecture

2 18-hole USGA-rated golf courses
2 outdoor pools, 1 kiddie pool
48 boat slips (10×18 feet)
4 lighted outdoor tennis courts
Clubhouse, exercise room

1 indoor pool
2 lakes, 29 miles of shore
Hiking trails, picnic areas
Stables with 2 bridle paths
Steam/sauna

INTRODUCTION

Fairfield Mountains, a private recreational and residential community, is located on the northern shore of Lake Lure (known as the "Gem of the Carolinas") and surrounded by the majestic Blue Ridge Mountains. Lake Lure has been described by *National Geographic* as one of the most beautiful man-made lakes in the world.

This part of the Blue Ridge Mountains has been blessed with an isothermal belt, which means winter is warmer, summer is longer, and autumn is more colorful than in most of the Carolinas. In Asheville, only 31 miles from the site, you can visit the Biltmore house and gardens or shop at factory discount outlets and mountain stores. Linville Caverns, 45 miles away, and, the Oconaluftee Indian Village, 80 miles from the community, are ideal for family outings. Other local attractions include Carl Sandburg's home, Chimney Rock Park, Grandfather Mountain, and the High Country snow ski resorts.

Fairfield Mountains is being developed by Fairfield Communities of Little Rock, Arkansas. Building began in 1977. Asheville, the nearest large town, has a population of 62,000. Interstate 40, 25 miles from the site, is the closest major highway to the community. Air transportation is provided by the Asheville Regional Airport, 34 miles away. Police protection is provided by local, county, and state police. A volunteer fire department is nearby. Rutherfordton Hospital, the nearest facility with emergency care, is 20 miles from Fairfield Mountains.

A fair amount of services (a medical clinic, a grocery and liquor store, a restaurant, and retail shops) can be found within the community. The closest hair salon is five miles away; the nearest pharmacy, dry cleaners, and movie theater are 20 miles from the site.

RECREATION AND SOCIAL ACTIVITIES

Fairfield Mountains has two 18-hole championship courses. The Bald Mountain club course is located on the main site and was the first course built at the community. Bald Mountain features bermuda tees and fairways with bent grass greens; the course has 31 sandtraps, 10 water hazards, and four sets of tees. The Bald Mountain country club excels in live entertainment such as comedy routines, dance troupes, live bands, and dinner theaters. The golf course at Apple Valley Club is rated one of North Carolina's top 50 courses. Designed by Dan Maples, the 6,900-yard, par 72 course has been open for about three years.

Lake Lure boasts a 50-slip marina with private docks and a full selection of rental boats and water recreational equipment. The marina also offers lake tours on pontoons. Waterskiing is available through mid-October, and fishing is fun all year round.

The community's recreation center contains an indoor pool, a large whirlpool, fully equipped exercise rooms, and an entertainment room with a giant-screen TV. There is an "adults only" pool at the Bald Mountain club; the family pool is located near the recreation center. Other outside activities offered at this community include miniature golf, basketball, shuffleboard, hiking trails, picnic areas, stables and two bridle paths, and outdoor tennis. The Fairfield Mountains Lakefront Tennis Complex, in full view of the spectacular Blue Ridge Mountains, has four lighted, all-weather courts.

The entire community participates in monthly festivities such as Winter Wonderland, Mardi Gras, Autumnfest, the North Carolina film festival, and Mountain

Heritage. Fairfield Mountains employs a recreation director and publishes a monthly newsletter. Valet, concierge and maid services are available. The association organizes outside trips and on-site crafts, provides seasonal daycare for children, and offers activities for teens.

Fairfield Mountains is a highly secured community. There are guarded access gates for entry to the site and a 24-hour patrol within the development.

HOMEOWNER ASSESSMENTS, TAXES, AND UTILITIES

There are 1,800 lots at Fairfield Mountains; to date, 244 single-family homes, 220 garden-style condos and 214 time-share units have been built. The condominiums range in price from $80,000 to $200,000, and owners pay an average of $100 per month in community association assessments. The single-family homes cost between $80,000 and $250,000. The owners pay $400 per year in community association assessments. Lots run from $30,000 to $80,000.

Both cable and community television channels are available. Electricity provides the primary heating fuel. The community is on a septic system for sewer waste disposal, and water is provided by wells. All utilities are underground. There are no extra storage facilities within the community.

RESTRICTIONS IN THE COMMUNITY

There are 14 neighborhood associations at Fairfield Mountains and membership is mandatory. The associations provide maintenance for buildings and grounds for the condominium and time-share units, as well as all association-owned facilities and infrastructure. Single-family homeowners provide their own maintenance. All exterior modifications are regulated by the architectural control committee. Single-family homeowners may install their own landscaping, but the condominium and time-share owners must have prior approval from the board of directors to install landscaping.

There are no age or length-of-stay restrictions. Only permanent residents of the community are allowed to have pets. Time-share units have a designated maximum occupancy per unit. There are no rental restrictions, nor are there any resale restrictions. Operating a business from a home is prohibited. There are designated parking areas for condominium and timeshare owners. Single-family owners park on their own lots. The community provides a special area to park recreational vehicles, boats, and other large vehicles.

SEA TRAIL PLANTATION

651 Clubhouse Road
Sunset Beach, North Carolina
28468
800-624-6601

$109,900 to $250,000+
200/2,000 Garden-style
Condos, Townhomes, and
Single-Family Homes
Contemporary/Colonial
Architecture

3 USGA-rated golf courses
10 lakes
Hiking trails
2 large clubhouses

2 outdoor pools, 1 kiddie pool
1 mile to Atlantic Ocean
2 lighted outdoor tennis courts
Exercise room, steam/sauna

INTRODUCTION

Golf is the heart of the Sea Trail Plantation; three championship courses enhance this private recreational and residential paradise. Sea Trail Plantation encompasses some 2,000 acres of the most beautiful property found along the Carolina coast. Stately oaks, cypresses, longleaf pines, and holly trees can be found alongside the community's streams, lakes, and inlets. Large ridges of white sand are also found throughout the Plantation. The South Brunswick Islands, full of charm and appeal, are just a short drive across the Intracoastal Waterway.

Brunswick County, where Sea Trail is located, is one of the fastest growing areas in North Carolina. The new schools, health care facilities, offices, and retail centers enhance all of the local communities. Development, however, is being closely watched by a protective consortium of local governments to ensure that the atmosphere of the area is preserved for many years to come.

Sea Trail is being developed by the Sea Trail Corporation, founded in 1976. The first home at Sea Trail was built in 1985.

The Myrtle Beach and Wilmington airports, both about 30 miles from Sea Trail, are served by major carriers with hourly connections to principal cities across the nation. Major highway improvements, including the I-40 link between Raleigh and Wilmington and the widening of U.S. 17 to four lanes throughout Brunswick County, will soon make access to this private community much easier. Police protection is provided by both local and county sheriff authorities; there is a volunteer fire department nearby. Brunswick City, the nearest hospital with emergency facilities, is 12 miles from the site.

Sea Trail only offers a restaurant on site; however, most other services are quite close. Within one mile you will find a pharmacy, a hair salon, a grocery and liquor store, and retail shops. The closest medical clinic is four miles away; the nearest dry cleaners is six miles away. For movie theaters, you will have to drive 20 miles.

The Wilmington area boasts a number of lovely gardens and museums and hosts the colorful North Carolina Azalea Festival each spring and the River Fest each fall. You can experience the rich past of the Cape Fear region in such places as the Orton Plantation, the U.S.S. North Carolina Battleship Memorial, and Old Brunswick Town near Southport.

RECREATION AND SOCIAL ACTIVITIES

Recreation abounds at Sea Trail Plantation, both inside and outside the community. This lively resort area has become one of the most popular tourism centers in the nation. Over 50 championship golf courses, 1,000 restaurants, many nightclubs, and scores of malls, shops, and outlet centers can be enjoyed all year long.

Because the three golf courses at Sea Trail Plantation were designed to maximize the benefits of the surrounding environment, each course has a distinct character and provides a unique challenge. Sea Trail's 54 signature holes of golf were designed by Dan Maples, Reese Jones, and Willard Byrd. Also within the Plantation is Oyster Bay golf links, which *Golf Digest* named the best new resort course in the country for 1983. Membership to the Sea Trail courses is included with property ownership, with various stipulations for activating your membership privileges. There is a 20 percent discount for social golf; resident families pay $1,200 per year; families whose second home is at the Plantation pay $950 per year.

Overlooking the golf courses are two clubhouses with dining and lounge facilities, meeting rooms, and card rooms. The new activities center overlooks the Maples course and a crystal lake. Within this center you will find a fitness room, a sauna, a whirlpool, swimming pools, shuffleboard courts, and lighted tennis courts. Private parking facilities are located on beautiful Sunset Beach.

Sea Trail does not employ a recreation director but does publish a quarterly newsletter. Catering from the community's restaurant and maid service are also available for homeowners or guests. Access to the community is through guarded gates, and there is also a patrol.

HOMEOWNER ASSESSMENTS, TAXES, AND UTILITIES

Sea Trail Plantation offers a distinctive selection of beautiful fairway homesites, custom-built homes, and villa townhomes. You can choose views of the golf course, the lake, or the forest. Currently there are 33 garden-style condominiums, 48 townhomes, and 125 single-family homes. Upon completion there will be between 1,500 and 2,000 units at Sea Trail Plantation.

The condominiums range in price from $109,900 to $129,900, and owners pay monthly community association assessments of $128. The condominiums are either two-, three- or four-bedroom homes. Townhomes cost between $159,000 and $179,000, and owners pay $97 per month to the community association. The 125 single-family homes range in price from $109,900 to over $250,000 with monthly assessments of $50. Single-family homes have a 1,500 square foot minimum. The developer also offers homesite lots (from one-third to one-half acre) ranging in price from $44,900 to $85,000. There are currently 25 finished homes that have not yet been sold. Some of the features that the developer offers include lot landscaping, two-car garages, private courtyards, and screen porches.

Both cable and community television channels are available to homeowners. Homes are heated primarily by gas or electricity. The community's sewer waste disposal is by septic system; water is provided by the local municipality. All utilities are underground. Sea Trail provides extra storage space for homeowner use.

RESTRICTIONS IN THE COMMUNITY

Sea Trail Plantation has a community association and membership is mandatory. The association handles exterior building and grounds maintenance for the association-owned amenities and attached housing units. Single-family homeowners provide their own building and grounds maintenance. All building, remodeling, and landscaping must be approved by the architectural review committee.

There are no restrictions on age or length-of-stay for visitors. Rental units may not harbor pets; resident owners are allowed to have pets. The community enforces restrictions on how many people may occupy a single unit. There are some rental restrictions but no restrictions on the resale of homes. Operating a business from a home is prohibited. The association does provide storage areas for recreational vehicles, boats, and the like.

THE VILLAGE AT NAGS HEAD

Hwy. 158 Bypass Mile Post 15
P.O. Drawer 1239
Nags Head, North Carolina
27950
919-441-8533

$135,000 to $990,000
200/750 Single-family Homes
Outer Banks Style Architecture

18-hole USGA-rated golf course	3 outdoor pools
1 kiddie pool	9 small lakes on golf course
Over a mile of ocean shore	Over a mile of Roanoke Sound shore
Boating	150 acres open space
4 picnic areas	5 lighted outdoor tennis courts
Beach club	Clubhouse with exercise room

INTRODUCTION

Seaside living on over a mile of clean, unspoiled beach is what you'll find at the Village at Nags Head. This elegant community offers nineteenth-century charm and twenty-first-century convenience. Homes are designed with the distinctive touches of outer banks architecture: weathered shakes, gabled roofs, and shady porches.

Great efforts have been taken to keep this community's natural surroundings intact and pristine. The Village at Nags Head is being developed by the Ammons Dare Corporation of Nags Head, North Carolina, which has been developing communities for over 20 years.

The Village at Nags Head is located on the Outer Banks Islands off the state of North Carolina. The village is approximately 75 miles from the Norfolk/Newport News/Virginia Beach area. The nearest interstate, I-64, is 75 miles away. Police protection is provided by local authorities, the county sheriff's department, and the North Carolina state police. Both volunteer and staffed fire departments are nearby. The Outer Banks Medical Center, the nearest hospital with emergency facilities, is ten miles from the community.

Within the Village at Nags Head you will find a pharmacy, a dry cleaners, a hair salon, a grocery store, restaurants, retail shops, and a movie theater. A medical clinic and liquor store are three miles from the community.

Other area attractions include the Jockey's Ridge state park, the Elizabethan gardens, the Wright memorial, the Cape Hatteras lighthouse, the lost colony outdoor drama, and the North Carolina Aquarium.

RECREATION AND SOCIAL ACTIVITIES

The Nags Head golf links is a challenging 18-hole, par 71 golf course designed in true Scottish links style. It winds along the shores of Roanoke Sound, following the natural contours of the dunes. Carefully engineered to incorporate the natural beauty of the land, Nags Head golf links offers state-of-the-art technology and computerized irrigation to keep the course in top form. The golf links clubhouse, overlooking Roanoke Sound, has a pro shop, the Links Room restaurant, and a specially designed members' quarters featuring two private locker rooms and cozy lounges for members' relaxation. The Nags Head country club has a $6,000 initiation fee and monthly fees of $110.

The Village beach club is a fully completed oceanfront beach and tennis club. It boasts an olympic-size swimming pool, a children's wading pool, and 13,000 square feet of decks. Light lunches are served from the beach club cafe or at poolside, and the recreation center features games and lounging areas for large social functions or friendly get-togethers. The Village beach club has a $2,500 initiation fee and a $50 monthly fee.

Fishing is fine on the two Sound side piers in the Village at Nags Head. The shallow Sound access is the perfect place to launch your small vessel (canoe, sailboat, or sailboard) and the perfect swimming spot for small children.

The Village at Nags Head also features four picnic areas and five lighted outdoor tennis courts. For homeowners, the Village offers a private beach, complete with showers and ocean boardwalk.

The association also has a shuttle bus that follows a regular schedule throughout the village and makes stops at nearby shopping areas, grocery stores, and the Village beach club and golf links clubhouse. Nags Head also employs a recreation director and publishes a quarterly newsletter. Valet/concierge services, trips, on-site entertainment, catering, and activities for teens are all provided. There are no perimeter restrictions, but a 24-hour patrol operates within the community.

HOMEOWNER ASSESSMENTS, TAXES, AND UTILITIES

The 200 single-family homes built at the Village range in price from $135,000 to $990,000. At completion, there will be approximately 750 homes. There are currently 15 homes that have been built but not sold. Each of the single-family home owners pay between $10 and $70 a month in community association assessments. Yearly property/municipal taxes are $1 per $1,000 of assessed value. Upon completion of the community, there will be 300 homes with three bedrooms, 300 homes with four bedrooms, and 150 homes with more than four bedrooms.

Cable television is available; however, there are no community television channels. Gas and electricity provide the primary heat source for homeowners. The community has its own sewer waste disposal service; the local municipality provides water. All utilities are underground. There are no extra storage facilities within the community.

There are a variety of homes available for lease; they are furnished with rattan and bentwood furniture and decorated in pastel hues. Anyone leasing a home is provided with fresh linens, towels, and a basket of freshly baked bread.

RESTRICTIONS IN THE COMMUNITY

There is a community association at the Village at Nags Head and membership is mandatory. Each neighborhood is set up differently; some neighborhoods provide building and grounds maintenance for the home, others do not. The community association is responsible for all common areas in the development. Any exterior modifications, landscaping modifications, or installations must be approved by the architectural review committee.

Pets are allowed in private homes but not in rental homes. No dogs are allowed on the golf course. There are no age or length-of-stay restrictions for visitors. An owner who chooses to rent may stipulate the rental policy of maximum occupation and length of the lease. Operating a business from a home is prohibited according to deed restrictions. Upon resale of a home, signs must comply with community restrictions. Parking is only allowed in driveways and in other designated parking areas, not on the streets. The community provides additional space to park recreational vehicles and boats.

CHICKASAW POINT

Chickasaw Point Association
P.O Box 200
Fairplay, South Carolina 29643
803-972-3680

$60,000 to $260,000
208/700 Townhomes and
Single-family Homes
Mixed Architecture

18-hole USGA-rated golf course
1 lake with 962 miles of shore
Hiking trails
2 lighted outdoor tennis courts

1 olympic-size pool
42 boat slips
Picnic area, beach
Clubhouse

INTRODUCTION

Located in the foothills of the great Smokey Mountains, Chickasaw Point offers wooded, golf course, and lake front lots. With its 962 miles of shoreline, Lake Hartwell is considered one of the three best fishing lakes in the South. The center of the lake is over 170 feet deep, and the entire lake covers 56,000 acres. The first home at Chickasaw Point was built in 1972. Over 200 homes (out of an expected 700) homes have been built.

This private recreational community is located 50 miles from Greenville, South Carolina, and is only four miles from Interstate 85. Homeowners are never more than five hours from the Atlantic coast at Charleston, Myrtle Beach, or Savannah, Georgia. In Greenville, only 1 1/2 hours north of the community, there are seven airlines that serve the area. The Atlanta airport is about 100 miles from the development.

Chickasaw Point has on-site security; a volunteer fire department is within one mile. The Oconee Memorial Hospital, the nearest facility with emergency care, is just 12 miles from the site. There are no services within the community; however, a grocery and a convenience store are within half a mile. The nearest restaurant is three miles away. All other necessary services (pharmacy, medical clinic, dry cleaners, hair salon, retail shops, and movie theaters) are within 12 miles of the community.

Points of interest include Clemson University and the Duke Nuclear Power Plant. Many state and federal parks are nearby, including the beautiful Blue Ridge Mountains. Chickasaw Point is located close to Georgia, North Carolina, and Tennessee.

RECREATION AND SOCIAL ACTIVITIES

The unspoiled natural beauty of the area offers many outdoor activities for homeowners. Boating and waterskiing are very popular at Chickasaw Point. Winter is short (from January to March) and usually mild. Spring and fall are long and lovely. Golf, tennis, and fishing continue year-round.

The site has an 18-hole golf course, a playground, a sandy beach at Lake Hartwell, a cabana, a marina, and boat-launching ramps. The 42 boat slips can accommodate boats 10×20 feet and 16×20 feet. The association offers many activities for homeowners, including aquacize classes in the pool, dances, holiday parties, bridge classes and tournaments, bowling league, crafts, theater parties, and gardening. Also, the association publishes a quarterly newsletter.

Concerts, theaters, regional and seasonal festivals, craft shows, and six nearby universities provide great entertainment. You will find many opportunities for volunteering in charitable, political and civic organizations and for visits to historic sites.

Security is tight at this development. The single entry road has a 24-hour guard on duty. Although many of the residents at Chickasaw Point are retired, there are no age restrictions within the community. Homeownership at Chickasaw Point automatically entitles you to membership in all the club and recreation facilities.

Over the next five years the association plans on building an additional pool, a clubhouse, and boat slips. They will also be expanding the beach and picnic area. The Chickasaw Point golf course is a privately owned facility with 18 holes, a putting green, a practice range, golf carts, and a pro shop. There is a $200 initiation fee. Family memberships for homeowners currently cost $135 per quarter.

HOMEOWNER ASSESSMENTS, TAXES, AND UTILITIES

Originally developed in 1971 as a private vacation community, Chickasaw Point has now become a year-round community. It is a property owners' association, and is governed by a seven-member board of directors. Currently there are eight townhomes that cost approximately $125,000 and 200 single-family homes that range from $60,000 to $260,000. Lots sell from $5,000 to $50,000. Annual community association assessments for the townhomes and single-family homes are $300; undeveloped lot owners pay $120 per year.

Cable television is not yet available. Heat is provided by propane, electric, and solar sources. Public water and sewer facilities are provided by a private company, Hartwell Utilities. Fees are approximately $45 per quarter. Telephone and electrical utilities are both above and below ground. There is a secured and locked storage area for boats, trailers, and motor homes.

RESTRICTIONS IN THE COMMUNITY

Membership in the community association is mandatory, and a code of covenants and restrictions is in force. The association provides maintenance for all grounds, buildings, amenities, and roads. Individual homeowners are responsible for their own lots and homes. Owners who want to make exterior modifications must abide by covenants and restrictions of the association.

There are no age or length-of-stay restrictions for visitors at Chickasaw Point. Pets are allowed but must be under the control of the owner at all times. Only family members may occupy a dwelling. If owners plan to rent their home, they must notify the association. Operating a business from a home is prohibited. There are no restrictions on the resale of units or lots.

HARBISON

Harbison Community
Association
106 Hillpine Road
Columbia, South Carolina
29212
803-781-2214

$48,000 to $300,000
2,209/6,900 Condos,
Townhomes, Single-family
Homes, and Apartments
Mixed Architecture

224 acres of parks
3 ball-playing fields
Racquetball courts
2 lakes

Hiking trails
8 lighted tennis courts
Indoor pool, sauna
Clubhouse with gym, exercise room

INTRODUCTION

Initiated in 1971 and opened in 1976 as one of the planned communities started under the National Housing Act of 1970, Harbison has become one of the few integrated communities in the country, achieving a high degree of economic, social, and racial integration. Harbison was designed to provide educational, health, recreational, shopping, and employment opportunities in one location.

The executive director of the Harbison association notes that, of the six major real estate developments in the Columbia area, three are in Harbison. A recent association board member captured the spirit of the community, writing, "Nowhere [else] that I know of do you find people of different races, origins, educational backgrounds, pulling together to create a thriving community."

Harbison is eight miles from Columbia and a few hours from the golfing and ocean resorts of Myrtle Beach, Hilton Head, and Charleston. The community is also a few hours from the Blue Ridge Mountains where you can ski, camp, or fish for trout. Just four miles away is Lake Murray.

Most residents can walk to the downtown area in twenty minutes or less. The town center has a large air-conditioned shopping mall on one side of Interstate 26, a discount mall, a neighborhood strip shopping center, and a variety of self-standing facilities, including a medical service center. Children will be able to reach every school by bike paths or greenways that have underpasses at all major roads. About 13 percent of Harbison is open space, either left wild or developed into parks and playgrounds.

There are many nearby attractions in Columbia, including the campus of the University of South Carolina, the Koger Center for the Performing Arts, the South Carolina State Museum, and numerous landmarks on the historical register.

RECREATION AND SOCIAL ACTIVITIES

Harbison applies a special philosophy to athletics. Taking an unusual approach in its recreation programs for all ages, the community has made a concerted effort to downplay the intensely competitive atmosphere that permeates athletics in most of the nation.

The Harbison community center, which can be reached without having to cross any major streets, has a gym, racquetball courts, a pool, several lounges, tennis courts, basketball courts, an exercise room, and saunas.

There are 224 acres of parks and greenways with eight miles of completed hiking trails. At completion there will be 14 total miles of hiking trails. The community also has eight illuminated tennis courts.

A daycare center that emphasizes early learning experiences offers care for children from six months to five years as well as after school supervision for first through sixth graders. There are organized programs for all ages and special activities for teenagers. The swim program has sent competitors to the Senior Nationals, the World Games, and the Olympic Trials.

The association employs an athletics supervisor, a program supervisor, and a pool supervisor. Harbison does publish a monthly newsletter.

HOMEOWNER ASSESSMENTS, TAXES, AND UTILITIES

When completed, Harbison will be home to about 23,000 residents. Of the planned total of 6,900 units, about 2,200 are completed. The 110 completed condos range from $48,000 to $63,000; the 32 townhouses cost between $52,000 and $68,500; the 963 single-family homes vary in price from $62,000 to $300,000. Each of the single-family homes is designed by the builder according to plans which must be approved by the design and development review committee. At the end of 1990, there were over 1,100 apartments, duplexes, and four-plexes available for rental. All property owners are subject to monthly community association assessments based on the appraised value of the property. These assessments provide the funds for street lighting and the upkeep of the greenways, bike paths, lakes, recreation centers, the clubhouse, and other common facilities.

A complex for retirees, elderly, and disabled individuals was opened in 1981. In 1984, the Baptist Medical Center opened a medical campus in Harbison, including doctors' offices and a diagnostic and treatment center.

The community is served by cable television. A separate system permits the use of fire and smoke detectors, medical alert devices, and intrusion alarms to be monitored by appropriate agencies to provide immediate emergency response. Electricity and telephone wires are underground. There are municipal water and sewage systems. The community plans to make gas heat systems available.

RESTRICTIONS IN THE COMMUNITY

All residents (including renters) are eligible for membership in the Harbison community association. The association must approve any additions or changes to any property, including the building of a fence, the change of a color of paint, and the removal of trees over four inches in diameter. Individual homeowners are responsible for their own maintenance activity.

No residence may be used for any commercial activity that would bring heavy traffic or be otherwise outwardly visible in the community. Parking restrictions are in effect for boats, trailers, and recreational vehicles.

KINGSTON PLANTATION

c/o Quadrant, Inc.
P.O. Box 1555
North Myrtle Beach, South
Carolina 29598
803-272-5300

$200,000 to $400,000
1,018/2,000 High-rise and
Garden-style Condos
Contemporary Architecture

2 indoor pools
1 lake
3 picnic areas
9 lighted outdoor tennis courts
Over 15,000 square feet of meeting
  space
Exercise room

4 outdoor pools, 2 kiddie pools
More than 10 acres of open space
6 ball-playing fields
Racquetball/squash
Gymnasium
Steam/sauna facilities
Full service hotel

INTRODUCTION

Located on half a mile of secluded beach, Kingston Plantation consists of 145 acres highlighted by a 20-acre freshwater lake and a terrain filled with large oaks, hickories, myrtles, and dogwoods. Owners and their guests share this private master planned community with a large variety of wildlife including bream, bass, swans, egrets, ducks, and sea turtles.

The development of Kingston Plantation has undertaken an unusual and profound dedication to preserving its natural environment. The developer, Rank Development, Inc., has demonstrated an uncompromising commitment to this endeavor and has received special recognition from the South Carolina state legislature for its efforts to protect the natural beauty of Kingston Plantation

Building began at the site in 1986; 1,018 homes have been built and sold. At completion there will be approximately 2,000 homes. Currently, there are 15 units which have been built but not yet sold. The community association is managed by Quadrant, Inc. of North Myrtle Beach.

The closest interstate (I-95) is located 70 miles away. The nearest major airport is at Myrtle Beach, 12 miles from Kingston Plantation. Local, county, and state police provide protection. Both a staffed and a volunteer fire department are nearby. The Grand Strand Hospital, the nearest facility with emergency medical care, is three miles from the site.

Many services are located within Kingston Plantation: a hair salon, a grocery and liquor store, a restaurant, and retail shops. A pharmacy, a medical clinic, a dry cleaners, and a movie theater are within three miles. The Myrtle Beach area is known far and wide for its golf courses: There are more than 80 championship courses in and around Kingston Plantation. Other area attractions include the Myrtle Beach Pavillion and Brookgreen Gardens.

RECREATION AND SOCIAL ACTIVITIES

The centerpiece of the Plantation's amenities is the $4 million sport and health club. Over 50,000 square feet, it is recognized as the finest facility of its kind in South Carolina. This multi-level center provides year-round, on-site recreational fitness, and relaxation opportunities. The club features a large indoor swimming pool, a sauna and whirlpool, an aerobics studio, squash and racquetball courts, and a wide range of weight-training machines. Outside, you will find a large pool and deck area, a lighted tennis facility with clay and hard courts, and a stadium court for tournament play. A pro shop, the Center Court Cafe, and a lounge are located inside the club.

In addition to the natural attractions of sea, sand, and sun, Kingston Plantation has events and planned activities for all ages. Such events as the Myrtle Beach Classic 10 km run, the USAir All-American Collegiate Tennis Tournament, and the Young Americans Pro Challenge have been held at the community. The Plantation has volleyball, a play area for the kids, and an entertainment center with a sunken dance floor. During the summer, families can also take advantage of a fully staffed, supervised children's program and an on-site childcare center.

The hotel employs a recreation director and offers a full complement of services such as valet/concierge services, a monthly newsletter, organized trips for homeowners, and on-site entertainment. Catering and maid service are also available. There is 24-hour patrol within the community, and access is restricted by manned gates. The use of all recreational facilities is included in the community association monthly assessment fee.

HOMEOWNER ASSESSMENTS, TAXES, AND UTILITIES

Kingston Plantation offers buyers several different kinds of homes: oceanfront condominiums, lakefront villas, and townhomes near the golf course or tennis courts.

The oceanfront condominiums offer two-, three-, and four-bedroom floor plans. Units have expansive decks overlooking the Atlantic Ocean, large gourmet kitchens, and walk-in closets. Within the building there is a lounge, a private indoor heated pool, a whirlpool, and covered parking. Units range in price from $189,000 to $347,000.

Townhomes have six units per building. Each building boasts its own private courtyard with special lighting and elaborate landscaping. These two-bedroom homes feature cathedral ceilings, whirlpool tubs, fireplaces, skylights, arched windows, and spiral stairs leading to a loft. New construction prices start at $138,000.

The lakefront villas, the developer's newest design, feature one-, two-, and three-bedroom units that overlook the freshwater lake. You may choose either a first or second floor unit. Special features include woodburning fireplaces, large decks, and carports with enclosed storage. A lakefront swimming pool is also available for homeowner use. Pre-construction prices begin at $115,000. For all units, community association assessments average about $225 per month. Property taxes range from $1,950 to over $2,700 per year.

Cable and community television channels are available for homeowner use. Electricity provides the primary heat source; both water and sewer waste services are provided by the local municipality. All telephone and electrical utilities are underground. There are no extra storage facilities within the community.

RESTRICTIONS IN THE COMMUNITY

There is a community association at Kingston Plantation and membership is mandatory. Exterior modifications cannot be made unless the owner obtains prior authorization from both the individual condo association and the master association architectural committees and the boards of trustees. All exterior landscaping is controlled by the master association.

Depending on the condo association, there may be restrictions on length of stay for visitors. Pets are not allowed on master association property. There are no restrictions on how many people can occupy a unit, nor are there any rental restrictions. No businesses are permitted. There are no restrictions for resale. Depending on which part of the community you live in, there may be parking restrictions. The community does not have assigned parking. They do, however, offer special parking areas for recreational vehicles and boats.

WILD DUNES

P.O. Box 1410
Charleston, South Carolina
29402
800-845-8880

$68,500 to $780,000
1,357/2,334 Mid-rise and
Garden Condos, Town-
houses, and Single-family
Homes
Mixed Architecture

2 golf courses
15 Har-Tru tennis courts
Boat slips on Intracoastal Waterway
Jogging paths and bike trails
Clubhouse

18 outdoor pools (3 oceanside)
Over 2 miles of Atlantic shoreline
Picnic areas
Conference center
Beach pavilion

INTRODUCTION

Only 15 miles from historic Charleston, Wild Dunes is an island resort hideaway, replete with dunes, secluded white beaches, palmettos, and wildlife.

Wild Dunes considers itself a part of Charleston, one of the South's most charming cities. Home of Fort Sumter, the oldest landscaped gardens in the United States, pre-revolutionary houses, America's oldest museum, and antique stores, Charleston is a historical treasure. Charleston's nightlife includes fine dining, dancing, and carriage rides along quaint cobbled streets.

Interstate 26, 13 miles from Wild Dunes, is the nearest major highway. Air transportation is available in Charleston, 25 miles from the community. The city of Isle of Palms provides police protection and fire protection. East Cooper Community Hospital, the nearest facility with emergency care and the nearest medical clinic, is located 12 miles from Wild Dunes.

A restaurant and retail shops are located within the community. Within three miles you will find a dry cleaners, a hair salon, and a grocery and liquor store. The nearest pharmacy is nine miles away and the nearest movie theater is 13 miles from the community.

RECREATION AND SOCIAL ACTIVITIES

Wild Dunes Links is a true links-style golf course, designed by Tom Fazio and ranked in the top 50 by both *Golf Magazine* and *Golf Digest* three years after it opened. In 1986 the Wild Dunes harbor course was added, featuring narrow fairways weaving through marshland along the Intracoastal Waterway. In 1991 a third course, of championship caliber and designed by Arthur Hill, will open in the residential community of Dunes West, just minutes away.

Wild Dunes' tennis facilities are ranked among the nation's top 50 by both *Tennis Magazine* and *Tennis Week*. Instruction, clinics, camps, and tournaments are held virtually year-round. Wild Dunes also provides boating and fishing on inland waters or on the high seas for mackerel, marlin, yellowtail, and flounder. Residents can enjoy swimming, shopping, or sunning on the beach.

For the business-minded, Wild Dunes has a conference center that can handle groups from 15 to 350. Professional conference coordinators handle catering, banquets, sports, and entertainment.

Whether you stay for a day, a week, or a lifetime, Wild Dunes will make your visit memorable with its full-time social director, valet and concierge service, maid service, catering service, and organized on-site entertainment. The island is a year-round resort with more moderate temperatures than on the mainland. Shopping, dining, and entertainment are available on the island as well as in nearby Charleston.

HOMEOWNER ASSESSMENTS, TAXES, AND UTILITIES

Because over half of the permanent residents first came as guests, Wild Dunes advises visitors to plan to stay. As a guest you have a choice of daily rates from $95 to $370, three-day rates at about 15 percent below the daily rate, and weekly rates from $480 to $2,010, with the majority in the $1,200 range. Rental rates for private homes are available on request. Deposits are necessary, and the rates are subject to state and local taxes.

Buyers have a choice of home sites, single-family homes, townhouses, and condos; some condos sell at one-fifth equity on a partnership basis. Homesites at Ocean Point neighborhood, adjacent to the seventeenth and eighteenth Links' holes, begin at $89,000, with full club membership included. Homes overlooking both the Atlantic Ocean and the seventeenth and eighteenth holes of the Links start at $425,000. At Seahorse and Ensign Court, adjacent to the front nine on the harbor course, the lots range from $80,000 to $299,000, with full club membership included. Most of the homes are in the $300,000 to $400,000 range.

Condo villas with two bedrooms and Links golf course views are in the $160,000 range. Three-bedroom condo villas with Links golf course views sell at one-fifth equity for $68,500. Other homes and villas are available.

Ownership doesn't automatically include membership in the club and access to recreational facilities. The Wild Dunes club has a schedule of dues and membership categories. For example, the regular initiation fee is $16,000; monthly dues are $150 for a resident family and $99 for a non-resident family. A one-fifth owner's initiation fees are $4,320 and dues are $32 per month. Green fees for a member's guests are $45 at the Links course and $30 at the harbor course; cart fees at both courses are $10 per person per round.

Cable television is available. Electricity provides the primary heat source. A private company provides sewage and water services. All utilities are below ground. Police and fire protection are available on the island, the community's entrance is guarded, and the area is regularly patrolled.

RESTRICTIONS IN THE COMMUNITY

All owners are members of the Wild Dunes community association, which provides maintenance for common roads, grounds, and a community building. Each condominium complex has its own separate association that maintains condo buildings and grounds. Homeowners provide their own maintenance for single-family dwellings. The association exercises strict architectural control over both buildings and grounds.

Owners have no restrictions on renting their properties. Restrictions on home businesses deal with signs, excessive traffic, and nuisance factors. There are parking restrictions. Recreational vehicles are not allowed. Private boats must be stored out of sight.

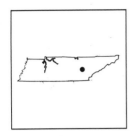

**FAIRFIELD GLADE
COMMUNITY CLUB**

P.O. Box 2000
Fairfield Glade, Tennessee
38557
615-484-3780

$60,000 to $250,000
2,442/14,837 Garden-style
Condos, Townhomes, and
Single-family Homes
Mixed Architecture

4 USGA-rated golf courses
2 outdoor pools, 2 kiddie pools
12,000 acres
5 picnic areas
8 lighted outdoor tennis courts
Gymnasium

1 indoor pool
11 lakes, boating
4 miles of hiking trails
1 ball-playing field
Horse stables, 2 bridle paths
Steam/sauna

INTRODUCTION

Fairfield Glade Community Club is a breathtaking panorama of rolling hills and lush, manicured greens. Its towering pines and fragrant dogwoods surround you, forming a natural buffer against the outside world. Nestled in the heart of the Cumberland Mountains, Fairfield Glade is a fully-contained community, located just beyond the reach of commercial growth. It provides the perfect lifestyle for those who appreciate beautiful scenery and natural surroundings. The gorgeous mountain views from the community's 2,000-foot elevation are complimented by pleasant summer days, cool nights, and mild winters.

Seventy-five miles from Knoxville, Tennessee, Fairfield Glade is located in Cumberland County, on top of the Cumberland Plateau (the largest wooded plateau in North America). The plateau covers 679 square miles, over 80% of which is covered by virgin forest. Walden's Ridge forms the easternmost escarpment of the plateau, the highest vertical rise between the Smokies and the Rockies. At 3,500 feet, Hinch Mountain is the highest point in Cumberland County.

Due to temperate climate, the area claims the second highest number of plant species in the world. Only a region in remote China boasts more diversity of plant life. The average altitude of 2,500 feet above sea level and the actual geographical location of this temperate zone enable the community to grow species that normally thrive much farther north as well as native southern species.

Within an hour's drive of Fairfield Glade there are no less than 10 waterfalls. Other attractions include Rugby (an English utopian community dating from 1850), Big South Fork (America's newest national park), Sewanee University's Gothic architecture and music concerts, and the Highland Winery, featuring Tennessee wines and champagnes. Nearby is the Catoosa wildlife management area, consisting of 84,000 acres of protected forest. Fairfield Glade is only 45 miles from Fall Creek Falls state park and only 12 miles from the Cumberland Mountain state park.

Within the community you will find a pharmacy, a hair salon, a grocery store, a restaurant, and retail stores. A medical clinic, a dry cleaners, and a movie theater are located ten miles away. The nearest liquor store is 65 miles away.

Just six miles off Interstate 40, the community is within a 120-mile radius of the vibrant cities of Nashville, Knoxville, and Chattanooga, all of which are serviced by major air carriers. The nearest hospital with emergency facilities is ten miles away in Crossville. The area has local, county, and state police protection and a volunteer fire department with 85 members.

Cumberland County is the second fastest growing county in Tennessee. The annual growth rate is 16 percent as compared to 5 percent for other counties in the Upper Cumberland area. A 1988 survey indicated that the median age of Cumberland County residents is 34.2 years.

This private community is being developed by Fairfield Communities, one of the nation's largest builders. The first home at Fairfield Glade was built in 1970.

RECREATION AND SOCIAL ACTIVITIES

At Fairfield Glade, you can choose from all the recreational amenities you would expect to find at a premier vacation resort and from many you would not find anywhere else. The community's 12,500 acres are home to 11 clear, unpolluted lakes, three swimming pools, and the famous John Newcombe tennis center with its lighted indoor and outdoor courts. Indoor basketball, volleyball, and badminton are also available, as well as a health and fitness club, complete with a sauna and exercise classes. The community also features equestrian facilities for rides through the same hills once scouted by Daniel Boone.

The community association employs a recreation director, publishes a weekly newsletter, organizes trips for residents, sponsors on-site entertainment, and provides internal bus service and food catering. There are organized on-site crafts, daycare facilities for children, activities for teens, and a 24-hour patrol within the community.

All recreational facilities are included with homeownership; however, user rates may apply. For example, for a member 18 holes of golf costs $14 ($30 for nonmembers). The marina offers boat rentals (paddleboat, canoe, rowboat, sailboat), fishing supply rentals, and boat slips ($200 annual fee). You can also rent bicycles, take bus tours, use the fitness room or tanning beds, and play miniature golf for a minimal fee.

HOMEOWNER ASSESSMENTS, TAXES, AND UTILITIES

Fairfield Glade is made up of 14,837 lots. Currently, there are 322 garden-style condos, 147 townhomes, 1,345 single-family homes, 339 timeshare units, and 202 modular/mobile units. Homes range in size from 1,291 square feet to 2,215 square feet. Lots in the community cost $15,000 and up. Home prices range from $60,000 to $250,000. All property owners pay $16 per month in community association assessments. Neighborhood assessments, if any, are separate. Municipal taxes cost about $200 per year.

Both cable and community television channels are available. Electricity provides the primary heat for the homes. Fairfield Glade utilizes both septic and city sewer services and both well and city water. All utilities are above ground. There are extra storage facilities within the community.

RESTRICTIONS IN THE COMMUNITY

There is a community association and membership is mandatory. Each condominium association handles all exterior building/grounds maintenance for the condominium owners. Single-family homeowners are responsible for their own exterior maintenance. The association also handles maintenance for all common roads and recreational facilities. All exterior improvements or landscaping changes must be approved by the architectural control committee.

There are no restrictions on age or length-of-stay for visitors. Pets must be on a leash, and breeding of animals is prohibited. Only one family may occupy a unit. There are no rental restrictions, nor are there restrictions on resales. Operating a business from a home is prohibited. Parking restrictions prohibit parking on roadways and extended parking of recreational vehicles on personal property. The association does provide a special area to park recreational vehicles, boats, and the like.

AQUIA HARBOUR

1221 Washington Dr.
Stafford, Virginia 22554
703-659-3050

$100,000 to $400,000
1,865/2,814 Single-family Homes
Mixed Architecture

9-hole USGA-rated golf course
1 kiddie pool
3 nautical miles to Atlantic Ocean
127 boat slips
Hiking trails
3 ball-playing areas
Horse stables
Large clubhouse

2 outdoor pools
12 miles of natural river
Boating activities
168 acres of open space
3 picnic areas
2 outdoor tennis courts
31 miles of bridle trails
Gymnasium, exercise room, steam and sauna facilities

INTRODUCTION

The Aquia Harbour property owners' association is located on Aquia Creek, which feeds into the Potomac River. The community is approximately 40 miles southwest of the Washington, D.C. metro area and 13 miles away from Fredericksburg, Virginia. The complex was originally developed by the Aquia Corporation; the first home was built in 1968.

The Washington, D.C. metro area boasts an average household income of $62,000 per year and is home to seven of the Fortune 500 companies: Martin Marietta, Gannet Publishing, Washington Post, Lafarge, Mohasco, Danaher, and Fairchild Industries. The Washington metro area also has 55 private golf courses, 13 daily fee courses, and 17 municipal courses. Within this metro area there are over 30 national forests, parks, and wildlife areas.

Interstate 95 is only one mile from Aquia Harbour. Richmond, one of Virginia's most beautiful cities, is located 70 miles from this development. The community has security officials within its confines and very strict perimeter restrictions. A county sheriff's department is three miles away, and the state police headquarters is 13 miles from the development. Both a volunteer and a staffed fire department are located three miles from the community. The nearest hospital with emergency facilities is the Mary Washington Hospital, 13 miles from the site.

Other area attractions include an amusement park in King's Dominion, 45 miles away; historical Fredericksburg, 10 miles from the site; and all the cultural activities and museums of the Washington, D.C. metro area. Within the confines of the community are a restaurant and retail shops. All other services are one mile away, including a pharmacy, a medical clinic, a dry cleaners, a hair salon, a grocery and liquor store, and a movie theater.

RECREATION AND SOCIAL ACTIVITIES

Water sports abound at Aquia Harbour, but the association offers many other recreational and social activities such as golf, swimming, boating, hiking, and picnicking. Many of the homes are situated on Aquia Creek and have private boat slips for easy access. There are horse stables and 31 miles of riding trails. The large clubhouse has gymnasium facilities, an exercise room, and steam and sauna rooms.

The association does not employ a recreation director, but it does publish a monthly newsletter and provide on-site entertainment. Internal bus service and catering service are available. The community offers organized on-site craft classes in its clubhouse, as well as many committee and volunteer activities. The community is highly restricted: There is a 24-hour patrol, and access is through guarded gates.

Within the next five years, the community plans to build a new community center, additional trails and paths, and a new swimming pool. Homeownership at the Aquia Harbour association automatically entitles you to all the club and recreational facilities except the marina, golf course, and horse stables, which require extra fees. The marina has monthly fees of $1.65 per foot for uncovered boat slips and $2.05 for covered slips. A family golf membership costs $440 per year, a single membership costs $285 per year, and a junior membership costs $100 per year.

HOMEOWNER ASSESSMENTS, TAXES, AND UTILITIES

Currently 1,865 single-family homes have been built out of an expected total of 2,814. The building lots at Aquia Harbour range from $30,000 to $75,000; the most expensive lots are those adjacent to the creek. Homes cost between $100,000 and $400,000. Owners of lots pay $435 per year in community association assessments. Owners of single-family homes pay an additional $65 per year to the association. The annual community association assessments are due on July 1. Property/municipal taxes for homeowners average about $500 per year.

Cable television is available to homeowners. Homes are heated primarily by electric sources. The local municipality provides both the sewer waste disposal and water systems. Telephone and electrical wires and poles are both below and above ground. There are no extra storage facilities within this community.

RESTRICTIONS IN THE COMMUNITY

Membership in the Aquia Harbour owners' association is mandatory. Individual homeowners provide their own exterior building/grounds maintenance. The community association provides maintenance for all the roads, grounds, and amenities owned by the association. All additions to the exterior of a home or to the property must first be approved by the community's architectural committee. Any landscaping must also be approved by this committee.

There are no restrictions regarding age or length-of-stay for visitors. The association requests that only a reasonable number of household pets be kept in each home. The association also restricts maximum occupancy: All homes are single-family residences only. Any one person is allowed to own no more than five rental properties. Operating a business from a home is prohibited by the by-laws of the association. There are no restrictions regarding the resale of homes or lots. Parking is prohibited along the roadways and easements. There are special areas within the community to park recreational vehicles, boats, and other large vehicles.

BRANDERMILL

3001 East Boundary Terrace
Midlothian, Virginia 23112
804-744-1035

$60,000 to $500,000
3,850/4,000 Single-family
Homes
Mixed Architecture

18-hole USGA-rated golf course	5 outdoor pools, 5 kiddie pools
1700-acre lake	583 boat slips
450 acres of open space	31 miles of hiking trails
15 picnic areas	22 outdoor tennis courts
4 lighted tennis courts	Clubhouse
1 community center	1 ball-playing field

INTRODUCTION

The residents of the private Brandermill community live in neighborhoods that border the shores of the largest freshwater lake in the Richmond area. Whatever architectural style or price range you prefer, chances are you will find a neighborhood in Brandermill to suit you. In fact, Brandermill features over 80 distinctive neighborhoods, ranging from traditional to contemporary architectural styles. Neighborhoods each contain a variety of homes in style and size ranging in price from $60,000 to $500,000.

This unique community association was selected as the winner of the Grand Award for sensible growth, design, and planning by the National Association of Homebuilders. It has been featured in many magazines and journals, including *Southern Living, Better Homes and Gardens,* and the *Journal of the National Association of Homebuilders.*

Brandermill is located just 15 miles from Richmond, Virginia, which has a population of 230,000. Air transportation is provided by the Richmond International Airport, 25 minutes from the site. Interstate 95, 12 miles from the community, makes access by car fairly easy. The complex was developed by East-West Partners (originally the Sea Pines Company) of Midlothian. The first unit was built in 1975; presently 3,850 units have been built and sold. The final build-out will be 4,000 homes.

Protection is provided by county and state police, and volunteer and staffed fire departments are nearby. The Johnston-Willis Hospital, the nearest facility with emergency care, is located seven miles from Brandermill. Almost every service you might need is located within Brandermill (pharmacy, medical clinic, dry cleaners, hair salon, grocery store, restaurant, retail stores, professional offices, and schools). A liquor store and a movie theater are located about three miles from the community.

Other area attractions include several local plantations, Agecroft Hall, the Virginia Museum of Fine Arts, the science museum, the Richmond Braves, the University of Richmond, King's Dominion theme park, confederate museums, and a farmer's market.

RECREATION AND SOCIAL ACTIVITIES

At Brandermill, you can go sailing or fishing on the 1,700-acre lake or play tennis on one of the many clay courts. Within the community there are 583 boat slips and over eight miles of shoreline. There are assigned spaces for sailboats, T-racks for canoes and jonboats, and special areas for boats with trailers. The 18-hole championship golf course was designed for the Brandermill country club by Gary Player. You can keep fit by working out on Nautilus™ equipment or swimming in one of Brandermill's five luxurious pools. Thirty-one miles of interconnecting jogging and biking trails, complete with underground tunnels, allow you and your children to walk or ride within Brandermill without having to cross major thoroughfares. There are also horse stables within two miles of the development.

Brandermill does not employ a recreational director, but it publishes a monthly newsletter, provides on-site entertainment and catering services, runs a local day-care center for children, and plans activities for teens. Scouting troops, athletic leagues, and church groups are active in Brandermill. Your children will enjoy year-round use of the community's playgrounds, including the Sunday Park, located on a 15-acre peninsula that can only be reached by bicycle paths. Although no perimeter access restrictions exist in Brandermill, there is a 24-hour police patrol within the community.

HOMEOWNER ASSESSMENTS, TAXES, AND UTILITIES

There are only 150 new homes left to buy at Brandermill; the community is almost finished. The 136 garden-style condominiums range in price from $60,000 to $200,000, with monthly community association assessments between $117 and $219. The 155 townhomes at Brandermill also cost from $60,000 to $200,000. Their monthly assessments range from $43 to $87. The 3,259 single-family homes in the development vary from $80,000 to $500,00. Annual assessments are $228. The current yearly property/municipal taxes are $1.09/$100 of assessed value.

Cable television is available. Homes are heated by either electricity or gas. Water and sewer waste disposal systems are provided by the local municipality. All utilities are underground. There are extra storage facilities on site. Use of the country club facilities (clubhouse, golf, tennis, and pools) requires a separate membership. The parks, bike trails, lake, boats, and playgrounds are available to all homeowners as part of their ownership privileges.

RESTRICTIONS IN THE COMMUNITY

There is a community association and membership is mandatory. Individual homeowners provide their own exterior building/grounds maintenance. The architectural review board must approve all new construction, and any exterior modifications to existing homes must conform with all covenants and restrictions of the association.

Topographic features of properties may not be altered by removal, reduction, or cutting; burning leaves is banned within the community. No trees measuring six inches or more in diameter at a point two feet above ground may be removed without prior written approval. No lot in a single-family area may have more than one detached single-family dwelling and one small one-story accessory building. After construction begins, the exterior of a home built in Brandermill must be completed within one year. Houses may not be occupied until they are completed. Each house must have a screened area in which to conceal garbage receptacles, fuel containers, air conditioning equipment, clotheslines, and other unsightly objects. Television antennas may only be attached to a home with prior approval from the association.

There are no age or length-of-stay restrictions for visitors. County ordinances govern pet ownership. Pets must be licensed, and leash laws apply within the community. Only one family may occupy any single home. There are no rental restrictions. Local county government approval is required for certain types of businesses operated from a home. There are no restrictions on resale of homes. Recreational vehicles, boats, and the like must be screened from view if they are parked on private property. The association provides a special area for recreational vehicles and boats. Permission from the association is required for all signs, and there are restrictions on the size, color, and content of signs. One real estate sign is permitted on each property for sale, but it must be at least six feet back from the street.

**FORD'S COLONY AT
WILLIAMSBURG**

One Ford's Colony Drive
Williamsburg, Virginia 23188
804-565-4000

$225,000 to $600,000
487/3,250 Mid-rise, Town-
homes, and Single-family
Homes
Georgian Federal and
Colonial Architecture

27 holes of USGA-rated golf
4 lakes with 6 miles of shore
2 miles of hiking trails
4 outdoor tennis courts
Clubhouses, gymnasium

1 outdoor pool, 1 kiddie pool
550 acres of open space
1 picnic area
Stables and riding ring
Exercise room, steam/sauna

INTRODUCTION

Located on Longhill Road, just four miles from the historic village of Williamsburg, Ford's Colony is a 25-minute drive from Jamestown and Yorktown and a
one-hour drive to Virginia Beach and the Atlantic Ocean. Richmond and Norfolk
are approximately 50 miles away, and the nation's capital is only 150 miles from
Ford's Colony.

A visit to Williamsburg is like stepping back in time to a period when the great
architects of our democracy helped set the framework for a bold and powerful
nation. The town began in the early seventeenth century at Middle Plantation.
An early outpost against Indian attack, Middle Plantation evolved into a small
village of scattered houses, a tavern, a church, and several stores. In 1695, it became an educational community with the founding of the College of William
and Mary. Williamsburg was one of America's first urban planned communities.
Functionally designed with wide boulevards, stately commerce buildings, and
open public greens, the visual appeal of Williamsburg was evident even in colonial times. George Washington, Thomas Jefferson, Benjamin Franklin, and Patrick
Henry are but a few of the influential patriots who helped to form Williamsburg's
glorious history.

After the Revolution, Richmond became the permanent capital of Virginia.
Williamsburg continued to prosper as a quiet college and market town into the
twentieth century. In 1926, through the benevolence of John D. Rockefeller, Jr. and
the vision of Reverend W.A.R. Goodwin, the restoration of the authentic colonial
village of Williamsburg began. For more than thirty years, Mr. Rockefeller con-
tributed the necessary funds to return Williamsburg to its aesthetic and historic
greatness. Today, Williamsburg is one of the most enchantingly beautiful towns
in America.

Ford's Colony at Williamsburg is being developed by Realtec Inc. of Atlanta,
Georgia. The first home was built in 1984. Ford's Colony has been the recipient of
many awards, including the Virginia "Take Pride in America" Award, the Award
of Excellence from the Department of Agriculture, a commendation from the Fish
and Wildlife Service and a merit award from the Soil Conservation Service.

Access to Ford's Colony is provided by Interstate 95, 30 miles from the community. The Richmond International Airport is 30 miles away. Police protection for
Ford's Colony is provided by local, county, and state authorities. The community

is completely secure with a 24-hour patrol and manned and electronic access gates. James City County provides fire and emergency services and is only one mile from the site. Emergency hospital care can be found in Williamsburg, five miles away.

Except for a restaurant, Ford's Colony has virtually no services within the community. However, all needed services are within six miles. Besides historic Williamsburg, other area attractions include Jamestown Landing, Busch Gardens, Water Country USA, the Mariner's Museum, outlet malls, and Chesapeake Bay.

RECREATION AND SOCIAL ACTIVITIES

Except for the private golf course, all of the recreation facilities at Ford's Colony are paid for out of the monthly community association assessment. Currently, there is one outdoor pool with kiddie facilities; three more pools are planned. The community has 550 acres of open space, and two of the planned 12 miles of hiking trails are complete. You can picnic, canoe, fish, or play tennis on one of the community's four courts, or just relax in the steam/sauna facilities.

Future plans include three additional recreation areas with pools, tennis courts, and hobby rooms, a canoe clubhouse and storage area, and more picnic areas and trails. All of these facilities will be built by 1998.

Ford's Colony employs a recreation director and publishes a monthly newsletter. The association sponsors a swim team, sportsman clubs, health/exercise classes, professional guest lectures and exhibits, a monthly supper club, and a weekly visit from a mobile library.

The private Ford's Colony country club offers memberships to residents and limited memberships to nonresidents. Ultimately, three 18-hole golf courses will be constructed at the site. Currently, 27 holes are in play, another nine holes will be in play by the end of 1991, and the remaining 18 holes will be completed on an as-needed basis. Designed by golf architect Dan Maples, the course blends into the hills and valleys of Ford's Colony; lakes, creeks, and small ponds add to the challenge of the course. Large white and red oaks line the natural wood bridges that take you through undisturbed forest to the next tee. Touring golf pro Fuzzy Zoeller, who is a property owner at Ford's Colony, can often by seen playing the course.

The country club features an elegant clubhouse which offers a formal dining room, a men's grill, a formal lounge, a casual cafe, and a pro shop. Tucked away in the far reaches of the club's lower level is an environmentally perfect cellar that holds 800 select wines. Membership to the country club requires a $10,000 bond, a $7,500 initiation fee, and annual dues of $2,600.

HOMEOWNER ASSESSMENTS, TAXES, AND UTILITIES

Georgian federal and colonial architecture provide a backdrop for gracious living. Mid-rise condominiums, townhomes, and single-family homes are all available. Ultimately, there will be 3,250 homes at this exclusive development. To date, 1,400 homesites have been sold; 400 single-family homes have been built. Also, 80 townhomes and 24 mid-rise condominiums have been built.

The mid-rise condos sell for $250,000, and owners pay community association assessments of $295 per month. Townhomes cost about $225,000 each, with a monthly assessment of $206. The 400 single-family homes range in price from $225,000 to $600,000, with assessments of $55 per month. Homesite lots can cost anywhere from $55,000 to $250,000. Property taxes for this part of Virginia are $.69 per $100 of value.

Both cable and community television channels are available. Gas and electricity provide the primary heating sources. Water and sewer services are provided by the local municipality. All utilities are underground. The community provides extra storage areas for homeowner use.

RESTRICTIONS IN THE COMMUNITY

Community association membership is mandatory at Ford's Colony. Maintenance for the townhomes and condominiums is provided by the association; single-family homeowners provide their own building/grounds maintenance. The environmental control committee reviews and approves all residential construction, which must conform with association covenants. This committee also approves all landscaping plans. Owners must observe tree preservation rules. The association provides a community garden spot.

There are no age or length-of-stay restrictions for visitors at Ford's Colony. All dogs and cats must be licensed, and a leash law is enforced. Only household pets are allowed. Home occupancy is limited to single families and domestic servants. There are no time restrictions for rentals, nor are there restrictions regarding the resale of units (except for restrictions of signs). If operating a business from a home, you may not create a nuisance, increase traffic, or cause roadway parking. Parking is restricted to driveways and garages. The association provides a fenced yard for recreational vehicles and boats.

LAKE OF THE WOODS

Box 1-LOW
Locust Grove, Virginia 22508
703-972-2237

$60,000 to $500,000
1,800/4,250 Single-family Homes
Mixed Architecture

18-hole USGA-rated golf course
2 kiddie pools
59 boat slips owned by the association
Over 100 acres of open space
Hiking/walking/beaches
Softball field
4 lighted outdoor tennis courts

2 outdoor pools
2 lakes (550 acres; 25 acres)
Individual boat slips on lots
4 parks
Soccer field
8 outdoor tennis courts
Horse stables, paths, and show ring

INTRODUCTION

The Lake of the Woods association, located about 17 miles from Fredericksburg, Virginia, was historically a community where families built vacation cottages.

Today it has become a complex private residential area offering many amenities to its homeowners. Lake of the Woods was originally developed by Virginia Wildlife Clubs, Inc. The first home was built in 1967. All of the 4,250 lots have been sold, but not all have yet been improved by their owners.

This community is ideally situated between Washington, D.C. and Richmond, Virginia. I-95 is located 15 miles from the community. Washington National Airport is located 70 miles from the site. The nearest hospital with emergency facilities is located in Fredericksburg, about 17 miles away.

Local historical attractions include Civil War battlefields, Washington's boyhood home, Williamsburg Colonial Historical Park, and King's Dominion amusement park. Lake of the Woods is strictly residential and recreational, but there is a restaurant on site. Within one mile of Lake of the Woods association, you will find a pharmacy, a medical clinic, and a hair salon. Fifteen miles away are a dry cleaners, a grocery and liquor store, retail shops, and movie theaters.

Police protection is provided by local authorities, the county sheriff's department, and the Virginia state police. There is a volunteer fire department within the community.

RECREATION AND SOCIAL ACTIVITIES

Lake of the Woods offers an incredible array of recreational activities for its homeowners. To begin, there is an 18-hole USGA-rated golf course. The golf pro at the course, Bruce Lehnhard, was chosen Player of the Year for the Middle Atlantic Section of the Professional Golfer's Association in 1990.

One of the two lakes at the community is quite large (550 acres); the association owns 59 boat slips on this lake. Individual owners of lots that are situated on the lake may also build boat slips. There are beaches on the lake, soccer and softball fields, two outdoor swimming pools with kiddie facilities, and four parks.

Horseback riding is very popular at this community. There are boarding facilities for horses, a show ring, and bridle paths. The association offers riding lessons for both children and adults as well as riding competitions.

The community has a large clubhouse and publishes a monthly newsletter. The community provides on-site entertainment and crafts for its homeowners. Every Thanksgiving, the clubhouse hosts an arts and crafts show where local artisans present their wares. There is a youth activities committee that organizes many activities for the children in the community, including Boy Scouts, Girl Scouts, Little League, a ski club, and golf, tennis, and swim teams. The community also has a cooperative nursery school for its young children.

This lake community has 105 campground sites for recreational vehicles or tents. There are seven beaches and one marina. Use of the restaurant, lakes, beaches, parks, and the marina is free to all homeowners, but there are some user fees for some of the recreational activities. For example, the annual family membership for golf is $680, an individual membership is $425, and a junior golf membership is $55. Fees for tennis courts, pools, campgrounds, and stables are collected separately from community association assessments.

HOMEOWNER ASSESSMENTS, TAXES, AND UTILITIES

In 1967, the Lake of the Woods association was begun as a vacationer's community. Things have changed, and the community is now mainly residential.

Although there are still some vacation cottages, the minimum square footage for new homes is now 1,400 square feet. Currently there are 1,800 single-family homes built on the 4,250 lots. All of the lots have been sold.

The homes range in price from $60,000 to $500,000, with an annual community association assessment of $440. Lots on which no homes have yet been built also have an assessment of $440. The current yearly property/municipal taxes are $.68 per $100 of assessed value. Owners can contract with any local builder to construct their homes. Almost all the homes are custom-built.

Both cable and community television channels are available to homeowners. Primary heating sources, including solar, can be chosen by the homeowners depending on their preference. The local municipality provides the sewer waste disposal services. Both a well system and the local municipality provide water to the community. Utilities are both above and below ground. There are no extra storage facilities within the community.

RESTRICTIONS IN THE COMMUNITY

There is a community association at Lake of the Woods and membership is mandatory. Individual homeowners are responsible for their own single-family residence building/grounds maintenance. The community association handles the maintenance for all the common areas, such as roads, buildings, and amenities. Any exterior modifications to a home must have prior approval of the environmental control committee.

There are no restrictions on age or length-of-stay for visitors. Only domestic animals are allowed at this site. There are no restrictions regarding how many people may occupy a home. In order to rent your home, you must have the prior approval of the association. There are no landscaping restrictions at Lake of the Woods. Only a "home occupation" type of business is permitted to be operated out of a home. The association has the right of first refusal on the resale of homes and lots. No trucks, recreational vehicles, or trailers may be parked on a lot unless they are in a garage. The association provides special areas to park recreational vehicles, boats, and the like.

**LAKE RIDGE PARKS
AND RECREATION ASSOCIATION**

12350 Oakwood Drive
Lake Ridge, Virginia 22192
703-550-2982

$65,000 to $1,000,000
6,550/7,500 Garden-style
Condos, Townhomes, and
Single-family Homes
Victorian/Colonial
Architecture

5 outdoor pools, 5 kiddie pools
2 ball-playing fields
18 playgrounds
3 community centers
Boat landing

Hiking trails
6 lighted outdoor tennis courts
Steam/sauna
14 basketball courts

INTRODUCTION

Lake Ridge Parks and Recreation Association is a private, family-oriented, environmentally conscious community with a hometown atmosphere. It offers year-round recreational activities with close proximity to shopping, professional services, and medical care. The community provides a variety of lifestyles, and the association ensures preservation of aesthetic integrity. Emphasis is placed on conservation of the mature hardwood trees, natural vegetation, and manicured landscapes that cover 1,000 acres of community land.

Ridge Development of Woodbridge, Virginia is developing the community. The first home was built in 1972. To date, 6,550 homes have been completed out of an expected total of 7,500.

Just 30 miles from Washington, D.C. and 20 miles from Washington National Airport, Lake Ridge is only two miles from I-95. Local, county, and state police authorities provide protection; both a staffed and a volunteer fire department are nearby. Potomac Hospital, the nearest facility with emergency care, is five miles from the site.

Services within Lake Ridge include a pharmacy, a medical clinic, a dry cleaners, a hair salon, a grocery store, a restaurant, retail shops, and a movie theater. Local attractions include Williamsburg, King's Dominion, Potomac Mills mall, Lake Ridge county park, and all of our capital's museums and cultural sites.

RECREATION AND SOCIAL ACTIVITIES

Over 15,000 people utilize the recreational facilities within Lake Ridge, which include five swimming pools with children's facilities, hiking trails, over 1,000 acres of open space, ball-playing fields, and lighted tennis courts. All of the facilities are available for homeowner use, but there may be nominal user fees for some activities.

The community's recreation director organizes events and activities for children and adults alike. Lake Ridge's community centers are fairly large and have steam and sauna facilities as well as meeting rooms. A monthly newsletter, published by the association, announces all of the community's organized trips, on-site entertainment, crafts, and activities for teens. The community also provides daycare for children. There are no perimeter restrictions for access.

HOMEOWNER ASSESSMENTS, TAXES, AND UTILITIES

Lake Ridge consists of condominiums, townhomes, single-family homes, 11 commercial properties, and two apartment complexes. Architectural styles include contemporary, victorian and colonial. Both a master association and neighborhood associations govern life at Lake Ridge.

The 749 garden-style condominiums belong to both associations, with monthly neighborhood association fees between $102 and $140, an annual fee of $142.20 to the master association, and $58 per year for the pool assessment. The association handles buildings and grounds maintenance for the condos.

Townhomes number 2,703 and belong only to the master association. They cost from $85,000 to $185,000, with $8 to $15 monthly fees for street maintenance and snow removal, master association fees of $142.20, and $58 per year for the pool assessment. Owners are responsible for their own home maintenance; the association provides street work, snow removal, and common grounds maintenance.

The 3,070 single-family homes are all located on streets maintained by the local municipality. Therefore, the owners are members of the master association and only pay the $142.20 and $58 yearly charges. Single-family homeowners are responsible for their own building and grounds maintenance. All of the owners at Lake Ridge pay municipal taxes of $1.405 per $100 of assessed value.

Both cable and private community television channels are available for use by homeowners; electric sources provide all heating. The local municipality provides both sewer waste and water systems, and all utilities are below ground. There are extra storage areas within Lake Ridge for homeowner use.

RESTRICTIONS IN THE COMMUNITY

Community association membership is mandatory at Lake Ridge. There are strict architectural guidelines for homeowners to follow. Once construction or changes are approved by the committee, work must be completed within six months. Landscaping changes and installations must also receive prior approval.

At Lake Ridge, only one exterior antenna will be approved on any individual structure; any enclosure for the care of domestic pets must be minimally visible from surrounding properties; temporary clotheslines must be located in the rear yard of properties and must be removed as soon as possible after use; raised or tiled solar panels may only be installed on the rear roof; front roof solar panels must be flush mounted; and fencing may only be installed on the backyard perimeter property lines.

There are no restrictions on how many people may occupy a single unit nor are there any rental restrictions. Operation of a business from a unit must first be approved by the board of directors of the association. Parking restrictions are extensive and enforced strictly. There are no special on-site lots for parking oversized vehicles.

LITTLE ROCKY RUN

6201 Sandstone Way
Clifton, Virginia 22024
703-830-0411

$157,000 to $550,000
2,091/2,364 Townhomes and
Single-family Homes
Victorian/Colonial
Architecture

Golf course within one mile
3 miles of hiking trails
5 ball-playing fields
3 clubhouses

3 outdoor pools, 3 kiddie pools
Picnic areas
7 outdoor tennis courts
900 total acres

INTRODUCTION

The Little Rocky Run homeowners association is located in the Centreville area of west Fairfax County, Virginia. It has been carved out of over 1,000 acres of heavily forested land. The forest consists primarily of hardwoods and has many specimen trees within its interior. A private arborist guided the development in preserving these natural assets. Buffer and conservation areas were delineated along the perimeter to shield the project from major roadways. In some cases, the conservation areas contain Civil War bunkers.

The Little Rocky Run community was originally planned by Hunter Development Company of Fairfax. The first home was built in 1984. Currently, four builders have qualified to construct homes at Little Rocky Run.

In the early planning of the project, 13 acres of interior land was set aside for the construction of Union Mill elementary school; current enrollment is in excess of 950 students. Forethought enabled the construction of the school to meet the needs of the growing population rather than responding to a demand for larger schools after the community was completed.

Fairfax County is responsible for providing fire and police protection, public sewer and water services, schools, libraries, and other general public welfare services. Upon completion, the public streets will be permanently maintained by the Virginia Department of Transportation. The private streets and parking areas in the townhouse neighborhoods are maintained by the association.

Washington, D.C. is just 20 miles from this private community, and Interstate 66 is 1.5 miles away. Dulles International Airport, 11 miles from the site, provides air transportation. Fair Oaks Hospital, the nearest facility with emergency medical care, is ten miles from the community.

There are no services within Little Rocky Run; however, all needed services are within two miles: a pharmacy, a medical clinic, a dry cleaners, a hair salon, a grocery and liquor store, restaurants, retail shops, and movie theaters.

Area attractions include Wolftrap Cultural Arts, many Civil War battlefields and museums, Patriot Center on the campus of George Mason University, Bull Run regional park, Mount Vernon, and many antique stores.

RECREATION AND SOCIAL ACTIVITIES

Except for nominal user fees, use of the community's recreational amenities are included in the homeowners' assessments. Hiking trails, swimming pools with kiddie facilities, tennis courts, and three clubhouses provide hours of entertainment. Community activities include a brunch for new members, blood donor drives, Easter egg hunts, Las Vegas Night, yard sales, a luau, the Lollipop swim meet, youth swim parties, the Fall Festival, the Halloween parade, breakfast with Santa, and an oldies party.

Although Little Rocky Run does not have a golf course within its boundaries, a Fairfax County park authority course is within one mile.

The community does not employ a recreation director, but it does publish a monthly newsletter. The community has a neighborhood watch program, co-op babysitting, and aerobic/fitness classes. There are no perimeter restrictions for access, but there is a 24-hour patrol within the community.

HOMEOWNER ASSESSMENTS, TAXES, AND UTILITIES

At completion there will be 2,364 homes in the community. To date, 2,091 homes have been constructed and sold.

The 722 completed townhomes range in price from $157,000 to $172,000, with $50.55 per month in community association fees ($29.05 for the general fund and $21.50 for the individual neighborhood fund). Property taxes average about $1,700 per year.

Single-family homes number 1,369 and range from $289,000 to $550,000. The owner pays $29.05 each month to the general fund. In addition, single-family homeowners who live on a pipestem driveway and share a common drive with other owners pay an annual maintenance fee for future asphalt replacement. Currently, this fee is $36.52 per year. Property taxes for the single-family homes average about $3,300 per year.

Some of the features offered by the builders at Little Rocky Run include crown molding, hardwood floors, raised hearth brick fireplaces, beamed cathedral ceilings, full basement, two-car garage, concrete driveway, ceramic tile floors in full baths, french doors, sun room, jacuzzi in the master bath, bay windows, alarm systems, and complete landscaping packages.

Both community and cable television channels are available. Gas and electricity provide the primary heat source. The local municipality supplies both sewer waste and water systems. All utilities are underground. There are no extra storage facilities within Little Rocky Run.

RESTRICTIONS IN THE COMMUNITY

Membership is mandatory in Little Rocky Run's homeowners' association. All open space is maintained by the association. Strict architectural guidelines are published by the association regarding building and renovations. Vegetable gardens must be located between the rear of the house and sides of the house.

There are no restrictions regarding age or length-of-stay for visitors. Residents with pets must conform to county ordinances such as leash laws. There are no rental or resale restrictions. Recreational or commercial vehicles may not be parked or stored in open view on residential property, private streets, or open space. The community does not provide a separate area for oversized vehicles.

**RIVER WALK ON
THE ELIZABETH**

701 River Walk Parkway
Chesapeake, Virginia 23320
804-547-3893

$60,000 to $250,000
500/1,350 Condos,
Townhomes, and Single-
family Homes
Traditional Architecture

2 outdoor pools
Clubhouse
2 lighted tennis courts
Great Meadow Park for picnics

Hiking trails
2 ball fields
Boat launching ramp (planned)
Storage slips (planned)
Children's playground (planned)

INTRODUCTION

River Walk's developers combined the "tidewater lifestyle" with the Chesapeake
wetlands environment and a colonial setting, creating a community attractive to
both young and old. River Walk parkway threads two miles through the center of
the site and connects 16 separate residential villages, each with its own character.
The community plans to have neighborhood shopping, an office park, and service
areas at the two entrances. Eventually there will be a childcare center, an elementary school, and a public recreation center. The city of Chesapeake will operate
the recreation center which will feature a gymnasium, a health room, meeting
rooms with kitchen facilities, and an exercise and game room. The community
already has a private club, tennis courts, pools, and a park.

The development lies on a mile of frontage along the Elizabeth River which
opens the entire Intracoastal Waterway to residents. Commuters to the Norfolk
and Virginia Beach areas avoid the long waits at the frequent drawbridges further
south.

Located in the city of Chesapeake, River Walk is only a mile from Interstate
64 and ten minutes from downtown Norfolk. River Walk is about an hour's drive
from colonial Williamsburg, the warm and sandy shores of Virginia Beach are
nearby, and Kitty Hawk and Nag's Head are only an hour away.

Begun in 1988, River Walk has already claimed the attention of professionals and trendsetters. In its initial year, River Walk was the site of the Tidewater
Builders' Association's Homearama, and in 1989 it earned the coveted Community of the Year award. In 1990 River Walk was one of 20 projects out of 788
entries to earn a citation for urban design and planning from *Progressive Architecture*, a leading professional magazine. The citation recognized the "pageantry
of civic spaces" and the complex preservation of wetlands and forests at the site.
Twenty percent of the land will never be developed. There are three lakes, one
with a fountain that is brightly illuminated at night.

RECREATION AND SOCIAL ACTIVITIES

The River Club is a dark brick building with an elegant exterior and an interior
featuring a dramatic circular lobby that provides access to all parts of the club-

house. The west wing has a conversation bar, a stately fireplace, and comfortable chairs, exuding the atmosphere of a private club. The east wing has a grand room used for meetings, receptions, dances, and so on. A pool and a tennis court are linked to the club but have separate dressing facilities.

The community is studying the feasibility of building a marina that would house approximately 200 boats. Several governmental agencies have expressed an interest in additional public marina facilities, making the development of commercial facilities more likely.

Homeownership automatically entitles you to membership in all of the club and recreation facilities at River Walk; there are no extra membership dues.

HOMEOWNER ASSESSMENTS, TAXES, AND UTILITIES

Currently, River Walk has sold about 500 units; the estimated total is 1,350. The units are located in 16 residential villages that each provide a unique lifestyle. In Queen's Gate, a buyer can choose condominiums priced from $60,000 to $80,000. In King's Ford (now sold out) are 92 coach-house condominiums that resemble single-family houses. At Creekside, colonial townhouses start in the $70,000 range. In Echo Cove and Beacon Point, single-family homes begin at $120,000. The Island villages offer lots with an array of single-family houses (you can choose from 20 custom-builders) valued at $160,000 to over $250,000. All homeowners pay $17 per month in community association assessments. Neighborhood association assessments, if any, are separate from the master association fees.

A senior citizen program, managed by nearby Chesapeake General Hospital, offers assisted living in elegant Georgian Manor. The 40-unit facility, served by licensed nurses, can provide meals, housekeeping and laundry services, and transportation for shopping and appointments.

Despite its rustic surroundings, the community has modern services: gas and electricity for heat, municipal water and sewer systems, and cable television. All utilities are below the ground; there are no overhead poles or wires.

RESTRICTIONS IN THE COMMUNITY

River Walk's community association is responsible for the care and maintenance of common property. Every owner is automatically a member. Individual homeowners are responsible for the upkeep of their living unit. The association imposes some restrictions that are designed to maintain curb appeal and improve property values, such as the architectural review of plans by the developer for the custom units to be built. Individual landscaping plantings also require review and approval by the association.

There are no restrictions on the sale or rental of units. Only city restrictions apply to operating a business out of the units. However, there are carefully controlled sign standards for shops and realtors. There are no pet restrictions within River Walk. Recreational vehicles are prohibited on the site, but the community plans to provide a special parking lot.

WOODLAKE

14900 Lake Bluff Parkway
Midlothian, Virginia 23112
804-739-4344

$75,000 to $500,000
1,850/2,600 Garden-style
Condos, Townhomes, and
Single-family Homes
Mixed Architecture

1 indoor pool
1 lake with 5 miles of shore
Over 300 acres of open space
6 picnic areas
8 outdoor tennis courts
Clubhouse

3 outdoor pools, 2 kiddie pools
200 boat slips
8.5 miles of hiking trails
5 ball-playing fields
6 illuminated tennis courts
Exercise room

INTRODUCTION

Voted 1990's Best Planned Community by the Urban Land Institute, Woodlake community association is a superb example of what a recreational and residential community should be. Built on the shores of a spectacular 1,700-acre lake, the community's homes are built with a high regard for privacy and quiet. All of the neighborhoods are small, averaging no more than 50 homes. Cul-de-sacs reduce traffic for a safer, quieter, and more secure environment.

Connecting each neighborhood, a network of biking and jogging trails lead to Woodlake's recreational facilities and wind along the lakeshore. You won't need to carpool to get your children to the recreational centers; they can get there safely on their own. Within the community are two elementary schools, a daycare center, and two churches. A middle school and high school are nearby.

Woodlake is being developed by East-West Partners of Virginia, the same company that is developing Brandermill. The first home at Woodlake was built in 1984. To date, 1,850 homes out of an expected 2,600 homes have been sold.

With a population of 214,000, Richmond is 20 miles from the site. Within 15 miles of Woodlake you will find I-95 (actually a four-lane highway to Richmond); air transportation is available in Richmond. Police protection is provided by local, county, and state authorities. Both a staffed and a volunteer fire department are nearby. Two hospitals with emergency facilities are within ten miles of the development.

At Woodlake's village square you will find a pharmacy, a dry cleaners, a grocery store, and a restaurant. A medical clinic and a hair salon are four miles from the site; six miles away you will find a liquor store and retail shops. The nearest movie theater is five miles from Woodlake. The Virginia Museum of Fine Arts and King's Dominion theme park are but a few of the area attractions.

RECREATION AND SOCIAL ACTIVITIES

A $2 million indoor/outdoor swim and racquet club is a major amenity offered to Woodlake residents. It features an eight-lane competition pool, one- and three-meter diving boards, and spectator seating. One of the outdoor pools at Woodlake has a unique 60-foot waterslide that adults and children both enjoy. There are eight outdoor tennis courts, six of them illuminated for nighttime play.

With Woodlake's 1,700-acre lake, there is actually more water than land in the development. The lake provides sailing, fishing, and romantic strolls along the water's edge. Throughout the year, entertainment is featured for all ages at the Woodlake Waterside Amphitheater.

Woodlake's Central Park is ideal for everything from organized soccer to baseball, softball, and volleyball. The miles of paved biking and jogging trails that connect each neighborhood pass through tunnels to avoid major streets and provide safety.

Probably the most intriguing area of this private community is Tom Sawyer's Island, a playground located in Woodlake's shallow cove and filled with interesting activities. It is easily accessible by bike path.

Although the community does not employ a recreation director, it does publish a monthly newsletter. All of the recreational facilities are free for homeowners except for the swim and racquet club, which has membership packages starting at $350 per year.

HOMEOWNER ASSESSMENTS, TAXES, AND UTILITIES

Woodlake's small and unique neighborhoods offer a variety of styles, including classic Victorian, contemporary, brick traditional, and painted Williamsburg designs. Waterfront condominiums and single-family homes are also available.

To date, the 78 garden-style condominiums and 35 townhomes have sold at prices from $75,000 to $130,000, with neighborhood association assessments between $52 and $115 and annual master association fees of $220. The 1,577 single-family homes cost from $95,000 up to $500,000. The owners only pay master association assessments of $220 per year.

Cable television is available, but there are no exclusive community channels. Both gas and electricity provide the primary heating source for homes. Water and sewer services are provided by the local municipality. All utilities are underground. Woodlake provides extra storage areas for homeowner use.

RESTRICTIONS IN THE COMMUNITY

Community association membership is mandatory at Woodlake. The condominiums and townhomes must have membership in both the master and the neighborhood associations. Individual single-family homeowners provide their own exterior building and grounds maintenance. The neighborhood association provides maintenance for the condominiums and townhomes as well as for all recreational facilities and infrastructure. All modifications are subject to review and approval by the architectural review board.

For single-family homeowners, there are no restrictions on maximum occupation, rentals, or resales. Individual condominium and neighborhood associations have varying levels of restrictions for these activities. Every single-family home has a space for off-street parking. The association provides extra space to park recreational vehicles and other large vehicles.

Chapter 9

Sun-Belt South
Florida

AMELIA ISLAND PLANTATION

Highway A1A South
Amelia Island, Florida 32034
800–874–6878

$95,000 to $950,000
1,100/2,200 High-rise,
Mid-rise, and Garden
Condos, Townhomes,
and Single-family Homes
Contemporary/Spanish
Architecture

45 holes of golf	1 indoor pool
Outdoor pools	Kiddie pool
Oceanfront acreage	Boating
Picnic areas	Hiking and biking trails
3 lighted outdoor tennis courts	25 outdoor tennis courts
Gymnasium, exercise room	Racquetball facilities
	Steam/sauna facilities

INTRODUCTION

The southernmost of the Golden Isles and the only one located in Florida waters, Amelia Island is 13 1/2 miles long and gently tapers in width from two miles at the northern end to less than a quarter mile in the south. Named the Isle de Mai by the French, the island was so coveted that eight flags have flown there, charting the ebb and flow of world powers from the sixteenth century to the present day.

Located on the southern end of the island, Amelia Island Plantation is a 1,250-acre private sanctuary nestled between the Intracoastal Waterway and the Atlantic. The island is still as beautiful as it was more than two hundred years ago, when it was named for the daughter of King George II.

The Plantation is only 22 miles from the Jacksonville International Airport and 15 miles from Interstate 95. Police protection is provided by local, county, and state police authorities. The community is fully secured by both manned and electronic gates. There is a staffed fire department nearby. The nearest hospital with emergency facilities is Nassau General, located eight miles from the Plantation.

Within the community you will find a dry cleaners (that picks up laundry), a hair salon, a grocery store, restaurants, and retail shops. A liquor store is two miles away; a pharmacy and a movie theater are five miles from the site. The nearest medical clinic is eight miles from the island.

Other local attractions include historic Fernandina Beach, the Amelia Island Museum of History, the Little Talbot Island state park, the Kingsley Plantation state historical site, the Jacksonville Symphony, the Gator Bowl, and the Cumberland Island park.

RECREATION AND SOCIAL ACTIVITIES

Recipient in 1989 and 1990 of *Golf Magazine*'s Gold Medal award as one of the 12 best golf resorts in America, the Plantation is home to 45 holes of unsurpassed golf. The nines of Oysterbay, Oakmarsh, and Oceanside form the Amelia Links; designed by Pete Dye, these 27 holes combine overhanging oaks and small greens with saltwater marshland and towering sand dunes. Long Point, the newest course, was designed by architect Tom Fazio. This championship 18-hole layout challenges the golfer with unusual hazards, highly elevated fairways, large bodies of water, and both marshland and duneside play. There are two pro shops, private and group lessons, and a strict dress code. Full membership which includes golf, costs $12,000 for initiation as well as additional monthly dues.

The Plantation's Racquet Park is truly one of the finest tennis complexes in the nation. Recognized as one of the top 50 American tennis resorts by *Tennis Magazine* and as a five-star destination by *World Tennis,* Racquet Park annually hosts the prestigious Bausch and Lomb Championships in April and the DuPont All-American Tournament in September. Twenty-five courts are scattered among the moss-draped oaks of Racquet Park; three courts have lights for night play. Racquet Park offers private and group lessons, and a pro shop; it also enforces a dress code.

Adjacent to Racquet Park is the community's health and fitness center. This center is a full-service resort spa offering racquetball, aerobic, aquadynamic, and conditioning classes, fitness consultation, a heated indoor pool, a jacuzzi, and a state-of-the-art workout room with Keiser progressive resistance strength-training machines, exercycles, a treadmill, and a ski simulator. The men's and women's locker rooms include saunas, steam rooms, and whirlpools. Throughout the year the center sponsors special road runs and walks, cycling events, triathalons, racquetball tournaments, and fitness lectures. There is an $8,000 social club initiation fee, which includes use of the health club (monthly dues are additional).

Deep-sea fishing in the Gulf Stream, surf casting on uncrowded, sandy beaches, and freshwater angling in the creeks and rivers make the Plantation a fisherman's paradise. A wide variety of charters are available. Offshore fishermen will enjoy the search for blue marlin, wahoo, sailfish, and king mackerel on a charter run to the Gulf Stream. Other charter trips visit offshore wrecks and ledges, looking for catches of red snapper, grouper, and sea bass.

Amelia Island Plantation's recreation department organizes programs for children of all ages throughout the year, such as fishing, swimming, arts and crafts, games, and exciting field trips. Special sports clinics for children ages 9 to 12 are scheduled with Amelia's resident pros. Teens can choose from DJ parties, bonfires on the beach, and video game tournaments. Organized programs for adults include casino nights, shopping excursions, trips to dinner theaters and dog races in nearby Jacksonville, and many special holiday activities.

The most romantic offering at Amelia Island is a horseback ride along the beach. One of the few stables on the Atlantic coast to offer beach riding, Sea Horse Stables is located less than two miles south of the Plantation. The daily rides last approximately 1 1/2 hours and cost $25.

HOMEOWNER ASSESSMENTS, TAXES, AND UTILITIES

Amelia Island Plantation is being developed by the Amelia Island Company. The first home was built in 1974. Currently, 1,100 units have been sold. Final build-out is expected to be 2,200 homes. The homes are a mix of contemporary and Spanish architecture. Ranging in size from 1,850 to over 5,000 square feet, homes with wooded, fairway, lagoon, or ocean views are available. Homesites are also available in either full or patio size to allow custom home designs.

There are 295 high-rise condominiums ranging in price from $125,000 to $465,000 with monthly community association assessments between $164 and $370. Property/municipal taxes average $1,700 to $6,000 per year. The 82 mid-rise condominiums vary in price from $100,000 to $650,000 and cost between $173 and $424 per month in association assessments. Their property/municipal taxes cost between $1,300 and $7,000 per year. Garden-style condos number 139 and range in price from $95,000 to $268,000. Each costs between $168 and $350 in monthly association assessments and from $1,200 to $3,600 in annual taxes. The 215 townhomes cost between $115,000 and $258,000. Their association assessments range from $195 to $380 per month; taxes are $1,500 to $3,700 per year. Single-family homes number 300 and cost between $198,000 and $795,000. They are exempt from community association fees but do pay between $2,600 and $8,000 per year in property/municipal taxes.

Both cable and community television channels are available. Electricity provides the primary heating source, and the local municipality provides both sewer waste and water services to the community. All utilities are underground. There are extra storage facilities within the community for homeowner use.

RESTRICTIONS IN THE COMMUNITY

There is a community association at Amelia Island Plantation and membership is mandatory. The community association handles all exterior building/grounds maintenance for condominium owners. Single-family homeowners provide their own exterior building/grounds maintenance. All construction, changes, or modifications, including landscaping, must be approved by the association's architectural review board.

There are no restrictions on age or length-of-stay for visitors. Maximum occupancy of a home is governed by local fire codes. There are no rental restrictions. The Amelia Island Company retains a right of first refusal on resale of homes. Condo owners are allotted a certain number of parking spaces. Boats and recreational vehicles must be parked in the association's special lots.

BLACK DIAMOND RANCH

3333 W. Black Diamond Circle
Lecanto, Florida 32661
904–746–7400

$250,000 to $500,000
75/599 Single-family
Homes
Traditional Architecture

18-hole USGA-rated golf course
2 lighted outdoor tennis courts

16 miles to the Gulf of Mexico
Clubhouse

INTRODUCTION

Black Diamond Ranch golf and country club community is a private equity residential club that encompasses 1,240 acres of magnificent Florida terrain. One category of equity membership is offered: a private club limited to 750 members. Memberships are mainly limited to homeowners, but a few select outside memberships are granted. An equity golf membership costs $20,000.

The initial development was built around a stunning 18-hole championship golf course. The focal point and signature holes for the course are the five golf holes that surround Black Diamond Lake. Eighty-foot cliffs soar above the lake and rock quarries, providing spectacular views for the residents.

Black Diamond Ranch prides itself on quality, low-density land planning (only .48 units per acre), and a serene, rural atmosphere. The community was voted most outstanding in the 1989 Aurora Awards design competition held by the Southeast Builders' Conference. According to the judges, the designers of the project gave considerable attention to the overall effect of the landscaping and the placement of streets and signs. The site is being developed by Black Diamond Properties, Inc. and was designed by Henigar and Ray Engineering of Crystal River, Florida. The first lot was sold in 1987.

A master association maintains Black Diamond's private roads, streetlights, and common grounds, and the development is secured by a guardhouse that is manned 24 hours a day. Police protection is provided by the county sheriff's department and the Florida state police. Volunteers staff a local fire department. The nearest hospital with emergency services is in Inverness, 12 miles from Black Diamond Ranch. The nearest interstate (I-75) is 28 miles from the community.

There is a club restaurant in the community. Within one mile you can find a pharmacy, a medical clinic, a dry cleaners, a hair salon, and a grocery and liquor store. Inverness, 12 miles away, has retail shops and movie theaters.

Black Diamond Ranch is located in central Citrus County, approximately 8 miles east from the spot where the beautiful Crystal River and its tributaries empty into the Gulf of Mexico. Less than 20 miles northeast, the Dunnellon and Inverness freshwater rivers and lakes offer excellent freshwater fishing and boating. The Ranch is about 80 miles north of Tampa airport and 80 miles northwest of Orlando airport and Disneyworld™. Some local attractions include the Homosassa and Crystal River flea markets, the Indian Mounds Museum, and the Homosassa Springs.

RECREATION AND SOCIAL ACTIVITIES

The first 18-hole championship facility, designed and built by Tom Fazio, was voted the best new private course of 1988 by *Golf Digest*. From the Black tees, the course measures 7,159 yards; from the front tees, it plays a little over 5,300 yards. The front nine is built on some of the most beautiful hills in the area, and five of the back nine holes are built in and around two old limestone quarries. To complement the native sandhill vegetation and add color to the course, the community completed an extensive landscaping program, including the planting of over 1,000 oaks, 1,000 dogwoods, 800 myrtles, 150 magnolias, and over 5,000 azaleas. Upon completion of the community, there will be a total 36 holes of golf.

The first building of the clubhouse complex is open; approximately 4,500 square feet, it includes a pro shop, locker rooms, a lounge, and grill room facilities. The main clubhouse and swimming facilities will commence operations with 350 memberships. When complete, the swimming pool and sun deck will be built around the hilltop clubhouse, offering panoramic views of the entire community.

At present there are two lighted Har-Tru™ tennis courts adjacent to the clubhouse. Four more courts will be added as the community grows. The first clubhouse will house the tennis pro shop when the main building is completed.

The association does not employ a recreation director but does publish a quarterly newsletter. Organized trips and on-site entertainment are provided for homeowners.

HOMEOWNER ASSESSMENTS, TAXES, AND UTILITIES

Black Diamond Ranch offers two basic homesites: estate lots and golf cottage lots. The estate lots range in size from three fourths of an acre to $1\frac{1}{2}$ acres, and the home must have a minimum of 2,300 square feet of air-conditioned space. Golf cottage lots range in size from one-fourth of an acre to one-third of an acre. The golf cottages are located in the villages of Bermuda Dunes, Plantation Pines, and Bent Tree. Lots range in price from $55,000 to over $150,000. Homes range in price from $110,000 to $500,000. Each homeowner pays $30 per month to the master association. To date, 75 homes have been built and 150 lots have been sold. At completion there will be 599 homes.

Generous corridors for golf and deep setbacks for homesites protect the integrity of the golf course and the privacy of the property owners. No housing will be allowed around the quarry in order to preserve its natural beauty and the unique design of the golf course.

Cable television is available, but there are no community television channels. Heat is provided by electric sources. Both a septic and a municipal system provide sewer waste disposal. Water is provided by the local municipality. All utilities are underground. There are no extra storage facilities within the community.

RESTRICTIONS IN THE COMMUNITY

Black Diamond Ranch has a master association and membership is mandatory. All construction, renovations, or landscaping work must be approved by the architectural review board. Lawn maintenance services are available to homeowners for additional fees.

There are no restrictions for age or length-of-stay for visitors. Rentals are subject to length-of-stay restrictions. Operating a business from a home is prohibited. There are some restrictions on the resale of homes. Boats and recreational vehicles are not allowed to park within the development.

BLUEWATER BAY

P.O. Box 247
1950 Bluewater Blvd.
Niceville, Florida 32588
904–897–3613

$62,000 to $500,000
1,800/3,600 Mid-rise Condos, Townhomes, and Single-family Homes
Mixed Architecture

27 holes of golf
10 lakes
Boating
Ball-playing fields
12 lighted outdoor tennis courts

5 outdoor pools (1 heated)
30 miles to Gulf of Mexico
Hiking trails, picnic areas
21 outdoor tennis courts
Handball/racquetball

INTRODUCTION

Located in the heart of Florida's Emerald Coast, Bluewater Bay is surrounded by some of nature's most splendid handiwork: a freshwater bay to the south, 38 miles of sparkling Choctawhatchee Bay to the west, government reserve lands to the east, and a state park to the north. With 2,000 acres of unspoiled land, the community is a premier private recreational resort community, offering extensive amenities and a vast array of housing options. The community was developed by the Bluewater Bay Development Company; the first home was built in 1978.

The community's new 4,000-square-foot conference center can accommodate groups from 5 to 80, and the on-site conference coordinator caters to your every need. The two main conference rooms feature a cathedral ceiling, a public address system, and projection equipment. Guests at the conference center are also allowed to use the community's amenities.

Bluewater Bay is 15 miles from Ft. Walton Beach, and only nine miles from Elgin Airport, where daily flights to and from Atlanta and Memphis are available. Interstate 10 is 18 miles from the site. Police protection is provided by the Okaloosa County sheriff's department and the Florida state police. There is a staffed fire department nearby. A hospital with emergency facilities is five miles from Bluewater Bay.

Currently, the community contains a medical and dental clinic, a dry cleaners, a hair salon, five restaurants, and retail shops. By the end of 1991, a full-service neighborhood supermarket will be completed on site. The nearest movie theater is two miles away.

Area attractions include the Fred Gannon state park, the Air Force Armament Museum, the Destin Fishing Museum, Eden state park, the Indian Mound Temple, the Gulfarium, and the Museum of Sea and Indians.

RECREATION AND SOCIAL ACTIVITIES

Bluewater Bay offers everything for active living, no matter the season. The community's 18-hole championship golf course was designed by Tom Fazio and Jerry Pate. The golf pro is always available to help with your game or match you up with a foursome.

The Bluewater Bay International Invitational Golf Tournament draws players from all over the world. In its eleventh year, the tournament consisted of 180 players who represented five continents and 18 countries. Participation in this prestigious event is by invitation only.

Bluewater Bay has 21 tennis courts: ten with clay courts, nine with hard surfaces, and two with synthetic grass. Twelve courts are lighted for night play. The facilities include a stadium court, a clubhouse with a viewing deck, a fully stocked pro shop, a snack bar, and fully equipped locker rooms. Organized men's and women's programs operate year-round. The community has an excellent junior tennis program that produces state-ranked players.

Bluewater Bay's full service, 120-slip marina provides access to Choctawhatchee Bay. The Intracoastal Waterway, leading to the Gulf of Mexico, is only a cruise away. Rental boats, fishing charters, and windsurfing equipment also enhance life on the Bay.

The private bayside beach island and the five swimming pools provide many hours of relaxation. You can also jog, hike, or bike on miles of wooded trails. The association's Leisure Services department plans organized trips, on-site entertainment, crafts classes in the community's clubhouse, activities for teens, and a bimonthly newsletter. There are no perimeter restrictions for access, but there is a 24-hour patrol within the community. Three subdivisions (Parkwood Estates, Windward, and Southwind) have restricted access with a security gate.

Future amenities include an additional recreation center with an eight-lane olympic-size pool, and nine additional holes of golf designed by Tom Fazio and Jerry Pate.

Club and recreational facilities cost extra at Bluewater Bay. A single golf membership is $2,000 plus annual dues; couples pay $2,500 plus annual dues. A tennis membership costs $350 plus annual dues; recreational/social memberships cost $200 plus annual dues.

HOMEOWNER ASSESSMENTS, TAXES, AND UTILITIES

You can choose from a full selection of affordable housing alternatives and unique neighborhoods at Bluewater Bay. Single-family homes have been created by the area's best builders; garden patio homes offer the golf course for your backyard; lakeside and bayside condos and townhomes feature tranquil views; and wooded lots provide you with a chance to build your dream home.

To date, 1,800 homes have been sold within the community. Final build-out is expected to be around 3,600 homes. The 102 low-rise condominiums range in price from $62,000 to $200,000. Currently, townhomes number 241 and are priced from $70,000 to $150,000. The 1,481 single-family homes range in price from $70,000 to over $300,000. Community association assessments range from $15 to $200 per month depending on the neighborhood and the services provided.

Both cable and community television channels are available for homeowner subscription. Heat is provided by electricity or natural gas; the local municipality provides both sewer services and water distribution. All utilities are underground.

RESTRICTIONS IN THE COMMUNITY

Currently, 18 neighborhood associations are operating at Bluewater Bay. All of the multi-family dwellings are maintained by their association. Single-family homeowners provide their own maintenance but may contract with the on-site provider. All exterior modifications must be authorized by the architectural review board. Landscaping restrictions vary with each neighborhood association.

There are no age or length-of-stay restrictions at Bluewater Bay. Pets are prohibited for short-term rentals, and there are pet size restrictions for long-term rentals. Pets are allowed in owner-occupied units; however, in all cases, the county leash law is in effect. Signs advertising business activities that operate from a home are prohibited, and an occupational license is required. There are no resale restrictions within Bluewater Bay. The community provides an extra parking and storage area for boats, motor homes, and oversized vehicles.

EDGEWATER BEACH RESORT

11212 Front Beach Road
Panama City Beach, Florida
32407
904–235–4044

$90,000 to $273,000
691/973 Garden-style, mid-rise, and High-rise Condos, and Golf Villas
Contemporary & Caribbean Architecture

9-hole golf course
Outdoor free-form pool
Oceanfront view
12 outdoor tennis courts

Clubhouse and convention center
Lake
3 picnic areas
6 lighted tennis courts

INTRODUCTION

Along Panama City Beach's white sands and emerald waters lies Edgewater Beach Resort, a private recreational and residential community of incomparable beauty. Surrounding Edgewater's 110 acres is a privacy wall featuring white stucco columns with hundreds of lights. Three gatehouses ensure security for all homeowners and visitors.

A unique feature of the community is the 10-foot-wide pedestrian overpass which links the towers, the pool, and 2,100 feet of beach frontage to all the other amenities in the development. This concrete and steel bridge accommodates pedestrians and shuttle trams, allowing all parts of the community to be within walking distance.

The community also has excellent conference facilities. The 12,500-square-foot center offers 7,000 square feet of meeting space that is divisible into 13 rooms, complete catering facilities, and a staff of conference specialists who plan activities for 10 to 750 people.

Edgewater Beach Resort is located seven miles from Panama City. The nearest major airport is in Panama City, and Interstate 10 is 48 miles from the site.

Building began in 1979; currently 691 of a planned 973 homes have been built and sold. In January 1991, there were 63 finished units yet to be sold.

The Shops at Edgewater, an ultra-modern shopping center, offers a supermarket, six theaters, restaurants, a dry cleaners, a hair salon, a liquor store, and retail shops. Gulf Coast Hospital, the nearest facility with emergency care, is within seven miles. A pharmacy and medical clinic are within two miles.

RECREATION AND SOCIAL ACTIVITIES

Few pools rival Edgewater's huge Polynesian-style masterpiece. The 11,500-square-foot free-form pool is graced with islands, waterfalls, and over 20,000 tropical plants. It is surrounded by two heated whirlpools, six reflection ponds, walking paths, bridges, and expansive sun decks facing the Gulf of Mexico.

The 8,000-square-foot clubhouse is a two-story facility featuring a second-story restaurant and lounge with a casual atmosphere. The nine holes of par 3 golf are made challenging by 12 lakes and imaginative island greens and tees. Twelve championship-quality, two-tone, all-weather tennis courts with night lighting are available as well. The resident tennis pros offer lessons, clinics, and programs. Edgewater also has a golf and tennis pro shop with clothing and equipment for purchase or rental.

The Hombre, an 18-hole championship course and the site of the Ben Hogan Panama City Beach Golf Classic, is only minutes away from Edgewater.

Homeownership automatically includes membership in the club and recreation facilities (golf, tennis, pool) at Edgewater Beach. There are some nominal user fees. Association management publishes a monthly newsletter, organizes trips, and provides on-site entertainment. An internal tram service, catering, on-site crafts, and maid service are available as well.

HOMEOWNER ASSESSMENTS, TAXES, AND UTILITIES

The Edgewater Towers, 12 stories high, offer one-, two-, and three-bedroom units with panoramic views of the Gulf and the lagoon pool. The Golf Villas are contemporary, Caribbean-style, two-story buildings with white stucco, cedar trim, and tile roofs. Each villa enjoys its own special view, privacy, adjacent parking, and a nearby community pool. The Villas are nestled among 12 stocked lakes, several with spouting fountains. Efficiencies, one-, two-, and three-bedroom units are available. Windward and Leeward, two six-story condominum buildings within Edgewater, are positioned parallel to each other and are in close proximity to the water. Windward and Leeward residents enjoy full privileges at Edgewater's recreational amenities in addition to their own pool and social game room.

All of the homes feature wall-to-wall carpeting, insulated glass, furnished appliances, custom kitchen floors, illuminated kitchen ceilings, cultured marble vanities, and individually metered electrical service.

Currently, 388 high-rise, 107 mid-rise, and 302 garden-style homes have been sold at Edgewater Beach Resort. They range in price from $90,000 to $273,000. Monthly community association assessments for the high-rise condos range from $104 to $344; for mid-rise condos, from $135 to $210; for garden-style condos, from $150 to $300. The property tax rate is .0138968.

Cable and community television are available. Electricity provides the primary heat; water and sewer services are provided by the local municipality. All utilities are underground. The association provides extra storage areas within the community.

RESTRICTIONS IN THE COMMUNITY

Edgewater has a community association and membership is mandatory. Any exterior modifications must be authorized by the architectural control committee. Homeowner landscaping is not allowed at Edgewater. The association handles all building/grounds and landscaping maintenance for the community.

No pets are allowed at Edgewater. Maximum occupation restrictions are four people to a one-bedroom unit, six people to a two-bedroom unit, and eight people to a three-bedroom unit. Renters must be at least 25 years old. Residents are prohibited from operating businesses in units. There are no resale restrictions. Only passenger vehicles may be parked at buildings. The community provides a special area to park recreational vehicles and boats.

**GRENELEFE RESORT AND
CONFERENCE CENTER**

3200 State Road 546
Haines City, Florida 33844-9732
800–421–4722

$30,000 to $600,000
1,188/1,324 Garden-style
Condos, Townhomes, Single-
family Homes, Duplex, and Lots
Mixed Architecture

3 18-hole USGA-rated golf courses
6,400-acre lake
Hiking trails
13 lighted outdoor tennis courts

4 outdoor pools
Boating
20 outdoor tennis courts
Condo hotel and resort center

INTRODUCTION

Grenelefe, a 1,000-acre private planned community in Central Florida, is set among deep woods and lush vistas. Whether you're looking for a vacation home, a year-round residence, or a place for your retirement, Grenelefe can offer all the lifestyle benefits of Florida. Just 45 minutes from Orlando, this community offers an array of on-site recreational amenities and is located near many other area attractions.

Within the boundaries of Grenelefe you will find a dry cleaners, a hair salon, a grocery and liquor store, and restaurants. A pharmacy and a medical clinic are six miles from the site; retail shops and movie theaters are ten miles away. Interstate 4 is 15 miles from the development. The nearest airport is in Orlando, about 35 miles away. The Polk County sheriff's department provides police protection, and a volunteer fire department is nearby. Haines City Hospital, the closest facility with emergency care, is 11 miles from Grenelefe.

Grenelefe residents enjoy close proximity to some of central Florida's famous attractions. Sea World Marine Life Park, Disneyworld, Epcot Center, and Universal Studios are within 30 minutes of the community. Busch Gardens and Florida's west coast beaches, also nearby, offer some of the finest fishing and sailing in the state. Within a short drive are many baseball teams' spring training sites, including the Boston Red Sox, the Minnesota Twins, the Detroit Tigers, and the Houston Astros.

RECREATION AND SOCIAL ACTIVITIES

Grenelefe has three excellent golf courses to choose from. The 6,869-yard South Course, designed by Ron Garl, features a wide variety of length, terrain, and traps, demanding every conceivable shot. Grenelefe's 6,802-yard East Course was designed by Ed Seay. Compared to the large, rambling West Course, it is much shorter and tighter, requiring precise shot placement. Designed by Robert Trent Jones, the West Course has a traditional layout with long, tight fairways lined with tall pine trees and large, treacherous bunkers. There are two clubhouses and pro shops as well as a golf school. There is an initial fee of $2,800 for golf privileges. Yearly dues cost between $1,450 and $2,000.

Grenelefe has recently added two new grass courts to their 20-court tennis complex. Thirteen of the courts are illuminated for nighttime play. Group and private lessons are held at the tennis academy.

The community is situated on Lake Marion, a 6,400-acre lake famous for its bass fishing. Lake Marion has been featured on many nationally televised fishing shows and was the 1985 site for the swimsuit segments for the Miss USA Pageant. The Lake Loft Marina provides fishing tours, bass guides, boat rentals, and other necessary supplies. Covered boat slips are available for $45 per month.

The condo hotel and resort center within the community offers 75,000 square feet of convention space, two restaurants, and a pro shop. Other amenities within the community include five swimming pools, nature trails, and special discounts and privileges for owners. This "owners' courtesy" program offers a 10 percent discount from April 16 to January 14 and a 20 percent discount from January 15 to April 15 for all food and beverage purchases in the resort's restaurants and lounges, and purchases in the golf and tennis pro shops. In addition, owners are privy to special sales held twice a year, receiving a 35 percent discount on most merchandise.

There is a recreation director on site, a daycare for children, and activities for teens. The association does not publish a newsletter. There is a 24-hour patrol within the community; there are no perimeter restrictions for access.

HOMEOWNER ASSESSMENTS, TAXES, AND UTILITIES

Grenelefe is a mixed housing and commercial development, with garden-style condominiums, townhomes, single-family homes, duplexes, golf villas, lake villas, the hotel and conference center, and lots. Building began at the site in 1974.

The 777 garden-style condos range in price from $30,000 to $110,000. The 85 townhomes range from $94,000 to $164,000. Condo and townhome owners pay between $110 and $225 per month in community association assessments. Single-family homes number 100 and cost between $135,000 and $600,000, with assessments of $250 per year. The golf and lake villas range in price from $95,000 to $215,000 and have monthly community association assessments of $134. The 92 duplexes cost between $95,000 and $155,000. Lots range from $30,000 to $75,000 each; of the 118 total lots, 114 have been sold.

Both cable and community television channels are available for homeowner use. Electricity provides the primary heat source; the local municipality provides both sewer waste and water services. All utilities are underground.

RESTRICTIONS IN THE COMMUNITY

Grenelefe has a community association and membership is mandatory. The association handles all exterior building/grounds maintenance for the common areas and the condominiums. Single-family homeowners maintain their own homes and landscapes. All exterior modifications, construction, and landscaping must be approved by the association.

Pet restrictions vary in the different neighborhoods throughout the community—some allow pets, others don't. There are no restrictions on age or length-of-stay for visitors. The association does set limits for maximum occupation, both for homeowners and for renters. Some of the condominium associations have the right of first refusal on resales. The association provides a special area to park recreational vehicles, boats, and the like.

THE HEMISPHERES

1980 South Ocean Drive
Hallandale, Florida 33009
305-457-9732

$40,000 to $250,000
1,295/1,295 High-rise Condos
Contemporary Architecture

2 outdoor pools, 2 kiddie pools
27 boat slips (14' × 35')
Clubhouse, exercise room
Bocci ball
18-hole putting green and golf cage

Oceanfront property
Intracoastal Waterway property
2 lighted tennis courts
Steam/sauna
Shuffleboard
Basketball court

INTRODUCTION

The Hemispheres condominium association offers its owners fantastic beachfront and Intracoastal Waterway property in Hallandale, Florida, just seven miles from Ft. Lauderdale. As the general manager of the association said, "The Hemispheres offers its residents the amenities of any city plus more." The community not only has a wealth of on-site recreational amenities but also has a social calendar full of events for young and old alike.

I-95 is just three miles from the Hemispheres. The Ft. Lauderdale Airport is only seven miles away. Local police and fire departments provide protection and rescue services. The community has its own security force with access through manned or electronically guarded entrances. An emergency medical care facility is only one mile from the site.

Within this luxurious high-rise, you will find a dry cleaners, a hair salon, a grocery store, a restaurant, and retail shops. All other needed services, such as a pharmacy, a medical clinic, a liquor store, and a movie theater are within a half mile of the community. The area has many beach activities and two racetracks: the Gulf Stream Racetrack and the Hollywood Dog Track. The Ft. Lauderdale area has many fine golf courses.

The Hemispheres courtesy bus, free to all residents, makes trips to local shopping centers on a regular basis.

RECREATION AND SOCIAL ACTIVITIES

Recreation amenities are quite diverse at this oceanfront community. Two outdoor pools, both with kiddie pools, provide hours of relaxation in the Florida sun. The community's 27 boat slips can moor boats up to 14 feet × 35 feet. Both outdoor tennis courts are illuminated for night games, and there are also shuffleboard and bocci courts within the property. The community also contains a basketball court, an 18-hole putting green, and a golf cage.

The community's clubhouse (over 15,000 square feet) is the center for many activities. A full-time recreation staff organizes shows, movies, trips, and activities; the staff also acts as a liaison for outside organizations and seminars. All of the association's recreational facilities are free for homeowners, with occasional nominal user fees for some events.

The association's newsletter contains information about the community's activities. There are all kinds of educational classes and lectures, dances, off-Broadway shows, groups for singles, youth activities, video game rooms, ceramics, woodworking, art facilities, singing groups, bus trips, a library, blood pressure checkups, chess and bridge groups, shuffleboard tournaments, game nights, and special events for grandchildren visiting seniors who live at the Hemispheres. Civic and social groups also meet at the Hemispheres.

HOMEOWNER ASSESSMENTS, TAXES, AND UTILITIES

Developed in 1970, the Hemispheres has 678 units with one bedroom, 408 with two bedrooms, 134 with three bedrooms, and 75 studio units—a total of 1,295 units. These high-rise condos range in price from $40,000 to $250,000, and owners pay between $172 and $500 per month in community association assessments.

Cable television is available, but there are no community television channels. Both natural gas and electricity provide heat sources, and the local municipality provides both sewer and water services to the Hemispheres. All utilities are located underground. The association provides extra storage space within the buildings for homeowners to use.

RESTRICTIONS IN THE COMMUNITY

Community association membership is mandatory at the Hemispheres. The association handles all building, grounds, recreational amenities, and infrastructure maintenance. Unit owners may not change any exteriors of a building nor install landscaping.

Age and length-of-stay restrictions do not exist here. Cats are permitted; dogs are prohibited. Maximum occupancies for units are enforced: two people for a studio unit, three people for a one-bedroom unit, four people for a two-bedroom unit, and six people for a three-bedroom unit. Renters must agree to a minimum three-month lease. No units may be used to operate a business. There are no resale restrictions for owners. You are entitled to one parking space but must pay extra to park additional vehicles. The association does not provide a special lot to park oversized vehicles such as recreational vehicles, campers, and trucks.

Residents using the swimming facilities are required to use full-length contoured towels when on the chaise lounges at the poolside. Eating and drinking at the pool area is also prohibited.

When you are driving in the community's garages, you are required to use your headlights. A nice feature at the Hemispheres allows residents who are driving into the garage late at night to press the gate button and request a security escort to their building.

THE HIGHLANDS

675 Shepard Road
Winter Springs, Florida 32708
407-327-0640

$50,000 to $120,000
1,125/1,647 Garden-style
Condos, Townhomes,
Duplexes, and Single-
family Homes
Mixed Architecture

18-hole USGA-rated golf course
3 streams
6 picnic areas

Olympic-size pool, 1 kiddie pool
5 miles of hiking trails
16 lighted outdoor tennis courts

INTRODUCTION

The Highlands homeowners' association is located on 550 acres of prime land in Winter Springs, just five miles from Orlando. The community offers a wide variety of housing options, including condos, townhomes, duplexes, and single-family homes. A private 18-hole golf course runs through the community.

There are 15 sub-associations within the Highlands. Each sub-association governs its own neighborhood, and the master homeowners' association governs and maintains all common property in the development. Community association assessments have only increased 5 percent since 1985. The property is staffed with three employees who supervise the day-to-day affairs of the association. The first home at the Highlands was built in 1973.

The development is conveniently located just three miles from Interstate 4 and only 20 miles from the Orlando International Airport. A local police station is three miles from the site, the County sheriff's department is six miles away, and a Florida state police station is four miles from the Highlands. Both a staffed (28 firefighters) and a volunteer fire department are nearby. South Seminole Hospital, the nearest emergency facility, is two miles from the community.

The Highlands does not offer services within its property, but most needed services (pharmacy, medical clinic, dry cleaners, hair salon, grocery store, liquor store, restaurants, and retail shops) are within a half mile of the development. The nearest movie theater is three miles away.

The area around Winter Springs and Orlando offers a wealth of outdoor activities and attractions such as Disneyworld, Epcot Center, Universal Studios, Sea World, golf courses, flea markets, and shopping centers.

RECREATION AND SOCIAL ACTIVITIES

Except for the private golf club, all the recreational facilities at the Highlands are included in the monthly community association assessment.

Five miles of bicycle and hiking paths wander through the 550-acre property. The Soldier Creek nature trail abounds with wildlife. The Lake Audubon Park is perfect for picnics and fishing. The Highlands also has a junior olympic pool with a wading pool for the children. The association's 16 illuminated tennis courts provide action both day and night.

The community also provides several unique, fully equipped playgrounds for the children and a 4,000-square-foot clubhouse for the exclusive use of residents. The community recently engaged an interior designer to assist with clubhouse renovations, including new carpeting, ceramic tile, and furnishings and a complete overhaul of kitchen facilities.

The Highlands residents' civic association plans numerous social events for the adults and children of the community, such as a Halloween children's party, the community Christmas party and Christmas carolling, a Labor Day pool party, Hawaiian luaus, and a semi-annual garage sale. Most of these events are paid for with advertising profits from the association's newsletter.

The Winter Springs golf club offers a challenging 6,559-yard, 18-hole, par 71 course. Architects Robert Von Hagge and Bruce Devlin placed the course in a 140-acre nature preserve; thousands of huge cypress trees line well-maintained fairways bordered by natural lakes and ponds. The club is open year-round and provides a lighted driving range, chipping and putting areas, daily golf and lunch specials, lessons by PGA professionals, a fully stocked pro shop, rentals, clubs and carts, and advance annual greens fee memberships. There are no initiation fees at the club. Annual greens fee memberships cost $890 for singles and $1,250 for couples.

HOMEOWNER ASSESSMENTS, TAXES, AND UTILITIES

Several types of affordable housing options are offered at the Highlands. Currently, 1,125 homes out of a total 1,647 have been sold. The 448 garden-style condos range in price from $50,000 to $70,000. The 82 townhomes cost $60,000 to $80,000. There are 515 single-family homes that range in price from $85,000 to $100,000, and the 80 duplexes cost about $120,000. All owners pay $330.75 per year to the homeowners' association. Annual assessments are due on January 1. In addition, those areas with sub-associations have separate, additional fees. Property taxes average between $500 and $700 annually.

Cable television is available, but there are no private community channels. Both gas and electricity provide heat, and the local municipality provides both sewer and water services. All utilities are underground. Extra storage facilities are unavailable at the Highlands.

RESTRICTIONS IN THE COMMUNITY

Community association membership is mandatory. The architectural review board must give prior approval for any exterior alterations. If owners neglect to maintain their residence, the association will take corrective action including fines and charging owners for any repairs.

The homes must adhere to strict guidelines set forth by the association: All screening material for screened porches must be gray or black; temporary buildings or sheds may not be constructed; exterior lighting must be shielded from neighbors' views; no carports are permitted; trees with a diameter larger than 6 inches cannot be removed without the authorization of the city of Winter Springs; only standard curbside mailboxes painted black or dark earth tones are permitted; no wire or chain link fences are allowed, and wood fences must be kept painted and in good repair.

There are no pet restrictions within this community, nor are there restrictions regarding age or length-of-stay for visitors. Operating a business from a unit is against city codes. There are restrictions imposed on the resale of condominium units, but none for single-family homes. Parking is only allowed in garages or driveways. The association does not provide a special area for oversized vehicles.

INDIGO LAKES

301 Indigo Drive
Daytona Beach, Florida 32114
904–252–2807

$72,000 to $450,000
300/450 Mid-rise, Garden-style Condos, Townhomes, and Single-family Homes
Mixed Architecture

18 holes of USGA-rated golf	1 outdoor pool, 1 kiddie pool
7 miles to Atlantic Ocean	Hiking trails, picnic areas
10 lighted outdoor tennis courts	Racquetball
Clubhouse, gymnasium	Steam/sauna

INTRODUCTION

The Indigo Lakes association is located within the Hilton at the Indigo Golf and Tennis Resort. Indigo Lakes is an excellent example of a master planned community and is featured in Chapter 1. Indigo is a four-star Hilton resort with one of the top golf courses in Florida. This private community houses the national headquarters for the Ladies' Professional Golfers' Association. A resort and conference center, encompassing 22,000 square feet and able to accommodate up to 300 people for receptions and meetings, is also within the community.

The Charles Wayne Group, developer and builder of Indigo Lakes, is known throughout Florida for applying advanced concepts of energy-efficient construction, innovative home designs, and a dedication to preserve the natural environment. The company has achieved all these goals at Indigo Lakes since completing the first home in 1978.

Orlando, the nearest major city, has a population of 381,500 and is 45 miles from the community. The site is two miles from the Daytona Beach airport and 1½ miles from Highway 95. Police protection is provided by local, county, and state authorities. Both a volunteer and a staffed fire department are nearby. Halifax Hospital, the nearest facility with emergency care, is 3½ miles from the site.

Within the community, there are two restaurants. Within one mile of the development, you will find a pharmacy, a hair salon, retail shops, and a movie theater. A medical clinic, a dry cleaners, and a grocery and liquor store are all within three miles.

Indigo Lakes is situated seven miles from the Atlantic Ocean, where many different types of water sports are available. All of Orlando's major attractions are within 65 miles of the development. Locally, there are flea markets, the Ocean Convention Center, and a museum of arts and sciences.

RECREATION AND SOCIAL ACTIVITIES

Indigo Lakes' 7,123-yard golf course, ranked one of Florida's 10 best and designed by Lloyd Clifton, recently underwent considerable renovation. All greens, tees, and fairway bunkers were demolished, and everything was rebuilt from scratch, at a reported cost of $1.5 million. All greens were raised, (some as much as six feet) to provide better drainage and a better target. Even the huge driving range, which measures 100 × 400 yards, was raised by two feet. For those who need to sharpen their skills, there are putting and chipping greens with a practice sandtrap. The club sports a pro shop and locker rooms.

The Indigo health club, completed in January 1991, offers a wide variety of activities for homeowner members. Under the direction of M.N. Fulton, M.D., the club provides members with general fitness programs. There are also special programs for golfers and tennis players. One-on-one supervised workout sessions, massage therapy, and pool aerobics are also offered to members. For outside exercise, a 15-station, one-half mile fitness trail is open during daylight hours.

Tournament-quality tennis on 10 all-weather outdoor illuminated courts will provide many hours of exercise and fun. A complete service pro shop, private lessons, group clinics, and host play are available. Two racquetball courts, a large swimming pool, and a kiddie pool are also on site.

The Hilton association employs a recreation director and publishes a quarterly newsletter. Catering, maid service, an internal bus service, and on-site entertainment are provided for homeowner convenience. The association organizes daycare for children, activities for teens, and a security patrol within the development.

Homeownership does not automatically entitle you to all the recreational amenities at Indigo Lakes. An all-inclusive (golf, tennis, health club) annual family membership costs $1,850 per year; a single membership costs $1,550. Tennis privileges cost $700 per year for a family. Pool privileges cost $300 per year for a family; an annual social membership costs $225.

HOMEOWNER ASSESSMENTS, TAXES, AND UTILITIES

Both golf course and lakefront homes are available at Indigo Lakes. At completion, there will be 450 residential homes. Currently, there are 36 mid-rise condominiums, 332 townhomes, and 112 single-family homes. There are also 300 garden-style rental condominiums within the development.

The mid-rise condos range in price from $72,000 to $92,000, and owners pay $133 per month in community association assessments. Their property taxes cost between $800 and $900 per year. The 332 townhomes vary in price between $95,000 and $140,000, with an additional $65 to $90 per month in assessments to the homeowners' association and between $1,200 and $1,700 per year in property taxes. Single-family homes cost between $185,000 and $450,000 at Indigo Lakes, with $18 monthly assessments and property taxes between $1,800 and $3,900 per year.

Architecture within the community is mixed. Special features offered by the developer include vaulted ceilings, wet bars, screen porches, cultured marble roman tubs, double stainless steel sinks, finished garages, eat-in custom kitchens, pantries and linen closets, concrete driveways, sidewalks, and patios, skylights, and mirrored closet doors.

Both cable and community television channels are available. Homes are heated primarily by electricity. The local municipality provides both sewer waste disposal and water systems. All utilities are underground. There are no extra storage facilities within the community.

RESTRICTIONS IN THE COMMUNITY

There is a community association at Indigo Lakes, but membership is not mandatory in all areas. The association provides building and grounds maintenance in some of the neighborhood areas; single-family homeowners provide their own building and grounds maintenance. Regardless of the neighborhood, all homes and landscaping installations must conform to the association's architectural guidelines.

There are no age or length-of-stay restrictions for visitors. Only two pets per home are allowed. Homes are intended for single-family occupation only. For rentals, a six-month minimum lease is required. Operating a business from a home is prohibited. There are no restrictions on the resale of homes. The association does not provide any extra parking areas for recreational vehicles, boats, and the like.

THE MEADOWS

5037 Ringwood Meadow
Sarasota, Florida 34235
813-377-2300

$100,000 to $350,000
3,300/3,700 Garden-style
Condos and Single-
family Homes
Mixed Architecture

54 holes of golf
16 tennis courts
250 acres of open space
Recreation fields

Outdoor pools
80 lakes
11 miles of hiking and
    bike trails
Clubhouse at the country club

INTRODUCTION

Taylor Woodrow Homes Limited, known globally for integrity and leadership in engineering, construction, and development, picked Sarasota for the site of its award-winning private recreational community, the Meadows. Sarasota, one mile from the Meadows, has long enjoyed the reputation of being the cultural center of southwest Florida. The Ringling Museum houses over 1,000 paintings by such masters as Rembrandt, Rubens, El Greco, and Gainsborough. Such cultural showcases as the Van Wezel Performing Arts Hall, Sarasota's Opera Company, Asolo Theatre, the Selby Botanical Gardens, and the Sarasota Jungle Gardens can be found at Sarasota.

Siesta Key beach, only a few miles away from Sarasota, was recently judged to have the whitest and most powdery sand in the world, prevailing over 29 other entries, including Waikiki in Hawaii and Nassau in the Bahamas. A 40-acre nature preserve and bird sanctuary is within the Meadows Country Club. Sarasota's Memorial Hospital is only five miles away.

With a population of 250,000, Sarasota County provides air transportation for residents at the Meadows. Interstate 75 is only 2 1/2 miles from the site. The county sheriff's department and the Florida Highway Patrol provide police coverage. The city and county staffed fire departments provide protection and emergency services.

Many services are located at the Meadows: a dry cleaners, a hair salon, a convenience and liquor store, a restaurant, and retail shops. Two miles away, you will find a movie theater and a medical clinic. The nearest pharmacy is two miles from the development.

RECREATION AND SOCIAL ACTIVITIES

Set among 80 lakes on a 1,600-acre spread, the Meadows provides more than its share of golf and tennis facilities. The Meadows sports two championship golf courses and an 18-hole walking course, just three of the total 54 golf courses in the Sarasota area. The Meadows has an outstanding 16-court tennis center with lighted courts and a championship center court. Sarasota offers water sports such as boating, fishing, swimming, wind surfing, and waterskiing. The Meadows contains eleven miles of paved paths for bicyclists and pedestrians. For walkers and joggers, there is an 18-station exercise course. Lakes are stocked for fishing.

The Meadows Country Club's two private restaurants and the dining facilities at the nearby Highlands Golf Club are among the finest in Florida. The Shopping Village offers a variety of retail stores, professional services, and restaurants. *The Meadoword,* the community newspaper, carries reports on crafts, golf, tennis, social, and seasonal events.

No full-time recreation director is needed: The Good Neighbor program sponsors events such as pool parties, deep-sea fishing trips, theater trips, visits to art centers, and shopping forays. Several times a year the Sarasota Community Blood Bank Bloodmobile holds a blood drive at the Meadows to provide a reserve for homeowners in the community.

HOMEOWNER ASSESSMENTS, TAXES, AND UTILITIES

The Meadows offers over twenty homestyle choices of garden-style condos, villas, and single-family homes. The garden homes range from $100,000 to $125,900, with quarterly maintenance fees of $255. The villas cost $132,900 to $268,000, with quarterly maintenance fees from $327 to $435. The single-family homes sell at prices from $160,000 to over $300,000. In addition, all owners pay an average annual assessment of $400 to the master association.

Membership in the country club currently requires a $7,000 equity value investment in the club (with an additional initiation fee of $750) as well as a $5,500 fee for golf and a $1,700 fee for tennis. All other amenities, including at least one outdoor pool per condo association, do not require extra fees.

Started in 1977, the community has to build only 175 units to complete the final total of 3,700 units. Cable television is available, the primary heat source is electricity, and all utility wires are underground. Water and sewage services are provided by municipal systems. The community has an active recycling program. No extra storage facilities are available.

RESTRICTIONS IN THE COMMUNITY

The community association handles the maintenance of all common areas; the condominium associations handle common elements and exterior maintenance in the individual neighborhoods. Single-family home and grounds maintenance is the responsibility of the owner. Architectural restrictions are enforced; details are available upon request. There are no landscaping restrictions for single-family homeowners.

There are rental restrictions for some condo associations but none for single-family homes. Business operation is not permitted in any residence. Parking restrictions prohibit commercial vehicles, trucks, and recreational vehicles, except in certain designated areas. Pet restrictions vary with each condo association; only household pets are permitted, and leashes are required when pets are outside.

OAK RUN COUNTRY CLUB

9232 S.W. 110th St.
Ocala, Florida 32676
904-854-5775

$57,900 to $127,900
1,371/4,926 Single-family
Homes
Traditional Architecture

9-hole golf course	1 outdoor pool
Over 100 acres of open space	2 ball-playing fields
4 lighted outdoor tennis courts	Clubhouse with exercise room
Steam/sauna facilities	Billiard room
Bocci court, croquet court	Horseshoe pits

INTRODUCTION

The Oak Run Country Club, a private adult community, is located in the heart of Florida's "Big Sun Country." The community's crystal lakes, lazy rivers, and rolling hills provide a backdrop for thoroughbred horse farms and century-old oaks. Exploring the area around Oak Run Country Club will provide you with many hours of enjoyment. Orlando, just 70 miles south of the community, provides attractions such as Disneyworld, Epcot Center, MGM Studios, Sea World, and Universal Studios. Tampa's many cultural activities, including the Busch Gardens and the Tampa Bay Buccaneers, are all within easy reach.

Just 36 miles away, Florida's Gulf Coast offers sandy beaches and serene sailing. To the east is the exciting deep sea fishing of the Atlantic. A few miles from Oak Run, some of the finest freshwater fishing in the country awaits you. The famous attraction of Silver Springs is nearby, as well as shopping, dining, theater, and other diversions. Oak Run even has a free community bus to provide transportation to many locations. Oak Run is being developed by Kulbir Ghumman of Ocala, Florida. The first home was built in 1985.

Interstate 75 is seven miles from the site. Gainesville, the nearest large town, is located 45 miles from Oak Run. Police protection is provided by local authorities, the county sheriff's department, and the state police. There is a volunteer fire department within three miles of the community. The nearest hospital with emergency facilities is located in Ocala, 12 miles away.

There are no services provided within the community; however, within two miles are a pharmacy, a medical clinic, a dry cleaners, a hair salon, a grocery and liquor store, a restaurant, and retail stores. There is a movie theater nine miles from the community. The University of Florida is located 40 minutes north of Oak Run.

RECREATION AND SOCIAL ACTIVITIES

Oak Run Country Club promises affordable living with a country club lifestyle. Homes are clustered in small neighborhoods throughout the community's 1,400 lushly landscaped acres. The privacy of the residents is protected by a manned gatehouse just inside Oak Run's Grand Entry, which boasts illuminated pools and waterfalls.

The lifestyle at Oak Run is active, relaxed, and friendly. Nowhere is that spirit more apparent than at the community's ten-acre recreational resort complex, the Orchid Club. The acoustically perfect auditorium is ideal for movies, plays, live musical performances, bingo nights, and dances. Other rooms are equipped for ceramics, arts and crafts, billiards, card games, and club meetings. The building includes a fully equipped kitchen, a complete fitness center, a well-stocked library, and a reading room. Outside, you'll find tennis and shuffleboard courts, horseshoe pits, and bocci; a year-round schedule of tournaments attracts competitors and spectators alike. The community also provides a huge swimming pool and hot tub. Oak Run's private cable TV channels keep residents posted on the community's many activities, trips, tournaments, and special events.

A challenging round of golf on the 9-hole executive course at the Oak Run country club can test the skill of players of all abilities. The club offers a chipping and putting area and a fully equipped pro shop with a snack bar. Although there is no recreation director at Oak Run, the association does publish a monthly newsletter.

HOMEOWNER ASSESSMENTS, TAXES, AND UTILITIES

Only single-family homes are currently being built at Oak Run. However, the developer is planning to build some attached housing units in the future. So far, 1,371 single-family homes have been sold. The total build-out is expected to be 4,926 homes. The developer at Oak Run offers eight different models to choose from. Homes can range in size from 1,421 square feet to 2,882 square feet. All homes are provided with a custom-designed landscaping package (including sodded lawn and chemically treated subsoil), a concrete driveway, a walkway, a full-size garage, covered entry with lighting, a spacious screened porch, and lever-action door handles. The homes range in price from $57,900 to $127,900. The average municipal taxes are $650 per year.

Residents at Oak Run own both the single-family home and the homesite; therefore, there are no maintenance fees. However, there is an amenities fee of $67 per month that provides 24-hour security, basic cable television, access to the Oak Run cable TV channel, membership to all recreation facilities, maintenance of all recreation facilities and common areas, and curbside trash collection service. Any yearly adjustment is limited to the amount of fluctuation of the Consumer Price Index. A monthly road fund fee of $6 is held in escrow for use in maintaining and repairing roads and drainage areas. As with the amenities fee, any yearly adjustment of the road fund fee is limited by the Consumer Price Index. Electricity provides the primary heat source, and the developer of the community has provided a private waste water treatment plant and water purification system. All utilities are underground. There are no extra storage facilities on site.

RESTRICTIONS IN THE COMMUNITY

Oak Run Country Club is an adult community, allowing no one younger than 18 years old to live in the development. However, children may visit for 30 days each year. No more than two pets are allowed per home, and they must be confined on the owner's property or on a leash.

There is a community association and membership is automatic upon purchase. Individual homeowners provide their own exterior building and grounds maintenance. Any exterior modification to a home must be submitted to the architectural review board for approval to ensure harmony of exterior design. No gardens may be grown in the front yard, and backyard gardens may not exceed two percent of the gross footage of the lot. Outside builders are not allowed within Oak Run: Only the developer of the community is allowed to build homes.

The maximum occupancy at Oak Run Country Club is four permanent residents per home. Homes may not be rented for less than three months. No business, commercial enterprise, or business activity may be conducted from a home. No window signs are permitted; other signs must be approved to assure uniformity. No more than two automobiles are permitted per home, and they must be parked in the homeowner's driveway. There are extra parking areas available for recreational vehicles and boats.

RIVERWOOD PLANTATION

6200 Riverwood Drive
Port Orange, Florida 32127
904-788-4164

$66,200 to $400,000
300/450 Townhomes and
Single-family Homes
Contemporary and Spanish
Architecture

1 outdoor pool
7 miles to Atlantic Ocean
2 picnic areas

4 lakes
Boating
2 outdoor tennis courts

INTRODUCTION

Riverwood Plantation, a bayfront community located along 180 acres of the Spruce Creek in Port Orange, Florida, offers seven separate and distinct neighborhoods with homes designed for different lifestyles. One of the major attractions at this development is the private recreation area at Spruce Creek. An attractive gazebo, made for lazy afternoons, sits unobtrusively on a clearing near the creek. Just beyond the gazebo is the only private boat ramp in the Daytona area.

The Charles Wayne Group, developer of Riverwood Plantation, is one of the largest and most respected builders in Florida, having built over 6,000 homes in many Florida communities. The Group is known for applying advanced concepts of energy-efficient construction, innovative designs, and a dedication to preserve the environment. Committed to quality and value, the Group has won numerous awards for its homes and communities, including several of the Southeast Builders' Conference's prestigious Aurora Awards for excellence in design and energy efficiency.

Just ten miles from the Riverwood Plantation, Daytona Beach has a population of 65,000 and provides the nearest air transportation. Interstate 95 is only four miles from the community. The Port Orange police department, Volusia County sheriff's department, and the Florida state police provide protection for the community. Within the estate section of Riverwood there are electronic perimeter restrictions. Port Orange's staffed fire department is near the community. The

Halifax Medical Center, ten miles from the development, provides emergency care.

Strictly a residential community, Riverwood Plantation offers no commercial services to residents. However, all services are within two or three miles. Two miles away you will find a pharmacy, a dry cleaners, a hair salon, a grocery store, a liquor store, and restaurants. A medical clinic, retail shops, and a movie theater are three miles from the site.

Area attractions include the Daytona International Speedway, jai alai, the dog tracks, the Ocean Center, Peabody Auditorium, the Museum of Arts and Sciences, Daytona's flea market, Disneyworld, Sea World, the Church Street Station, the Kennedy Space Center, and the Atlantic Center for the Arts.

RECREATION AND SOCIAL ACTIVITIES

All Riverwood Plantation residents enjoy full recreational facilities including an award-winning clubhouse, a pool, racquet and tennis courts, nature trails, picnic areas, wooded parks, four lakes, and a boat ramp on the bay. The Atlantic Ocean, only seven miles from the site, also offers a tremendous amount of water sports and activities. There are numerous golf courses in the area as well.

The association does not employ a recreation director; however, it publishes a monthly newsletter and organizes trips and entertainment for homeowners. The community has an evening patrol provided by local authorities, and there are electronic gates at the entry to the estate section of the community.

HOMEOWNER ASSESSMENTS, TAXES, AND UTILITIES

Homes at Riverwood Plantation are divided into seven neighborhoods: Glenbrook, Greenbriar Villas, Riverwood, Sable Cove, River Pointe, Baytree, and the new Palmas Bay Club. Out of an expected total of 450 homes, 300 have been sold to date. Townhome owners pay $75 per month in community association assessments; single-family homeowners pay $20 per month. Owners of the eleven homes located in the Palmas Bay Club pay $78 per month in association fees.

The Riverwood, Glenbrook, and Baytree neighborhoods offer custom-built executive homes ranging in price from $102,900 to $141,900. Features include vaulted ceilings, cultured marble vanity tops, sodded lawn and landscaping, a pantry and linen closets, a two-car finished garage, and concrete walkways, driveway, and patio.

Sable Cove, a neighborhood of single-family homes, offers two-, three-, or four-bedroom houses ranging from $82,900 to $98,900. Features include a pantry, coat and linen closets, a walk-in closet in master bedroom, a two-car finished garage, and landscaping and sodded lawn.

Riverpointe is a neighborhood of contemporary single-family homes, that range in price from $79,900 to $88,400. Two- and three-bedroom homes with one- or two-car garages are offered; some models have lofts.

Greenbriar Villas is the community's townhome neighborhood. Landscaping at the Villas is taken care of by the association. Homes cost $66,200 to $77,200 and feature vaulted ceilings, large walk-in closets, and attached garages.

The Palmas Bay Club, Riverwood's estate neighborhood, offers homesite lots from $60,000 to $103,000; lots on the creek are the most expensive. Homes constructed here must be a minimum of 3,000 square feet. You may have the Charles

Wayne Group design your home or contract with your own architect, but all the homes within this section must adhere to strict architectural standards set forth by the association. Entrance is controlled by security gates that may be opened and closed from any home within the community. These homes range from $200,000 to $400,000.

Cable television is available, but there are no community television channels. All homes are heated by electricity, and the local municipality provides both water and sewer services. All utilities are underground. There are no extra storage facilities within the community.

RESTRICTIONS IN THE COMMUNITY

Membership in the Riverwood Plantation community association is mandatory. Two of the neighborhoods offer building and grounds maintenance services; the other five require owners to handle their own maintenance. The association maintains all common property and amenities. Any exterior or landscaping modification must be approved by the architectural committee.

There are no age or length-of-stay restrictions for visitors at Riverwood. Pets are allowed but must be leashed when outside private property. Homes are restricted to single families and are not to be used for commercial purposes. There are no rental or resale restrictions imposed by the association. Parking on streets is prohibited. RVs or boats are not allowed in driveways and must be parked in garages or storage areas. A plan for a special area to park oversized vehicles is currently in the process of receiving city approvals for construction in the next phase of the development.

SEASIDE

P.O. Box 4730
County Road 30-A
Seaside, Florida 32459
800-635-0296

$217,000 to $400,000
180/300 Single-family
Homes and Lots
Florida Vernacular
Architecture

2 outdoor pools, 2 kiddie pools
1 hiking trail
2 outdoor tennis courts

½ mile of ocean shoreline
Located on beach
Picnic areas

INTRODUCTION

Maybe the March 1988 issue of *Travel & Leisure Magazine* said it best: "Seaside is, in its simplest sense, a beachfront tract of about 80 acres in the process of development. But it is much more complicated and far-reaching than that...something that has seized the attention of urban-planning theorists and brought them down to see for themselves. It has become the subject of seminars among municipal officials across the country, and it contains the seed of a land-development philosophy that could influence the way America lives in the 21st century."

Seaside has been featured in virtually every major national publication, including *Time, The Wall Street Journal,* and *Atlantic Monthly. Atlantic Monthly* called it "the most celebrated new American town of the decade," and it received *Time's* award for "community design of the decade." Seaside has won awards for urban design from *Progressive Architecture,* the American Institute of Architects, the National Association of Homebuilders, and *Southern Living.*

Real estate developer Robert Davis wanted to build a "traditional American small town." Seaside is his dream come true. The community is a combination of American and European town planning and uses forms and elements usually seen in older buildings of the Southeast. Mr. Davis also made an environmental statement with Seaside. The beach has been left undeveloped and simple wooden pavilions were placed at the ends of major streets. This has the effect of distributing property values more fairly, and the oceanfront property is treated with dignity.

Architectural rules at Seaside are very strict. Homes must be low, free-standing, and of wood frame construction; they must have exposed rafters, deep front porches, and gentle roof pitches. They can only be painted in approved pastel colors with approved contrasting trim. Windows may only be vertical or square, and roofs must be made of metal or wood shakes. All homes must have yards landscaped with sand and native scrub. Each house must have its own white picket fence, with no fence pattern repeated on any one street.

Mr. Davis believes that these architectural factors can foster sociability among neighbors at Seaside. For example, the distance allowed between a front porch and sidewalk is so small that residents sitting on their front porches can easily strike up a conversation with a passersby. Formal footpaths are placed between the homes, bringing neighbors even closer together.

Seaside is 35 miles from Ft. Walton Beach, where air transportation can be found. The county sheriff's department provides police protection; both a volunteer and a staffed fire department are nearby. Destin, just 25 miles away, has the nearest hospital with emergency facilities.

The community contains a grocery store, restaurants, retail shops, and a movie theater that operates in the summer. The nearest hair salon is one mile away, a medical clinic is three miles away, a pharmacy is ten miles away, and the nearest dry cleaners is 20 miles from Seaside. The completed community will have dozens of stores and workshops, a town hall, a post office, an outdoor theater, two hotels, several small inns, and related business and recreational facilities.

RECREATION AND SOCIAL ACTIVITIES

Life at this lovely little community revolves around the sea and the arts. The Seaside Institute, founded in 1981, promotes educational and cultural activities in the community. During the past seven years, the Institute has sponsored a variety of performing arts and literary events, such as chamber music recitals, poetry readings, arts and crafts shows, and theater and dance performances.

An internship program for architectural students was established in 1987. With the completion of housing and studio space for students and faculty, the program is expected to grow to include artists-in-residence and lecture series by visiting artists and scholars. An annual symposium on urban design attracts architects and planners from throughout the country. Similar programs will be implemented in other visual and performing arts disciplines, with the eventual development of a music camp and festival at Seaside.

Residents can also enjoy two pools, two tennis courts, a world-class croquet court, shuffleboard, bicycle and boat rentals, a hiking trail, picnic areas, and a half mile of white sandy beach. Membership in the swim and tennis club currently costs $500 per year.

Other activities include musical theater, cooking demonstrations, an annual giant garage sale, foot races, and many holiday events. Christmas at Seaside is very special: The month of December is filled with fun events. The surrounding area also offers activities such as golf, deep sea fishing, diving trips, boating and river tours.

Seaside publishes a quarterly newsletter, organizes activities for teens, and even provides maid service to vacationers. There are no perimeter restrictions, but there is a 24-hour patrol within the community.

HOMEOWNER ASSESSMENTS, TAXES, AND UTILITIES

In keeping with the original plans for a small town atmosphere, maximum build-out at Seaside will be only 300 dwellings. To date, 280 lots have been sold and 180 homes have been built. Lots range in price from $99,000 to $180,000. Homes cost from $217,000 to $400,000. All owners pay between $500 and $600 per year to the community association. Property taxes are $16 per $1,000 of assessed value; the county assesses homes at 80 percent to 85 percent of market value.

Cable television is available, but there are no community television channels. Electricity provides the primary heat source, and the local municipality provides both sewer and water systems. All utilities are underground. There are no extra storage facilities within Seaside.

RESTRICTIONS IN THE COMMUNITY

Membership in the Seaside community association is mandatory for all owners. Building and grounds maintenance for homes is the responsibility of the owner. The association maintains all common areas and infrastructure. Attached garages are prohibited. As noted before, architectural guidelines are very strict: The guidelines even spell out what types of hidden hinges can be on cabinets.

There are no age or length-of-stay restrictions for visitors in the community. A leash law is in effect for all outdoor pets. Rental and occupancy restrictions are also in effect at Seaside. Operating a business from a home is prohibited. There is a special area within the community for parking oversized vehicles.

**TOPS'L BEACH
AND RACQUET CLUB**

5550 Highway 98 East
Destin, Florida 32541
904-267-9222

$110,000 to $800,000
186/700 Garden-style and
High-rise Condominiums
Contemporary and Spanish
Architecture

45 holes of USGA-rated golf	Indoor pool
Outdoor pool	Kiddie pool
2 lakes	Situated on beach
100 private boat slips	Hiking/walking trails
Picnic areas	Volleyball court
12 outdoor tennis courts	10 lighted outdoor tennis courts
Handball/racquetball/squash	Large clubhouse
Gymnasium, exercise room	Steam, sauna room

INTRODUCTION

Tops'l Beach and Racquet Club encompasses 55 acres in south Walton County, Florida. Located ten miles east of Destin and midway between Pensacola and Panama City, the property extends from Highway 98 to the Gulf of Mexico. The community is being developed by the Tops'l Management Corporation of Destin, Florida. The developer also provides management services to the community. The first unit was built in 1985.

Unsurpassed tennis facilities, world-class pros, and extensive programs promise an exhilarating challenge for the accomplished competitor. There are 12 clay and hard courts, ten of which are illuminated. In fact, *Tennis Magazine* rated this community as one of the top 50 tennis resorts in the United States. The Tops'l Beach and Racquet Club has also received a four-star rating from Mobile. The Tops'l staff includes resident professional Steve Pennyton and two assistants who conduct numerous regular and special events.

Interstate 10 is 15 miles from the site. The nearest major airport is at Fort Walton Beach, about 20 miles away. There is a private air strip located 7 miles from the project. Police protection is provided by local authorities, the county sheriff's department, and the state police. There is a staffed fire department nearby. The nearest hospital with emergency facilities is in Destin, seven miles from the community.

Local attractions include area beaches, amusement parks, water parks, Sea World, and private and charter boat fishing. Within the confines of Tops'l Beach and Racquet Club, you will find a hair salon, a liquor store, and a restaurant. Within one mile of the community there are retail shops and a pharmacy. Seven miles away you will find a movie theater, a dry cleaners, and a medical clinic.

RECREATION AND SOCIAL ACTIVITIES

Even though it is primarily a tennis community, Tops'l Beach and Racquet Club offers many other exciting activities.

Golfing along the Emerald Coast is simply sensational. Through a reciprocal agreement with the Sandestin Country Club, Tops'l Beach's resident members have privileges at both clubs. The Sandestin Club has excellent golfing facilities, with 45 holes designed by Tom Jackson. Long a legend among Florida courses, Links offers a challenging layout along the beautiful Choctawhatchee Bay. And the newer Baytown golf courses feature three challenging tracts: the Dunes, with views of the Gulf of Mexico, the Harbor, near Baytowne Marina, and the new Troon course, which includes an unparalleled island green.

Tops'l residents also have access to an indoor and outdoor swimming pool (along with kiddie facilities) and two small lakes with approximately one mile of shoreline. There are boating facilities with 100 private boat slips, hiking trails, picnic areas, and outdoor volleyball courts.

The community has a large clubhouse that holds a gymnasium, racquetball courts, an exercise room, and steam and sauna facilities. The community employs a recreation director, offers valet/concierge services, and publishes a monthly newsletter. The association organizes trips and provides on-site entertainment. Homeowners have access to bus service, catering services, and maid service. This association provides daycare for children and activities for teens.

Tops'l Beach and Racquet Club is a highly secured community. Perimeter restrictions include both manned and electronic gates. There is also a 24-hour patrol within the community.

HOMEOWNER ASSESSMENTS, TAXES, AND UTILITIES

The tile roofs and geometric design of Tops'l Tennis Village accent the lush greenery, and the 65 garden-style villas cluster around the lake and tennis courts. Tennis Village residents may choose from six appealing floor plans with two- and three-bedroom designs and a selection of interior decors. Each villa also features covered parking, enclosed exterior storage, a wood-burning fireplace, a gourmet kitchen, and double common walls for quiet privacy. These homes range in price from $110,000 to $200,000, with a current monthly community association assessment between $117 and $250. Yearly property/municipal taxes average $1,500.

The Tops'l Beach Manor offers every resident a magnificent view of the sea. The 14-story Manor is designed for luxury and comfort. Its 121 units, in two- and three-bedroom styles, are each equipped with a balcony, a wood-burning fireplace (in specified units), nine-foot ceilings, a gourmet kitchen, luxurious baths, and an optional wet bar. All windows are insulated to ensure security. There are fire detection and sprinkler systems, and all residents are provided with covered parking. These homes range in price from $150,000 to $800,000. The current monthly community association assessment for the high-rise condos ranges from $150 to $500, and their yearly property/municipal taxes average $1,800.

Both cable and community television channels are available to homeowners. Electricity is the primary heat source. The local municipality provides both sewer waste disposal and water systems. All telephone and electrical utilities are underground. There are extra storage facilities within the community.

RESTRICTIONS IN THE COMMUNITY

There is a community association at the Tops'l Beach and Racquet Club, and membership is mandatory. There are no restrictions for age or length-of-stay for visitors. Pets are allowed only by special exception.

Currently, both the community association and the developer provide exterior building and grounds maintenance. The developer is still in control of this community because the community is not completely sold out. Any exterior modifications of the homes must be approved by the association and developer of the community. Additional landscaping is prohibited by the association.

Maximum occupation is restricted to the bed capacity of the home. Rental restrictions include a minimum stay for renters during certain times of the year. Operating a business from your unit is strictly prohibited. There are no restrictions regarding resales at the Tops'l Beach and Racquet Club. The association provides a special parking area for recreational vehicles, boats, and the like.

Chapter 10

Southwest
Arizona
Texas

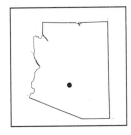

THE DOBSON RANCH

2719 South Reyes
Mesa, Arizona 85202
602-831-8314

$60,000 to $200,000
4,950/4,950 Garden-style
Condos and Single-family
Homes
Mixed Architecture

18-hole USGA-rated golf
1 kiddie pool
Boating
Handball/racquetball

4 outdoor pools
7 lakes with 5 miles of shore
12 lighted outdoor tennis courts
Clubhouse

INTRODUCTION

Dobson Ranch was established in a land-use plan by the city of Mesa in April 1973. Mesa has a population of 300,000 and is just east of Phoenix. The Ranch covers approximately 1,600 acres. Since 1973, the Ranch has grown to include over 4,950 families, making up a total population of approximately 12,000 individuals.

Highway 360 is located at the entrance of the community. The Sky Harbor International Airport is seven miles away. A police department, a fire department, and a public library are within the community. The nearest hospital with emergency facilities is the Good Samaritan Hospital, two miles from the community.

This large community has most needed services on site, including a pharmacy, a medical clinic, a dry cleaners, a hair salon, a grocery and liquor store, a restaurant, and retail shops. A movie theater is within a few miles of Dobson Ranch. Arizona State University, located in Mesa, has an enrollment of 40,000 students.

RECREATION AND SOCIAL ACTIVITIES

The Ranch has three major recreation facilities and an 18-hole USGA-rated golf course. The use of the recreation facilities are restricted to Dobson association members and their guests. Members delinquent in their association dues are not allowed to use the facilities.

Some of the programs offered include tot time (a recreation and socialization program for children three-to-five years of age), a soccer league for both boys and girls, private piano lessons for both adults and children, a 150-member swim team for children 5 through 17, that holds practices five days a week during the summer months and competes in various local meets, a friendship sports league that offers football, basketball, and tee-ball for children age 5 through 17, and instruction for adults and children in tae kwon do, a Korean martial art that incorporates the philosophy of a disciplined mind and body. The association also sponsors holiday events, a women's club, and adult programs ranging from instructional classes such as CPR training to social events such as dances.

Within the community are seven small lakes with a total of five miles of shore-line. Boating is allowed; all boats operated on the lakes must be powered man-ually, by sail, or by an electric motor, with a maximum of three horsepower. Sailboats cannot exceed 18 feet in length, and canoes cannot exceed 16 feet. Sailboards are not allowed on the lakes. All boats must be registered with the association and the state of Arizona. Association decals are $3 annually. Wading, swimming, and diving in the lakes are strictly prohibited for both residents and their pets. Fishing is allowed but is limited to a total of six fish a day per license. Lakes are stocked each year.

All 12 of Dobson's outdoor tennis courts are lighted. There are handball and racquetball facilities in the clubhouse. Lessons are available from the resident pro.

The community has a fairly large clubhouse and employs a recreation director. The community association publishes a monthly newsletter and provides daycare facilities for children. The Dobson association is a private community, but there are no perimeter restrictions for access. The community expects to complete a new, 7,000-square foot clubhouse in September 1991. Homeownership at Dobson automatically entitles you to use of all the club and recreation facilities.

HOMEOWNER ASSESSMENTS, TAXES, AND UTILITIES

The Ranch offers single-family homes, patio homes, condominiums, and town-houses. All of the intended homes have been built, but resales are occurring. There are 850 garden-style condominiums that range in price from $60,000 to $120,000. The 4,100 single-family homes cost $60,000 to $200,000. All homeowners pay $17.25 per month in community association assessments. Neighborhood associ-ation assessments, if any, are separate.

There is a variety of architectural styles within the community, primarily con-temporary and Spanish architecture. Both cable and community channels are available. The primary heat source is electricity, and the local municipality pro-vides both sewer waste disposal and water systems. All telephone poles and electrical wires are underground. The community does not provide extra storage facilities for its homeowners.

RESTRICTIONS IN THE COMMUNITY

Dobson Ranch has a community association and membership is mandatory. In-dividual homeowners provide the exterior building and grounds maintenance for their homes. The association provides maintenance for all the common areas and amenities. Any exterior modifications to a home must have prior approval of the architectural review committee. Most landscaping is allowed within the community, but gardens are only allowed in the rear yard.

There are no restrictions on age or length-of-stay for visitors at Dobson. No more than three household pets are allowed per home, and they must be kept on a leash when outside. Maximum occupation is limited to a single family or no more than three nonrelated persons. If you choose to rent your home at this community, you must inform the association and decide whether you will retain the right to use the recreational facilities or give that right to the renter.

There are no restrictions on the resale of homes. Operating a business from your unit is allowed, but it must not create any additional pedestrian or vehicular traffic. There is a three-quarter ton limit for trucks, and no recreational vehicles or trailers may be parked on streets or in driveways. If an oversized vehicle is parked in the rear yard, it must not exceed the height of the fence and must not be visible from the sidewalk, street, common area, or neighboring property. The community does not provide any special parking areas for recreational vehicles or boats.

THE FOOTHILLS AT SOUTH MOUNTAIN PARK

2231 E. Camelback Road
Suite 332
Phoenix, Arizona 85016
602-468-6180

$80,000 to $350,000
600/7,000 Townhomes and Single-family Homes
Southwestern Architecture

18-hole USGA-rated golf course
Boating
Picnic area

5 small lakes
Hiking trails
Clubhouse

INTRODUCTION

Whether you prefer golfing, hiking, jogging, biking, or picnicking, the Foothills offers abundant opportunities to enjoy the outdoors. The 4,140 acres of the Foothills at South Mountain Park makes it the largest master plan development in the history of Phoenix. Publicly owned and listed on the New York Stock Exchange, the Del Webb Corporation of Arizona, along with Burns International, is creating an imaginative and beautiful Sonoran desert community.

The Foothills at South Mountain Park is located 3 1/2 miles west of the I-10 interchange at Chandler Boulevard, close to Sky Harbor Airport, downtown Phoenix, and the Southeast Valley communities. Future construction of the South Mountain Freeway will make the Foothills even more accessible. The Southeast Valley communities already account for over 25 percent of the Phoenix metropolitan area's population. By the year 2000, these communities are expected to account for half of the metro area's growth and a third of the metropolitan Phoenix population. In 1989 the Southeast Valley was already home to 60 companies of at least 300 employees. With over 80 business and industrial parks and more in the planning stages, employment opportunities in this area continue to increase rapidly.

South Mountain Park (the largest municipal park in the United States) spans 16,000 acres on the northern boundary of the Foothills. Its rugged contours combine the beauty of the desert and the hills, creating a peaceful setting. Residents bike, hike, and explore the many trails laced across these mountains. A planned 40-acre city park will incorporate a full scope of facilities and playground activities.

Property values at the Foothills are protected by high architectural standards. Colors, styles, landscaping, and lighting are coordinated to blend with the environment. The developers of the Foothills have worked to ensure a conscientious and practical approach to the use of water, the desert's most valuable resource. Landscaping with native, drought-tolerant vegetation is one measure used to reduce the demand on water. Runoff and recycled effluent are used to irrigate the golf course and maintain the water features.

In order to maintain and enhance property values, all elements from traffic patterns to landscaping and lighting have been carefully planned.

Over the next decade, the Foothills will become a self-sufficient community encompassing single- and multi-family homes, churches, schools, businesses, municipal and medical facilities, retail shops, restaurants, and a wide variety of recreational opportunities. At this time 600 homes have been sold in the community.

Police protection is provided by local authorities, and there is a staffed fire department nearby. The nearest hospital with emergency facilities is Tempe Lutheran, 10 miles from the site. At this time there are no services within the community. Within one mile you will find a dry cleaners, a hair salon, and a grocery and liquor store; two miles away you will find retail shops, restaurants, and a pharmacy. A medical clinic is four miles from the community and a movie theater is five miles away.

RECREATION AND SOCIAL ACTIVITIES

The 18-hole championship golf course, designed by Tom Weiskopf and J. Morrish, is one of the focal points of this desert community. A daily fee course, it features high-quality fairways and greens, multiple tee boxes, and expansive practice areas. Clinics, seminars, private instruction, and group tournaments are all under the supervision of a staff of PGA professionals. The pro shop offers a full line of golf equipment and sports attire.

As homes continue to sell at the Foothills, many more amenities are planned. The city of Phoenix will be building a softball field, eight lighted tennis courts, six lighted volleyball courts, three lighted basketball courts, four ramadas, two soccer fields, a playground, and restroom and storage facilities. At present there are five small lakes with boating areas, hiking trails, picnic areas, and a large clubhouse. Although the Foothills does not employ a recreation director at this time, the developer at the community does employ an information director to help organize recreation events for homeowners within the community. The community also publishes a quarterly newsletter.

HOMEOWNER ASSESSMENTS, TAXES, AND UTILITIES

Currently seven builders are building within the Foothills' fourteen different neighborhoods. Homes range in size from 1,348 to 4,200 square feet and in price from $80,000 to $350,000. Currently 600 homes have been completed and sold. Homes and homesites with golf, lake, and hillside views are available, and some of the neighborhoods have their own guarded gates.

The townhome owners at the Foothills currently pay $30 per month in community association assessments. Single-family homeowners pay $15.15 per month to the community association. Neighborhood association assessments, if any, are separate. Townhomes average $400 per year in property/municipal taxes, and single-family homes average $1,000 per year.

Both cable and community television channels are available. Homes are heated by either electricity or solar sources. The local municipality provides the sewer waste disposal and water services. All utilities are underground. There are no extra storage facilities within the community at this time.

RESTRICTIONS IN THE COMMUNITY

The Foothills has a community association and membership is mandatory. Individual homeowners are responsible for their own exterior building and grounds maintenance. All building or exterior modifications must have prior approval from the Foothills design committee. There are strict guidelines covering every aspect of building within the community.

All landscaping installed must be drought-tolerant and harmonious with the Sonoran desert habitat. Whenever economically feasible, all desert washes, natural rock, outcroppings, and existing plants should be preserved. Exterior surfaces of buildings should blend with the mountain backdrop and desert landscape: Adobe, masonary, local stone, or stucco are predominant. Large expanses of wood surfaces or sidings are not suited to desert conditions and therefore are not permitted.

Passive and active solar design is encouraged at the Foothills. Solar collectors must be placed on south-facing roofs, must be flush mounted, and must resemble skylights. Any other configurations should be screened from view.

Single-family homeowners may build swimming pools and spas, which should be screened from the street and, whenever possible, from the neighboring property's view. Any swimming pool to be located on a lakefront lot must be approved by the design review committee.

Swimming or wading in the lakes is prohibited. Any water craft must be approved in advance by the association for lake use. U.S. Coast Guard approved flotation gear should be carried on each water craft. Children under six years of age must always wear a life vest when in the craft. Windsurfing is prohibited on the lakes. Propulsion is limited to electric motors only, and boat speed should never exceed 5 mph at any time.

There are no age or length-of-stay restrictions within this community. The zoning codes of the city of Phoenix restrict maximum occupation and the operation of a business from a home, which is also covered by the community's regulations. There are no rental restrictions within the community. There are no restrictions on the resale of the units. Parking on the roadways or adjacent properties is prohibited. On-street parking in single-family areas is discouraged except during special occasions. Recreational or commercial vehicles are not allowed to park on the streets, in driveways, or in the yards of any development. Currently, the community does not provide any place to park recreational vehicles.

GAINEY RANCH

7720 Gainey Ranch Road
Scottsdale, Arizona 85258
602-998-1411

$100,000 to $500,000+
467/962 Garden-style
Condos, Single-family
Homes, and Homesites
Contemporary Architecture

27-hole USGA-rated golf course
7 lakes on golf course
Hyatt Resort Hotel
2 picnic areas
Clubhouse with exercise room

City park, two ramadas
Over 100 acres of open space
7 tennis courts with lights
Steam/sauna facilities

INTRODUCTION

In the heart of the Valley of the Sun, this 560-acre retreat is a private master planned community of remarkable beauty. Surrounded by mountains (the McDowells, the Superstitions, and the famous Camelback Mountain), Gainey Ranch evokes the comfortable lifestyle of a small town. In 1956, Daniel C. Gainey named the land Via de Vaquero—the Way of the Cowboy. The Gainey family's prized Arabian horses and purebred Hereford cattle roamed the 640-acre ranch, miles away from urban Phoenix. Today, Gainey Ranch still feels like a world apart.

The community is being developed by Markland Properties, Inc. of Scottsdale. The first home was built in 1984. Gainey Ranch is located just four miles from downtown Scottsdale, Arizona, which has a population of 138,000. It is ten miles from downtown Phoenix. The nearest interstate is I-10, located ten miles from the development. The nearest airport is Phoenix Sky Harbor, also about ten miles from the site. Police coverage is provided by local, county, and state police. The staffed fire department is located nearby. Scottsdale Memorial Hospital is five miles from the development.

Gainey Ranch has its own small downtown called the Town Center. This growing area includes the world-class Hyatt Regency resort hotel and the Gainey Ranch Financial and Corporate Center, home to many local and national companies. The final section of the Town Center will eventually include exclusive shops, restaurants, and services for Gainey Ranch residents. Within one mile of the community you will find a pharmacy, a medical clinic, a dry cleaners, a hair salon, a grocery store, and a liquor store. Movie theaters are a few miles away.

There are over 14 golf courses in Scottsdale, including the USGA Tournament Players Club course that hosts the prestigious Phoenix Open. Scottsdale also has more than 120 art galleries. Other area attractions include Rawhide (an 1880s western town with shops and restaurants), Taliesin West (the western campus of the Frank Lloyd Wright School of Architecture), Cosanti (an earth-formed structure and gallery designed by Paolo Soleri), the Scottsdale Center for the Arts, and the Scottsdale Symphony.

RECREATION AND SOCIAL ACTIVITIES

The Gainey Ranch golf course is the focal point of this resort. Three million cubic yards of earth were moved to transform flat desert land into a lush tropical oasis.

The course features three different 9-hole layouts: the Dunes, the Arroyo, and the Lakes, each with its own distinctive character and challenges. *Golf Digest* rated the 27-hole golf course among the top resort golf courses in the country. *Golf Illustrated* named the ninth hole of the Lakes course one of the 18 best water holes in the country.

The community also offers tennis, swimming, croquet, bicycling, jogging, and miles of walking paths. The seven lighted tennis courts provide shaded areas with chairs between the courts and refrigerated drinking fountains on the courts.

The community employs a recreational director and publishes a monthly news-letter. There is on-site entertainment and catering services. The community is surrounded by a perimeter wall, and entry must be through 24-hour guarded gates or several remote controlled gates. The Estate Club, former home of the Daniel C. Gainey family, has been meticulously restored to its earlier splendor and is now the social center for Gainey Ranch residents. Tennis courts and a 25-meter swimming pool surround the club's showpiece: a tournament croquet lawn. Inside the Estate Club, members can relax by the fireplace, play bridge with their neighbors, and exercise in the fitness center. Every Gainey Ranch resident is automatically a member of this unique and exclusive club.

HOMEOWNER ASSESSMENTS, TAXES, AND UTILITIES

Currently over 500 homes out of a total 962 have been sold in the community. The Oasis neighborhood at Gainey Ranch is a unique mix of townhomes, casitas, and carriage homes set among mature tropical palms, waterfalls, and a swimming pool and spa. The three models range in price from $169,500 to $185,500, with current monthly community association assessments of $136.

Situated right on the course, the golf villas have tile roofs and arched win-dows. The villas range in price from $199,500 to $299,500. There are also 137 single-family homes priced from $199,000 to $340,000. Their monthly commu-nity association assessments range from $50 to $200 (depending on neighbor-hood). Gainey Ranch also allows custom building within the community. You can purchase a homesite (lots range in size from 9,000 square feet to more than one acre) and design your own home. In addition to the community association fees, each homeowner pays a monthly master association assessment of $120.

Cable and community television are available. Currently there is one channel exclusively for Gainey Ranch residents. The community association provides all exterior maintenance for the condominium communities. Single-family home-owners provide their own maintenance except for landscaping, from front yards to streets, and common areas. Electricity provides all heat, and the local mu-nicipality provides both water and sewer services. All utilities are underground. There are no extra storage facilities on site.

The Gainey Ranch golf club requires a $20,000 initiation deposit and $225 monthly dues for residents. All other recreational facilities are included with homeownership. There are nominal user fees for tennis and fitness activities.

RESTRICTIONS IN THE COMMUNITY

There is a community association and membership is mandatory. Any architec-tural changes must be approved by both the neighborhood and master association architectural committees. Any landscaping a homeowner would like to install is allowed, but all plants must be chosen from the list of approved plants and plans must be submitted for approval to the master association architectural control committee.

There are no restrictions on age or length-of-stay for visitors. Only domestic pets are allowed. Dogs must be leashed and are not allowed on the golf course. Owners must clean up after their dogs. Only a single family may occupy a unit. If a unit is to be rented, leasing rules require registration of all tenants, and no property may be leased for less than 30 days. No businesses may be operated from a home. No "for sale" signs are allowed other than authorized Gainey Ranch "open house" signs. Parking restrictions prohibit vehicles over three-fourths ton, campers, and mobile homes; residents and guests must park in garages, driveways, or designated areas. The community does not provide a special place for recreational vehicles or boats.

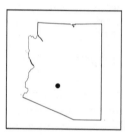

LEISURE WORLD

908 S. Power Road
Mesa, Arizona 85206
602-832-0003

$40,000 to $300,000
2,537/2,656 Garden-style
Condos and Single-family
Homes
Spanish Architecture

2 18-hole USGA-rated golf courses
Over 100 acres of open space
6 outdoor tennis courts
Clubhouse, exercise room

2 outdoor pools
2 picnic areas
4 tennis courts with lights
Steam/sauna

INTRODUCTION

Set beneath the legendary Superstition Mountains, Leisure World community association is just 30 miles east of metropolitan Phoenix and 25 miles from Sky Harbor International Airport, where shuttle service is available at any hour. Leisure World is easily accessible from the Superstition Freeway (Hwy. 360). Leisure World is established exclusively for adults: One resident of the home must be at least 55 years of age and no resident may be younger than 45. This private adult community was developed by Western Savings and Loan. The first home was built in 1973.

The Phoenix metropolitan area offers many museums, concert halls, historical monuments, and flea markets. Within the community you will find a medical clinic, a restaurant, and a movie theater. Other services, such as a pharmacy, a dry cleaners, a hair salon, a grocery and liquor store, and retail shops are all within a half mile of the complex. The Valley Lutheran Hospital is located just outside Leisure World's gates. The county sheriff patrols the area, and both a volunteer and staffed fire department are nearby. Provided by the association, free buses carry Leisure World riders to and from shops, medical centers, and church services on a regular basis. Reserve a seat and you will be picked up and returned to your own front door.

RECREATION AND SOCIAL ACTIVITIES

The two private golf courses, totaling 36 holes, are set in a dramatic setting of lakes and the Superstition Mountains. Two fully equipped pro shops handle all equipment needs. Several multi-million dollar recreation centers offer a host of possibilities for leisure time pursuits. Each recreation center is equipped with its own large heated swimming pool and jacuzzi. Adjacent to the pool area at Recreation Center 1 are separate exercise rooms and saunas for men and women. There is a full complement of programs, including dances, special events, classes, entertainment, speakers, and local bus excursions. You can enjoy lawn bowling, billiards, or pool. The community library is stocked with several thousand volumes and a variety of magazines and newspapers. The complex contains six outdoor tennis courts, two of which are illuminated for nighttime play, numerous picnic areas, and over 100 acres of open space. The 12 shuffleboard courts are also illuminated for residents to enjoy nighttime games.

The woodworking shop is equipped with almost every woodworking tool, including two lathes and an eight-foot panel saw. Classes provide instruction on individual machines, wood carving, and marquetry. The lapidary shop is equipped with a 24-inch rock saw, tumblers, ovens for gold and silver casting, diamond-grinding wheels, and a jeweler's faceting machine. Silversmithing and lapidary classes are taught by resident experts, who show how to turn turquoise and other stones into handsome jewelry.

Leisure World employs a recreation director and publishes a monthly newspaper. Through its health services department, Leisure World also provides round-the-clock nursing services administered by registered nurses. Security guards patrol the community, and a privacy wall encloses the entire community. Homes are only accessible through manned gates. All security personnel are trained in CPR and assist the nursing staff in responding to emergencies.

HOMEOWNER ASSESSMENTS, TAXES, AND UTILITIES

Currently, there are 525 garden-style condominiums and 2,018 single-family homes at Leisure World. The condominiums range in price from $40,000 to $80,000, and owners pay monthly association assessments of $205. The single-family homes range in price from $90,000 to $300,000 and, depending on services provided to the owners, cost $86, $164, or $179 per month in assessments. Homeownership automatically entitles you to all recreational and social activities except for golf. Golf has a separate membership: the annual rate for all courses is $864 per member, and the executive course costs $552 per year per member.

All of the homes have a Spanish theme. Cable television is available, but there are no community television channels. The primary heating source is electricity and the local municipality provides sewer waste and water systems. All utilities are underground. There are no extra storage facilities within the community.

RESTRICTIONS IN THE COMMUNITY

There is a community association at Leisure World and membership is mandatory. The association provides exterior building/grounds maintenance for all condominiums and grounds maintenance only for single-family homes that have lawns. Any exterior modifications to homes must be approved by both county authorities and the association architectural control committee. There are no real restrictions on what types of plants you can install around your home; however, the association does discourage plants that need heavy watering. If a single-family home has desert landscaping, responsibility for upkeep reverts to the individual owner.

Even though this is an age-restricted community, children and other guests are allowed to visit a maximum of sixty days in a twelve-month period. Pets are allowed, but they must be kept on a leash and owners must pick up any droppings. No more than three people are allowed to live in a two-bedroom home, and no more than four people in a three-bedroom home. Renters must also meet the community age requirements. Operating a business from a unit is prohibited. There is a right of first refusal for resales. Any vehicles you own must fit inside your garage; however, a special parking area is provided for recreational vehicles, boats, and the like.

SUN CITY WEST

13323 Meeker Blvd.
Sun City West, Arizona 85375
800-341-6121

$70,000 to $200,000
10,200/13,000 Garden-style Condos, Townhomes, and Single-family Homes
Spanish Architecture

7 18-hole golf courses
Boating half hour north of site
2 parks
20 lighted outdoor tennis courts
3 multi-million dollar recreation centers
1 indoor pool, 2 outdoor pools

Downhill skiing 2 hours north
1 ball-playing field
Handball/racquetball/squash
Exercise room, steam/sauna
Largest single-level theater in the world
300-seat performing arts theater

INTRODUCTION

Sun City West is being developed on 5,700 acres by the famous Del Webb Corporation and is home to over 20,000 people. At final build-out, a population of 25,000 is expected. The company is now looking into expanding the project by adding more homes, another golf course, and another recreation center. The first home was built in 1978. The Del Webb Corporation has been building active adult communities for over thirty years. Today, over 72,000 people live in communities developed by Del Webb.

Sun City West is an age-restricted community where at least one resident must be 55 years or older. Phoenix, with a population of one million, is just eight miles from the community. Interstates 17 and 10 are located 12 and 16 miles away, respectively. Air travel is provided by Sky Harbor International Airport, 40 miles from the site. The area is patrolled by the county sheriff's department, and there is a volunteer sheriff's posse that patrols within the community 24 hours a day. There is also a local staffed fire department. The Del Webb Memorial Hospital is located within the boundaries of this active adult community.

Throughout the community are more than 80 stores, restaurants, financial institutions, and other businesses. The community even offers one dollar movies every Thursday at the recreation center's performing arts theater.

RECREATION AND SOCIAL ACTIVITIES

Sun City West is a totally self-contained, private, recreational community. It is home to the nation's largest single-level theater, the 7,169-seat Sundome Center for the Performing Arts, which attracts world-class entertainment all year long. There are also a 95-piece symphony orchestra and a 300-seat theater for resident productions.

Sun City West's recreation centers feature sports, hobbies, social events, and creative activities. You will find swimming and therapy pools, three fitness gyms, 24 bowling lanes, billiards (25 tables), two 18-hole miniature golf courses surrounded by palms, and a quarter mile running track with a synthetic surface and special pacing lights. Adjoining the running track is an 18-station fitness circuit, incorporating a series of exercises that develop flexibility and conditioning.

There are 20 regulation tennis courts, eight platform tennis courts, handball, racquetball, and squash courts, croquet and badminton areas, an arcade offering a wide assortment of electronic games and pinball machines, and a 1,200-seat social hall. Available year-round, an outstanding arts and crafts village allows you to create your own ceramics, silvercraft, sewing, woodworking, painting, and weaving.

Other facilities include an outdoor softball field, a metal and wood shop, a photography lab, a greenhouse, and a children's playground for visiting grandkids. Serious readers can spend days in the community's private library, which houses over 40,000 volumes.

Seven 18-hole golf courses are located within the boundaries of Sun City West. Five courses (Pebblebrook, Stardust, Grandview, Echo Mesa, and Trail Ridge) are reserved exclusively for residents. Hillcrest is open to the general public. Briarwood is the community's first private country club, with dining facilities and recreational amenities. The Hillcrest Golf Club of Sun City West has been the five-time host of the Senior PGA tour and has hosted the Ladies Professional Golfers Association's Sun City Classic. An annual resident's golf pass costs $575 for the five courses reserved for their use.

The recreation center publishes a monthly newsletter for residents. There are no perimeter restrictions for access.

HOMEOWNER ASSESSMENTS, TAXES, AND UTILITIES

Seventy-five percent of the homes at Sun City West are single-family dwellings. The remaining homes are garden-style condominiums, duplexes, and townhomes. Standard features for all homes include tinted dual-pane windows, pre-wiring for cable TV, electric garage door openers with remote control and vacation switches, fully finished garage interiors, selection of contemporary flooring and carpeting, cultured marble bath vanity tops, laminated kitchen countertops, window screens, wood cabinets, and garbage disposal.

There are 11 models of single-family homes to choose from, ranging from 1,038 to 2,047 square feet. The single-family homes cost from $70,000 to over $200,000. Duplex buyers have four models to choose from, ranging in size from 1,165 to

1,880 square feet and in price from $81,500 to $120,500. The casita condominiums are available in three models, ranging in size from 1,102 to 1,390 square feet, with prices from $69,900 to $81,000. All of the townhomes, duplexes, and condominiums have garages, landscaping, and irrigation systems in the front yard.

Owners of the townhomes, duplexes, casitas, and terraces have automatic membership in a homeowners' association, with a monthly assessment fee of $40 to $60 for building/grounds maintenance. All residents are required to join the recreation centers of Sun City West with a per person yearly fee of $112 to cover recreational expenses. There are currently 10,200 completed homes out of an expected build-out of 13,000. Property/municipal taxes cost half of one percent of the purchase price.

Most homes are of Spanish design and architecture. Most of the homes have two bedrooms, with a small percentage opting to convert some plans to three-bedroom homes. Cable television is available; however, there are no community television channels. The homes are heated primarily by gas and electricity. The local municipality provides sewer waste disposal; water is provided by a well system. All utilities are below ground, with the exception of one roadway. There are no extra storage facilities within the community, but there are storage facilities nearby.

RESTRICTIONS IN THE COMMUNITY

At least one resident must be 55 years or older to live at Sun City West. Children are not allowed to live in the community but may visit for three months per year. There are no restrictions on length of stay for adult visitors.

There is a community association for the condominium owners; membership is mandatory. Exterior building/grounds maintenance for the condos is provided by the association. Single-family homeowners provide their own exterior building/grounds maintenance. There are restrictions on exterior modifications of homes. For planting and landscaping, there are restrictions regarding height and proximity to neighbors.

There are no restrictions on how many people may occupy a single home. Renters must meet the age requirements of the community. Operating a business from a home is prohibited. Other than age requirements, there are no resale restrictions at Sun City. There are no pet restrictions at Sun City West. Recreational vehicles may only be parked in a driveway for 72 hours at a time, but the association does provide a special parking area for recreational vehicles, boats, and other large vehicles.

SUNLAND VILLAGE EAST

2150 S. Farnsworth Drive
Mesa, Arizona 85208
1-800-777-7358

$59,900 to $114,000
900/2,500 Townhomes and
Single-family Homes
Traditional and Southwest
Architecture

18-hole USGA-rated golf course
3 lakes on the golf course
4 lighted outdoor tennis courts
Billiards room
Clubhouse, exercise room

2 outdoor pools with a spa
Over 100 acres of open space
Shuffleboard and horseshoes
10,000 square foot auditorium

INTRODUCTION

Sunland Village East is the third and newest adult community developed by the Farnsworth Development Company of Mesa, Arizona, which has built over 7,000 units for adult communities since 1959. The first home in this community was constructed in 1984. Sunland Village East is an age-restricted community (one resident must be 55 or older) located in the city limits of Mesa, Arizona, which has a population of 300,000.

Residents at this community, surrounded by the Superstition Mountains, will enjoy all the benefits of a happy and active retirement, including an incredible array of recreational and social activities. The community benefits from Mesa's dry, mild climate. The sun usually shines between 295 and 306 days of the year. The annual rainfall for the area is only about seven inches. High and low temperatures in December average about 66 degrees and 38 degrees; March averages 75 degrees and 44 degrees.

The Superstition Freeway is located just a half mile from the site. Air transportation is provided by the Sky Harbor International Airport, 20 miles from the development. Local police and a staffed fire department provide protection. The Valley Lutheran Hospital is three miles from the site, and the Superstition Springs Regional Mall is only two miles from the homes at Sunland Village East. Downtown Phoenix is 30 minutes away, providing museums, concert halls, and historical sites. Arizona State University is 15 miles from the community.

There are no services within the community; however a pharmacy, a medical clinic, a dry cleaners, a hair salon, a grocery and liquor store, restaurants, retail stores, and movie theaters are all within a five-minute drive.

RECREATION AND SOCIAL ACTIVITIES

Besides the golf, swimming, and tennis facilities, there are many other amenities at the community's multi-million dollar recreation center: shuffleboard, horseshoes, softball, arts and crafts, sewing, dancing (ballroom, square, and round), woodshop, lapidary, ceramics, siversmithing, and billiards. A library, card rooms, and aerobics classes are available for homeowner use. Within the recreation center there is a 10,000-square-foot auditorium with a full-service kitchen.

The community's social calendar is always full. There are clubs, organizations, and committees for interests such as ceramics, gardening, stained glass, hiking, and bowling.

Sunland Village East employs a recreation director and publishes a monthly newspaper. The association sponsors organized trips and provides on-site entertainment. Catering services are also available. There is a 24-hour patrol within the community. Homeownership automatically entitles you to all the facilities except golf, which has an annual membership fee of $158 per home. There is also an option for unlimited golf for $550 per year or $925 per couple. Green fees cost $15.25 per 18 holes. All fees are for calendar year 1991.

HOMEOWNER ASSESSMENTS, TAXES, AND UTILITIES

Sunland Village East offers buyers eight different models to choose from. Homes range in size from 1,075 to 2,157 square feet. Golf course lots have a premium between $14,000 and $15,000. Some of the standard features offered by the developer include enclosed double car garages, pre-wired telephone jacks, front screen doors, 12-inch thick exterior walls, R-30 insulation in ceilings, formica countertops, self-cleaning ovens, ceramic tile around tubs and showers, deadbolt locks, and smoke alarms.

There are currently 280 townhomes and 620 single-family homes at Sunland Village East. The townhomes range in price from $59,900 to $83,500, with a monthly community association assessment between $56 and $63. Yearly municipal/property taxes average $500. The single-family homes range in price from $69,500 to $114,000, with a yearly community association assessment of $158 and municipal/property taxes on the average of $700 per year. Neighborhood association assessments, if any, are separate. The architecture at Sunland Village East is mostly Spanish. The developer builds two- and three-bedroom homes. Customized changes to floor plans are allowed.

Cable television is available, but there are no community television channels. The primary heating source is electricity. The local municipality provides both sewer waste disposal and water systems. All utilities are underground. There are no extra storage facilities within the community.

RESTRICTIONS IN THE COMMUNITY

There is a community association and membership is mandatory. Single-family homeowners provide their own exterior building/grounds maintenance. The association provides all exterior building/grounds maintenance for the townhomes. The single-family homeowners have no restrictions on exterior modifications, but townhome residents must abide by association rules regarding changes. Single-family homeowners may plant whatever they wish beside their homes, but townhome owners must abide by association restrictions.

At least one resident must be 55 years or older to live at Sunland Village East. Children are not allowed to live at the site. They may visit, but there are restrictions on length of stay. No pets are allowed in the townhome section of the community. Single-family homeowners are allowed to have pets, but dogs must live within fenced yards and be on a leash when walking with the owner.

There are no set restrictions regarding maximum occupation, but the association will step in if the number of occupants becomes a nuisance. There are no rental restrictions within the community. Resale restrictions exist only for townhomes. Parking is only allowed for 48 hours on the street and 72 hours in a driveway. There is a special place within the community to park recreational vehicles, boats, and the like.

GREAT NORTHWEST

8809 Timberwilde Drive
San Antonio, Texas 78250
512-681-2983

$50,000 to $90,000
4,330/4,750 Single-family Homes
Mixed Architecture

2 outdoor pools
50 acres of open space
3 playing fields
Medium-size clubhouse
2 basketball courts

2 kiddie pools
1 picnic area
6 lighted outdoor tennis courts
1 playground
2 volleyball courts

INTRODUCTION

The Great Northwest Community Improvement Association is located in northwest San Antonio, in Bexar (pronounced "bear") County, Texas. As a result of annexation, the Great Northwest became part of the city on December 31, 1989. The city of San Antonio, with a population of 1.3 million, is by far one of Texas' most romantic destinations. The famed Riverwalk, with its boats, restaurants, and beautiful landscaping, has the same romantic atmosphere of Venice.

The area that is now the Great Northwest was purchased in 1976 by Wayne Nance for residential development; the first homes were constructed that year. There are now 4,330 homes and 17,000 residents in the Great Northwest Community Improvement Association.

Interstate 10 is just ten miles away, and air transportation is provided by San Antonio International Airport, 15 miles from the site. Police protection is provided by local authorities, and there is a staffed fire department nearby. A private security patrol within the community supplements the efforts of the local police. The nearest hospital with emergency facilities is the south Texas Medical Center, only five miles away.

This community is entirely residential; there are no services within its borders. However, all needed services are within a few blocks: a pharmacy, a medical center, a dry cleaners, a hair salon, a grocery store, liquor stores, restaurants, retail shops, and movie theaters. Other area attractions include the San Antonio Missions National Park, the Alamo, Sea World of Texas, Fiesta Texas Park, and the San Antonio Fiesta.

RECREATION AND SOCIAL ACTIVITIES

Great Northwest recreation facilities are private; use is limited to association members in good standing and their guests. Members in good standing are those who have paid all association assessments to date, are not otherwise restricted from using the facilities, and have a current association membership card.

The Lodge of the Great Northwest is the association's community center, containing meeting rooms and a kitchen that are available at a nominal charge for use by association members. The association sponsors crafts classes, provides on-site entertainment, and plans organized trips for its homeowners. The association plans on hiring a recreation director during 1991.

The Emerald Valley Recreation Complex includes an outdoor swimming pool, basketball and tennis courts, and a children's playground. The swimming pool is open from May through September each year. The Silver Creek Recreation Complex has a swimming pool, basketball and tennis courts, playing fields, and picnic areas.

There are no perimeter restrictions around the community, but there is a 24-hour patrol. The association publishes a monthly newsletter. In 1991, the association plans to begin the construction of a third recreation center. Homeownership at this community automatically entitles you to participate in all the club and recreational facilities. There is a strong committee system, and homeowners actively participate in many civic matters and community organizations.

HOMEOWNER ASSESSMENTS, TAXES, AND UTILITIES

As a result of restrictions on the deeds to all residential properties in the Great Northwest, all homeowners in the development are members of the Great Northwest Community Improvement Association, Inc., a nonprofit Texas corporation that is authorized to provide recreation, security, and other services to its members and that is required to enforce all restrictions and guidelines. Membership is mandatory, not optional. The association is governed by a seven-member board of directors who are elected from members-at-large. Directors serve three-year terms. The board employs a full-time community manager as well as other full- and part-time staff. The board has established a number of standing, select committees in areas such as safety, welcoming, public relations, municipal relations, and recreation.

Currently, 4,330 single-family homes have been built in this community. At final build-out a total of 4,750 homes is expected. The homes range in price from $50,000 to $90,000, with a yearly community association assessment of $137. Property/municipal taxes range from $900 to $1,500 per year, depending on home and lot size.

Both cable and community television channels are available. Heat is provided primarily by gas or electricity. The local municipality provides both sewer waste disposal and water services. All utilities are below ground. Although there are no extra storage facilities on site, there are some nearby.

RESTRICTIONS IN THE COMMUNITY

There are no restrictions regarding age or length-of-stay for visitors. Only domestic pets are allowed, and a leash is required when pets are outside the home. Any exterior changes require advance approval by the architectural control committee. Most types of exterior landscaping are allowed, except for landscaping that might affect views of traffic.

No more than one family may occupy a single home within the community. There are no rental restrictions, nor are there restrictions regarding the resale of homes. You should, however, notify the association office when you plan to rent or sell your home. Operating a business from a home is strictly prohibited. Recreational vehicles may not be parked in a front yard. Derelict or inoperable vehicles are never allowed to be parked in the community. There are no special lots for recreational vehicles, boats, and the like.

KINGWOOD

700 Rockmead Drive, Suite 110
Kingwood, Texas 77339
713-358-2111

$60,000 to $1,000,000
12,725/18,000 Garden-
style Condos and Single-
family Homes
Mixed Architecture

4 18-hole USGA-rated golf courses
14 outdoor pools, 14 kiddie pools
60 miles to Gulf of Mexico
45 miles of greenbelts
16 picnic areas
33 outdoor tennis courts
Handball/racquetball/squash

1 indoor pool
6 lakes
Boating
43 miles of hiking trails
20 ball-playing fields
28 tennis courts with lights
Stables and 10 miles of bridle paths

INTRODUCTION

Kingwood is a 13,000-acre private master planned land development project of the Friendswood Development Company (a subsidiary of Exxon Corporation) and King Ranch, Inc. Friendswood serves as the managing developer. The project is located 20 miles northeast of downtown Houston; Houston's Intercontinental Airport is only a 10 minute drive away.

One visit to Kingwood and you'll understand why it's called "The Livable Forest". The Akokisa Indians, the first known human inhabitants of the area, shared their habitat with an astonishing variety of wildlife, most of which can still be found in Kingwood today. There are over 25 different species of trees within the development, over 80 species of nonmigratory and migratory birds, and over 20 species of woods and wetlands amphibians and reptiles. There are at least 10 different kinds of fish in Kingwood's lakes, rivers, and streams. Mammals found in this development include armadillos, beavers, bobcats, coyotes, deer, deer mice, foxes, opossums, racoons, squirrels, swamp rabbits, white-footed mice, and wood rats.

Kingwood is a complete, self-contained community with schools, churches, parks, restaurants, a library, service stations, a YMCA, and a metro "park and ride" facility for those commuting out of the development. There is also a hospital located within the project. The first home was built in 1971.

The master plan for Kingwood includes 14 residential villages, each with its own special charm, price range, and distinguishing characteristics. In addition, each village is self-sustaining, with community associations that perform community services. Carefully planned expansion will allow the population to grow to over 60,000 by the late 1990s while still maintaining the village atmosphere. Upon completion there will be approximately 18,000 homes. Large-scale commercial areas have been set aside to accommodate office buildings, corporate office sites, and research and development facilities. The business areas are carefully planned to be compatible with the residential development areas.

Kingwood's law enforcement protection is provided by Precinct 4 constables. Kingwood's crime prevention committee offers assistance to residents in setting up their own neighborhood programs for fingerprinting, drug prevention, and bicycle safety.

Fire protection is provided in Kingwood by the Kingwood fire department. The department consists of three full-time, salaried firefighters and 55 volunteer firefighters, many of whom are fully certified. The fire department has two stations, and a third is in the final stages of planning.

Kingwood has seven elementary schools, two middle schools, and a high school. Approximately 9,000 students attend Kingwood schools. There is also a private religious school within Kingwood. There are eight daycare centers and five preschools as well as seven "Mother's Day Out" programs at Kingwood churches. The east campus of North Harris County College, a fully accredited two-year public community college, is located within Kingwood with an enrollment of approximately 2,500 students.

RECREATION AND SOCIAL ACTIVITIES

Kingwood offers four 18-hole, par 72 golf courses and two private country clubs. Both clubs are owned and managed by one of the premier country club and resort operators in the country, Club Corporation of America (CCA). There are driving ranges, putting greens, and pro shops. Both country clubs are located on the shores of Lake Houston.

The Deerwood Club is the home of the annual Doug Sanders Kingwood Celebrity Classic, a Senior PGA-sanctioned event, playing host each spring to top senior professionals including Arnold Palmer, Gary Player, Chi Chi Rodriquez, Lee Trevino, and Jack Nicklaus. Celebrity participants in the past have included Bob Hope, Clint Eastwood, Andy Williams, George Strait, Flip Wilson, Willie Nelson, and Ed McMahon.

The Kingwood Country Club offers dining and meeting facilities and many social events. The club has 25 tennis courts and five swimming pools. Group and private lessons in golf, tennis, and swimming are available. Scattered throughout the community are more swimming pools, six lakes with boating facilities, 43 miles of hiking trails, 16 picnic areas, 20 ball-playing fields, and horse stables with 10 miles of bridle paths.

The community publishes a monthly newsletter, provides organized trips and on-site entertainment, has an internal bus service, and offers daycare for children and activities for teens.

The River Grove Park borders the north bank of the San Jacinto River and provides access to Lake Houston, where you can fish, waterski, or sail. The 45 miles of greenbelt trails that wind throughout the residential villages and commercial areas are designed to provide walkers, joggers, and bicyclists with a safe, naturally forested environment; therefore, motorized vehicles are prohibited.

The Lake Houston YMCA in Kingwood provides a wide range of programs for residents, including basketball, soccer, teen dances, day camp, swim lessons, karate, and Indian Guide and Indian Princess classes. Plans are underway for a capital program to raise funds for a new, full-scale YMCA facility to be built in Kingwood.

Homeownership does not automatically entitle you to membership: The health club costs $25 per month; a country club membership is $65 per month, and golf costs $160 per month. Kingwood also offers an incredible number of social and civic groups.

HOMEOWNER ASSESSMENTS, TAXES, AND UTILITIES

Kingwood is governed by community and trail associations, non-profit organizations designed to provide many of the needed services in the community. These services include street lighting and cleaning, mowing and maintenance of common areas, mosquito fogging, and maintenance of village pools, parks, and greenbelt paths. Also, community associations contract for garbage and refuse pickup within their designated areas of responsibility.

Every property owner in Kingwood is a member of a community and trail association. Dues are assessed annually, based on the value of your property. Residents elect representatives to serve on the board of trustees.

The majority of the housing offered at Kingwood is single-family dwellings. Currently, there are over 11,000 single-family homes, 1,575 garden-style condominiums, and over 1,600 rental units in six apartment complexes. Homes range in price from $60,000 to $1 million. All homeowners pay a monthly community association assessment of $30. The property/municipal taxes are $3.10 per $100 value. There is a wide array of architectural styles and landscape designs in this community. You'll find traditional, French provincial, Tudor, and contemporary homes built by the 18 different builders active in Kingwood. Most of the homes at the site have four or more bedrooms.

Both cable and community television channels are available. Homes are heated by gas, and the local municipality provides both sewer waste and water systems. All telephone wires are below ground; electrical utilities are both above and below ground. There are extra storage facilities on site for homeowner use.

RESTRICTIONS IN THE COMMUNITY

There is a community association, and membership is mandatory. Single-family homeowners provide their own exterior building/grounds maintenance. The association provides maintenance for all the common areas and the garden-style condominiums. Deed restrictions require prior approval for any exterior modifications to homes. Landscaping is allowed but must not impede drainage.

There are no restrictions on age or length-of-stay for visitors. All outdoor pets must be leashed at all times. Deed restrictions limit occupation of a home to a single family. There are no rental or resale restrictions. Parking restrictions extend to limiting the size of garages and setbacks; recreational vehicles and boats are not permitted to be seen from the street.

THE WOODLANDS

2220 Buckthorne Place
P.O. Box 7859
The Woodlands, Texas 77387
713-367-5647

$30,000 to over $1,000,000+
9,550/25,000 Garden-style
Condos, Townhomes, and
Single-family Homes
Mixed Architecture

3 18-hole USGA-rated golf courses	1 indoor pool
7 outdoor pools	5 kiddie pools
25 lakes	60 miles to Gulf of Mexico
Boating	56 miles of hiking trails
30 picnic areas	20 ball-playing fields
Tennis	Clubhouse

INTRODUCTION

The Woodlands is a 25,000-acre private planned community consisting of residential villages, commercial developments, schools, churches, and extensive recreational amenities. Just 27 miles north of downtown Houston on I-45 and 14 miles north of the Houston Intercontinental Airport, the community has a convenient location.

Since late 1974, more than 30,000 people have come to live in the Woodlands. More than 390 businesses have located here, providing more than 7,850 jobs. About one-third of the employed residents work within the community. When the community is completed in the next century, it will be home for over 100,000 people and 3,100 businesses, offering nearly 82,000 jobs. More than 25 percent of the community's 25,000 acres will be designated as forest reserves, parks, golf courses, lakes, and open spaces.

The Woodlands is being developed by the Woodlands Corporation, a subsidiary of Mitchell Energy and Development Corporation. To date, the developers have invested almost $2 billion in the community. At completion, total investment will reach $12 billion. The master plan of the development envisions a self-sustaining community in which people can live, work, and play. Careful attention has been paid to preserving the natural environment of the east Texas forest so that people may live in harmony with nature.

The Woodlands' business complex forms a 5,000-acre crescent alongside and across Interstate 45. Early in the next century, its forested lands will support more commercial office and industrial space than that which existed in Houston's central business district in 1970.

The Woodlands Corporation and Montgomery County jointly operate a "park and ride" lot located inside the community. The Woodlands Express, the first commuter bus to serve Houston business centers from Montgomery County, operates numerous runs each weekday between Houston and the Woodlands. Daily and monthly fees are reasonably priced.

Within the community, nine public schools located in village neighborhoods offer grades kindergarten through twelve. There are also a number of preschools and daycare centers within the Woodlands.

The Woodlands community association manages fire and police protection. A special branch of the Montgomery County sheriff's department, headquartered at the public safety building in the village of Grogan's Mill, provides 24-hour police protection. The Woodlands has two fire stations with full-time staffs and modern firefighting and emergency medical equipment. The Woodlands was cited as one of America's safest communities in a recent Rice Center study.

Two village shopping centers within the Woodlands, Grogan's Mill's shopping center and Panther Creek's village square, each contain a supermarket and numerous retail shops that provide a wide range of goods and services.

RECREATION AND SOCIAL ACTIVITIES

The Woodlands Country Club, a private membership facility, includes three 18-hole golf courses, one of which was designed by Arnold Palmer. The Woodlands Country Club also has complete health spa facilities. Its tennis program and complex are directed by Peter Burwash International, one of the world's leading tennis management companies. The club has 24 indoor and outdoor courts, including clay surfaces. Membership to the Woodlands Country Club costs $10,000 for initiation plus a $200 monthly fee. The PGA Tournament Players course, a separate 18-hole facility, is the site for the annual Independent Insurance Agents' Open every spring.

The Woodlands' athletic center features olympic-class swimming and diving facilities and has been the site for many national and international competitions, including the 1986 U. S. Olympic Festival. Fitness classes of all types are held for residents of all ages.

A regional YMCA is located in the village of Cochran's Crossing. It offers fitness programs, operates a child development center, and contains an outstanding weight room, a gymnasium, and swimming facilities.

The 31 neighborhood parks throughout the community feature swimming pools, playgrounds, playing fields, picnic pavilions, tennis courts, and lakes and ponds for fishing. The parks are connected to residential neighborhoods by a 53-mile network of wooded hiking and bicycle trails. Lake Woodlands, a 200-acre stocked lake in the village of Panther Creek, provides sailing and fishing for the community. Its eight-mile shoreline offers outstanding sites for homes and businesses.

Homeowners at the Woodlands have access to all association-owned parks, trails, and swimming pools. Annual user fees for the pools are imposed.

HOMEOWNER ASSESSMENTS, TAXES AND UTILITIES

The Woodlands offers a full range of housing opportunities, from affordable homes in the $70,000 price range to luxurious estates with lakefront or golf course views. Estate lots, where some of the community's most prestigious neighborhoods are located, are priced from $60,000 to $250,000. There are more than 2,350 apartments, ranging from government-assisted apartment homes to luxury apartments with golf course views. Special lifestyle buildings are also available for senior citizens, and more are in development. In three separate neighborhoods, there are 660 assisted-living apartments (with income-based rent) for residents who are age 62 or older, or who are handicapped. Heritage Manor, a luxurious 181-bed retirement living and nursing center, opened in 1986. Chambrel is a retirement living neighborhood with 303 rental apartments and cottages.

There are approximately 600 garden-style condominiums and townhomes at the Woodlands. The garden-style condominiums range in price from $30,000 to $150,000. The townhomes cost between $100,000 and $150,000. Currently there are over 9,000 single-family homes built within the community, with prices from $80,000 to over $1 million.

Sewer and water charges are separate. The community association is operated like a municipality; instead of a monthly assessment, the association collects an ad valorem tax of $.60 per $100 of assessed value. Homeowners also pay other property/municipal taxes to support the hospital, county, schools, utilities, and roads.

Both cable and community channels are available to homeowners. Homes are heated by both gas and electricity. The local municipality provides both sewer waste disposal and water systems. All utilities are underground. There are extra storage facilities within the community.

RESTRICTIONS IN THE COMMUNITY

There is an active community association at the Woodlands, and membership is mandatory. Individual homeowners are responsible for their own exterior building and grounds maintenance. The community association handles maintenance for all common property. Any exterior modifications must be approved by the residential design review committee, and the community has reasonable development standards. Guidelines are also issued regarding landscaping for your home.

There are no age or length-of-stay restrictions for visitors except in the neighborhoods set aside for senior citizens. Only two pets per home are allowed at the Woodlands. In some of the apartment projects, no pets are allowed.

Only single families may occupy a home. Some of the apartment and condo buildings have other maximum occupation restrictions. Generally, there are no rental restrictions, but no investor is allowed to make excessive purchases for rental purposes. If you want to operate a business out of your home, you must present an application to the association. There are no restrictions on the resale of homes at the Woodlands. Vehicles should not be kept on the street, and every home must have a functional garage. There are other parking restrictions in the apartment, townhome, and condo projects. The community provides a lot for oversized vehicles.

Chapter 11

Pacific Coast

California
Hawaii
Oregon
Washington

ALISO VIEJO

Mission Viejo Company
26137 La Paz
Mission Viejo, California 92691
714-837-6050

$100,000 to $300,000
5,100/20,000 Condominiums
and Single-family Homes
Mixed Architecture

3 18-hole USGA-rated golf
  courses within 3 miles
3 to 5 miles to the ocean
27 hiking trails
Dozens of picnic areas
10 outdoor tennis courts

Outdoor swimming pools
40-acre lake within one mile
2,600-acre regional park within
  the community
5 ball-playing fields
Clubhouses

INTRODUCTION

Aliso Viejo lies among rolling hills where cattle and sheep once grazed. More than a decade ago the Mission Viejo Company began building a unique, carefully balanced environment where people could live, work, and play. Aliso Viejo is a 6,600-acre private community situated in the heart of south Orange County, California.

Aliso Viejo rests upon land which was once part of the 26,000-acre Moulton Ranch. The Moulton family took title in the 1890s to land that was originally granted to Juan Avila by the Mexican government in 1842. Over the years, portions of the ranch were sold, becoming Leisure World of Laguna Hills and Laguna Niguel. In 1976, the Mission Viejo Company purchased the remaining 6,600 acres; the first home was sold in 1982.

The community is located about 50 miles south of Los Angeles and 70 miles north of San Diego, just west of Interstate 5. It is 22 miles south of Disneyland and adjacent to the city of Laguna Beach. The master plan of the community calls for 36 percent of the land to be devoted to residential neighborhoods, 51 percent to parks, schools, and community facilities, and 13 percent to business, office, and retail buildings.

Aliso Viejo has been designed to provide a balance between the number of on-site jobs and the resident work force, allowing residents to live and work in the same community. Pacific Park, a 900-acre business, corporate, and research park centered in Aliso Viejo, is Orange County's second largest business park. A projected 22,000 job opportunities provided by Pacific Park will afford many Aliso Viejo residents a chance to bicycle or walk to work.

Within the property are the 2,600-acre Aliso and Wood Canyons regional park and the Orange County Natural History Museum. You will also find within the boundaries of Aliso Viejo a pharmacy, a medical clinic, a dry cleaners, a hair salon, a grocery store, a liquor store, a restaurant, and retail stores. A movie theater is just a half mile away. A hospital with emergency facilities is within one mile of the development. The community is under the jurisdiction of the county sheriff and has a staffed fire department.

RECREATION AND SOCIAL ACTIVITIES

California's Mediterranean climate provides ample opportunities for outside activities. The Casta del Sol public golf course, with a restaurant and lounge, is just four miles east in nearby Mission Viejo. There are three USGA-rated 18-hole golf courses within three miles of the community. Aliso Viejo is within a convenient drive or easy bicycle ride of the Laguna Niguel regional park, which offers a 40-acre stocked lake for fishing and boating. The famous beaches of Laguna Beach and Dana Point Harbor are only a short drive away.

Sheep Hills Park, Glenbrook Park, Pinewood Park, and Hummingbird Park, the first of many local parks to be developed in Aliso Viejo, offer softball and soccer fields, tot lots, picnic areas, and open play areas. Individual neighborhood associations have their own swimming pools, clubhouses, and other recreational facilities. The Aliso Viejo events committee, a group of community volunteers, coordinates a number of annual events, including Santa's arrival, the Fourth of July community picnic and concert, and an Easter egg hunt and pancake breakfast.

The master association publishes a quarterly newsletter, and most of the neighborhood associations publish a monthly newsletter. County programs provide security, bus service, and visiting nurse services. Daycare is provided by various private programs.

HOMEOWNER ASSESSMENTS, TAXES, AND UTILITIES

Aliso Viejo offers a variety of housing options and architectural styles, including townhomes, condominiums, apartments, garden homes, and single-family homes. All homes are located within 1 1/2 miles of the businesses at Pacific Park.

There are currently 5,100 homes out of an expected 20,000. The developer expects the project to be complete around the year 2005. Seventy percent of these homes will be condo/townhomes, and the remaining 30 percent will be single-family dwellings. There are 29 neighborhood associations within the community, and homeowner assessments vary according to services provided by the association. Property taxes are about 2 percent of assessed value.

Both cable and community television channels are available. Gas provides the primary heat for the community, and water and waste services are provided by the local water district. All utilities are underground. At this time, there are no extra storage facilities on site.

RESTRICTIONS IN THE COMMUNITY

This community has a master association that handles all facilities and property common to the entire development and 29 neighborhood associations that handle all relevant matters within each neighborhood. Most condo and townhome associations maintain full building and grounds maintenance. Most single-family homeowners provide their own yard and building maintenance. Any modifications to a home must be approved by the architectural review committee. Any planting must be on your own property. Remember that rules may vary from neighborhood to neighborhood.

There are no pet restrictions, nor are there restrictions regarding age or length of stay for visitors. County ordinances on maximum occupation of homes apply in this community. There are no rental restrictions. Daycare and home offices are permitted; however, no traffic-generating businesses may be operated from a home. Most of the associations prohibit parking an RV and repairing a car on the streets. Within three miles of the community you will find special parking areas for recreational vehicles and boats.

CANYON LAKE

22200 Canyon Club Drive
P.O. Box 5A
Canyon Lake, California 92380
714-244-6841

$75,000 to $1,000,000
4,802/4,802
Garden-style Condos,
Townhomes, Single-
Family and Mobile Homes
Mixed Architecture

18-hole USGA-rated golf course	1 outdoor pool
Lake with 15 miles of shore	Boating facilities
75 rental boat slips	50 acres of open space
Clubhouse	9 picnic areas
2 ball-playing fields (1 lighted)	4 outdoor tennis courts
2 lighted outdoor tennis courts	Horse stables

INTRODUCTION

If you're looking for a little privacy in the midst of southern California's cosmopolitan madness, the Canyon Lake property owners' association might be the place for you. This private community is built around a 400-acre waterski lake and offers an abundance of outdoor activities. In addition to the 4,000 homes in this private community, there is a 105-site recreational vehicle campground.

Canyon Lake is located just 25 miles from Riverside, California, southeast of Los Angeles. Riverside has a population of just over 200,000. Canyon Lake was developed by the Corona Land Company of Corona, California. The first home was built in 1968. All lots have been sold; 80 percent have homes built on them. Interstate 15 is only $3\frac{1}{2}$ miles from the site. Air transportation is provided by the Ontario International Airport, located 38 miles from Canyon Lake. Police protection is by the county sheriff and the California state police. Both a volunteer and a staffed fire department are nearby. The nearest hospital with emergency facilities is the Menifee Valley Medical Center, located eight miles from Canyon Lake.

Located within the confines of Canyon Lake are a dry cleaners, a hair salon, a grocery and liquor store, restaurants, and retail shops. A pharmacy is four miles away; a medical clinic is seven miles away. The closest movie theater is 19 miles from the community. Other area attractions include Old Town, Temecula, local wineries, and hot air balloons.

RECREATION AND SOCIAL ACTIVITIES

At Canyon Lake, you can golf, swim, ride, picnic, or sunbathe. The 18-hole USGA-rated golf course offers many hours of pleasure for the golf enthusiast. The community also has an outdoor swimming pool.

The 400-acre lake has 15 miles of shoreline, and waterskiing is one of the main attractions. Seventy-five association-owned boat slips are available for member use and can accommodate boats up to 21 feet in length. Owners with lakefront property may build private slips and docks. The 50 acres of open space within the community contain nine picnic areas and two ball-playing fields, one of which is lighted. There are also four outdoor tennis courts, two of which are lighted. Horse stables and a community clubhouse are other features of Canyon Lake.

Canyon Lake does not have a recreation director, but a wide variety of community and social organizations plan activities. The association publishes a weekly newsletter and provides on-site entertainment. There is a 24-hour security patrol within the community, and perimeter restrictions include both manned and electronic gates. The travel club organizes many trips for homeowners. Additional meeting facilities and an additional sports field will be built in 1991. In 1992 the association plans to build another outdoor swimming pool with kiddie pool facilities.

Homeownership automatically entitles you to membership in all the club and recreation facilities. However, the golf course has greens and cart fees, and there are boat registration fees for any boat you might own.

HOMEOWNER ASSESSMENTS, TAXES, AND UTILITIES

At Canyon Lake, there are 164 garden-style condominiums and 14 townhomes. The condominiums and townhomes all range in price from $150,000 to $200,000. The 4,000 single-family homes cost between $150,000 and $1 million. There are also 123 mobile homes located at Canyon Lake, with prices from $75,000 to $100,000. The single-family and mobile home owners each pay $105 per month in community association assessments. The garden-style condominium and town-home homeowners pay $105 a month in community association assessments, and also pay additional neighborhood association fees. The current yearly property/municipal taxes are one percent of the assessed value. Each single-family home was custom-built by the owner; the community has a mix of architectural styles.

Cable and community television channels are available. Electricity provides the primary heat source for the community. The local municipality provides both the sewer waste disposal and water systems. All telephone wires are below ground.

Most of the electrical wires are below ground; however, a few are above ground. There are no extra storage facilities within the community.

RESTRICTIONS IN THE COMMUNITY

Canyon Lake has a community association, and membership is mandatory. Individual homeowners are responsible for their exterior building and grounds maintenance. The community association provides maintenance for all the common areas and amenities. All improvements to homes are subject to the architectural review committee's review and approval. The association does impose minimum landscaping requirements.

There are no restrictions on age or length-of-stay for visitors. Within this community, the municipal leash laws apply. No dogs are allowed on beaches, in parks, or in the lake. There are no restrictions regarding how many people can occupy a single unit, nor are there any resale restrictions. If you choose to rent your home, you are still responsible for the tenant's interaction with the association. To operate a business out of your unit, you must conform with municipal zoning requirements. Parking restrictions designate a limited time for cars to be parked on streets. Commercial vehicles are not allowed at all. The association does not provide special areas to park oversized vehicles.

LAKE FOREST

22921 Ridge Route Drive
Lake Forest, California 92630
714-837-6100

$150,000 to $450,000
1,702/1,702 Garden Homes,
Condos and Single-family
Homes
California Ranch, Spanish, and
Contemporary Architecture

3 outdoor pools, 1 kiddie pool
10 miles to Pacific Ocean
200 acres of open space
6 lighted outdoor tennis courts

2 lakes with 5 miles of shoreline
Boating
Hiking trails
Clubhouse, exercise room

INTRODUCTION

The Lake Forest community association is a unique private development with homes located in a large eucalyptus forest and around two manmade lakes. The community was developed by Occidental Land Development of Newport Beach, California. Building began at the site in 1968. All of the homes have been sold: There are a total of 1,702 garden homes, condominiums and single-family homes.

Lake Forest, California is located in Southern California, midway between Los Angeles and San Diego. The John Wayne Airport is ten miles from Lake Forest. Interstate 5 and Interstate 405 are just two miles from the development. The county sheriff's department and the California highway patrol provide police protection; both staffed and volunteer fire departments are nearby. Saddleback

Memorial Hospital, the nearest facility with emergency services, is three miles from the site.

Lake Forest is virtually self-contained; located within the community are a pharmacy, a medical clinic, a dry cleaners, a hair salon, a grocery and liquor store, restaurants, and retail shops. A movie theater is one mile from the development. Southern California offers many activities for its residents, such as Disneyland, Knott's Berry Farm, Irvine Meadows, the Pacific Amphitheater, Orange County Performing Arts Center, Dana Point and Newport Beach Harbors, Mission San Juan Capistrano, the Orange County fairgrounds, Wild Rivers Water Park, the Laguna art museum, and the Laguna Beach Festival of the Arts.

RECREATION AND SOCIAL ACTIVITIES

The Lake Forest Beach and Tennis Club contains two swimming pools, a swimming lagoon, a wading pool, an indoor spa, six lighted tennis courts, outdoor volleyball and basketball courts, an exercise room, a billiards room, and an adult lounge with a bar and large-screen TV. This adult lounge, along with an official association bar, also offers liquor lockers for homeowners to store their liquor for use when the association bar is closed. There is an initial fee of $15 and an annual fee of $15 for use of the liquor locker. In addition, several rooms are available in the clubhouse for club functions and private parties.

Some of the clubs at the community include the men's club, the handmaidens' craft and hobby club, Boy Scouts, Girl Scouts, ceramics, swim team, tennis association, garden club, yacht club, and a ladies' tennis club. The community also provides youth activities and preschool programs.

The two lakes within the community have about five miles of shoreline. No swimming is allowed in the lakes. All homeowners may use the large lake for boating, but only residents of the lakefront properties may dock boats on the lake overnight. All other boats must be removed from the lake daily. The small lake is a private lake, solely for the use of homeowners in certain neighborhoods. The maximum boat size for both lakes is limited to 14 feet in length and eight feet in width. Boats may only be powered by electric motors which do not exceed one horsepower. All boats must be registered with the association; the annual cost is $5 per boat.

Lake Forest employs a recreation director and publishes a monthly newsletter. The association plans organized trips and provides on-site entertainment. There are no perimeter restrictions for access to the community. Homeownership automatically entitles you to all the association's recreational and clubhouse facilities and activities, but there may be nominal participation fees for some activities.

HOMEOWNER ASSESSMENTS, TAXES, AND UTILITIES

Lake Forest is a private planned community governed by a master declaration of covenants, conditions, and restrictions. Responsibility for executing the provisions of the master plan and for managing the finances and business of the community is placed upon the Lake Forest community association, and, in particular, upon the board of directors of the association.

Lake Forest is a master association and has two sub-associations that govern the condominium projects. There are 126 condominiums in the development which range from $150,000 to $300,000, with monthly community association assessments of $50. Their sub-association assessments, if any, are separate. The 1,576 single-family homes cost from $75,000 to $450,000 with community association assessments between $50 and $130 per month.

Cable television is available, but there are no community television channels in service. Both gas and electricity provide heating sources; the local municipality provides both sewer waste disposal and water services to the community. All utilities are underground. There are no extra storage facilities within the community.

RESTRICTIONS IN THE COMMUNITY

Lake Forest has an active community association, and membership is mandatory. Single-family homeowners provide their own exterior building/grounds maintenance. In the case of the two condominium neighborhoods, the sub-association provides exterior maintenance. Common grounds and facilities are maintained by the community association. Architectural committee approval is required for all exterior modifications including, but not limited to, painting, room additions, patio covers, and awnings. Landscaping installations or changes must also be in accordance with the standards of each particular neighborhood.

There are no restrictions on age or length-of-stay for visitors at Lake Forest. Only household pets are allowed within the community. Orange County health standards govern how many people may occupy a single home. There are no rental restrictions within Lake Forest, nor are there any restrictions on the resale of homes. Operating a business from a home is prohibited. Community regulations govern all parking within the development. There are no extra parking lots within the community, but there are private storage facilities within ten miles of the association.

LAKE SHASTINA

Lake Shastina Civic Services
15440 Juniper Peak Rd.
Weed, California 96094
916-938-3281

$45,000 to $5,000,000
563/4,071 Townhomes and
Single-family Homes
Chalet, A-frame, and Split-level Architecture

USGA-rated 18-hole golf course
2 outdoor pools
Cross-country skiing
  within a half hour drive
Boating
Hiking trails, picnic areas

9-hole golf course
Lake with 15 miles of shoreline
Downhill skiing with chair lifts
  within a half hour drive
Over 100 acres of open space
2 outdoor tennis courts

INTRODUCTION

Lake Shastina is located on the north slope of majestic Mount Shasta, one of California's most spectacular mountains. A private residential resort community, it is built around the "Magnificent Monster"—the community's 27-hole championship golf course.

The city of Weed, home to this private community, was established in the late 1800s as a bustling lumber town and it still retains much of its small town charm today. Weed is surrounded by national forests and high desert plains. Backpacking, camping, and fishing the local rivers in this part of California is quite an experience. Most exhilarating of all is waterskiing on Lake Shasta, right below 14,162-foot Mt. Shasta.

Lake Shastina golf resort is located 75 miles north of Redding, California and 75 miles south of Medford, Oregon, each of which have a population of about 100,000. Interstate 5 is just seven miles from the development. The site is governed by local and county police, and a volunteer fire department is nearby. Mt. Shasta Hospital, an emergency care facility, is located 15 miles from the community.

The famous Oregon Shakespearean Theater is just an hour away. The College of the Siskiyous in Weed has many excellent programs for students to choose from. This beautiful community college offers art exhibits, theatre presentations, and plenty of activities for sports enthusiasts.

Within the community you will find a hair salon and a restaurant. In Weed, you will find a pharmacy, a medical clinic, a dry cleaners, a grocery and liquor store, retail stores, and a movie theater.

RECREATION AND SOCIAL ACTIVITIES

The "Magnificent Monster" at Lake Shastina was designed by the renowned golf architect, Robert Trent Jones. Almost every hole is within view of majestic Mount Shasta. The course features four sets of strategically placed tees leading to broad fairways sculptured from native shrubland and pine forests, large undulating greens, well-placed sand traps, and ingenious water hazards.

The community contains two outdoor swimming pools with a spa and a lake with 15 miles of shoreline. Skiing, boating, diving, and snorkeling provide unexcelled summer fun. Other activities in the area include whitewater rafting trips on the Klamath, McCloud, or Salmon Rivers, hunting, rock hounding, arrowhead hunting, and gold panning. There are also numerous downhill and cross-country ski trails with chairlifts to take you to the top of the mountain.

The association publishes a monthly newsletter, sponsors an RV club which organizes trips, and provides on-site entertainment. The golf course restaurant provides catering, and some private maid services are offered. There is a 24-hour patrol within the community. The community center has a kitchen and bar facilities and can only be rented to property owners.

Homeownership does not automatically include membership in the club or recreational facilities. For a $500 initiation fee and a monthly fee of $65 per family or $50 per single, you can enjoy golf, pool, and tennis facilities. An associate membership for golf costs $30 per year, which includes savings of over 50 percent on green fees and less than one half price golf after 2:00 P.M.

HOMEOWNER ASSESSMENTS, TAXES, AND UTILITIES

Currently, over 500 units are complete at this site. Total build-out will be 4,071 homes. There are 35 duplex units, 28 townhomes, and 501 single-family homes at Lake Shastina. The duplex homes range in price from $45,000 to $80,000. Townhomes cost between $65,000 and $150,000. Single-family homes range in price from $100,000 to $5 million. Owners of duplexes and townhomes pay $208 per year in community association assessments. For single-family homes, community association assessments range from $144 to $173 per year. Water and sewer service charges are separate. Municipal taxes average $600 to over $1,500 per year.

Cable television is not available, but there are community television channels. Heating options at Lake Shastina include electricity, oil, propane, and wood. Water is provided by wells. Waste disposal is handled by both septic systems and city sewer systems. All utilities are underground. There are no extra storage facilities on site.

RESTRICTIONS IN THE COMMUNITY

Lake Shastina has a community association and membership is mandatory. Homes built on private lots must meet 20-foot front and back setback requirements and have 5-foot easements on each side. Additions must be compatible with the surrounding area. Any fencing must be approved by the environmental control committee.

There are no restrictions on age or length-of-stay for visitors. Pets must be under the owner's control at all times. Only one family (consisting of immediate family members) may occupy a unit. There are no rental restrictions. No signs may be erected to advertise a business operating from your unit. Restrictions on resales do not exist. Vehicles must not be parked in the right-of-ways. There are no special parking facilities for RVs or boats.

LEISURE VILLAGE

200 Leisure Village Drive
Camarillo, California 93012
805-484-2861

$130,000 to $350,000
2,136/2,136 Single-
family, Duplex,
Triplex, and Four-plex
Contemporary Architecture

18-hole golf course	1 outdoor pool
10 miles to Pacific Ocean	Bocci courts
1 picnic area	2 outdoor tennis courts
Handball/racquetball	Large clubhouse
Shuffleboard, horseshoes	Hobby shops

INTRODUCTION

In Camarillo, California, Leisure Village is a vibrant, active retirement community of 3,500 residents. This age-restricted (55 years and older) community is 50 miles northwest of Los Angeles. The first home was built in 1973 by Leisure Technology, one of America's largest builders of adult communities.

The Ventura Freeway and Route 101 are two miles from the development. Police protection is provided by local, county, and state police authorities. The community also provides 24-hour manned security that can respond to emergency calls and provide oxygen and CPR when needed. There is a staffed fire department nearby. Pleasant Valley Hospital, the nearest facility with emergency care, is three miles away.

Leisure Village is close to Santa Barbara and Ventura and only ten miles from the Pacific Ocean. There are no services offered within the community, but within half a mile you can find a pharmacy, a medical clinic, a dry cleaners, a hair salon, a grocery and liquor store, banks, restaurants, and retail stores. A movie theater is just three miles from the site.

RECREATION AND SOCIAL ACTIVITIES

The social and recreational life at Leisure Village is very active, with many committees and social clubs. There are over 80 different clubs in the community.

Some of the organizations at this time include architectural and landscape, buildings and grounds, education and recreation, emergency services, finance, insurance, nominating, security and safety, and "meet your neighbor" committees. Social clubs include book review, billiards, gem and mineral, ceramics, woodshop, keyboard, dance, camera, amateur radio, racquet, golf, and women's clubs.

Recreational amenities include an 18-hole golf course, a swimming pool, tennis courts, picnic areas, bocci courts, shuffleboard courts, horseshoe pits, and a large clubhouse. The association's internal TV cable channel provides its residents with information and special programming related to the community. Two monthly communications provide additional information. The official association bulletin provides the needed details regarding current events and the second newsletter is prepared by homeowners and includes commentary on current issues within the Village.

Even though the development does not employ a recreation director, the association does plan organized trips for homeowners, provide on-site entertainment, and sponsor on-site crafts and activities.

HOMEOWNER ASSESSMENTS, TAXES, AND UTILITIES

The Village sits on 500 acres and has extensive greenbelts throughout the development. All of the 2,136 homes at Leisure Village have two bedrooms; units are either single-family, duplex, triplex, or four-plex. All of the homes are single-story units and vary in size from 900 to 2,000 square feet. The homes range in price from $130,000 to $350,000 and, based upon the size of the home, have monthly association assessments between $140 and $210.

The community's 1991 budget includes $80,000 for new state-of-the-art irrigation controls to help reduce water consumption throughout the community, an important measure considering California's drought problem. The community has also earmarked funds to begin a pilot program to eliminate high-maintenance shrubs and plants, reducing pruning and water consumption. The 1991 budget also provides for three additional employees to be added to the landscaping department, raising its personnel from 42 to 45 people.

Both cable and community television channels are available to all residents. Electricity provides the primary heat source, and the local municipality provides both sewer waste disposal and water systems. All utilities are underground. There are no extra storage facilities within the community. Monthly association assessments include all exterior maintenance, security, free use of all facilities, cable TV, RV parking, water, trash and sewer services, and insurance. The community has just approved a plan to begin curbside recycling similar to the program recently instituted by the city of Camarillo.

RESTRICTIONS IN THE COMMUNITY

There is a community association at Leisure Village and membership is mandatory. The community association provides all exterior building/grounds maintenance for the complex, including homes and recreational facilities. Any exterior modifications must be approved by the architectural committee. Alterations to the landscaping around a home are allowed, but the owner must then maintain any special plantings.

As noted before, you must be 55 years or older to live in the complex. No children are allowed to live at the site. There are no restrictions on age of visitors, but there are restrictions on how long visitors can stay. Only two pets are allowed at each residence. There is a maximum occupation of four people per home. If you choose to rent your home, there is a minimum rental period of 90 days, and renters must meet age requirements. Businesses are not allowed to operate from any unit. Other than the age requirement, there are no restrictions regarding the resale of units. There are no parking restrictions, and the association does provide a free place to park recreational vehicles, boats, and the like.

**LEISURE VILLAGE
OCEAN HILLS**

4600 Leisure Village Way
Oceanside, California 92056
619-758-7080

$250,000 to $350,000
1,375/1,640 Single-family
Homes
Spanish Architecture

18-hole golf course
5 miles to Pacific Ocean
4 outdoor tennis courts
Clubhouse
Bocci courts, croquet
Billiards parlor

1 olympic-size outdoor pool
50 acres of open space
2 tennis courts with lights
Gymnasium
Aquatic sports
Photo printing lab

INTRODUCTION

Emulating Aegean hill towns, Leisure Village Ocean Hills features curving streets with romantic Greek names and bougainvillea blossoms that spill over white stucco walls of tiny villas. In some parts of this lovely community, you can even see the Pacific Ocean five miles away. This age-restricted community is made up of six different neighborhoods, all offering their own unique charm and housing options. In all, the community has won more than ten major and regional building industry awards.

The community's developer, Leisure Technology, is currently building active adult, single-family, or full-service retirement communities in New Jersey, New York, Florida, Illinois, and California. Founded in 1957, the company is one of the country's largest builders of adult communities. The first unit at Leisure Village Ocean Hills was built in 1984.

In 1989, Leisure Village Ocean Hills was the top seller of residential homes in San Diego County, selling more than 200 homes. The project, a $235 million community located on 353 acres, has sold over 1,300 homes since its opening in 1984.

The community is located just 30 miles from San Diego in the city of Ocean-side. Highway 78 is the closest major road, three miles from the development. Police coverage is provided by local, county, and state authorities. There is a 24-hour security force, and the community has both manned and electronic gates. A professionally staffed fire department is nearby.

There are no services within the community; however, within five miles you will find a pharmacy, a medical clinic, a dry cleaners, a hair salon, a grocery and liquor store, a restaurant, retail stores, and a movie theater. All of southern California's major attractions are within a short drive.

RECREATION AND SOCIAL ACTIVITIES

Community amenities, which are clustered around and within the private Ocean Hills country club, include an 18-hole golf course, a pool and spa, lighted tennis courts, paddle tennis courts, bocci courts, shuffleboard courts, and a Nautilus exercise room. The heart of the community is the Maurice Abravanel Hall for the Performing Arts, a 750-seat professionally equipped auditorium that is the venue for regular performances by entertainers and classical musicians.

The Ocean Hills Country Club also has studios for chamber music, lapidary, woodworking, ceramics, painting, color photography, and broadcasting. Other amenities include a library, a billiards room, and the Wall Street Club, which has a computer terminal to monitor investments.

Social clubs include a computer group, a dinner and dance club, an arts and crafts group, the anglers' association, an audio visual club, an art appreciation group, a ballroom dance club, a backgammon club, the "bon appetit" club, a bocci club, a bridge club, a garden club, a country-western dance group, the chorale society, a swim club, a weight loss group, the lady golfers' club, the library association, a rotating dinner club, a travel club, a theater group, and an organ club.

The association employs a recreation director, publishes a monthly newsletter, and provides an internal bus service. Homeownership at Leisure Village automatically entitles you to all club and recreation activities within the community without extra membership dues.

HOMEOWNER ASSESSMENTS, TAXES, AND UTILITIES

Homes at Leisure Village range in size from 1,594 to 2,630 square feet; all homes have two or three bedrooms and $2\frac{1}{2}$ or $3\frac{1}{2}$ baths. Berkus Group Architects designed the homes, including such features as courtyards, leisure rooms, curvilinear walls, skylights, French doors, and illuminated display niches.

Currently, there are 1,375 completed homes at Leisure Village Ocean Hills. The total build-out is expected to be 1,640 homes. Homes range in price from $250,000 to $350,000, with community association assessments from $185 to $250 per month. Municipal/property taxes average about one percent. Upon completion, there will be 440 two-bedroom homes and 1,200 three-bedroom homes. The community association assessments cover operation of the Ocean Hills country club, all facilities, amenities, and staff; 24-hour guarded entry and dusk-to-dawn patrols; exterior painting and roof maintenance of homes; landscape maintenance, including irrigation of common areas and slopes; fire insurance on individual villa homes and community facilities; insurance for common areas throughout the community; street maintenance and sweeping; community bus service; and maintenance of utilities, electricity, water, and sewer services in common areas. Maintenance of home exteriors and front yard landscaping is managed by the individual neighborhood associations.

Cable and community television channels are available. Gas provides the primary heat source. The local municipality provides both water and sewer services to the community. All utilities are underground. There are no extra storage facilities on site.

RESTRICTIONS IN THE COMMUNITY

There is a community association and membership is mandatory. The community association handles all building/grounds maintenance for the development. Any exterior modifications must be approved by the architectural control committee. There are also restrictions regarding individual plantings next to your home.

Leisure Village Ocean Hills is an age-restricted community. At least one of the buyers must be 55 years of age. No children are allowed to live at the development, and, although they may visit, there are restrictions on length of stay. Currently, there are no pet restrictions at the site. Only one family may occupy a single home. There are no rental restrictions, nor are there restrictions (except for the age restriction) regarding resales. Local zoning laws are in effect regarding operation of a business from your home. There is a special place within the development to park recreational vehicles and boats.

**LEISURE WORLD OF
LAGUNA HILLS**

P.O. Box 2220
23522 Paseo de Valencia
Laguna Hills, California 92653
714-951-2262

$45,000 to $650,000
12,736/12,736 Condos,
Cooperatives,
Townhomes, and Single-
family Homes
Contemporary and Spanish
Architecture

9- and 18-Hole USGA-rated golf
5 miles to Pacific Ocean
8 outdoor tennis courts
Horse stables and bridle path
Gymnasium, exercise room

5 outdoor pools
Walking trails
2 lighted tennis courts
6 clubhouses
192 clubs and organizations

INTRODUCTION

Leisure World of Laguna Hills opened on September 10, 1964, and within six months nearly 900 families had moved into the soon-to-be largest community in the country for active senior citizens. More than 21,000 people now reside on 2,100 acres at Leisure World. The minimum age for at least one resident of the household at this community is 55 years. Retirement is not a necessary pre-requisite for residency at Leisure World. The community was developed by the Rossmoor Corporation.

Leisure World of Laguna Hills is approximately halfway between Los Angeles and San Diego, five miles from the Pacific Ocean. Interstates 5 and 405 are located one mile from the community. Air transportation is provided by the Orange County airport, just 15 miles away. Police protection is provided by the county sheriff's department, and the Orange County Fire Station #22 provides fire-fighting and rescue services. Saddleback Memorial Medical Center, the nearest facility with emergency care, is just a half mile from the development.

Orange County's new $89 million Performing Arts Center, Laguna Beach's Pageant of the Masters, three excellent dinner theaters, three colleges, and a university are all within a fifteen-mile radius of the community. Through its emeritus program, Saddleback Community College conducts 60 classes each semester in and around the Leisure World community, offering courses in accounting and investments, foreign languages, arts and crafts, physical fitness, and so forth. Over 3,600 residents participate in these classes annually. Leisure World has a community newspaper, library, cable TV, and TV studio. The Anaheim Convention Center, Anaheim Stadium (home of the California Angels and Los Angeles Rams), and Disneyland are less than 25 miles north of the community.

There are no business services within the community, but all necessary services are within one mile, such as a pharmacy, a medical clinic, a dry cleaners, a hair salon, a grocery and liquor store, restaurants, retail stores, and movie theaters.

RECREATION AND SOCIAL ACTIVITIES

Leisure World has 192 clubs and organizations that meet in recreation facilities valued at more than $25 million. Every conceivable club is represented at Leisure World, from bridge to chess to table tennis to travel.

There are six clubhouses (one of which has an 834-seat theater), five pools and spas, 18 shuffleboard courts (12 enclosed courts), two lawn bowling greens, eight tennis courts (two lighted), 10 crafts workshops, stables with 40 stalls and three and a half miles of equestrian trails, two garden centers, 14 security gates, and 2 recreational vehicle storage areas.

The community employs a recreation director and provides organized trips, on-site entertainment, and crafts classes. Twenty-four-hour motorized patrol and both guarded and electronic perimeter restrictions as well as an internal bus service, are also provided.

There are two professional golf courses: a challenging championship 27-hole course and a 9-hole 3 par executive course. In addition, you will find a driving range, putting greens, a chipping area, a well-stocked pro shop, two full-time golf professionals, and electric cart rentals.

HOMEOWNER ASSESSMENTS, TAXES, AND UTILITIES

In this community, you can find a home to meet your specific needs and lifestyle. You may select a single-family home, a one- , two- , or three-bedroom condominium, or a cooperative in a single- or multi-story building. You can enjoy the ultimate in luxury carefree living by selecting a condominium in the twin Rossmoor Towers located across from the 9-hole executive golf course. With its 311 luxury condominiums, the Towers is one of the best retirement facilities of its type on the West Coast. Besides enjoying all the facilities of Leisure World, Towers residents enjoy additional amenities. However, the Towers is not a convalescent or health care facility, but simply an environment where retirees can enjoy retirement free from cooking and housekeeping chores. Tower residents are provided three balanced meals a day and weekly maid service. These units can cost as much as $350,000 or be leased for as little as $8,000. They have an average monthly maintenance fee of $1,276 and municipal/property taxes average about $1,500 per year (with a property value of $125,000).

The mid-rise buildings, consisting of condominiums and cooperatives, average $96,000 with monthly community association assessments of $294. Their yearly property taxes average $1,200. The 1,345 garden-style condos cost about $116,000, with an additional $286 per month in association assessments. Their property taxes are about $1,450 per year. Townhomes number 696 and cost about $85,000, with a monthly community association assessment of $286 and property taxes of $1,065 per year. The 421 single-family homes average about $350,000, with monthly association assessments of $284 and property taxes of about $4,300 per year.

Contemporary and Spanish architectural styles are prevalent within the community. There are 879 one-bedroom homes, 10,587 two-bedroom homes, and 1,270 three-bedroom homes. Both cable and community television channels are available. Electricity provides the primary heating source. The local municipality provides both water and sewer waste services. All utilities are located underground. Except for the RV storage lots, there are no extra storage facilities on site.

The governmental structure at Leisure World includes three housing corporations and the Golden Rain Foundation. Each owner in Leisure World is a member of one housing corporation and a resident member of the Golden Rain Foundation. The housing corporations are responsible for services directly related to housing and adjacent land. The Golden Rain Foundation directs operation of all community-owned facilities, including the bus system, entrance gates, clubhouses, swimming pools, golf courses, stables, and so forth.

Each of the three housing corporations have a board of directors elected by their members. The board members then elect directors to the Golden Rain Foundation. In addition to the boards of directors, there are 26 volunteer advisory committees that assist in the complex task of governing this multi-faceted community. The community also contracts with a professional management company to handle financial, security, recreational, maintenance, and landscaping services.

RESTRICTIONS IN THE COMMUNITY

There is a community association and membership is mandatory. The association provides exterior building grounds maintenance for the homeowners. Any exterior modifications must meet established standards and receive board of trustee approval. All common landscaping is maintained by the association. If you want to install special landscaping, you must abide by special rules.

The major restriction in the community is age; at least one of the residents must be 55 years old. Children are not allowed to live in the development, but they are allowed to visit. All pets must be licensed and kept on leashes; owners must clean up after their pets. No more than three dogs per home are allowed. Maximum occupation is limited at only two people per bedroom. There is a leasing office on site to assist owners in renting their homes. No businesses are allowed to be operated from a dwelling. The association has a right of first refusal on resales but seldom uses it. There are garages, carports, guest parking areas, and two special areas to park recreational vehicles and boats.

MISSION VIEJO

26522 La Alameda, Suite 190
Mission Viejo, California 92691
714-582-2489

$150,000 to $1,000,000+
25,400/30,783 Single-family
Homes and Condominiums
Mixed Architecture

1 public 18-hole golf course
6 recreation centers
8 miles to Pacific Ocean
30 community parks
Over 30 ball-playing fields
Over 30 tennis courts with lights
Gymnasium, exercise room

1 private 18-hole golf course
124-acre lake with 3 miles of shore
Over 150 boat slips
Hiking trails, over 30 picnic areas
Over 60 outdoor tennis courts
Handball/racquetball/squash
Steam/sauna

INTRODUCTION

Mission Viejo, a 10,300-acre master planned community in south Orange County, California, is included here as an example of what can happen to a private planned community. Mission Viejo is now an incorporated city but is still operated and managed as a community association. Mission Viejo's original master plan was to provide a wide range of housing opportunities within a private community. The master plan calls for 52 percent of the land to be devoted to residential uses, 29 percent to parks, open space and recreation, 10 percent to schools and churches, and 9 percent to business properties.

The land that Mission Viejo rests on was part of the 53,000-acre Rancho Mission Viejo with the title to the land dating back to 1769 and the beginning of Spanish rule in California. In 1963, Mission Viejo Company began the purchase of 10,000 acres for a new planned community. The first residential units were offered for sale in late 1965. The city of Mission Viejo has a current population of 74,000 people living in 25,400 dwelling units. When completed in 1995, the community is expected to have a population of about 90,000 residents occupying 30,783 dwelling units.

On November 3, 1987, the residents of Mission Viejo voted to incorporate. On March 31, 1988, the City of Mission Viejo became the 27th city in the County of Orange. Mission Viejo is located about halfway between Los Angeles and San Diego, along the east side of Interstate 5, 22 miles south of Disneyland and five miles northeast of Laguna Beach. All services can be found within the boundaries of Mission Viejo, including a dry cleaners, a hair salon, grocery and liquor stores, retail shops, and movie theaters. Mission Viejo has over a dozen community and neighborhood shopping centers.

More than 900 acres have been set aside to serve the community's commercial, professional, and business needs. The Mission Viejo Regional Medical Center is a full service, acute-care facility with 212 beds and plans to expand to 375 beds within the next year. With a staff of 350 physicians representing 22 specializations, it has been designated south Orange County's regional trauma center. In addition, four full service medical and dental centers with clinical laboratories, pharmacies, and radiology facilities serve the community.

RECREATION AND SOCIAL ACTIVITIES

Upon completion, Mission Viejo will have approximately 2,100 acres for permanent non-urban uses, including 1,122 acres in parks and open space areas and more than 900 acres in private recreation areas and community school sites. A recent countywide study showed the city of Mission Viejo ranking highest among south Orange County cities in per capita park acreage.

Currently, Mission Viejo has 30 completed parks. A nature trail and a 113-acre natural area with large sycamore and oak trees make up Wilderness Glen. Approximately 40 acres north of Lake Mission Viejo have been developed into a youth athletic park to accommodate Little League and soccer teams. The 41-acre Oso Viejo Community Park features a multi-purpose community center, a senior center, and lighted softball, baseball, and soccer fields. Alicia Park contains four lighted softball fields for youth and adult play. Every home in Mission Viejo is within one mile of a community park.

Mission Viejo operates four voluntary membership recreation centers. Facilities include three competition swimming pools (including one 50-meter Olympic pool), a large play pool, one free-form pool, three wading pools, four hydrotherapy pools, a 25-meter Olympic diving pool, 19 lighted tennis courts, 10 handball/racquetball courts, one grass and two sand volleyball courts, two outdoor basketball courts, men and women's saunas, billiard tables, four weight rooms with Nautilus, Olympic, and Universal equipment, two free-weight rooms, lounges, locker rooms, and a sporting goods store, a children's indoor play area, and four outdoor playgrounds. A multi-purpose mini-gym is available for basketball, volleyball, and gymnastics, and a large cultural/multi-purpose indoor facility is used for classes, shows, and community events.

One example of Mission Viejo's dedication to its youth is the Nadadores swim team, a 300-member competitive swimming program for young people ages five and up. Since 1968 the senior swim team has won 47 national championships, and the diving team boasts 38 national team titles. Nadadores swimmers and divers earned ten gold medals in the 1984 Olympic Games. Mission Viejo also offers more than 40 organized youth athletic organizations, including baseball, softball, football, soccer, swimming, diving, basketball, tennis, track and field, and gymnastics.

Lake Mission Viejo is a private 124-acre man-made recreational lake providing facilities for sailing, swimming, fishing, and picnicking. The lake is surrounded by single-family homes, condominiums, five beaches, boat launching facilities, and two picnic areas.

The Casta del Sol 18-hole golf course is privately owned and open to the public. The private Mission Viejo country club offers a championship-length 6,680-yard golf course, eight tennis courts, a swimming pool, and a clubhouse.

Mission Viejo also has nearly 50 adult organizations, ranging from gardening to hospital support to singing. The Mission Viejo activities committee, a group of community volunteers, coordinates a number of annual events, including the St. Patrick's Parade, the 4th of July Street Faire, and the Five Nights of Christmas program.

Homeownership automatically entitles you to lake and association facilities. Health club membership has a $200 initiation fee and a $50 monthly fee. The private country club has a $25,000 membership fee. The public golf course costs $13 per round on weekdays. Lake facilities have a $13.50 monthly fee for use.

HOMEOWNER ASSESSMENTS, TAXES, AND UTILITIES

Homes at Mission Viejo can range from $100,000 to $500,000. Homes built on the lake exceed $1 million. Property taxes average 2 percent of the assessed valuation. Condominium assessments vary with the neighborhoods. The predominant architectural style of homes built between 1965 and 1983 is Spanish; homes built since 1983 are varied in their architectural styles. Both cable and community television channels are available. The primary heating fuel is gas. A local water district provides both sewer and water systems. All utilities are underground. There are extra storage facilities within the community.

RESTRICTIONS IN THE COMMUNITY

Although there are no general age restrictions within Mission Viejo, there are two senior projects (2,000 units and 900 units) that are restricted to age 55 and older. There are 25 neighborhood community associations within Mission Viejo. Membership is mandatory except for owners of houses built from 1965 to 1969, before Mission Viejo established associations. Single-family homeowners are generally responsible for their own building/grounds maintenance, but there are some exceptions. The community association provides building/grounds maintenance for common areas and condominiums. Any exterior building modifications must be reviewed by the association's architectural committee. There are no restrictions regarding landscaping as long as it is done on your own property: Owners are not allowed to plant in common areas.

There are city ordinances (overcrowding statutes) governing how many people can occupy a single home. There are no rental restrictions, nor are there restrictions governing resales. Only daycare and home office businesses are permitted; traffic-generating businesses are not allowed. RVs and boats are not permitted to park for long periods on the streets or in driveways. There are two special parking areas for recreational vehicles and boats.

NORTHSTAR

Box 1910
Truckee, California 95734
916-562-0322

$55,000 to $1,000,000+
1,153/1,252 Townhomes,
Single-family Homes, and Lots
Mixed Architecture

18-Hole USGA-rated golf course
Steam and sauna facilities
22 lifts
Snowmaking capabilities
4 picnic areas
Horse stables with 3 bridle paths

1 outdoor swimming pool, 2 spas
49 downhill ski trails
45 km of cross-country trails
3 hiking trails
10 outdoor tennis courts
Clubhouse with exercise room

INTRODUCTION

The Northstar property owners' association located in Truckee, California, is a private recreational community in the Sierras. The Trimont Land Company of Truckee is developing the community; the first home was built in 1970. Within 35 miles of both Reno and Lake Tahoe, the Northstar property owners' association offers many recreational activities for its homeowners, including skiing, hiking, golfing, and swimming.

With a population of 140,000, Reno is the nearest large city to Northstar. Interstate 80 is just six miles from the development. The area is provided police coverage by the county sheriff's department, and there is a staffed fire department nearby. The nearest hospital with emergency facilities is eight miles from the community. Within the confines of Northstar, you will find a grocery and liquor store and restaurants. A pharmacy and a medical clinic can be found seven miles from the community. A dry cleaners, a hair salon, retail shops, and movie theaters are eight miles away.

Although this mountain resort is secluded in the Sierras, it is near many attractions. For example, Lake Tahoe is only six miles away, and the Nevada casinos are as close as eight miles. There are many other historic and cultural activities for homeowners to visit in the area.

RECREATION AND SOCIAL ACTIVITIES

You'll never be bored at this mountain resort. You can play 18 holes of golf surrounded by beautiful evergreens, or you can relax in one of the community's pools or spas. There are 49 downhill ski trails with a myriad of lifts, including one gondola, two quads, three triple, and six doubles. The 45 kilometers of cross-country ski trails cover some of the most beautiful land in the Sierras. The community also has snowmaking capabilities. In the summer, you can take a walk on one of the three community hiking trails or plan a picnic at one of the four picnic areas. There are 10 outdoor tennis courts, horse stables with three bridle paths, and a small clubhouse that includes an exercise room and steam and sauna facilities.

Northstar employs a recreation director and publishes a newsletter two or three times a year. The association organizes trips and provides on-site entertainment for homeowners. An internal bus service and catering are also available. The association sponsors daycare for children and many activities for teens. There is a 24-hour patrol within the community, but there are no perimeter restrictions.

The recreation center has a $110 quarterly fee that also provides part of the funds for the busing system. Golfing and skiing fees are extra. Future plans include the construction of an additional 1,000 units and a second recreational facility.

HOMEOWNER ASSESSMENTS, TAXES, AND UTILITIES

Currently, there are 653 mid-rise condominiums at Northstar, varying in size from studios to four bedrooms. These homes range in price from $55,000 to $200,000, with a monthly community association assessment between $140 and $215. Current property/municipal taxes are between $800 and $2,500. All 599 lots within the community have been sold. To date, 500 single-family homes have been built. These homes range in price from $200,000 to over $1 million, with a monthly community association assessment fee of $35. Property taxes for the single-family homes average between $2,500 and $11,000. Single-family homes start at two bedrooms; there are even some eight-bedroom homes within the community.

Both cable and community television channels are available. Gas provides the primary heat source for the community. Both sewer waste disposal and water services are provided by the local municipality. All utilities are underground. There are no extra storage facilities within Northstar.

RESTRICTIONS IN THE COMMUNITY

All homeowners at Northstar belong to the master community association, which runs the recreation center and enforces the restrictions in individual home areas. There are also five condominium associations. Each association is responsible for its own neighborhood's building and grounds maintenance. Owners of individual homes are responsible for their own maintenance. The master association must approve any changes and all new construction of homes. Each condo association has control of the exterior of the condos. Landscaping installations must also have approval from both the master and the neighborhood associations.

There are no age or length-of-stay restrictions for visitors. Pets are allowed, but they must be under the control of the owner at all times. There are no restrictions on how many people can occupy a single unit, nor are there any rental restrictions. Operating a business out of a home is not allowed if it generates traffic. There are no restrictions on the resale of units within the community. Trailers, boats, and motor homes are not allowed to park overnight within the community. All parking must be in the paved parking areas, not on the streets. During the summer months, the community provides storage for boats, motor homes, and other oversized vehicles.

OAKMONT

6637 Oakmont Dr.
Santa Rosa, California 95409
707-539-1530

$200,000 to $500,000
2,700/2,855 Single-family
Homes
California Ranch Architecture

2 18-Hole USGA-rated golf courses
1 pond with a quarter mile shore
50 acres of open space
2 picnic areas
6 outdoor tennis courts
Exercise room

3 outdoor pools
20 miles to Pacific Ocean
Hiking trails
Ball-playing fields
Clubhouse
Steam and sauna facilities

INTRODUCTION

Northern California's rugged coastline, ancient redwoods, lazy rivers, and rolling hills are all within easy access for Oakmont's active adults. Oakmont, located in the middle of Sonoma County's wine country, is an age-restricted community where homeowners must be 55 years of age or older. The community is being developed by Oakmont Developers of Santa Rosa. The first home was built in 1964.

There are currently 2,700 single-family homes out of an ultimate build-out of 2,855. Located just five miles from the community, Santa Rosa has a population of 115,000. California's Highway 101 is located seven miles from the complex. San Francisco is a little over an hour's drive away. Air transportation is provided by the Sonoma County airport, located 12 miles away. Police coverage is provided by local authorities, the county sheriff's office, and the California state police. Both a volunteer and a staffed fire department are nearby.

Within the confines of the community, homeowners have access to a dry cleaners, a hair salon, a grocery and liquor store, and restaurants. All other services are located within five miles of the community, including a pharmacy, a medical clinic, retail shops, and movie theaters. The nearest hospital with emergency facilities is Memorial Hospital, five miles from the development. Oakmont plans to build more office and retail buildings by 1995.

RECREATION AND SOCIAL ACTIVITIES

Oakmont has two 18-hole USGA-rated golf courses, three outdoor swimming pools, and a small pond with about a quarter mile of shoreline. Walking the many trails of Oakmont is a favorite pastime in this adult-oriented community; there are also two picnic areas. The community has six outdoor tennis courts. A large clubhouse contains an exercise room and steam and sauna facilities.

The association employs a recreation director and publishes a monthly newsletter. Organized trips, on-site entertainment, and on-site crafts are provided. There is a 24-hour security patrol within the community, but there are no perimeter restrictions for access. All recreational facilities are available to homeowners for a monthly fee of $10 per person. Golf membership is separate, and there is a special annual rate available to residents. As with most adult communities, there is a vast array of clubs and social organizations.

HOMEOWNER ASSESSMENTS, TAXES, AND UTILITIES

Oakmont is almost completed, with room only for 155 more homes in the community. The 2,700 homes that have already been built and sold average in price from $200,000 to $500,000. California Ranch is the only architectural style in this community. If your home is in a designated maintained area, then you may have an assessment fee of up to $120 per month. The current property/municipal taxes are 1 percent of the sales price.

Both cable and community television channels are available. Gas is the primary heat source. The local municipality provides both sewer waste disposal and water systems. All telephone and electrical utilities are located below ground. The community provides extra storage facilities.

RESTRICTIONS IN THE COMMUNITY

The most important restriction at Oakmont is the age restriction: Homeowners must be 55 years of age or older to live at this community. Children are not allowed to live here. There are restrictions on the age and length-of-stay for visitors. Only two pets are allowed in each home, and they must be leashed at all times.

There is a community association and membership is mandatory. The community association provides all exterior building/grounds maintenance for the common areas. The individual homeowners are responsible for their own maintenance. The architectural control committee governs all modifications to homes and any additional landscaping.

There are no restrictions regarding how many people can occupy a single unit. There are no rental restrictions except the age restriction. Operating a business out of your unit is not allowed at this community. There are no restrictions on the resale of units. Parking is not allowed on the streets at Oakmont; all parking must be done on a driveway or in a garage. The community provides a special parking area for recreational vehicles, boats, and the like.

PALM DESERT GREENS

73-750 Country Club Drive
Palm Desert, California 92260
619-346-8005

$70,000 to $200,000
1,850/1,922 Single–family
Homes
Mixed Architecture

18–hole USGA golf course
4 small lakes on golf course
3 picnic areas
7 outdoor tennis courts
Clubhouse

3 outdoor pools, 1 kiddie pool
100 acres of open space
1 ball-playing field
6 illuminated tennis courts
Steam/sauna

INTRODUCTION

Palm Desert Greens, located just south of Palm Springs, California, is a community that offers an incredible amount of recreational and social activities for its single-family homeowners. The first home was built in 1971.

Homeowner association business is administered by a seven-member board of directors. The board is elected by residents for two-year terms, except that the candidate with the highest number of votes receives a three-year term, which staggers the terms so that each year there are three vacancies. Each December, three board members are elected. Each lot has one vote regardless of the number of family members. The board of trustees is assisted by voluntary committees of association members and on-site management staff. Current standing committees are adult center/social activities, architectural review, communications, finance, food and beverage, golf, maintenance, recreation, and security.

Palm Desert Greens operates with an annual budget of over $3.15 million to maintain streets, buildings, grounds, security, and other services. Currently, there are 1,922 property owners.

Palm Desert Greens is adjacent to the town of Palm Desert, which has a population of 23,000. The community is just ten miles from the Palm Springs Regional Airport. Highway 10 is two miles from the development. Police protection is provided by the county sheriff's department. This community has a 24-hour patrol, and access is only through guarded gates. There is a staffed fire department nearby. Eisenhower Hospital, the nearest facility with emergency care, is two miles from the site.

There is a restaurant within the community. Within a half mile you will find a pharmacy, a dry cleaners, a hair salon, a grocery and liquor store, and retail shops. Two miles away are a medical clinic and a movie theater.

Situated south of the Los Angeles metropolitan area, the community is within a few hours of many area attractions. You can visit the Bob Hope Cultural Center, the Living Desert, and the area's numerous golf courses.

RECREATION AND SOCIAL ACTIVITIES

All recreational amenities are included in the monthly community association assessment, entitling you to unlimited golf, three swimming pools, picnic areas, ball-playing fields, lighted tennis courts, and use of the clubhouse, with its steam and sauna facilities and its meeting rooms.

Club activity is endless: There are CPR classes, holiday programs, a nonsmokers' poker group, a travel club, blood bank drives, golf clubs, the library association, weight watchers, bridge players, a shuffleboard club, Friday night bingo, a drama club, exercise classes, community dinners, a bocci ball club, ceramics, aquaerobics, a choral group, jogging club, square dances, a tennis club, hula classes, oil painting classes, and a crafts club.

The community employs a recreation director, publishes an extensive monthly newsletter, organizes off-site trips, and provides on-site entertainment. Future plans include a new exercise room.

HOMEOWNER ASSESSMENTS, TAXES, AND UTILITIES

The major responsibility of the association at Palm Desert Greens is to protect the investment and enhance the value of the property owned by the members. The association provides security, trash collection, food and beverage services, clubhouse maintenance, golf course operations, and so forth.

There are 1,922 lots and 1,850 single-family manufactured homes at this development. Homes range in price from $70,000 to $200,000. With their price usually determined by their proximity to the golf course, lots can cost from $40,000 to $100,000. All of the property owners at Palm Desert Greens pay $115 per month to the association. This fee covers unlimited use of all the recreational amenities and maintenance of all association-owned property. Property taxes average 1.1 percent of value.

The majority of the manufactured homes have two or three bedrooms, and there is a variety of architectural styles throughout the community. Both cable and community television channels are available. Homes are heated by gas. The local municipality provides both sewer waste and water services. All utilities are underground. There is a privately operated RV facility on site.

RESTRICTIONS IN THE COMMUNITY

Palm Desert Greens has an active community association and membership is mandatory. Individual homeowners provide their own exterior building and grounds maintenance for their single-family homes. The association handles maintenance for all the property it owns. To assure that the integrity of the original community design is preserved, the association has an architectural review committee. This committee is composed of property owners, appointed annually, to review and approve all improvement plans and enforce maintenance and other standards. For building changes to a home or when building a new home, all homeowners must receive both the committee's and local governmental agency's authority to do so. Landscaping installation requires approval from the committee also.

There are no pet restrictions in this community. There are also no restrictions on how many people may occupy a unit, nor are there any rental restrictions. Operating a business from a home must receive the architectural review committee's approval to do so. Resale restrictions do not exist. Commercial vehicles, recreational vehicles, boats, trailers, etc. may not be parked on the streets or in driveways, however, the association does provide a special place to park oversized vehicles.

ROSSMOOR AT WALNUT CREEK

P.O. Box 2070
Walnut Creek, California 94595
415-939-1211

$100,000 to $400,000
6,300/7,600 Garden-style
& Mid-rise Condos and
Cooperatives
Contemporary Architecture

9-and 18-hole USGA-rated golf
30 miles to Pacific Ocean
Hiking trails, picnic areas
Horse stables

2 outdoor pools
695 acres of open space
6 outdoor tennis courts
4 clubhouse facilities

INTRODUCTION

Rossmoor at Walnut Creek, an age-restricted community, is located in Tice Valley, two miles from downtown Walnut Creek and 30 minutes on the freeway from downtown San Francisco. Walnut Creek has an ideal climate: Summers are clear and warm with cool evenings, and winters are moderately cool. The rainfall average is 20 inches per year, and humidity is in the dry middle range. There is an average of 3,200 hours of sunshine a year. Thirty-seven percent of the community is open green space, a total of 695 acres.

I-80 is two miles from the development; the Oakland International Airport is 15 miles away and the San Francisco International Airport is 25 miles from the site. Police protection is provided by the city of Walnut Creek and the Contra Costa County sheriff's department. Both a city and a county staffed fire department are nearby. In addition, Rossmoor has its own 24-hour public safety service. The entry plaza is manned around the clock, and there are frequent vehicle patrols throughout the community. Residents are given car identification stickers for immediate passage through the entry plaza. Guests merely show their passes and are waved through; door-to-door solicitations are prohibited.

The John Muir Medical Center, the nearest facility with emergency care, is three miles from the site. The Rossmoor Medical Clinic, a 30,000-square-foot medical facility is on-site and is open to all Rossmoor residents. The clinic has a staff of full-time physicians, nurses, and dentists and includes medical services such as x-rays, physical therapy, a laboratory, a pharmacy, an optical shop, a hearing aid shop, a home health agency, a blood bank, and 24-hour emergency nursing and medical services.

The community is being developed by UDC Homes, a limited partnership, of Pleasanton, California, which specializes in adult communities. UDC Homes constructs all residences and facilities in the community and maintains the exclusive sales department for new homes. Several realty firms, including UDC, offer resale services. There are currently 6,300 completed homes out of an expected build-out of 7,600 homes.

There are no commercial retail services within the development, but within a half mile of Rossmoor you will find a dry cleaners, a hair salon, a grocery store, a liquor store, restaurants, retail stores, and movie theaters. The San Francisco Bay area offers many cultural, historical, and recreational activities for residents.

RECREATION AND SOCIAL ACTIVITIES

At present, residents can enjoy four clubhouses, two swimming pools, picnic areas, three lawn bowling greens, shuffleboard courts, horseshoe pits, a 27-hole golf course, a driving range, and riding stables. There are art, music, and ceramic studios, woodworking, lapidary, and jewelry shops, and sewing, reading, and billiards. A photography lab, large meeting rooms, and a library are available. Over 200 clubs and organizations are also available to residents.

The Senior Dollar Clubhouse has card and game rooms, an art gallery, a solarium, and furnished social rooms. Rossmoor offers facilities for banquets, dances, and parties as well as an outdoor plaza and stage. Modest fees are charged for golf, stable boarding, and lawn bowling; there are also service charges for organizing certain social events.

The association employs a staff to coordinate recreation and clubhouse activities and publishes a weekly newspaper for all residents. An internal bus system operates within the community, and visiting nurse and caregiver services are available. A new clubhouse with a swimming pool, a spa, an exercise room, and a 5,500-square-foot multi-purpose room is scheduled for completion at the end of 1991.

HOMEOWNER ASSESSMENTS, TAXES, AND UTILITIES

Forty percent of the homes at Rossmoor are garden-style condominiums. The remaining homes are either mid-rise condos or cooperative housing. The homes vary in price from under $100,000 (cooperative) to $400,000. The co-operatives which were built 25 years ago, require an equity purchase. Property taxes are 1.25 percent of assessed value. The average homeowner pays $290 per month in community association assessments, which includes the fees of the master association and individual mutuals (neighborhood associations).

Both cable and community television channels are available, and electricity provides the primary heating source. The local municipality provides both sewer waste disposal and water systems. All utilities are underground. There are no extra storage facilities on site.

RESTRICTIONS IN THE COMMUNITY

There is a community association and membership is mandatory. The on-site professional property management group provides all exterior building/grounds maintenance at Rossmoor. Any exterior modifications require the approval of the architectural control committee. A permit approval is required in order to plant any special flowers, trees, or other plants.

Rossmoor at Walnut Creek is an age-restricted community: You must be 55 years old or older to purchase here. Children are not allowed to live at the site. There are no restrictions on age of visitors, but there are restrictions on length of stay. The association sets aside special swimming pool times for visiting youngsters.

The community only allows two pets (dog, cat, or bird) per home; no pet may weigh more than 20 pounds. Maximum occupancy is set at two people for a one-bedroom home and three people for a two-bedroom home. If you choose to rent your home, you may only do so under a one-year, nonrenewable lease. Operating a business from a unit is prohibited. There are some restrictions on the resale of units. Individual homeowner parking spaces are assigned. There is an extra area designed for the parking of recreational vehicles, boats, and the like.

SILVER LAKES

P.O. Box 179
Helendale, California 92342
619-245-1606

$75,000 to $450,000
1,804/5,000 Garden-style
Condos, Single-family
Homes, and Lots
Mixed Architecture

27-holes of USGA-rated golf
2 lakes, 300 total acres
Over 100 acres of open space
1 ball-playing field
30,000 square-foot clubhouse
Equestrian center

1 outdoor pool
Boating
3 picnic areas
4 lighted outdoor tennis courts
Exercise room, steam and sauna
2 parks with playground equipment

INTRODUCTION

Nestled in the middle of 2,000 private acres in San Bernadino County, California, Silver Lakes is located 15 miles from Victorville, east of Los Angeles. Victorville has a population of 30,000. All of the 5,000 lots in the community have been sold, and there are currently 1,480 completed single-family homes and 350 garden-style condominiums.

Interstate 15 is also 15 miles from the site. The Ontario Airport is 45 miles from Silver Lakes. The community was developed by Dart Industries, and the first home was built in 1975.

The area is provided police protection by the San Bernadino sheriff's department, and a volunteer fire department is nearby. The nearest hospital with emergency facilities is located in Victorville.

The community provides many services within its property, including a hair salon, a grocery store, a bar, a restaurant, real estate offices, a gift shop, a golf cart sales office, and retail shops. Other services, such as a pharmacy, a medical clinic, a dry cleaners, a liquor store, and a movie theater, are located in Victorville, 15 miles from the community.

Just a few hours away from Silver Lakes is the Los Angeles area, where there are many theme parks, museums, concert halls, historical sites, and flea markets. Future plans at Silver Lakes include a new five-acre park to be built in 1992.

RECREATION AND SOCIAL ACTIVITIES

Silver Lakes boasts a 27-hole USGA-rated golf course that has recently undergone extensive irrigation work to save on labor and improve turf conditions. Over 86,000 rounds of golf were played on the course in 1990. Active men and women's golf clubs operate at Silver Lakes, and there is also tournament play. A pro shop and driving range are also located at the golf club.

Silver Lakes contains an outdoor pool and two lakes with a total of 300 acres. The lakes have a beach area for swimming and boat launching facilities; however, there are no boat slips available for storage. The speed limit on both lakes is 10 mph in open water and 5 mph in the lakes' fingers. Waterskiing is not permitted.

Within the property are two parks with playground equipment, picnic areas, and ball-playing fields. Homeowners also have access to four lighted outdoor tennis courts. The six-acre equestrian center has a barn, corrals, hay lofts, and a riding ring. There are no bridle trails: All riding is done in the open space of the community.

The 30,000-square-foot clubhouse offers an exercise room, steam and sauna facilities, a bar and restaurant, a youth room, and areas for arts, crafts, and ceramics.

Silver Lakes has a very active social structure with many homeowner volunteers. There are 13 committees that coordinate events for residents. Dinner dances are provided on a monthly basis; many holiday events are also planned.

The community employs a recreation director and publishes a monthly newsletter. The recreation director organizes trips and on-site entertainment. Catering services are also available from the community restaurant. Access to Silver Lakes is through open entrances, and there is a 24-hour patrol within the community. Homeownership automatically entitles you to membership in all of the community clubs and recreational facilities.

HOMEOWNER ASSESSMENTS, TAXES, AND UTILITIES

Silver Lakes is governed by a seven-member board of directors. Each member serves a two-year term. Directors are voted from the membership at large, and terms of office are staggered.

The 350 garden-style condominiums at Silver Lakes range in price from $75,000 to $150,000, with a master association fee of $74.88 per month as well as individual neighborhood association fees. The 1,480 single-family homes cost $150,000 to $450,000, with a monthly community association assessment of $74.88.

Cable television is available, but there are no community television channels. Both gas and electricity provide primary heating for the homes. Sewer waste and water services are provided by a local water district. All utilities are underground. There are no extra storage facilities within the community, but private storage areas are nearby.

RESTRICTIONS IN THE COMMUNITY

There is a community association and membership is mandatory. Individual homeowners provide their own exterior building/grounds maintenance. The association provides all exterior building and grounds maintenance for the common areas, recreational amenities, and infrastructure. Neighborhood associations provide maintenance for the condominium units. Exterior modifications to homes are restricted: All changes must be approved by the environmental control committee, and a refundable deposit for construction and landscaping is required. Single-family homeowners must meet the association's minimum standards for landscaping.

There are no restrictions on age or length-of-stay for visitors, nor are there any pet restrictions. Only a single family may occupy a single home. There are no rental restrictions nor are there restrictions on the resale of units. Owners who rent units have the right to assign all recreation privileges to the tenant. Operating a business from a home is prohibited at Silver Lakes. There are no parking restrictions, and the association provides a special place to park recreational vehicles, boats, and other oversized vehicles.

SUNRISE COUNTRY CLUB

71601 Country Club Drive
Rancho Mirage, California
92270
619-328-6045

$160,000 to $250,000
746/746 Townhomes
Spanish Architecture

18-hole golf course
7 small lakes
6 lighted outdoor tennis courts

21 outdoor pools
13 outdoor tennis courts
Clubhouse

INTRODUCTION

The Sunrise Country Club lies amidst serene surroundings in the beautiful desert city of Rancho Mirage, California. The townhomes, set among knolls and fairways, afford views of lush greens and lakes that reflect the Santa Rosa Mountains.

The Sunrise Country Club was developed by the Sunrise Corporation of Palm Desert. The first home was built in 1973. All 746 townhomes have been sold; therefore, only resales are occurring.

Interstate 10 is only 10 miles away, and Palm Springs, 25 miles away, provides the nearest major airport. The community is under the jurisdiction of the county sheriff's department, and a staffed fire department is nearby. Security is tight at the Sunrise Country Club; access is through 24-hour guarded gates. The Eisenhower Medical Center, only one mile from the site, offers emergency medical care.

There is a restaurant within the property. Within five miles you will find a pharmacy, a medical clinic, a dry cleaners, a hair salon, a grocery and liquor store, retail shops, and a movie theater.

Downtown Palm Desert offers shopping at I. Magnin, Bullock's and Robinson's. Other attractions of interest include the Bob Hope Cultural Center, the Palm Springs tram, the College of the Desert, the Bob Hope Golf Classic, vintage car races, the Dinah Shore Golf Tournament, and foreign film festivals.

RECREATION AND SOCIAL ACTIVITIES

Sunrise Country Club offers golf, swimming, tennis, and a beautiful 15,000-square-foot clubhouse. Designed by Ted Robinson, an adventurous, executive-length, 18-hole golf course is lined with stately date palms. The lush greens and fairways offer ample opportunity to use every club in the bag, and the water hazards and sand traps provide exciting challenges. The golf shop is fully staffed by professionals and offers lessons, and repairs as well as a complete line of equipment, accessories, and the latest fashions.

Sunrise Country Club is an equity membership facility. There are 523 equity members, meaning each owner owns $1/523$ of the club's property and assets. Every equity member has one vote in electing the board that runs the club. An equity membership is real property and may be sold privately. However, the buyer must be approved by the club's membership committee, and the club must handle the transfer of ownership. The transfer fee is $500 and equity memberships sell for $5,000. Equity members also pay $2,100 per year for combined golf and tennis privileges. The annual fee for golf alone is $1,865. An equity member's tenants may also purchase a membership. Equity members also pay $330 per year for cart licensing, have a minimum purchase requirement in the club's restaurant, and so forth.

The community's 15,000-square-foot clubhouse is surrounded by shimmering blue lakes: The main dining room affords a breathtaking view of the club's largest lake and the first tee. From the adjacent lounge, you can look out over the championship sunken tennis court. The lower level of the clubhouse contains the men and women's locker rooms and golf and tennis shops. The snack shop is easily accessible from the front and back nines, the main pool, and the tennis clubs.

Scattered throughout the community are 21 sparkling swimming pools, 19 of which have companion therapy pools. The Sunrise Tennis Club facilities feature 13 courts, including six lighted courts and a recessed exhibition court. Located in the clubhouse, the tennis pro shop provides everything from equipment to accessories to repair accommodations.

Although the community does not employ a recreation director, it does publish an informative newsletter. Many activities and events are held at the clubhouse, including golf and tennis tournaments, dances, golf breakfasts, and Christmas and New Year's Eve parties. Sunrise Country Club HOA (homeowners' association) has a committee system in place, with homeowners volunteering for the architectural, landscaping, investment advisory, rules and regulations, and earthquake preparedness committees.

HOMEOWNER ASSESSMENTS, TAXES, AND UTILITIES

The 1991 budget for the association is over $2.6 million, with almost $500,000 earmarked for reserves to replace and repair major items at the development. Monthly assessments are determined by the type of unit you own. The five different models have monthly assessments of $265, $277, $297, $317, or $342.

Homes range in size from 850 square feet to 2,000 square feet with one-, two- and three- bedroom units. All of the homes are Spanish-style townhomes and line the golf course. Features include private courtyard entries, atriums, fireplaces, wet bars, enclosed two-car garages with golf cart areas, breakfast nooks, wardrobe closets, all-electric kitchens, and sunken bathtubs.

Both cable and community television channels are available, and gas provides the primary heating source. Sewer and water systems are provided by the local municipality, and all utilities are underground. There are no extra storage facilities on site.

RESTRICTIONS IN THE COMMUNITY

Community association membership is mandatory at the Sunrise Country Club. The association handles all maintenance for homes, recreational facilities, and infrastructure. All exterior modifications must be approved by the association, including landscaping changes. In 1990, 123 requests for architectural changes were made to the association; 116 were approved. Most of the requests were for routine changes involving new garage doors, mail slots, and the like.

Visitors of any age are allowed to stay for any length of time. There are no pet restrictions within the development; however, local leash laws do apply. There are also no restrictions regarding maximum occupation. Units may be sold or rented without association approval. Operating a business from a unit is prohibited. Parking restrictions are in place, and the association does not provide an area for oversized vehicle parking.

TAHOE DONNER

11509 Northwoods Blvd.
P.O. Box 11049
Truckee, California 95737
916-587-9400

$40,000 to $500,000
3,000/6,170 Garden-style
Condos and Single-family
Homes
Contemporary and Bavarian
Architecture

18-hole USGA-rated golf course
Leased land on Donner Lake
65km of cross-country ski trails
Over 2,000 acres of open space
3 picnic areas
Equestrian center
Clubhouse
60 campsites for tents and RVs

2 outdoor pools
Boating (launching only–no slips)
Downhill skiing (11 trails)
10 hiking trails
9 outdoor tennis courts
65km of bridle paths
Sauna facilities
Archery range

INTRODUCTION

Tahoe Donner, located 30 miles southwest of Reno and just northwest of Lake Tahoe, is a 6,000-acre private community in the Sierra Mountain range. Building began at the site in 1971 with an initial 11-phase plan. Over 3,000 homes (both condominium and single-family) have been built out of an expected total of 6,170. Growth in this area has picked up tremendously in the last few years. Building is now progressing at about 250 homes per year. Dart Resorts was the initial developer, but the site is now being developed by the Tahoe Donner association.

Tahoe Donner is a private recreational resort with activities for the entire family; such as camping, hiking, golfing, tennis, fishing, boating, and riding.

Interstate 80 is just two miles from the property. The nearest airport is 35 miles away in Reno. The area is protected by the county sheriff's department, and a staffed fire department is nearby. The nearest hospital with emergency facilities is just two and a half miles from the community.

All other needed services are within three miles, including a pharmacy, a medical clinic, a dry cleaners, a hair salon, a liquor store, and retail shops. A movie theater is five miles from the site. Within the confines of Tahoe Donner you will find a grocery store and restaurant. Other local attractions include the Donner Memorial Park, historical downtown Truckee, the beautiful Lake Tahoe and Donner Lake, and nearby casinos.

RECREATION AND SOCIAL ACTIVITIES

Golf, tennis, swimming, boating, horseback riding, downhill and cross-country skiing, camping, hiking, and an extensive social program for residents makes this mountain community a very special place. There are activities for teens, children, and adults.

Weekly events from mid-June through Labor Day include bingo, the tiny tot story hour, arts and crafts, archery clinics, slide shows, backgammon tournaments, aquatic games, the teen adventure program, children's movies, and a campfire circle. Special events sponsored by the association include world record day (residents try to set world records in flying paper airplanes, spitting melon seeds, blowing bubble gum, tossing grapes, and catching quarters tossed from your forearm), water carnival day, stargazing, a mountain bike tour, a scavenger hunt, a teen dance, a fun run, and a Monte Carlo night to benefit the Tahoe Donner ski teams.

The championship 18-hole golf course also sports a pro shop, provides lessons, and has a restaurant and bar. The tennis center has nine courts, a pro shop, lessons, and a practice board. The Tahoe Donner beach club offers sandy beaches, ping pong, video games, horseshoes, a snack bar, and barbecues. Fishing equipment, sailboats, sailboards, rowboats, and canoes can be rented. The Northwoods clubhouse, the center for many association activities, contains games, sports equipment, a volleyball court, a nature trail, an exercise course, and a color T.V.

The equestrian center at Tahoe Donner has 33 miles of riding trails, guided rides, lessons, and boarding facilities. The center also sponsors special events such as pony rides, breakfast and dinner rides, kids' camp, men's day, and ladies' day. The association's 60 campsites for tents and RVs provide hot showers, a sewer dump, picnic tables, and barbecues.

The association employs a recreation director and publishes a quarterly newsletter for residents. Beginning in 1991, Tahoe Donner will be providing a shuttle bus to its ski areas. Other future amenities include a recreation center, an olympic-size pool, a spa, a kiddie pool, a driving range, and four new tennis courts.

HOMEOWNER ASSESSMENTS, TAXES, AND UTILITIES

There are currently 290 garden-style condominiums ranging in price from $40,000 to $170,000. The 2,600 single-family homes in the community average from $75,000 to $500,000. All of the 6,170 lots in the community have been sold. All homeowners pay a yearly community association assessment of $480. Neighborhood association assessments, if any, are separate. Property taxes are 1.25 percent of the assessed value.

The association is now addressing the issue of user fees for some facilities. Currently, the association issues four passes per lot. If there is more than one owner on the deed, the additional owners can purchase extra passes that will allow use of the facilities. Everyone may use the country club and health club. Fees for golf are $18 per round (non-owner fees are $70). Fees for downhill skiing are $12 for owners and $20 for the general public.

Cable and community television stations are available, except to homes at the highest elevations. Heating is provided mainly by propane and wood stoves. The local municipality provides waste disposal and water systems. Utilities are both below and above ground.

RESTRICTIONS IN THE COMMUNITY

Tahoe Donner is governed by a master association and two condominium associations; membership is mandatory. The master association provides exterior building/grounds maintenance for all of the commonly held property and the recreational facilities. The condo associations provide maintenance for the condos. Single-family homeowners provide their own exterior building/grounds maintenance. The environmental control committee maintains strict regulations regarding structures built in the community. Because the board of directors want to "maintain quiet repose and harmony with the natural surroundings," prior approval for building or remodeling of present homes is required. Any application to construct or remodel homes in the development must be accompanied by payment of a deposit and fees.

There are no restrictions on age or length-of-stay for visitors. County ordinances govern pets. There are no rental restrictions within the community. Depending on zoning, there may be restrictions on how many people may occupy a unit. Any fencing must have prior approval. Operating a business from a home is allowed; however, signs can not be displayed, and there should be no increase in traffic due to the business. There are no resale restrictions. Parking is not allowed on streets during the winter season (November 1 to April 1). The association provides a boat storage lot at a nominal fee. The bylaws of the association are currently undergoing revisions, which means some of these restrictions may change.

**THE VILLAGES GOLF AND
COUNTRY CLUB**

5000 Cribari Lane
San Jose, California 95135
408-274-4400

$125,000 to $375,000
1,994/2,700 Garden-style
Condos and Single-family Homes
Mixed Architecture

9- and 18-hole USGA-rated golf
2½ miles of lake shoreline
Over 600 acres of open space
3 picnic areas
Stables and 7 bridle paths

3 outdoor pools, 3 spas
35 miles to Pacific Ocean
7 hiking trails
4 tennis courts
4 clubhouses

INTRODUCTION

The Villages Golf and Country Club is a private community exclusively for adults age 55 and over. Established in 1967, the Villages offers a spectacular championship golf course surrounded by distinctive neighborhoods. The Villages is being developed by UDC Homes of Pleasanton, California. Historically an area of vineyards and agricultural estates, the Villages remains a haven of natural beauty. Though secluded, the Villages is near shopping, transportation, and California's South Bay's burgeoning cultural community.

San Jose, with a population of 765,207, is 12 miles from the community. San Jose International Airport is just 10 miles from the Villages, and I-101 is three and a half miles from the entrance to the community. The area is protected by the San Jose police department, the Santa Clara county sheriff's department, and the California highway patrol. The staffed San Jose City Fire Station #11 is just a quarter mile from the entrance to the Villages.

Within the community you will find a doctor's office and a restaurant. Located within two miles of the Villages are a medical clinic, a dry cleaners, a hair salon, a grocery and liquor store, and retail stores. A movie theater is 12 miles away. The nearest hospital is the Santa Teresa Community Hospital, eight miles from the development.

San Jose and its surrounding area offer many local attractions, including the Winchester Mystery House, the Rosicrucian Egyptian Museum, the American Museum of Quilts and Textiles, the Center for Performing Arts, the convention center, and the Japanese Friendship Gardens. There are also numerous local wineries and the historical Mission Santa Clara, which was founded by the Spaniards. San Jose State University, Evergreen Community College, and the University of Santa Clara are all fairly close to the community. Stanford University is 30 miles away.

RECREATION AND SOCIAL ACTIVITIES

The Villages offers a wide range of social and recreational activities. There is a recreation director on site, and the community publishes a weekly newsletter. Organized trips, on-site entertainment, and crafts are just a few of the activities offered by the association. There is also a 550-acre nature preserve within the Villages.

The community features both a 9-hole golf course and an 18-hole course, as well as a pro shop, a driving range, and buildings for parking golf carts. At the Villages, homeowners automatically belong to the golf and country club. Membership fees are included in the monthly community association assessment. Residents do pay nominal green fees, however.

The Villages has over 80 organizations, committees, and clubs. The riding club has access to the community stables and seven bridle paths. The Villages' lakes have over two miles of shoreline. Four clubhouses provide specialized rooms for those interested in photography, woodworking, and billiards; a library and an auditorium with a stage are also available. Clubhouses range in size from 1,071 square feet to 5,179 square feet.

HOMEOWNER ASSESSMENTS, TAXES, AND UTILITIES

Homeowners at the Villages automatically receive cable television connections, private golf club membership, use of all recreational facilities, maintenance and operation of community centers, maintenance of private roads, 24-hour security, payment of taxes on all common buildings and grounds, exterior building and street lighting, landscaping maintenance, roof repair and maintenance, trash collection, water services, home exterior maintenance, fire and comprehensive insurance, and full-time property management.

Currently, there are 1,994 completed homes out of an expected build-out of 2,700 homes. The 1,843 garden-style condominiums range in price from $125,000 to $375,000, with monthly community association assessments from $172 to $528. The 151 single-family homes in the community have a monthly assessment of $131.31 and cost between $325,000 and $445,000. The yearly property/municipal taxes are 1.25 percent of the purchase price.

There are many styles of architecture within the community, but each village neighborhood has one consistent style. Both cable and community television channels are available. The homes are primarily heated by gas sources, and the local municipality provides both sewer waste and water services. Well water is used for irrigation of the golf course. All utilities are underground. There are no extra storage facilities within the community.

Future amenities include a larger clubhouse to be built in 1996, another small clubhouse planned for 1992, and a corporation yard and recreation park expected to be finished in 1991.

RESTRICTIONS IN THE COMMUNITY

There is a community association and membership is mandatory. Because this is an age-restricted community, children are not allowed to live in the Villages. There is no restriction on age of visitors, but there are restrictions on length-of-stay. Pet restrictions follow the local city ordinance.

The association provides exterior building/grounds maintenance for all the recreational facilities and for the condominiums. Single-family homeowners provide their own building/grounds maintenance. Any proposed exterior modifications must be approved by the architectural control committee. Patios may be landscaped as owners wish, but common areas in the community may not be landscaped without architectural control committee approval. There is also a community garden plot for homeowners to practice their gardening skills.

The maximum number of residents in a dwelling may only exceed the number of bedrooms by one individual. There are no rental restrictions; however, certain information about the renters must be given to the management office. When a home is resold, a $100 transfer fee must be paid to the association to cover transfer costs. There are restrictions concerning types of vehicles that can be parked, parking locations, and the number of vehicles per unit. There is a special place to park recreational vehicles and boats.

WOODBRIDGE VILLAGE

31 Creek Rd.
Irvine, California 92714
714-786-1800

$180,000 to $900,000
9,292/9,292 Condos,
Townhomes, Single-family
Homes, and Apartments
Mixed Architecture

33 outdoor pools, 10 kiddie pools
10 miles to the Pacific Ocean
250 acres of open space
Ball-playing fields
20 lighted tennis courts

2 lakes (36 and 29 acres)
25 boat slips (16-foot maximum)
Hiking trails, picnic areas
24 outdoor tennis courts
Clubhouse

INTRODUCTION

Woodbridge Village association, a private master planned community of approximately 2,000 acres, is located within the city of Irvine, which has a population of 90,000. The association is responsible for maintaining approximately 250 deeded common acres, including many recreational amenities and a considerable amount of parkway and paseo landscaping. The first homes closed escrow in 1976; currently, 7,656 single-family detached homes, condominiums, and townhomes and 1,636 apartment units house approximately 27,000 residents. The entire spectrum of real estate values, from affordable housing to lakefront estates, is available in the community. All of the homes are located in proximity to numerous parks, lakes, tennis courts, shopping centers, medical care facilities, and business offices.

Woodbridge Village has received numerous awards and accolades over the years. In 1989, the Woodbridge Village association was named "Association of the Year" by the Community Associations Institute (CAI), a national trade organization for community associations with over 10,000 members nationwide. In a 1985 article, *Parents* magazine cited Woodbridge as an excellent community in which to raise a family. As a result of that article, many families, including the Donny Osmond family, moved to Woodbridge. Recently Woodbridge was highlighted in an article in *Sunset* magazine concerning their unique architectural improvements to homes.

Local police provide protection and a staffed fire department is located within the community. The Irvine Hospital is just two miles from the community. Situated in Orange County, Irvine is close to many of southern California's most famous attractions, such as Disneyland, Knott's Berry Farm, Hollywood, Universal Studios, and the Orange County Performing Arts Center.

RECREATION AND SOCIAL ACTIVITIES

Not only does Woodbridge Village have excellent physical recreational amenities (including 33 pools, two lakes, hiking trails, picnic areas, 24 tennis courts, and a clubhouse), but the association sponsors many events and activities for its homeowners and youth throughout the year. There are tennis competitions, swim meets (the kids at Woodbridge have won many conference titles), foot races, a Halloween haunted house (which attracted 1,400 people in 1989), an Easter egg hunt, Santa's visit, the menorah lighting program, a cabbage patch doll party, concerts, and trips. The biggest event the association sponsors is its annual Fourth of July extravaganza. Over 3,000 residents and their guests participate in races, bingo, picnics, volleyball, and a spectacular fireworks display.

There is a recreational director, and the association publishes a monthly newsletter. There are organized trips, on-site entertainment and crafts, and daycamp for children. There is even a big-wheel park for the children, with bridges, tunnels, inclines, and a toy gas station.

The community is very oriented towards public service. Homeowners participate in blood drives, CPR and first aid classes, swap meets, babysitting seminars, water safety and lifesaving classes, and kids' safety day. The community provides programs such as jazzercise classes, prenatal and postnatal exercise classes, cooking classes, dog obedience classes, seniors' bridge, guitar lessons, ballroom dance, swimming lessons, sailing lessons, garden clubs, and Boy Scout and Girl Scout activities.

HOMEOWNER ASSESSMENTS, TAXES, AND UTILITIES

The 32 neighborhood associations within Woodbridge are primarily responsible for the maintenance within the common areas of their own association, including landscaping, dwellings, private streets, and so on. Homeowners are actively involved in all phases of association business, and the Woodbridge board of directors strongly supports the community's committee structure.

The Woodbridge Village association has always been a leader in setting aside reserve funds for capital improvements and replacement. Prior to the adoption of reserve legislation in California, the association already had on its records over $1.5 million set aside for replacement of its assets. Today the association has over $3 million set aside for continual upgrading and improvement of common areas adding funds of nearly $500,000 annually.

There are 1,636 garden-style apartments, 4,620 townhomes and condominiums, 3,036 single-family homes at Woodbridge Village, each with a monthly master association assessment of $46. Individual neighborhood association assessments are separate. The homes range in price from $180,000 to $900,000. Gas provides the primary heating source. Both cable and community television channels are available. The local municipality provides water and sewer systems, and all utilities are below ground. Fifteen to 20 percent of the homes are investment units.

The Woodbridge Village association has 32 community service personnel, 46 maintenance personnel, and a recreational staff of 29 to 57 members (more in the summer). The association's maintenance staff is responsible for the upkeep of all private facilities, including two manmade lakes and 70 boats, two swimming lagoons and beaches, 22 swimming pools, 13 spas, 13 wading pools, 20 lighted tennis courts, 63 restrooms, and many parks and trails.

RESTRICTIONS IN THE COMMUNITY

Membership in the community association is mandatory. Any exterior modifications must be approved by the architectural committee. Some neighborhoods provide building and grounds maintenance; others don't.

Restrictions on age or length-of-stay for visitors do not exist here. Pets must be on a leash, and owners must clean up any droppings. There are no restrictions concerning how many people may occupy a unit nor are there any rental restrictions. There are no restrictions on resales of units except for certain restrictions about signs. Recreational vehicles may not be parked in the community. There are no special parking places for RVs or boats; however, within a 5-mile radius, various private storage areas are available.

MILILANI

95-303 Kaloapau Street
Mililani Town, Hawaii 96789
808-623-7300

$120,000 to $550,000
9,312/16,000 Mid-rise and
Garden-style Condos
and Single-family Homes
Contemporary Architecture

18-hole golf course	4 outdoor pools, 2 kiddie pools
10 miles to Pacific Ocean	67 acres of common area
3 picnic areas	9 ball-playing fields
6 outdoor tennis courts	4 lighted outdoor tennis courts
3 clubhouses	Handball/racquetball in city gym

INTRODUCTION

The Mililani town association was started by Dole Pineapple, a subsidiary of Castle & Cooke, which recognized the need for top-quality, affordable housing on the island of Oahu. The idea began to take shape in 1958 when forecasters noted that pineapple growth and production would decline, leaving the Dole company with excess lands.

Tourism, which increased heavily in the early 1960s, caused vertical expansion in the urban environment of Honolulu. But high-rise development didn't meet the desires of everyone on Oahu. By 1962, Mililani's original 3,500-acre master development plan had been adopted, outlining the ultimate development of 15,000 units with 50,000 to 55,000 residents. This master plan called for a mix of residential and commercial property, schools, churches, and recreation centers. The first home was not built until 1968.

In keeping with the physical and climatic characteristics of the hillside site, Mililani contains wide tree-lined streets; creatively-designed homes that allow space and light; large lots with ideal yards for cookouts and family gatherings; uncluttered views free of TV antennas or utility poles; and lush green parks, playgrounds, and tot lots.

The most recent example of intelligent planning is the new Mililani town center, strategically located to provide easy access to the entire community. This will eventually be the third largest shopping center in the state of Hawaii. In addition to department stores, supermarkets, shops, and boutiques, the center will also contain a full service medical clinic and thousands of square feet of office space.

The Mililani town association is responsible for the upkeep and maintenance of all common areas in the community and the operation of all community recreation centers and facilities. The community employs a full-time staff of 30 as well as 30 part-time employees, including lifeguards, water safety staffers, various recreation instructors, and security guards.

H-2, a major Hawaiian highway, runs through the property. The nearest major airport is in Honolulu, 25 miles from the site. Local police provide coverage, and a staffed fire department is on site. A hospital with emergency facilities is eight miles from Mililani.

RECREATION AND SOCIAL ACTIVITIES

Mililani is certainly a complete community: There are churches, elementary schools, a state public library, and a high school within its property. Mililani's pedestrian walkway system offers residents a traffic-free route to schools, shopping, and other community destinations; it is also ideal for jogging or cycling. Mililani has over 50 acres of parks, and the four completed recreation centers offer tennis, basketball, and volleyball courts and swimming pools. The association employs a recreation director and publishes a monthly newsletter. Daycare facilities are also located within the community. Local police provide a 24-hour patrol, but there are no perimeter restrictions for access.

The community centers have rooms for meetings, games, and parties. Activities for children include the community Pop Warner leagues, bobby sox teams, the acclaimed Marlin swim team, carnivals, fairs, and holiday events of all kinds. Social groups within the community include parenting groups, the friends of the library, the bonsai club, the travel club, women's clubs, and many civic groups.

One of Oahu's most beautiful golf courses is located at Mililani. The superbly maintained 6,360-yard public course offers a challenging game and panoramic views of the island's Leeward Coast and Waianae Mountains.

HOMEOWNER ASSESSMENTS, TAXES, AND UTILITIES

Mililani offers mid-rise and garden-style condominiums, townhomes, and single-family homes to choose from. The 358 mid-rise condos range price in from $120,000 to $160,000, while the 1,227 garden-style units cost $140,000 to $350,000. Currently there are 1,307 townhomes with prices from $200,000 to $350,000 and 6,415 single-family homes with prices from $250,000 to $550,000.

All owners pay $16 per month to the Mililani town association. Neighborhood fees, if any, are separate.

Some of the features offered to buyers include an enclosed garage with an automatic door opener, bay windows, ceramic tile kitchen counters, double sinks in both baths, natural oak cabinets, mirrored wardrobe doors in the master bedroom, wood louvered pantry doors, and a covered lanai.

Homeowners have access to cable television, but there are no community channels. Electricity provides all heat sources. Sewer and water services are provided by the local municipality, and all utilities are below ground. There are no extra storage facilities within Mililani.

RESTRICTIONS IN THE COMMUNITY

Membership in the Mililani town association is mandatory. All building and exterior modifications must have prior approval of the design committee and must receive a permit. Installation of individual landscaping is permitted.

There are no restrictions on age or length-of-stay for visitors. Businesses operated from a home are only allowed if there are no employees working on the property, no signs, and no additional traffic. No more than five unrelated persons may occupy a single unit. Only house pets may be kept; breeding or sale of pets are not permitted. Other than canaries, parakeets, and other songbirds, no fowl may be maintained in any home. You are allowed to set up only one "for sale" or "for rent" sign with a maximum face area of three square feet. House trailers, mobile homes, and tents are prohibited. Trucks with a capacity over one ton are also prohibited. The association does not provide a special area for oversized vehicles.

WAILEA RESORT

161 Wailea Ike Place
Kihei, Hawaii 96753
808-879-4465

$400,000 to $5,000,000
1,400/1,400 Garden-style
Condos and Single-family
Homes, Hotels, and Lots
Mixed Architecture

2 18-hole USGA-rated golf courses
1 beachfront hiking trail
1 ball-playing field
5 lighted tennis courts
Exercise room

17 outdoor pools
6 picnic areas
11 hard-surface tennis courts
3 grass-surface tennis courts
Steam and sauna facilities

INTRODUCTION

Wailea Resort is a 1,500-acre private residential resort on the southwest coast of Maui. It lies at the foot of Mt. Haleakala, a 10,023-foot dormant volcano. Planned as a low-rise, low-density community, this development currently consists of luxury hotels, condominium units, and single-family homes and homesites. Hotels at the site include the Maui Intercontinental Wailea, the Stouffer Wailea Beach Resort, the Four Seasons Resort Wailea, the Grand Hyatt Wailea Resort and Spa, the Kea Lani Suite Hotel, and the Diamond Resort.

Wailea Development Company, a subsidiary of Alexander and Baldwin, Inc., directed the community's initial years of growth. In February 1989, Wailea was purchased by Wailea Resort Company, Ltd., a subsidiary of Shinwa International, Inc., a Hawaiian corporation. From the start, the development at Wailea has been guided by a philosophy of respect for the community and the natural environment. The maximum densities established by Wailea's master plan are 3,500 hotel rooms, 3,000 condominium units and 800 to 1,000 single-family homes.

Recently, Wailea widened its principal thoroughfare, Wailea Alanui, to four lanes separated by a tree-lined median. Air transportation is provided by the Kahului Airport, which is also on the island of Maui. Local police provide coverage, and a staffed fire department is nearby. The closest hospital with emergency facilities is located in Wailuku, 15 miles from the community.

Two dozen stores and restaurants occupy the 34,500-square-foot shopping village, which encloses a grassy mall. With services ranging from banking to real estate, the shopping village also serves as Wailea's town center and is the frequent site of cultural events. An expansion that will at least double the current size of the Wailea shopping village is in the planning stages. A pharmacy and a medical clinic are four miles away, and the nearest movie theater is 17 miles from Wailea Resort.

The community's central location puts you near the interesting sites of Maui: You can take a helicopter 10,000 feet to the top of Mt. Haleakala, see the island's only winery on the slopes of Mt. Haleakala, or visit the majestic Iao Needle. Wailea is just a short drive from historical Lahaina, Maui's famous whaling port of yesteryear.

RECREATION AND SOCIAL ACTIVITIES

Golf, tennis, and beachcombing provide hours of entertainment at this island paradise. Ownership at this community makes you eligible for golf and tennis club memberships and discounts on daily rates.

The Wailea Blue Course was completed in 1972. From the championship tees, it stretches more than 6,700 yards on rolling terrain dotted with natural lava rock formations. Hibiscus, plumeria, bougainvillea, and hundreds of flowering plants and trees line the course. Home of the women's Kemper Open, the Blue Course offers spacious fairways and spectacular vistas. This par 72 course's four lakes and 72 bunkers make it a great challenge.

The Orange Course is designed to test you, with higher elevations, narrower fairways, wicked doglegs left and right, and one of the world's most unusual hazards, ancient Hawaiian stone walls. Discovered on more than half the holes, these Hawaiian stone walls date back hundreds of years and have been left intact. This par 72 course is considered by the American Society of Golf Course Architects to be one of the best American courses built in the last 25 years. Both courses at Wailea Resort have been placed among the top 75 resort courses in the country by *Golf Digest*. Conveniently located between both courses is the Wailea golf clubhouse, providing a pro shop, a driving range, and lessons. Golf membership rates range from $425 to $1,150 per year.

The Wailea Tennis Club offers 14 courts. In all of Hawaii, only the Wailea Tennis Club has three grass courts (known as Wimbledon West) available to the public on a daily basis. Three of the courts are lighted for night games, and there is a half-court for practice. The pro shop carries the latest clothing, equipment, and accessories for rent or sale. Adjacent to the pro shop is the club's stadium court, the annual site of exhibitions and USTA-sanctioned tournaments. Tennis lessons are available at hourly rates, and the Wimbledon West Tennis Academy offers three- and five-day packages to improve your game. Tennis membership rates average $550 to $1,250 per year.

Each hotel employs a recreation director and offers valet and concierge and shuttle bus services. The community association publishes a monthly newsletter and provides management of beach accesses and common areas. Catering is available from community restaurants. There are organized on-site crafts, maid services, and 24-hour security by both patrol and electronic gates.

HOMEOWNER ASSESSMENTS, TAXES, AND UTILITIES

There are currently 1,111 low-rise condominiums that cost between $400,000 and $2.5 million with an average monthly community association assessment of $400 and average municipal taxes of about $2,500 per year. The 294 single-family homes range in price from $600,000 to $5 million, with an average monthy community association assesment of $125 and yearly municipal taxes of about $3,500.

Contemporary and Hawaiian architectural styles are prevalent. Housing areas are grouped in separate neighborhoods. Some of the neighborhoods have their own gate-guarded access as well as private neighborhood amenities such as pools, recreation centers, spas, and parks.

Cable television stations are available to all homes at the site. Home heating is not required. City authorities provide both waste and water services, and all utilities are underground. There are no extra storage facilities within the development.

RESTRICTIONS IN THE COMMUNITY

There is a community association and membership is mandatory. The associations provide all exterior maintenance for the condominiums and all common property. Any exterior building or landscaping changes must be approved by the association.

There are some pet restrictions in the community. There are no restrictions on age or length-of-stay for visitors. Only single families may occupy a home. Time-sharing of units and operating a business from a home are prohibited.

There are no restrictions regarding resale of units. Overnight parking on streets is prohibited. The community does not provide any extra parking areas for recreational vehicles or boats.

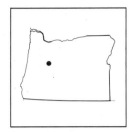

BLACK BUTTE RANCH

Hwy. 20, P.O. Box 8000
Black Butte Ranch, Oregon
97759
503-595-6211

$125,000 to $750,000
1,203/1,255 Single-family
Homes, Condos, and Lots
Contemporary Architecture

2 18-hole USGA-rated golf courses
1 lake with three quarter mile of shore
1,800 acres of forest
1 ball-playing field
3 lighted outdoor tennis courts

4 outdoor pools, 2 kiddie pools
Cross-country skiing
12 hiking trails, 4 picnic areas
19 outdoor tennis courts
Horse stables and bridle path

INTRODUCTION

Set among seven majestic mountains, Black Butte Ranch is surrounded by ponderosa pine forests, lush meadows, and streams lined with aspens. Located in the sun belt country of central Oregon, the community is 31 miles north of Bend on Highway 20 and just eight miles west of the western theme town of Sisters, the home of the Sisters Rodeo. Black Butte is a scenic two- to three-hour drive from Portland, Salem, and Eugene. The Redmond Municipal Airport, 30 miles northeast of the Ranch, provides the nearest air transportation.

Black Butte Ranch is virtually self-contained, providing its own fire department, police department, utilities (including water and sewer services), and maintenance staff. The nearest hospital with emergency facilities is located in Bend, 28 miles from the site.

Along with residential homes, Black Butte Ranch offers a guest lodge that provides a variety of accommodations from deluxe hotel-type bedrooms to one-, two-, and three-bedroom condominium suites, with all the amenities of a first-class resort. The community is being developed by the Black Butte Ranch Corporation. The first home was built in 1970.

Within the property of the Ranch, you will find a grocery store, restaurants, and retail shops. Other services are nearby. The Deschutes National Forest offers opportunities for hiking, fishing, boating, horseback riding, and some of the finest cross-country and alpine skiing in the Northwest. Other area attractions include the headwaters of the Metolius River, the Pacific Crest trail and the Sisters wilderness area.

RECREATION AND SOCIAL ACTIVITIES

The Ranch is known for its two meticulously-kept 18-hole golf courses, as picturesque as they are exciting. Homeownership does not automatically entitle you to golf privileges; there is an annual $600 fee.

There are 19 tennis courts, four outdoor swimming pools, and 16 miles of bike and jogging trails that thread throughout the 1,800 acres of forested grounds. Within the community are 12 hiking trails, four picnic areas, horse stables, and one bridle path. Pro and sports shops on the site offer recreational apparel, sports equipment, accessories, and gifts.

Guests at the lodge are provided with daily housekeeping services and a courtesy card that allows access to all the Ranch's amenities. Conference facilities for small groups are also available.

There is a recreation director on site, and the association publishes a monthly newsletter. The lodge offers on-site entertainment and catering services. The association organizes activities for teens but does not provide daycare for small children. Black Butte Ranch is highly secured; there are both guarded and electronic access gates as well as a 24-hour patrol within the community.

HOMEOWNER ASSESSMENTS, TAXES, AND UTILITIES

All of the 1,255 lots at the Ranch have been sold. To date, 1,100 single-family homes have been built. The single-family homes range in price from $125,000 to $750,000, with annual property taxes between $2,000 and $8,000 and community association dues of $54 per month (for both developed and undeveloped lots).

Many owners of the condominium units participate in the lodge's rental program. The 103 condominiums range in price from $100,000 to $130,000, with master community association fees of $54 per month.

There are 50 one-bedroom homes, 300 two-bedroom homes, 600 three-bedroom homes, and 150 homes with four bedrooms. Both cable and community television channels are available. Homes are primarily heated by electricity. The community has its own sewer waste and water system. All utilities are underground. There are no extra storage facilities within the community.

RESTRICTIONS IN THE COMMUNITY

Black Butte Ranch has a community association, and membership is mandatory. Single-family homeowners provide their own exterior building and grounds maintenance. The association provides maintenance for all amenities and infrastructure. All new construction or remodeling must be reviewed and approved by the community's architectural review committee. There are strict guidelines regarding landscaping at Black Butte Ranch. Homeowners may not plant any lawns, gardens, and so forth. All areas must be kept in a natural state.

There are no age or length-of-stay restrictions for guests. All dogs must be kept on a leash. There are no restrictions on how many people may occupy a single unit, nor are there any rental or resale restrictions. Operating a business from a home is prohibited. Parking is not allowed on roads; all vehicles must have a current identification sticker. The association provides a special area to park recreational vehicles, boats, and the like.

LITTLE WHALE COVE

Highway 101
Depoe Bay, Oregon 97035
503-636-0440

$85,000 to $550,000
150/312 Townhomes, Single-
family Homes, and Lots
Contemporary Beach Homes
and Cabins

1 indoor pool with spa	Freshwater ocean pond
Private beach	Located on a ½ mile of ocean headlands
2½ miles of hiking trails	3 gazebos for whale-watching
2 outdoor tennis courts	2 indoor tennis courts
Clubhouse	Sauna

INTRODUCTION

Sheltered by tall stands of Sitka spruce, Little Whale Cove is a secluded nook on the Oregon coast. It is a 142-acre planned development located a half mile south of Depoe Bay on Oregon's Highway 101. Depoe Bay is a small, quaint fishing village on the central Oregon coast. It boasts the world's smallest year-round navigable harbor and the famous "spouting horn" on its seawall. Portland is 100 miles from Little Whale Cove. The community was planned for a low density to lessen the impact on the varied ecosystem throughout the area.

The 142 acres that constitute Little Whale Cove were the site of the old Maling Estate. Bertrand Maling was an industrialist who pioneered frozen food processing and later sold his patent to Birds Eye. In the early 1930s, he built a four-level white brick mansion on the basalt cliff overlooking the Pacific. The house was used as a navigational marker and is still cited on navigational maps.

Maling weighed 320 pounds and the imposing mansion was constructed to fit his proportions, including made-to-order furniture such as his black bathtub, which was designed with giant-sized fixtures. The grounds were as spectacular as the house. There was a surrey track for show horses in the meadow along the long driveway leading to the house. There also was a heated poultry house and a large barn. Maling died in his mid-50s in 1943, but the house remained in the family until 1956. The estate then went through a number of owners, and the house fell in disrepair.

In 1972, Halvorson-Mason purchased the estate; in 1978, development plans were first made for a 150-unit condominium development, later expanded to add an additional 240 lots. The Halvorson-Mason Corporation was originally in heavy construction, building many roads and bridges in the Northwest and several dams on the Columbia River. Twenty years ago the corporation entered into land development.

There are no services offered within this unique community, but all needed services are nearby. Stores, services, and tourist facilities are set up for a thriving tourist trade. Retail shops, restaurants, a liquor store, and a hair salon are all within one mile of Little Whale Cove. A pharmacy, a medical clinic, a dry cleaners, and a movie theater are ten miles away. The nearest grocery store is three miles from the site.

Other area attractions include the Newport Performing Arts Center, the Mark Hatfield Marine Science Center, the Oregon Coast Aquarium, and factory outlet shopping in Lincoln City. The Oregon coast is spectacular and all beaches are public, except for the private beach at Little Whale Cove. Depoe Bay offers salmon and crab fishing, bottom fishing, clamming, bird- and whale-watching, deer and elk hunting, and beachcombing.

The area is provided police protection by the county sheriff's department. There is also a volunteer fire department. The nearest hospital is in Lincoln City, 12 miles from the site.

RECREATION AND SOCIAL ACTIVITIES

Little Whale Cove offers a recreation center, an indoor swimming pool with a spa, and both indoor and outdoor tennis facilities. There are over two miles of bicycle and hiking trails throughout the project, running along meadows, woods, and the coastline. Little Whale Cove has gazebos placed in strategic spots for whale-watching, as well as various other lookouts within the community. The clubhouse offers sauna facilities.

Little Whale Cove has a security entrance gate and private roads. As noted before, the beach at the community is reserved solely for the use of its residents. The first three phases of the community are complete. The final phases will add more destination points and bike and walking trails. The community is expected to be completed in 1998. All club and recreation facilities are available to home-owners as part of their membership in the association. However, indoor tennis has a $10 charge for 1½ hours of play.

HOMEOWNER ASSESSMENTS, TAXES, AND UTILITIES

The policy at Little Whale Cove is to keep the site as natural as possible, with low density and no polished or manicured look. Out of the 240 single-family lots, 110 have been sold, 127 are still available, and speculation homes in the $150,000 to $180,000 range are being constructed on three lots. Currently, 54 of the 110 lots hold finished houses. Out of the 35 townhome condominiums, 29 have been built. The townhomes average about $85,000, with a monthly community association assessment of $55. The single-family homes range in price from $150,000 to $550,000, with a monthly assessment of $45. Yearly property/municipal taxes for both townhomes and single-family homes are $19.20 per $1,000 of assessed value.

Most of the homes built are contemporary beach houses and cabins. Buyers have a choice of oceanview lots, wooded lots, or lots adjacent to common properties and paths. Both cable and community television channels are available. Homes are heated by gas or electricity. The local municipality provides both sewer waste and water facilities. All utilities are located underground. There are no extra storage areas within the community.

RESTRICTIONS IN THE COMMUNITY

There is a community association, and membership is mandatory. Individual homeowners are responsible for their own building/grounds maintenance. The association provides exterior maintenance for common areas and amenities.

Little Whale Cove has an architectural control committee that approves all building designs. Approval from the Depoe Bay planning commission must also be obtained. Landscaping and building guidelines have been established for all lots. There is no time requirement for commencement of construction once a lot has been purchased.

There are no age or length-of-stay restrictions for visitors. Animals may not be bred or raised for commercial purposes. A reasonable number of household pets are allowed if they are controlled and not a nuisance to others. All pets must be leashed. Short-term renters are not permitted to have pets.

Short-term (weekend) rentals are limited to six people per home. Operating a business from a home is prohibited. There are no restrictions regarding resale of units. Parking is not allowed on streets. Renters are limited to two cars per unit. Motorized vehicles are not allowed on the trails. Owners may not store or leave boats, trailers, mobile homes, RVs, and the like on any lot or common area.

Owners are asked to help preserve the balance of nature in the tidepools by not touching or removing any marine life.

MOUNTAIN PARK

#2 Mt. Jefferson Terrace
Lake Oswego, Oregon 97035
503-635-3561

$40,000 to $750,000
3,500/3,800 Mid-rise and Garden Condos, Apartments, Townhomes, and Single-family Homes
Mixed Architecture

1 indoor 50-meter pool
15 miles of hiking trails
1 ball-playing field
20,000-square-foot clubhouse
Exercise room

185 acres of open space
4 picnic areas
2 outdoor tennis courts
Gymnasium
Steam/sauna facilities

INTRODUCTION

Mountain Park is situated on 700 acres of wooded land on the slopes of Mount Sylvania, a small dormant volcano between Portland and the city of Lake Oswego. Mountain Park's boundaries enclose homes, townhouses, apartments, services (a dry cleaners, a hair salon, a grocery and liquor store, restaurants, and retail shops), a convalescent hospital, parks, and superb recreational facilities featuring a community-owned recreation center with a 50-meter indoor pool. Nearby is a privately owned, elaborate racquet club. A pharmacy, a medical clinic, and a movie theater are all within three miles of the development.

Mountain Park is an affluent, private planned community with a projected population of 12,000 people. The community is almost complete; 3,500 of its 3,800 homes have been sold. Mountain Park was developed by the Halvorson-Mason Corporation of Lake Oswego. The first home was sold in 1970.

Lake Oswego, home to Mountain Park, was once a small town and has grown into a thriving small city. The 30,576 residents are actively involved in their city's cultural, governmental, and scholastic activities. Built around the three-mile-long lake that shares its name, Lake Oswego has grown from a resort-like town into a thriving community.

Interstate 5 is just two miles away. Portland International Airport is located 25 miles from the community. Police coverage is provided by the local municipality, the county sheriff's office, and the Oregon state police. There is a staffed fire department nearby. The nearest hospital with emergency facilities is Meridian Park, just six miles from the complex. Portland Community College is located just outside the complex, and Lewis and Clark College is just two miles away.

RECREATION AND SOCIAL ACTIVITIES

The 20,000-square-foot clubhouse contains a 50-meter indoor pool, a weight room, a gymnasium, a game room, a billiards room, a lounge and party room, and two steam and sauna rooms.

The community has 185 acres of open space and 15 miles of walking and jogging trails. Some are lighted during evening hours for convenience and safety. There are four picnic areas, one ball-playing field, and two outdoor tennis courts.

The association employs a recreation director, publishes a monthly newsletter and provides activities for teens, daycare facilities for children, and on-site entertainment. Both Lake Oswego and the Willamette River are excellent for boating and fishing. By 1995, the association plans to add one or two miles of hiking paths. Homeownership at Mountain Park automatically entitles you to all the community facilities.

HOMEOWNER ASSESSMENTS, TAXES, AND UTILITIES

At Mountain Park, you can buy a building site, select an architect or builder, and build your own single-family home. You also have the option of buying a finished home ready for occupancy. Some of Oregon's finest builders build at the site. Besides the condominiums, the community also has a few apartment complexes.

Mountain Park is a diverse private community. There are 500 mid-rise condominiums and apartments, 1,000 garden-style condominiums and apartments, 1,000 townhomes, and 1,000 single-family homes. The mid-rise condos range from $40,000 to $90,000, and owners pay a monthly community association assessment of $16. The garden-style condos average $60,000 to $170,000, and owners pay monthly assessments of $26. The townhomes cost between $60,000 and $170,000, with owners paying $26 per month to the association. The existing single-family homes cost between $100,000 to about $750,000 (the price may be higher if you build your own home on one of the few remaining vacant lots), and owners pay $32 per month in community association assessments. Individual condominium association and neighborhood association assessments, if any, are separate. Depending on size, location and amenities, apartments rent from $550 to over $1,200 per month. Association assessments for each apartment unit are $16 per month and are included in the rent.

Both cable and community television channels are available. Homes are heated by either gas or electricity and the local municipality provides both sewer waste disposal and water systems. All utilities are underground. There is an RV storage lot on site.

RESTRICTIONS IN THE COMMUNITY

Mountain Park has a community association, and membership is mandatory. The association maintains all common property, amenities, and landscaping; homeowners maintain their own private property. Any exterior modifications must meet the "harmony of external design" criteria published by the association. There are minimum square footage requirements and height maximums for single-family homes built in this community.

There are no restrictions on age or length-of-stay for visitors. No animals or fowls may be raised on the property except for domestic dogs, cats, or caged birds kept within the dwelling. If a pet is outside the private property, it must be leashed. There are no restrictions regarding how many people can occupy a single unit, nor are there any resale restrictions. No businesses are allowed to operate from a dwelling. Recreational vehicles, boats, campers, and the like must be parked in garages. These types of vehicles may not be parked in driveways or on undeveloped lots within the community.

The association retains the right to limit the number of guests per household and to charge reasonable admission or user fees for recreational facilities.

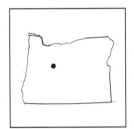

SUNRIVER

P.O. Box 3278
Sunriver, Oregon 97707
503-593-2411

$55,000 to $1,000,000+
2,800/4,100 Garden-style
Condos, Townhomes,
Single-family Homes,
and Lots
Northwest Contemporary
Architecture

2 18-hole USGA-rated golf courses	1 indoor pool
2 outdoor pools	2 kiddie pools
1 lake with 1 mile of shore	Downhill skiing 18 miles away
Cross-country skiing	28 hiking trails and paved bike paths
2 picnic areas	1 ball-playing field
28 outdoor tennis courts	3 indoor tennis courts
Handball/racquetball	Horse stables with 3 bridle paths
Private airstrip	Large clubhouse

INTRODUCTION

Sunriver is a 3,300-acre resort-residential community located 15 miles from Bend in central Oregon. In operation since 1968, the community currently contains approximately 1,850 single-family homes and over 775 condominiums. As of 1990, Sunriver had 1,400 year-round residents.

The community is also home to the Sunriver Lodge, which houses dining and lounge facilities including the Meadows Dining Room, the Provision Company, and the Owl's Nest Lounge. The Par Patio at the Sunriver Lodge and the 19th Hole restaurant at the North golf course are open during the golf season.

The Sunriver Village provides a grocery store, a liquor store, various restaurants, a bakery, beauty salons, a post office, a candy shop, a book store, gift and apparel shops, boutiques, banks, a florist, a sports shop, and a variety of professional services. Near the mall are a service station and a 24-hour family emergency center. Sunriver is a complete community, with public services such as a department of public safety, emergency first aid, a security force, the 911 emergency system, a volunteer fire department, an ambulance service, and street maintenance.

The Sunriver Utility Company provides water and sewer service to Sunriver residents. With its own water distribution facilities and waste treatment plant, the utility company can adequately service all existing dwellings. All electrical and telephone lines at Sunriver are underground.

Sunriver's 5,500-foot-long paved and lighted airstrip is the third busiest in the state of Oregon and one of the longest private airstrips in the west. The nearby Redland Bend Airport offers commercial service by Horizon Air and United Express.

Mt. Bachelor, only 18 miles from Sunriver, offers alpine and nordic skiing; the season extends from late November to July as a result of the summit lift. Nordic skiing is also popular at Sunriver and the adjacent Deschutes National Forest. Other winter activities include guided snowmobile rides in the Deschutes National Forest, sleigh rides, and an ice-skating rink. A ski shuttle is provided to Sunriver Lodge guests.

RECREATION AND SOCIAL ACTIVITIES

Recreational facilities at Sunriver include two 18-hole championship golf courses. The North golf course was designed by Robert Trent Jones. The course may be used on a daily greens fee basis, or owners may purchase annual memberships entitling them to unlimited play. Lessons are available from professionals at both courses. Men and women's golf groups play weekly.

The community also offers over 30 miles of paved bike paths, 28 outdoor tennis courts, two swimming pool complexes, an outdoor hot tub complex, stables, the racquet club (which includes three indoor tennis courts), a marina with canoe rentals, a nature center, an arts and craft center, and a bike shop.

Some of the clubs at Sunriver include the anglers' club, art competitions, a bridge club, a dining-out club, a flying club, a movie club, the women's club, a camera club, and so on.

Sunriver has set aside nearly 30 miles of paths for bicycle and pedestrian use only. Boats, canoes, rafts, and all necessary boating equipment are available at the marina. Local whitewater rafting trips can also be arranged. A well-designed children's playground is adjacent to the Lodge's tennis courts. You can fish on the Deschutes, Fall, or Spring rivers or on one of the many lakes that are close to Sunriver. Fishing seasons are variable, usually beginning in late April at lower elevations and in late May at the higher lakes.

In the Tennis Hill area, Fort Rock Park provides recreational facilities for softball, volleyball, and horseshoes as well as a large field that can be used for soccer, baseball, touch football, and so forth. The community's very popular Fourth of July picnic is held here. Mary McCallum Park, on the river adjacent to the marina, is only open to owners and has picnic and barbecue facilities and a shelter with a fireplace. Sunriver Stables offers lessons and trail rides during the summer season as well as boarding by the day, week, or month. The stables are situated along the river on the road to the airport.

Lake Aspen, a wildlife habitat near the nature center with observation points and paths, is the home of ducks, geese, otters, and other native wildlife.

Situated within the Tennis Village, the Sunriver racquet club offers three indoor tennis courts, five racquetball courts, an indoor pool and jacuzzi, a sauna, locker rooms, a pro shop, and an exercise room with a variety of equipment. You must be a member to use the club facilities. There is a $1,600 initiation fee and a monthly $60 fee.

The Sunriver owners' association publishes a monthly newsletter. Valet and concierge services are available for lodge guests. The restaurants within the community provide catering services. Daycare for children and activities for teens are also provided by the Lodge. There are no perimeter restrictions around Sunriver, but there is a 24-hour patrol within the community.

HOMEOWNER ASSESSMENTS, TAXES, AND UTILITIES

Currently, there are 2,035 single-family homes at Sunriver, ranging in price from $85,000 to over $1 million. The 754 garden-style condominiums and the 55 townhomes cost $55,000 to $250,000. Single-family homeowners pay $39.72 per month in community association assessments. Owners of garden-style condos and townhomes also pay this amount, as well as a monthly neighborhood association fee of $69 and up. Also available at Sunriver, lots cost from $25,000 to $250,000. Northwest contemporary architecture is the style of all homes in the community.

Both cable and community television channels are available. Gas and electricity provide the primary heat source for the community. All utilities are underground. There are extra storage facilities within the community.

RESTRICTIONS IN THE COMMUNITY

Sunriver has a community association, and membership is mandatory. Single-family homeowners provide their own exterior building and grounds maintenance. The condominium association provides building and grounds maintenance for the condo and townhome owners and for all association-owned facilities. Any exterior modifications or landscaping must first be approved by the Sunriver design review and control committee.

There are no age or length-of-stay restrictions for visitors. Pets are allowed, but leash laws for dogs and cats are enforced when these animals are outside. Maximum occupation of a single home is governed by Deschutes County. Generally there are no rental restrictions; however, in certain neighborhood condo associations and single-family areas, renters are restricted to minimum leases of 60 to 90 days. Operating a retail business from a home at Sunriver is prohibited. There are no restrictions on the resale of units. Parking on the streets is prohibited within the community. Recreational vehicles are not allowed to park on the property, but the association does provide a separate parking area for oversized vehicles.

SUDDEN VALLEY

2145 Lake Whatcom Blvd.
Bellingham, Washington 98226
206-734-6430

$50,000 to $100,000
2,500/4,000 Garden-style and
Mid-rise Condos and
Single-family Homes
Mixed Architecture

18-hole USGA-rated golf course	2 outdoor pools
2 lakes with 2 miles of shore	90 boat slips
7 hiking trails	25 picnic areas
2 ball-playing fields	5 outdoor tennis courts
3 lighted tennis courts	Clubhouse, gymnasium
Exercise room	Sauna facilities

INTRODUCTION

Sudden Valley community association, located eight miles from Bellingham and about 30 miles south of the Canadian border, has changed tremendously in its 20-year history. All of the 4,000 lots at the site have been sold, but only 1,400 single-family homes and condominiums have been built thus far. The community grew slowly until 1986 when Vancouver hosted Expo, causing hundreds of thousands of people to pass through the area. National magazines began to present the Pacific Northwest as a great place to live. By 1989, there was a wave of California and Alaskan buyers, with others from around the country. The first homes at Sudden Valley were weekend cottages, but after 1986, permanent residences began to appear.

The history of Sudden Valley reveals that its residents pull together in adversity. In 1983, rainstorms caused extensive flooding in Whatcom County; Sudden Valley alone suffered more than $1 million in damages along Austin Creek, where the community golf course is located. In the days following the flood, property owners scooped, scraped, and carried away debris and silt from the course. The managing agent and the board of directors negotiated long-term financing to rebuild the damaged course and property along the creek. This debt was paid off in 1989 by the association.

I-5 is just 8 miles from the site. Police protection is provided by the county sheriff's office, and both a staffed and a volunteer fire department are close to the site. The Bellingham International Airport is 25 miles away. A hospital with emergency care facilities is 15 miles from the complex.

Within a few miles of the community you will find a pharmacy, a medical clinic, a dry cleaners, a hair salon, liquor and grocery stores, retail shops, and movie theaters. A restaurant is located within the development. A large flea market and the Sudden Valley Summer Festival are also in the area.

RECREATION AND SOCIAL ACTIVITIES

The property is located on the west shore of Lake Whatcom, providing many recreational opportunities for residents. There are 90 boat slips (16-foot maximum) and a marina, hiking trails, many picnic areas, and two ball-playing fields.

The clubhouse offers a gymnasium, an exercise room, and sauna facilities. An 18-hole golf course is the site of summer golf tournaments. Other community activities include the Hobie Cat Regatta and the Summer Festival. From October through January, major events include the annual Halloween party (attended by hundreds of kids and adults), a Christmas gift exchange and potluck, the annual party to decorate the country club, the Christmas home tour, Santa Claus' visit to the Recreation Center, and the New Year's Eve party.

The association sponsors monthly potluck dinners with an average attendance of 50 to 100 people. The association also sponsors an annual Easter Egg hunt and a fishing derby. Sudden Valley employs a recreation director and publishes a monthly newspaper. There are organized trips and on-site entertainment for residents. Catering and maid service are available, and there is a 24-hour security patrol within the community. Future amenities include a craft studio and an interconnecting trail system as well as upgrading of many current facilities.

HOMEOWNER ASSESSMENTS, TAXES, AND UTILITIES

Sudden Valley offers both garden-style and mid-rise condominiums along with single-family homes. The current prices for homes at this community range from $50,000 to over $100,000. All homeowners pay an annual community association assessment of $340. Property taxes are paid to the local county.

Both cable and community television channels are available. Electricity provides the primary heating source, with natural gas becoming available in 1991. The local municipality provides both sewer waste and water systems. All utilities are below ground. There are extra storage facilities within the community.

The economy of Whatcom County has blossomed tremendously in the last few years, having a positive effect on Sudden Valley land sales and resort revenue. Therefore, the community association's board of trustees has recently begun to formulate a long-range plan for the community, including many homeowner suggestions and committee participation in the planning process. Even absentee owners were queried for input. The long-range plan for Sudden Valley should guide the community into the 90s.

RESTRICTIONS IN THE COMMUNITY

There is a community association, and membership is mandatory. Individual homeowners are responsible for their own building/grounds maintenance. Any exterior modifications to homes must meet association guidelines. There are no restrictions regarding landscaping.

There are no restrictions regarding age or length-of-stay for visitors. There are no pet restrictions. Guidelines also govern maximum occupation of a residence and rentals of a home. There are no restrictions on the resale of units. The association provides a special area to park recreational vehicles, boats, and the like.

Sudden Valley is a declared wildlife and bird sanctuary; therefore, use of firearms, molestation of birds and their areas or eggs, and the molestation of other wildlife are prohibited. Burning trash, paper, or leaves is also prohibited. It is the responsibility of property owners to remove dead trees, bushes, and the like from their property. Motorbikes and terrain vehicles are only allowed on paved roads within the community.

Chapter 12

Rockies
Colorado
Nevada
Wyoming

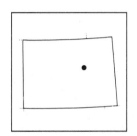

HEATHER GARDENS

2888 S. Heather Gardens Way
Aurora, Colorado 80014
303-755-0652

$38,000 to $250,000
2,426/2,426 Townhomes,
High-rise Condos, and
Single-family Homes
Contemporary Architecture

9-hole USGA-rated golf course
Over 100 acres of open space
Clubhouse over 15,000 square feet
Steam and sauna facilities

1 indoor pool, 2 outdoor pools
1 picnic area
Auditorium, exercise room
3 lighted tennis courts

INTRODUCTION

Just four miles from Denver, Heather Gardens is a 198-acre private adult community located in Aurora, Colorado. There are 4,000 residents living in 2,426 living units. This community is age-restricted: Owners must be at least 39 years of age, and no permanent residents under age 16 may live in the development. The first unit was built in 1973.

The Heather Gardens association took full control and responsibility for the community in 1983. At that time, ownership of the community center and recreational facilities, the golf course, and maintenance shops was still in the hands of the developer. On June 6, 1983 the association purchased the property from the developer for $2.3 million. To finance the purchase, the owners voted to establish the Heather Gardens metropolitan district and to issue $2.5 million of municipal bonds by the district, to be retired over a 20-year period. The bond proceeds were used to purchase the property, pay the underwriter's fee, and provide a reserve for interest and debt retirement.

Composed of the owners, the Heather Gardens association is directed by an elected board of trustees and a staff of 52 full-time employees. Composed of the residents, the Heather Gardens metropolitan district is a quasi-governmental authority that owns the principal recreational facilities (clubhouse, golf course, and so on) and is responsible for their oversight as well as the payment of the debt obligation to bondholders. The district is administered by its own separate board of directors, elected from among the residents. The district contracts with the association to manage the recreational facilities.

I-25 is three miles from the development and I-70 is six miles away. Denver's Stapleton Airport is 10 miles from Heather Gardens. The community has local police coverage and a staffed fire department. The nearest hospital with emergency facilities is three miles away.

A restaurant is within the community. All other services are within three miles of Heather Gardens, including a pharmacy, a medical center, a dry cleaners, a hair salon, a grocery and liquor store, retail stores, and a movie theater. Local attractions include the Denver Museum of Natural History, the Children's Museum, the Denver Botanical Gardens, the Denver Zoo, the U.S. Mint, and the Denver opera, theater, and ballet companies.

RECREATION AND SOCIAL ACTIVITIES

In 1989, the United States Golfers Association named the Heather Gardens' golf course "one of the absolute best" 9-hole courses in the mid-continent region. A record 42,424 rounds of golf were played in 1989, producing a total income of $178,500, which was an increase of more than $8,000 over the previous year.

The community center is a 30,000-square-foot building with two swimming pools, an auditorium, workshops, and other recreational facilities. In this center, the association sponsors an educational program that provides 159 individual courses taught by a staff of 31 part-time instructors, with a total yearly student registration of 1,500. Other activities at the center include blood pressure clinics, dance club meetings, religious services, pancake breakfasts, art shows, flea markets, craft fairs, municipal elections, and the New Year's Eve dance.

The community also has three lighted tennis courts and picnic areas, employs a recreation director, publishes a monthly newsletter, and organizes trips and on-site entertainment. On-site crafts, visiting nurse and caregiver services, and catering are also available. There is 24-hour security patrol within the community and electronic access to the RV parking lot. The association also provides a billiards room, a woodworking shop, an art room, and discounts on golf fees.

HOMEOWNER ASSESSMENTS, TAXES, AND UTILITIES

With 2,426 homes, Heather Gardens is totally built-out. The general manager and the community's staff are responsible for the year-round maintenance of 35 buildings, 316 townhomes, 252 patio homes, the community center, and 198 acres of real estate (including the golf course, landscaped grounds, private roads, and driveways). The staff maintains 3.6 million square feet of living area, 1 million feet of exposed roof, 10,900 windows and doors, 39 elevators, common area carpeting and furnishings, and all related electrical, plumbing, and heating systems.

The 1,536 high-rise condominiums range in price from $46,000 to $250,000, with monthly community association assessments of $153 to $344 and property/municipal taxes between $600 and $2,000 per year. The 574 mid-rise condominiums cost $38,000 to $180,000, with monthly assessments of $152 to $349. Their annual property/municipal taxes range from $550 to $1,700. Heather Gardens has 64 townhomes that cost between $85,000 and $115,000 with monthly assessments of $192 and property/municipal taxes between $800 and $1,300 per year. Single-family patio homes number 252 and cost $105,000 to $150,000, with monthly assessments of $164 to $192 and property taxes between $1,500 and $2,000 per year.

There are 146 units with one bedroom, 2,230 with two bedrooms, and 50 with three bedrooms. Both cable and community television channels are available at Heather Gardens. Gas is the primary heat source; waste disposal is provided by the local municipality. Water is provided by both well and city sources. All utilities are underground. There are extra storage facilities on site.

RESTRICTIONS IN THE COMMUNITY

There is a community association, and membership is mandatory. The community association provides all exterior building/grounds maintenance for the site. Any changes or additions to a home must be approved by the architectural control committee. Landscaping must be confined to specified areas, and there are some garden plots available for homeowner use.

Pets must always be leashed, and owners must clean up after their animals. There are no restrictions on how many people can occupy a single unit. Other than age restrictions, there are no rental restrictions, nor are there restrictions on resale of homes. Operating a business from a home is prohibited. Boats and RVs can only be parked off-site or in the specified RV parking lot.

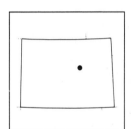

HIGHLANDS RANCH

Mission Viejo Company
8822 S. Ridgeline Blvd.
Highlands Ranch, CO 80126
303-791-8180

$40,000 to $650,000
5,707/35,900 Mid-rise and Garden-style Condos and Single-family Homes
Contemporary and Colonial Architecture

18-hole golf course
2 outdoor pools, 1 kiddie pool
8 neighborhood parks
11 lighted outdoor tennis courts
Full-size gymnasium
2 sand volleyball courts

1 indoor pool with jacuzzi
8,200 acres of open space
4 ball-playing fields
10 racquetball courts
Men and women's locker rooms
Indoor running track

INTRODUCTION

Highlands Ranch is a 22,000-acre private planned community in Douglas County, Colorado. Approximately 1½ miles west of Interstate 25, it is located in south metropolitan Denver along the Centennial Freeway. Denver's Stapleton Airport is just 15 miles from the community. Centennial Airport, one of the largest private airports in the country, is about 15 minutes from Highlands Ranch.

Approved by Douglas County in 1979, the Highlands Ranch master plan laid the foundation for the innovative development of a community with a variety of housing options. The master plan calls for 30 percent of the land to be devoted to residential uses, 61 percent to non-urban uses (including open space and recreation), and 9 percent to business properties.

The land upon which Highlands Ranch lies was part of the 1803 Louisiana Purchase. Homesteaders staked out claims that were consolidated into one holding of 23,000 acres by the turn of the century. The Ranch was purchased by the Mission Viejo Company in 1979, and the first residential units were offered for sale in July 1981. The current population is over 15,000 residents living in approximately 5,700 homes. Build-out of the community is expected to occur in the year 2010, with an estimated population of 90,000 residents occupying 35,900 homes.

More than 1,900 acres of land have been designated for corporate research and development, offices, industrial, commercial, and other business uses. Almost two million square feet of office, commercial, and industrial space have already been constructed.

Highlands Ranch is currently served by three public elementary schools, a public junior and senior high school, and a private elementary school. The master plan designates twenty-five school sites that will ultimately serve Highlands Ranch. Arapahoe Community College is just ten minutes from the community; the University of Denver and the Denver campus of the University of Colorado are about 30 minutes north. Lutheran, Methodist, Baptist, and Catholic worship services are just a few of those available at Highlands Ranch.

The community is just minutes from the Denver zoo, the state capitol, the Art Museum, the Museum of Natural History, and the Center for Performing Arts. On the site you will find a medical clinic, a dry cleaners, a hair salon, a liquor store, a restaurant, and retail stores. A pharmacy, a grocery store, and a movie theater are all within one mile. A hospital is also located one mile from Highlands Ranch.

RECREATION AND SOCIAL ACTIVITIES

Highlands Ranch is located only one hour from many of Colorado's premier ski resorts, and camping facilities are within a half hour from the community. The park at Highlands Ranch encompasses more than 480 acres of activity areas. Northridge activity area is the largest with over 250 acres; it features a physical fitness course, horseshoe pits, picnic areas, miles of biking and jogging paths, and areas for softball, basketball, and baseball. An extension of Northridge contains two flat, landscaped areas with picnic tables and barbecues. Highlands Ranch currently contains approximately eight miles of bicycle trails. Ultimately, trails will connect the links at the 18-hole golf course, the Highline Canal Trail System, and other major community facilities. Approximately 8,200 acres in the southern portion of Highlands Ranch have been designated an open space conservation area.

There are three clubhouses on site as well as the Highlands Ranch recreation center, a 54,000-square-foot building. Amenities at the recreation center include an outdoor swimming pool, an outdoor tot pool, a workout room equipped with Nautilus fitness equipment, 11 lighted tennis courts, an eight-lane indoor swimming pool with adjoining jacuzzi, 10 racquetball courts, an indoor running track, a full-size gymnasium, a babysitting room, several multi-purpose rooms, and two sand volleyball courts. A separate outdoor pool facility and a smaller clubhouse are also on site.

The community association employs a recreation director and publishes quarterly recreation program guides. There are also two independent newspapers within the community. Highlands Ranch provides a variety of holiday activities and events, internal bus service, on-site crafts, daycare for children, and activities for teens. Local sheriff's deputies patrol within the community, and some neighborhoods have perimeter restrictions.

HOMEOWNER ASSESSMENTS, TAXES, AND UTILITIES

Currently, 17 residential builders in the community offer a wide range of housing, including single-family and executive homes with contemporary, colonial, and traditional architectural styles. The 400 rental mid-rise condos and 116 garden-style condos cost $40,000 to $50,000. The 190 townhomes cost between $90,000 and $235,000, and the 5,000 single-family homes range from $80,000 to $650,000. The current quarterly homeowner assessment is $79.86, which covers use of all recreational facilities. The county provides maintenance for most roads.

Cable and community television channels are available. Homes are heated by gas, electricity, and solar sources. The local municipality provides both water and sewer services. All utilities are underground. There are extra storage facilities on site.

RESTRICTIONS IN THE COMMUNITY

There is a community association, and membership is mandatory. Any exterior modifications to homes must be authorized by the association's architectural control committee. The community is not age-restricted, but one neighborhood in Highlands Ranch is set aside for residents age 39 and older. Except for this neighborhood, there are no restrictions on age or length of stay for visitors.

There are no pet restrictions. County ordinances on maximum occupation apply. There are no rental restrictions. Daycare operations and home offices are permitted, but no traffic-generating businesses may be operated out of a home. There are no restrictions on resales. RVs may not be parked on the street; however, there is a special parking area for recreational vehicles and boats.

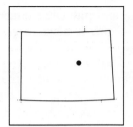

KEN-CARYL RANCH

7676 South Continental Divide Rd.
Littleton, Colorado 80127
303-979-1876

$40,000 to $750,000
2,839/5,800 Garden-style
Condos, Townhomes, and
Single-family Homes
Mixed Architecture

1 community center
60 acres of neighborhood parks
8 playgrounds
16 miles of hiking trails
6 picnic areas
11 outdoor tennis courts
4 outdoor volleyball courts
1 clubhouse
Exercise room
2 outdoor swimming pools

86 acres of greenbelts
2 outdoor basketball courts
16 miles of cross-country skiing
Over 3,000 acres of open space
3 ball-playing fields
6 lighted outdoor tennis courts
Horse stables
16 miles of bridle paths
5 miles of paved trails

INTRODUCTION

The 9,139-acre Ken-Caryl Ranch is located 18 miles southwest of Denver, Colorado. It is a private master planned community developed by the Manville Corporation. In 1972, after a year and a half of planning and public review, the official development plan for the former cattle ranch was approved by Jefferson County. To protect the natural wilderness of the property, it was determined that only one-third of Ken-Caryl Ranch would be developed.

The land itself has a colorful legacy. In the early 1800s, the Ute Indians were led to this site by their leader, Chief Colorow. Shortly after prospectors and settlers came to the area in the 1850s, Major Robert Bradford established a stagecoach stop in the north valley behind the Dakota Hogback. Most of the original building still stands and has been designated a historical site. In 1914, John Shaffer, cattle baron and one-time owner of the Rocky Mountain News, purchased the land and christened it the Ken-Caryl Ranch (after his two sons, Kent and Carroll). He also built the Manor House, where he entertained visiting presidents, royalty, and celebrities in grand fashion.

A massive forest fire ravaged 3,200 acres of Ken-Caryl Ranch in 1978, consuming much of the vegetation on lower slopes. Recovery measures, such as seeding grass, planting trees, and logging of dead trees, were completed by 1980. Vigorous regrowth has provided a fine habitat for the deer, songbirds, rodents, and predators that have returned in abundance. At an elevation of about 7,300 feet, there are aspen trees and, on the shady northern exposure, conifers such as ponderosa pines, spruces, and Douglas firs. Many of the trees on the northern exposures survived the fire intact, but the ponderosa pines on the ridgetops and mesas suffered heavy damage and will not be reestablished for centuries.

Ken-Caryl Ranch is part of unincorporated south Jefferson County, but a variety of services are close at hand. Law enforcement, planning and zoning, road maintenance, and snow removal are provided by the county. County clerk and commissioner's offices are located on the ranch, as is the crime prevention unit of the Jefferson County sheriffs department. Just north of the ranch is the Columbine branch of the U.S. post office.

Everyone in the community has easy access to on-site shopping and medical centers, elementary and high schools, daycare and business centers, and restaurants. A hospital with emergency care facilities is three miles from the site. The nearest movie theater is two miles from the community.

At full development, the Ken-Caryl business center will have 5 million square feet of retail, light industrial, and office space, with up to 20,000 employees. Currently, the business center is home to over 50 businesses and a neighborhood shopping center. There are 555 acres zoned for commercial or industrial use on the Ranch.

Ken-Caryl is served by Jefferson County's R-1 school district. There are three schools on the Ranch: Shaffer Elementary, Bradford Elementary, and Chatfield Senior High. Two additional school sites are available for future construction.

RECREATION AND SOCIAL ACTIVITIES

Established in 1988, the Ken-Caryl Ranch Metropolitan District is responsible for managing and operating the developed parks and greenbelts and the recreation facilities as well as providing quality leisure, cultural, and social programs for all residents.

The Ranch House is a 17-acre community center with 9 tennis courts, an olympic-size swimming pool, two soccer fields, a softball field, a frisbee golf course, croquet and shuffleboard courts, a game and exercise room, party and meeting rooms, a visitor's information center, and a basketball court. This facility is maintained and operated by the Ken-Caryl Ranch Metropolitan District.

Bradford Park offers residents a 30 × 60 foot swimming pool, wading pool, two tennis courts, volleyball, and horseshoe pits. The equestrian center provides indoor and outdoor boarding riding arenas, and English and Western instruction programs. There are 20 miles of hiking and horseback trails with marked picnic areas and campsites, 150 maintained acres of greenbelts with walkways and bike paths, and over 4,000 acres of open space. The Ken-Caryl Ranch Metropolitan District plans year-round recreation programs, activities, and events including seasonal swim and tennis programs for youth.

The association employs a recreation director and publishes a biweekly newsletter. The community has a vast network of committees and social organizations. There are organized trips, on-site crafts, and on-site entertainment. Catering services, visiting nurse and caregiver services, daycare for children, and activities for teens are also available. Maid service is available from local providers.

HOMEOWNER ASSESSMENTS, TAXES, AND UTILITIES

Encompassing 1,800 acres, the sweeping eastern side of Ken-Caryl Ranch is known as the Plains. It offers several appealing and diverse types of homes, from townhomes to single-family homes and custom-built homes. Situated between the Dakota Hogback and the foothills of the Rockies, the area known as the Valley consists of 2,000 acres of land. In the Valley, a few highly praised and skilled builders have crafted several exceptional neighborhoods of attached and detached single-family homes, luxurious traditional homes, and spacious and innovative custom-built residences.

At this time, about 3,000 homes have been sold at Ken-Caryl Ranch. The first home was built in 1976. The build-out is expected to be 5,800 homes. Currently, the 63 garden-style condominiums cost about $40,000, with monthly community association assessments of $77 and property/municipal taxes of about $400 per year. The 386 townhomes range from $40,000 to $120,000, with varied monthly community association assessments. The 2,500 single-family homes cost $60,000 to $750,000; their yearly property taxes average $800 to $6,000. There are also 90 duplex-style homes in the community, with monthly assessments of $110. The duplex homes range in price from $40,000 to $120,000. All homeowners also pay $22 per month to the master association at Ken-Caryl Ranch.

Homeownership automatically entitles you to use of all the park and recreational facilities. Both cable and community television channels are available. Homes are heated by gas, electric, oil, solar, and wood sources. The community uses a combination of well and city water services and a combination of septic systems and city sewer services. All utilities are underground. There are extra storage facilities on site. Ken-Caryl Ranch provides a unique recycling program, the cost of which is included in the monthly assessments.

RESTRICTIONS IN THE COMMUNITY

Any exterior modifications or landscaping installations must be approved by the architectural control committee. There are no restrictions in the community regarding age or length-of-stay for visitors. No more than two dogs or cats are allowed per home, and dogs must be on a leash when they are off private property. Homeowners must abide by Jefferson County restrictions of maximum occupation. There are no rental restrictions, nor are there restrictions on the resale of units. Recreational vehicles, boats, and other large vehicles may not be parked on the streets, but the association does provide special parking areas for these vehicles.

Rules regarding open space areas within the community include no vehicular traffic, no firearms (including BB guns, bows, or slingshots), no fires, no hunting or trapping, and no littering or vandalizing. Homeowners must stay on marked trails and carry a first aid kit.

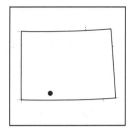

PAGOSA LAKES

230 Port Avenue
Pagosa Lakes, Colorado 81147
303-731-4141

$35,000 to $500,000
1,600/12,000 Garden-style
Condos, Single-family
Homes, Lots, Time-shares,
and Mobile Homes
Mixed Architecture

2 USGA-rated golf courses
6 lakes
Downhill skiing nearby
Hiking trails
Handball/racquetball
2 clubhouses

2 indoor pools
Boating
Cross-country skiing
7 outdoor tennis courts
Horse stables
14,000-square-foot recreation center

INTRODUCTION

The Pagosa Lakes property owners' association is the master association for own-ers in all but five of its subdivisions. The association was created in 1970 by the Navajo Trail Corporation. Owners of property in the five subdivisions where membership is not mandatory may voluntarily join the association. Only associ-ation members enjoy special access to facilities and vote in association elections. The nearest large city, Durango, has a population of 12,000 and is 60 miles away. Mercy Hospital, the nearest facility with emergency care, is located 60 miles from the community.

Over the last 20 years, the association has established itself as a mature instru-ment of community association management, overseeing a community which, if it were municipally incorporated, would be the third largest town in southwestern Colorado. In 1985, the association actually conducted a feasibility study concern-ing incorporation, but the referendum was defeated. The association is very active in the greater Pagosa Springs area: It was instrumental in the formation of a local humane society and the construction of a much needed animal shelter. In the 1970s, it formed a fire department and supported it with money and manpower. The Pagosa Lakes' department of public safety has four professionally equipped public safety officers who patrol the community.

Within the community of Pagosa Lakes, you will find a dry cleaners, a hair salon, a grocery store, a liquor store, a restaurant, and retail shops. A pharmacy, a medical clinic, and movie theaters are nearby. Other area attractions include the Mesa Verde National Park, the Durango and Silverton narrow gage railroads, and the Wolf Creek ski area, which has the most snow in Colorado.

RECREATION AND SOCIAL ACTIVITIES

The association owns, manages, and operates the Ralph Eaton Recreation Center, named after Pagosa Lakes' pioneer developer. This fine center offers an indoor swimming pool, a kid's wading pool, a sun deck, a jacuzzi, an exercise room with a Universal gym and exercycle, multi-use rooms, and two racquetball courts that double as basketball courts. The center sells a line of athletic wear and sports equipment. Future plans call for construction of outdoor recreational amenities on the six-acre site.

The association provides a variety of classes and activities including aerobics and water aerobics, swimming classes, fitness programs, racquetball tournaments, and CPR classes. The association sponsors the Pagosa Lakes Porpoises swim team for local youths, which has been very successful in statewide competition. Membership fees for the recreation center are set annually by the board of directors: Currently, user fees cover 35 percent of expenses of operation.

The association also owns and maintains two clubhouses: Trails and Vista. A portion of the Vista clubhouse holds the administrative headquarters for the association. The clubhouses may be rented by association members and are used by such association-sponsored activities as bridge, sewing, art, square dancing, and ballroom dancing.

At this time, the association is studying a proposal by the developer for the transfer to the association of ownership of the lakes and the resumption of management of the lakes as fisheries. The association has also received a proposal from the developer for the purchase of the golf courses, the tennis courts, and the marina. The board of directors has established a 14-member committee on the acquisition of recreational amenities to closely research these proposals for feasibility and impact on association operations.

HOMEOWNER ASSESSMENTS, TAXES, AND UTILITIES

The Pagosa Lakes property owners' association serves as the master association for the entire community. Within Pagosa Lakes there are 27 subdivisions, 16 condo associations, and eight time-share associations. Currently, there is a permanent population of about 1,600 people, with seasonal and time-share residents adding another 1,300 at any given time. Average occupancy is 2.55 persons per household compared to the national average of 2.62 and the Colorado average of 2.54.

There are over 10,000 lots, with prices from $2,000 to $40,000. The 325 garden-style condominiums range in price from $35,000 to $95,000, with annual property owners' association fees of $115. Neighborhood association fees are separate. The 1,125 single-family homes cost $26,000 to $500,000; the owners also pay $115 per year to the property owners' association. Time-shares number 150 units. There is also a mobile home subdivision where homes average $30,000.

Gas, electricity, and solar provide heat sources for Pagosa Lakes residents. There are special districts to handle sewer waste and water services for the community. Utilities are both above and below ground. There are no extra storage facilities within the community.

RESTRICTIONS IN THE COMMUNITY

There is a community association; except for five subdivisions, membership is mandatory. Condominium associations handle the building and grounds maintenance for their individual neighborhoods. Individual single-family homeowners handle their own building and grounds maintenance. The master association provides building and grounds maintenance for all recreational amenities and infrastructure.

Each individual neighborhood association has its own restrictions regarding exterior modifications, maximum occupancy, rental restrictions, and landscaping. Operating a business from a home at Pagosa Lakes is prohibited. There are no restrictions on the resale of units. The association does not provide any special parking areas for recreational vehicles, boats, and the like.

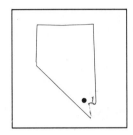

DESERT SHORES

2500 Regatta Dr.
Las Vegas, Nevada 89128
702-254-1020

$129,000 to $1,500,000
1,500/2,800 Single-family and Custom-built Homes
Spanish Architecture

21,600-square-foot swimming lagoon
Boating
37 acres of open space
5 picnic areas
Volleyball area

4 lakes
Private boat slips
8½ miles of walking paths
Clubhouse
Horseshoe pits

INTRODUCTION

Desert Shores is situated by the western foothills, with spectacular views of the mountains and the city lights. Part of the booming northwest section of Las Vegas, Desert Shores is bordered by the new Las Vegas Technology Center, Del Webb's Sun City Summerlin, and the city's new recreational center at Angel Park, which offers two golf courses designed by Arnold Palmer.

Desert Shores strives to achieve a balanced mix of homes, stores, open space, and recreational areas. More than 20 percent of the land has been reserved for common areas, including 37 acres of open landscape with grass and trees. You can walk anywhere on the eight miles of pathways and trails that wind through the community.

Desert Shores is the largest master planned community in the state of Nevada and the last "lake community" to be developed in Las Vegas. Located seven and a half miles from the city of Las Vegas, it is being developed by R.A. Homes of Las Vegas. The first home in this community was built in 1988. The complex is located only one mile from Interstate 95 and 12 miles from the Las Vegas McCarran Airport. Police protection is provided by local authorities, the county sheriff's department, and Nevada state police. There is a staffed fire department nearby. The nearest hospital with emergency facilities is seven miles from the community.

Other area attractions include Tule Springs in the Ralph Lamb State Park, Bonnie Springs, Red Rock Canyon, the Spring Mountain Ranch, and the Lorenzi Park Art Gallery. The following services were to have been completely constructed within the community by May 1991: a pharmacy, a dental office, a dry cleaners, a hair salon, a grocery store, and a restaurant. A movie theater is located one mile from the community.

RECREATION AND SOCIAL ACTIVITIES

The community has a spectacular 21,600-square-foot swimming lagoon surrounded by a sandy beach of imported Pacific Coast sand. The beach club and marina, 21,000 square feet in size, also sports a volleyball area, a children's playground, and a picnic area. The four lakes located within the property can accommodate boats from 8 to 14 feet and are fully stocked. The lakes stretch diagonally across the community for 1,000 to 2,000 feet; you can sail for almost a full straight mile on the longest lake. Five picnic areas are located at the beach club.

Desert Shores employs a recreation director, has a small clubhouse, publishes a monthly newsletter, and provides organized on-site entertainment. Some of the neighborhoods have guarded gates. Homeownership automatically entitles you to membership in the club and recreation facilities, with some nominal user fees.

HOMEOWNER ASSESSMENTS, TAXES, AND UTILITIES

At Desert Shores, you can choose from custom home neighborhoods, single-family homes, patio homes, and townhomes as well as two attached-housing neighborhoods. Nine lakeside neighborhoods offer homes along the water. All of the neighborhoods are within easy walking distance of the lakes and the beach club and marina.

Currently, 1,500 single-family homes have been built at Desert Shores. The ultimate build-out is expected to be 2,800 homes. There are 445 finished homes completed that have not been sold. Single-family homes cost $129,000 to $580,000, with a monthly community association assessment of approximately $60. Prices of custom homes range from $100,000 to $1.5 million. Custom homeowners also pay $60 per month in community association fees. Some neighborhoods also have a sub-association fee.

Cable television is available, but there are no community television channels. The heating fuel is gas. The local municipality provides both the sewer waste disposal and water systems. All telephone and electrical wires are underground. There are no extra storage facilities within the community.

RESTRICTIONS IN THE COMMUNITY

Desert Shores has a community association, and membership is mandatory. Individual homeowners provide their own exterior building/grounds maintenance. The community association provides maintenance for all common areas and recreational facilities. Desert Shores enforces full architectural control of exterior improvements. The association publishes a list of approved plants for landscaping. There are restrictions on the size of trees and, if your home is situated on the lake, types of lakefront landscaping.

There are no restrictions regarding age or length-of-stay for visitors. Only two pets per home are allowed, and the community enforces a leash law. Only a single family may occupy an individual home. There are no rental restrictions in the community, nor any restrictions of the resale of homes. Operating a business from a home is strictly prohibited at Desert Shores. Commercial vehicles, recreational vehicles, and vehicles over three-quarters of a ton may not be parked in the community. There are no special parking areas for these type of vehicles.

SPANISH TRAIL

7495 W. Mission Hills
Las Vegas, Nevada 89113
702-367-8747

$160,000 to $5,000,000
1,020/1,300 Condos,
Townhomes, and Single-family
Homes
Spanish Architecture

27-hole USGA-rated golf course
12 lighted outdoor tennis courts
Exercise room

7 outdoor pools
Large clubhouse, over 15,000 square feet
Steam and sauna facilities

INTRODUCTION

When the early pioneers traveled through the area now called the Las Vegas Valley, their route was known as the Spanish Trail. In 1953, Joe and Mary Blasco followed a similar path as they moved to Las Vegas. Joe started a sand and gravel company on a remote site south of the city in the shadow of the Red Rock Canyon, miles from the bustling downtown area. As Las Vegas expanded, the remote gravel company became linked to the Las Vegas Strip with new roads. As new residents settled along the Spanish Trail, the Blasco family started a development company. The first home in the community of Spanish Trail was built in 1984.

As construction began, the old gravel plant disappeared and more than 1.5 million cubic yards of soil were moved to shape the new golf course. Hundreds of trees were planted and huge lakes were added as the first homes were built. Situated at a slightly higher elevation than the Las Vegas Strip, Spanish Trail affords views of the city skyline to the east and the Spring Mountain Range and Red Rock Canyon to the west.

Over the past five years, Spanish Trail has won a total of 25 awards from the local builders' association; in 1990 the community was named the best sales center in the United States by the National Association of Homebuilders. More than 1,300 families will live within the community when it is completed.

Las Vegas has a population of 800,000 and is one of America's fastest growing cities. Interstate 15 is just three miles from the development. Police protection is provided by local, county, and state agencies. There is a hospital six miles from the community.

Local attractions include Las Vegas' famous casinos, museums, theaters, state and national parks, two theme parks, concert halls, and flea markets. Although there are no services within the community, within blocks of the homes you will find a pharmacy, a medical clinic, a dry cleaners, a hair salon, a grocery and liquor store, restaurants, and retail stores. A movie theater is just three miles away.

RECREATION AND SOCIAL ACTIVITIES

The magnificent golf course at Spanish Trail, recognized as one of the finest in the country, plays host to the PGA's Las Vegas Invitational Tournament. The 27-hole course was designed by Robert Trent Jones. The private Spanish Trail Golf and Country Club has over 500 active members, including some of the city's most elite residents. Spanish Trail residents have priority rights to purchase golf and social memberships at this exclusive club. Members enjoy full privileges at the magnificent clubhouse, which features a private dining room, a lounge, a grill, locker rooms, and a pro shop. The clubhouse is the site of numerous social events throughout the year and is available for special functions. A full membership in the country club costs $35,000, and a social membership costs $10,000. In addition, golfing privileges cost $200 per month plus $25 in green fees.

Spanish Trail offers swimming pools, tennis courts, and a health club and fitness center. Homeownership automatically entitles you to use these facilities. The swim and tennis center, open to all residents and their guests, has eight championship courts (five illuminated for night play), a large pool with a heated spa, a snack bar, and a pro shop. Many neighborhood pools and spas are also available for use throughout the year. The health club and fitness center offers four additional tennis courts, aerobic classes, a workout center, another large pool, and a spa.

The association employs a recreation director and publishes a monthly newsletter. Valet and concierge services are available, as well as on-site entertainment. The grounds are fully maintained by the master association, and a full-time security force patrols the grounds and monitors all incoming visitors. With the help of a modern computerized alarm system, all homes are monitored 24 hours a day. No activities for teens or daycare for children are offered within the community.

HOMEOWNER ASSESSMENTS, TAXES, AND UTILITIES

To date, there are 1,020 completed homes out of a total of 1,300. The 300 garden-style condominiums range in price from $160,000 to $250,000. The 200 town-homes cost $180,000 to $300,000, and the 520 single-family homes cost between $200,000 and $5 million. Monthly community association fees range from $210 to $255, depending on the type of home. Upon completion of the community, there will be 200 homes with two bedrooms, 400 homes with three bedrooms, 500 homes with four bedrooms, and 200 homes with more than four bedrooms.

Both cable and community television channels are available. Gas provides the primary heating source, and sewer and water services are provided by the local municipality. All utilities are located below ground. There are no extra storage areas within the community.

RESTRICTIONS IN THE COMMUNITY

A master association and neighborhood associations have been established within Spanish Trail. Membership in both associations is mandatory. Whether the individual homeowner or the association provides exterior building/grounds maintenance depends on the type of home. However, all exterior modifications must be approved by the architectural review committee.

There are no restrictions on age or length-of-stay for visitors. Only household pets are allowed: They must be under control at all times and must not cause a nuisance or excessive noise. When pets are outdoors, owners must clean up after them. Maximum occupancy restrictions for units do not exist here. If you choose to rent your home, you must secure a one-year minimum lease. As the owner, you are responsible for all your tenant's actions.

Operating a business from your unit is prohibited. There are restrictions on sales procedures for resale of homes. No parking on the street is allowed. Commercial vehicles and RVs are not allowed to park in the neighborhoods, but there is a special place to park these vehicles.

JACKSON HOLE RACQUET CLUB

Box 25003
Jackson, Wyoming 83001
307-733-5518

$80,000 to $475,000
473/473 Garden-style
Condos and Single-family
Homes
Mixed Architecture

1 outdoor pool	1 kiddie pool
Downhill skiing at Jackson Hole	Myriad of lifts
Cross-country skiing	Snowmaking capabilities
6 outdoor tennis courts	Clubhouse
Gymnasium	Exercise room
Steam and sauna facilities	18-hole golf course within walking distance

INTRODUCTION

The Jackson Hole Racquet Club is situated among Aspen groves along the base of the Teton Mountains. The community is centrally located between three ski areas, the town of Jackson, and the Grand Teton and Yellowstone National Parks. The first unit at the Jackson Hole Racquet Club was built in 1972.

Both within and outside its boundaries, this private recreational community offers a fantastic array of activities, such as the Grand Teton Musical Festival or whitewater rafting down the Snake River.

With jet service daily to most major cities, the Jackson Hole airport is eight miles from the town of Jackson. The community is 250 miles from Salt Lake City, Utah. The nearest interstate (I-80) is 160 miles away. The nearest major airport is also located in Salt Lake City. Police coverage is provided by local authorities, the county sheriff's department, and the Wyoming state police. A volunteer fire department is nearby. The nearest hospital with emergency facilities is in Jackson, six miles from the community.

Within the community, you can find a hair salon, a grocery and liquor store, restaurants, and retail shops. A pharmacy, a medical clinic, a dry cleaners, and movie theaters are within a few miles.

Though this private community contains 473 units, the buffering between the buildings and the architectural style of the homes give the community the appearance of being much smaller. Most of the homes afford a magnificent view of the Teton Mountains.

Homes at the Jackson Hole Racquet Club range in size from studios to spacious four-bedroom townhomes. All of the condominiums provide color cable television, a washer and dryer, and a private balcony.

RECREATION AND SOCIAL ACTIVITIES

The Jackson Hole Racquet Club provides a private athletic facility for home-owner use, with monthly fees of $50. The facility houses Nautilus equipment, free weights, a sauna, jacuzzis, and an outdoor heated swimming pool. John Gardiner's tennis clinics offer lessons for any level of skill. Indoor and outdoor tennis courts and racquetball courts are available.

During the winter, a shuttle bus provides free transportation to and from the Jackson Hole ski area, only five minutes away. The Jackson Hole ski area is known as one of the best skiing mountains in the west. Lifts include a tram, six chairlifts, and T-bars.

A short walk from the Jackson Hole Racquet Club, the Teton Pines Golf Course was designed by Arnold Palmer. This championship course features 18 holes of challenging golf on 188 acres of aspen woodlands, with lakes that mirror the mountains. In the winter, this area serves as a 10-kilometer double track cross-country skiing center.

Although the community does not employ a recreation director, it does publish a quarterly newsletter for homeowners. Maid service and free bus transportation also are available at Jackson Hole. The community provides daycare for children. Although there are no perimeter restrictions, the community does have a 24-hour patrol within its property.

HOMEOWNER ASSESSMENTS, TAXES, AND UTILITIES

There are 393 garden-style condominiums at the Jackson Hole Racquet Club, with prices from $80,000 to $260,000 and monthly community association assessments of $240. Property taxes average $350 per year. The 60 single-family homes range in price from $210,000 to $475,000. Single-family owners pay $15.70 a month in community association assessments as well as water and sewer charges for individual homes.

Cable television is available to homeowners, but there are no community television channels. Electricity provides the primary heat source. The community owns a waste water treatment plant, and a central well provides water to the community. All utilities are underground. The community has extra storage facilities.

RESTRICTIONS IN THE COMMUNITY

There is a community association, and membership is mandatory. Any exterior modification to a home or additional landscaping must be approved by the architectural control committee. The community has architectural guidelines in place.

There are no age or length-of-stay restrictions for visitors. Homeowners who live at the site are allowed to have pets. However pets are not allowed in rented units. Dogs are not permitted to roam freely in the community. The size of a unit dictates the number of people allowed. There are rental restrictions, and operating a business from a unit is strictly prohibited. There are no restrictions on the resale of the units. The community provides a special area to park recreational vehicles, boats, and the like.

Chapter 13

Midwest
Illinois
Indiana
Michigan
Missouri

APPLE CANYON LAKE

14A57 Canyon Club Drive
Apple River, Illinois 61001
815-492-2238

$40,000 to $150,000
452/2,727 Single-family
Homes, Lots
Mixed Architecture

9-hole golf course
440-acre lake with 15 miles of shore
Cross-country skiing trails
Hiking trails
2 outdoor tennis courts
Campground

1 outdoor pool
Over 400 boat slips
Snowmobile trails
Picnic areas
Clubhouse
Swimming beaches

INTRODUCTION

In a land of rolling hills and green valleys, Apple Canyon Lake spreads over 2,700 acres. In the center of this beautiful countryside is a 440-acre springfed lake. Remarkably clear and clean, the lake is three miles long, has more than 15 miles of shoreline, and reaches depths of 70 feet. Homesites are scattered throughout the varied terrain, near greenways that are set aside as miniature nature preserves. Because of the community's greenbelt system, 75 percent of the wooded shoreline will always remain in its natural state.

Apple Canyon Lake is a privately developed and owned lake community of homesites located in Jo Daviess County; approximately 17 miles from Galena and six miles from Apple River. Apple Canyon Lake is three hours from Chicago and two hours from the Quad Cities. The developer is Branigar Lake Properties, Inc., a wholly owned subsidiary of the Branigar Organization, Inc. The first lot was sold in 1968.

The nearest interstate (I-39) is 60 miles away. Rockford Airport is 60 miles from the site. Dubuque, Iowa, 45 miles away, also provides air transportation. Apple Canyon Lake security and state police departments provide patrols. A volunteer fire department is nearby. The closest hospital with emergency facilities is 25 miles away in Galena, Illinois. Except for a restaurant that operates seasonally, there are no services within the community. Within 15 miles of the site you can find a pharmacy, a medical clinic, a dry cleaners, a hair salon, grocery and liquor stores, retail shops, and movie theaters. Area attractions include the U. S. Grant House historical site, antique dealers, riverboating in Dubuque, Iowa, and many parks and museums.

RECREATION AND SOCIAL ACTIVITIES

Regularly stocked with panfish and bass, Apple Canyon Lake offers some of the best fishing in Illinois, as well as ice-fishing during the winter. Boating, sailing, canoeing, and waterskiing are popular. A full service marina operates 7 days a week in season. There are over 400 boat slips that can accommodate various boat sizes. There are four sand beaches for swimming and sunbathing. Best of all, the private lake is relatively uncrowded even on a busy summer weekend.

The community offers a clubhouse with a lakeside restaurant, a 9-hole golf course, tennis courts, a campground and many picnic areas, horseback and hiking trails, a hilltop swimming pool, snowmobiling, and cross-country skiing.

The association employs a recreation director, publishes a monthly newsletter, and organizes on-site entertainment and activities for teens. There is no perimeter security, but there is a 24-hour patrol within the community. Lot ownership automatically entitles you to membership in all the club and recreational facilities except golf. Community association members receive a discount on the fee for golfing privileges.

HOMEOWNER ASSESSMENTS, TAXES, AND UTILITIES

Part of the charm of Apple Canyon Lake is the diversity of the architecture, which is designed to blend into the environment and enhance the area's natural beauty. Property owners build the style of house that fits their individual tastes and needs. The architectural control committee assures that aesthetics and construction standards are met in order to maintain the character of the community. The average price of lots is between $5,000 and $15,000 but can be as high as $50,000 for choice locations. Homes have sold at prices under $50,000 to $150,000.

Currently, 452 homes have been built on the 2,727 available lots. Community association assessments are $150 per year. Property/municipal taxes for the single-family homes average $1,000 to $1,500 per year. Taxes for undeveloped lots are about $30 per year. Cable television is available, but there are no community television channels. Propane gas provides the primary heat source. Sewer waste is handled by a septic system, and the local municipality provides water services. Telephone and electrical utilities are located both above and below ground. There are no extra storage facilities within the community.

RESTRICTIONS IN THE COMMUNITY

Community association membership is mandatory. Individual lot owners are responsible for their own building/grounds maintenance. The association maintains all common grounds, private roads, and amenities.

Any exterior modifications must meet the requirements of the architectural control committee. There are also no restrictions regarding what type of landscaping you may install. The burning of grasses within the association complex is prohibited, except for controlled burns, under the supervision of the conservation committee.

There are no restrictions regarding age or length-of-stay for visitors. Pets must be leashed at all times and are not allowed in the clubhouse, pool, or beach areas. There are no restrictions on how many people may occupy a single unit, nor are there any rental restrictions. Operating a business from a home is prohibited. There are no resale restrictions at Apple Canyon Lake. Parking is controlled and regulated in certain areas of the community. There are no special parking lots for recreational vehicles.

Power boats, with the exception of pontoon boats, must be less than 19 feet in length. Pontoon boats, sailboats, or the like must not exceed 25 feet in length. Residents may register only one boat over 10 horsepower for lake use. All boats must be registered annually with the association. A valid Illinois fishing license is mandatory for owners who wish to fish.

Hunting, firearms, and fireworks are prohibited within the confines of the community. The use of archery equipment is restricted to private lots or approved ranges.

LAKE BARRINGTON SHORES

64 North Old Barn Road
Barrington, Illinois 60010
708-382-1660

$125,000 to $314,000
1,152/1,360 Garden-style
Condos and Townhomes
Contemporary Architecture

18-hole USGA-rated golf course
1 kiddie pool
Boating
Hiking trails
10 outdoor tennis courts

1 indoor pool, 1 outdoor pool
2 miles of lake shoreline
Cross-country skiing
1 ball-playing field
Exercise room, steam/sauna

INTRODUCTION

Lake Barrington Shores is Chicagoland's complete private resort community, with tennis, swimming, golf and many other recreational amenities, all located on the shores of a mile-long sparkling lake. The sloping hills and lush green fairways dotted by maples, willows, and oaks provide spectacular surroundings for all the community's condominiums and townhomes.

Lake Barrington Shores is located just 40 miles from Chicago and is being developed by Lake Barrington Associates of Barrington, Illinois. Building began at the site in 1973; currently 1,152 homes have been completed out of a build-out of 1,360. I-90 is located nine miles from the community. The area is patrolled by both the county sheriff's department and the state police. A staffed fire department is nearby. O'Hare Airport is just 25 miles from the site.

Within Lake Barrington Shores you will find a dry cleaners, a hair salon, a grocery and liquor store, a restaurant, and retail shops. A Great America theme park is near the community. A pharmacy, a medical clinic, and a movie theater are all within five miles of the site. The Good Shepherd Hospital is located four miles away.

RECREATION AND SOCIAL ACTIVITIES

Lake Barrington Shores' private 18-hole championship golf course, designed by E. Lawrence Packard, is one of the finest in the Midwest. Many residents enjoy an early morning game before they leave for work or an evening game to unwind after a hard day at the office. In addition to the course, Lake Barrington Shores offers a well-stocked pro shop, a putting green, and a driving range. The clubhouse features a lounge, an outdoor patio, and an elegant restaurant.

The jewel of Lake Barrington Shores is the magnificent mile-long natural lake. The lake is surrounded by heavily wooded paths ideal for biking, jogging, or strolling. Its sparkling clear waters and white sandy beach are perfect for swimming, sunning, and relaxing. Stocked with game fish, these 100 acres of scenic waters are a fisherman's dream. A marina houses a variety of rental boats.

A recreation center is available to all residents; its lower level houses an indoor pool, a whirlpool, a fully equipped workout room, a sauna, a library, a game room, a snack bar, and meeting rooms for the many clubs at Lake Barrington Shores. The upper level features a large fireplace lounge and a magnificent ballroom that may be used for private parties. Other amenities include an outdoor pool and sundeck, 10 tennis courts, playgrounds, a three-mile jogging path, and 35 acres of natural wildlife and forest preserves. The recreation director is busy year-round. The association publishes a monthly newsletter and organizes trips and on-site entertainment. Catering is also available. The community is protected by a 24-hour patrol as well as manned and electronic perimeter restrictions.

HOMEOWNER ASSESSMENTS, TAXES, AND UTILITIES

Designed for carefree ease and elegance by leading Californian architect Harry B. Reid, the residences at Lake Barrington Shores are spacious and filled with light. Private patios and courtyards, gourmet kitchens, lofts, skylights, and whirlpool baths are all available.

Currently, 650 garden-style condominiums and 550 townhomes have been completed at Lake Barrington Shores. The condos range in price from $125,000 to $190,000 with a monthly community association assessment of $175 and property/municipal taxes between $2,500 and $3,000 per year. The 550 townhomes cost between $170,000 and $314,000, with monthly community association assessments from $200 to $340 and yearly property taxes between $3,000 and $5,500. Upon completion there will be 600 units with one bedroom, 400 with two bedrooms, and 360 with three bedrooms.

Both cable and community television channels are available. Electricity provides the primary heating source, and the local municipality provides both the water and sewer services to the community. All utilities are underground. There are extra storage facilities within the community. Homeownership automatically includes access to all of the recreational facilities within Lake Barrington Shores except the golf club, which has an annual fee of $2,700.

RESTRICTIONS IN THE COMMUNITY

There is a community association, and membership is mandatory. The association provides all exterior building/grounds maintenance for the homes and recreational areas. Any exterior modifications must be approved by the board of directors. There are also restrictions regarding individual plantings.

There are no restrictions on age or length-of-stay for visitors. Pet and rental restrictions are in effect in this community. Operating a business from a home is prohibited. There are some restrictions regarding the resale of homes, and community parking rules are enforced.

WOODHAVEN LAKES

509 LaMoille Rd., P.O. Box 110
Sublette, Illinois 61367
815-849-5200

$6,000 to $15,000
6,000/6,156 Campsites
Park Model Trailers,
RVs, and Tents

2 outdoor pools	1 kiddie pool
7 Lakes with 10 miles of shore	Boating
Cross-country skiing	750 acres of open space
4 hiking trails	8 picnic areas
3 ball-playing fields	8 outdoor tennis courts

INTRODUCTION

Nestled in the gently rolling hills of the Rock River Valley, Woodhaven Lakes is the world's largest family camping resort where all campsites are privately owned. The community, included here because of its unique nature, has an incredible amount of recreational activities for its homeowners. The property was originally developed by American Lakes Development, which is no longer in business. The first campsite was sold in 1970.

Purchase of a campsite at Woodhaven eliminates many of the problems associated with seasonal renting, time shares, and divided interest. You can personalize your campsite any way you like, within Woodhaven's rules and regulations. When you become a Woodhaven property owner, you don't need to call ahead for reservations; your campsite will be waiting for you just as you left it.

The use of Woodhaven campsites and facilities is restricted to Woodhaven property owners and their guests. Membership passes are issued when a campsite is purchased and renewed each year when assessments are paid. Security is tight. You must have a pass to enter Woodhaven.

Woodhaven Lakes is located in north central Illinois near Dixon (the hometown of former President Ronald Reagan) and just 40 miles from Rockford, Illinois. I-88 is 15 miles away, and Chicago is about two hours away by car. The nearest airport is located in Rockford. The area is patrolled by local, county, and state police, and a volunteer fire department is located nearby. The closest hospital with emergency care facilities is located in Mendota, 11 miles from the site.

Within the community you will find a grocery and liquor store, a restaurant, and retail shops. A pharmacy, a dry cleaners, and a hair salon are four miles away. The nearest medical clinic is 11 miles away, and the nearest movie theater is 22 miles from the campground. The surrounding rural communities (Sublette, Amboy, Dixon and Mendota) provide a chance to do some sightseeing as well as browse in the local shops for unique items and good bargains.

RECREATION AND SOCIAL ACTIVITIES

Woodhaven Lakes' 6,156 lots are divided into 29 sections scattered around the seven man-made lakes on 1,756 acres. The campground is open 365 days a year, 24 hours a day. A full-time recreation staff ensures that there are activities for all ages in all seasons.

There are two pools (and a children's pool as well as one lake) where swimming is allowed. Woodhaven features eight tennis courts, three baseball diamonds, horseshoe pits, and a vast trail system for hiking, cross-country skiing, and snow-mobiling. The seven lakes are available for fishing, including ice-fishing in the winter.

The association publishes a newsletter (weekly during the summer months) and provides organized trips and on-site entertainment. Saturday night bingo, dances, arts and crafts, tennis and golf tournaments, cross-country ski tours, hikes, and nature activities are just a sampling of the offerings. The association also sponsors special theme weekends throughout the year, such as winter carnival; spring fling, summer main event (which features a Civil War battle re-enactment), and fall festival. There are also special holiday activities at Woodhaven.

Many residents at Woodhaven also participate in clubs, including the CB club, the nature club, the Sno-Riders club, the bass club, the square dancing club, and the Travelers' club.

There is a 24-hour patrol and controlled access at perimeters. Anyone entering the development must have a valid I. D. pass. The passes are reissued yearly when community association assessments are paid in full. Ownership automatically entitles you to all recreational and social activities at Woodhaven Lakes.

HOMEOWNER ASSESSMENTS, TAXES AND UTILITIES

Campsites at Woodhaven Lakes start at $6,000. Currently, 6,000 of the 6,156 lots have been sold. Each owner pays a yearly community association assessment of $46. Property/municipal taxes on the land average $120 per year.

Tents, travel trailers, pop-up campers, and park model RVs are all permitted, so you can camp in any style you prefer, from roughing it in a tent to the luxuries of a park model home. Woodhaven provides 17 comfort stations, with toilet and shower facilities.

Woodhaven's full-time maintenance staff maintains over 35 miles of paved roads and all amenities. The association employs a full-time arborist and natural resource consultant who is responsible for the maintenance and landscaping of Woodhaven's common grounds. The association even provides many of its own plants and shrubs from a greenhouse on site.

Cable and community television channels are not available at Woodhaven. The primary heating source for the trailers and RVs is propane gas. The local municipality provides both sewer waste and water systems. There are no telephone lines to the individual campsites. All other utilities are underground. There are no extra storage facilities within the community.

RESTRICTIONS IN THE COMMUNITY

There is a community association at Woodhaven, and membership is mandatory. No permanent homes are allowed to be built. Individual homeowners provide maintenance for their own lot. The community association maintains all common roads, grounds, and amenities. Established guidelines govern any landscaping.

There are no restrictions on age for visitors, but there are restrictions on length-of-stay. Pets are allowed but must be leashed. There are no restrictions on how many people may occupy a site. Rentals of sites is strictly prohibited. Operating a business from a site is prohibited. Parking is allowed in the development except in designated areas. The association provides a special parking area for boats and other recreational vehicles.

TIPTON LAKES

235 Washington Street
Columbus, Indiana 47201-6741
812-378-3353

$65,000 to $550,000
407/2,000 Condos, Town-
houses, and Single-
family Homes
Mixed Architecture

Outdoor pool	3 lakes with 120 acres
100 acres of open space	48 private boat slips
3 lighted outdoor tennis courts	Racquetball courts
6 indoor tennis courts	Hiking trails
Clubhouse	Ball-playing fields
Exercise room	2 picnic areas

INTRODUCTION

Tipton Lakes' first unit was built in 1979. Currently, the community is about a quarter of the way toward its goal of 2,000 residential units and 5,000 people. Tipton Lakes, "a great place to live," is located in Columbus, Indiana, a remarkable city of 30,000 people. Columbus is the headquarters for two of the Fortune 500 companies and claims the greatest concentration of buildings by nationally known architects in any small town. A local philanthropic organization donated the architectural fees for 25 of the 50 major structures.

Columbus is within 45 miles of five of Indiana's state parks, including the Monroe State Reservoir, which offers 190 miles of shoreline, water sports, hiking, hunting, fishing, and a championship golf course. Indiana University's Bloomington campus is just 35 miles away. The Indy 500 and professional football, basketball, hockey, and baseball teams are 45 miles away, and Louisville's Kentucky Derby is less than a two-hour drive from the site.

Indianapolis, 45 miles away, has a population of 700,807 and provides the nearest air transportation. Police protection is provided by the Columbus city police, the Bartholomew County sheriff's department, and the Indiana state police. A full-time, staffed fire department is located within the community of Tipton Lakes, and there are four other firehouses in the Columbus area. Bartholomew County Hospital, the nearest facility with emergency care, is three miles from the site.

Tipton Lakes does not offer any services within its property. Within half a mile of the community, you will find a pharmacy, a dry cleaners, a hair salon, a grocery and liquor store, a restaurant, and retail shops. The nearest medical clinic is three miles from the site; the nearest movie theater is two miles away.

RECREATION AND SOCIAL ACTIVITIES

At Tipton Lakes, shopping, professional, and recreational facilities and employment opportunities are within a few minutes' walk or bicycle ride. Tipton Lakes also offers a wide variety of leisure and sports activities for its residents. Three private lakes (Northlake, Eastlake, and Westlake) are interconnected by two canals and comprise 120 acres of water and seven miles of shoreline. Swimming, fishing, boating, and sailing are permitted; but only small electric motors are allowed. The lakes are stocked with bass, bluegill, and catfish. Residents who do not own lakefront homes have access to the lakes at the marina, which has a boat ramp, docks, a beach and picnic area, and a volleyball court. Boat rentals are also available.

Tipton Lakes offers a carefully planned network of pedestrian, jogging, and bike paths. Two underpasses link the walkways, which feature scenic views of the woods, ravines, and lakes. Nature trails wind through the woods, allowing residents to see the native timber, flora, and fauna up close. Guided nature trail tours have been held several times in the past.

The four-acre Harrison Ridge Public Park contains two outdoor tennis courts, a basketball court, a children's playground, a tot lot, a handball wall, a playing field, a gazebo, and a picnic area.

Tipton Lakes' racquet club features six indoor air-conditioned tennis courts, four racquetball courts, Keiser exercise equipment, childcare facilities, aerobics, saunas, a pro shop, and a lounge area with a large screen TV. Tipton Lakes' racquet club offers many organized tennis and racquetball leagues and clinics. Tipton Lakes' racquet club is open on a membership basis to anyone in Columbus and Tipton Lakes. Initiation fees are $50 to $100 for individuals and $75 to $150 for families (depending on which membership plan is chosen). The initiation fee is waived for new Tipton Lake residents. There are monthly dues and court fees for tennis and racquetball.

In addition to the active Columbus art and theater scene, the Tipton Lakes community association sponsors a variety of picnics and parties. The Harrison Lake country club, with golf, swimming, and tennis, is about three miles away.

HOMEOWNER ASSESSMENTS, TAXES, AND UTILITIES

Tipton Lakes offers a wide variety of condos, townhouses, apartments, and single-family homes, situated in about twenty different clusters. Apartments with one to three bedrooms rent for $400 to $700 a month. Condos with two to three bedrooms sell from $65,000 to $117,000; lakefront units start at $180,000. The monthly assessments for the condominiums, which includes exterior building/grounds maintenance, is $100 to $156 per month.

Single-family homes, depending on size and location, may cost as low as $67,000 or as high as $550,000. Community association assessments for single-family units are $16 to $50 a month. Residents of apartments pay the basic $15 assessment to the community association.

Most of the single-family homes are custom built and have three to four bed-rooms. The lakefront condos feature numerous amenities, including lofts, fire-places, whirlpool tubs, vaulted ceilings, wet bars, over-sized garages, decks, screen porches, private beaches, and boat decks.

Cable television is available to all residents. Primary heating sources are gas and electricity. All utilities are underground. The community uses the municipal water and sewage facilities of Columbus. Columbus also furnishes police and fire protection, trash pickup, street maintenance, and lighting.

RESTRICTIONS IN THE COMMUNITY

The Tipton Lakes community association includes all homeowners and renters. The association is funded through general assessment fees of $15 per month. Services and amenities that are for a particular cluster are supported by separate assessments, varying from neighborhood to neighborhood.

Except for condominiums, apartments, and one neighborhood of fee-simple townhouses, individual homeowners provide their own exterior building and grounds maintenance. A new construction committee, appointed by the devel-oper, reviews new house plans; a modifications committee reviews plans for ex-isting structures. Landscape plans must be approved by the design review com-mittee. Landscaping is required within one year of home construction.

There are no restrictions on rental of properties except that you must notify the association of all leases. Local city regulations require a zoning variance to operate a business in the home. There are protective covenants concerning nox-ious or offensive activities. There are no resale restrictions other than notifying the association. The association forbids the parking of junked, disabled, or unreg-istered vehicles unless they are kept in a garage out of public view. Recreational vehicles, boats, and the like must also be housed within a permanent structure. There are several self-storage rental facilities in the Columbus area.

WOODBRIDGE HILLS

4200 W. Centre
Portage, Michigan 49002
616-323-8876

$60,000 to $225,000
480/1,200 Garden-style
Condos, Townhomes, and
Single-family Homes
Mixed Architecture

18-hole USGA-rated golf course
Cross-country skiing
Hiking trails
Ball-playing fields
Clubhouse

4 lakes
Over 100 acres of open space
Picnic areas
16 lighted outdoor tennis courts
Handball/racquetball

INTRODUCTION

Woodbridge Hills is a private planned community that revolves around the home-owners. The developers, Woodbridge Development Company, located amenities and recreational activities for homeowners within the community.

Construction began at the site in 1980. The community is located in the city of Portage, which borders Kalamazoo. About 40,000 people live in the Portage/Kalamazoo area. Woodbridge Hills is midway between Chicago and Detroit. I-94 is only a half mile from the site. The nearest airport, Battle Creek International in Kalamazoo, is about five miles from Woodbridge Hills. Police protection is provided by local, county, and state police. Both a staffed and a volunteer fire department are nearby. The closest hospital is about seven miles away.

Within the community you will find a pharmacy, a medical clinic, a dry cleaners, a grocery and liquor store, a restaurant, and retail shops. A movie theater is five miles from the site. Other local attractions include the Portage Bicentennial Park, the Portage bandshell, four colleges, and Wings Stadium.

RECREATION AND SOCIAL ACTIVITIES

Woodbridge Hills offers a vast array of recreational activities for its residents, including 18 championship holes of golf and swimming, health club, and racquetball facilities. Cross-country skiing is offered in the winter. There are hiking and bike trails within the site and a nature preserve near the community. Woodbridge Hills also contains eight indoor tennis courts and 16 illuminated outdoor courts.

The association does not employ a recreation director but does publish a monthly newsletter and provides organized on-site entertainment. Homeownership does not automatically include use of club and recreation facilities. Golf privileges cost between $500 and $1,500 per year. The on-site health club is operated by the YMCA. Future amenities include child daycare facilities.

HOMEOWNERS ASSESSMENTS, TAXES AND UTILITIES

At Woodbridge Hills, 480 homes have been sold; total build-out is expected to be between 1,000 and 1,200 homes. There are currently about a dozen completed homes that have not yet been sold. The 75 garden-style condominiums cost $60,000 to $80,000, with a monthly association assessment of $60 to $75 and annual property/municipal taxes of $2,500. The 125 townhomes cost between $75,000 and $110,000, with assessments between $80 and $90 per month. The 200 single-family homes at Woodbridge Hills range in price from $150,000 to $225,000, with monthly association assessments of $12 and property taxes between $4,000 and $6,000 per year.

Woodbridge hills has 13 single-family home models and several townhome models to choose from. Most of the homes feature two-car garages, breakfast nooks, walk-in closets, and gourmet kitchens. Currently, there are 75 one-bedroom homes, 100 two-bedroom homes, 100 three-bedroom homes, 100 four-bedroom homes, and 75 homes with more than four bedrooms.

Both cable and community television channels are available. Homes are heated by either gas or electricity. The local municipality provides both sewer waste disposal and water systems. All utilities are underground. There are no extra storage facilities within the community.

RESTRICTIONS IN THE COMMUNITY

Woodbridge Hills has a community association, and membership is mandatory. The community association provides exterior building/grounds maintenance for the condominium and townhome owners, as well as all common areas. Single-family homeowners provide their own exterior building/grounds maintenance. Any exterior modifications must be approved by the architectural control committee.

There are no age or length-of-stay restrictions for visitors. Pets are allowed but must not weigh more than 40 pounds. There are restrictions on how many people can occupy a single unit, as well as restrictions concerning the rental of units. Operating a business from a home is prohibited. Resale restrictions are in effect. There are no special parking areas within the community for recreational vehicles or boats.

COMMUNITIES OF FOUR SEASONS

Four Seasons Lakesites, Inc.
260 Linn Creek Road
Four Seasons, Missouri 65049
314-365-6628

$90,000 to $1,500,000
843/4,100 Garden and Mid-rise Condos, Townhouses, and Single-family Homes
Contemporary Architecture

Robert Trent Jones golf course
Ken Kavanaugh golf course
Executive 9-hole course
14 outdoor pools
2 indoor pools
Hiking trails
Clubhouse
7 restaurants

19 tennis courts (indoor, clay)
Racquetball courts
Stables
400 boat slips
1 large public lake, 3 small lakes
Picnic areas
Exercise room
Sauna/massage

INTRODUCTION

The Communities of Four Seasons offers just one thing: "a magnificent nautical sporting relaxing well-seasoned resort." Located on the wooded shores of the Lake of the Ozarks, it is roughly halfway between St. Louis and Kansas City and just 40 miles away from Jefferson City, the capital of Missouri. U.S. highway 54 practically abuts the property, connecting with Interstates 44 and 70. The Communities of Four Seasons, accessible to the entire Midwest, has had over 25 years of popular success in resort entertainment.

St. Louis provides the nearest major airport and is 150 miles from the site. Local, county, and state authorities provide police protection. Thirty-five volunteers and two staff officers provide fire protection. The Lake of the Ozarks' General Hospital Trauma Center, ten miles from the site, provides emergency medical care.

Many services are located within Four Seasons: a dry cleaners, a hair salon, a grocery and liquor store, a restaurant, retail shops, and a movie theater. A pharmacy is seven miles away; the nearest medical clinic is five miles away.

Other local attractions include a water park, two state parks with camp sites and historical buildings, a county museum, an exhibition hall, and three convention hotel/resorts.

RECREATION AND SOCIAL ACTIVITIES

Four Seasons covers over 3,200 acres and fronts 72 miles of shoreline of the Lake of the Ozarks. The community offers outdoor activities such as golf, tennis, boating, fishing, swimming, riding, and hiking. Indoor facilities include four tennis courts, two pools, racquetball courts, an exercise room, saunas, and massage rooms. Dining and nighttime entertainment is available in the Fifth Seasons Lounge.

Chartered yachts are available for exploring the lake, and the Seasons' Queen can take you on a sightseeing cruise on the picturesque and historical lake. The marina offers complete boat maintenance and over 400 slips for boats up to 50 feet long. Rental powerboats and sailboats are also available.

The Robert Trent Jones Championship Golf Course was rated by *USA Today* as one of the nation's top ten resort courses. The Ken Kavanaugh course features a spring-fed lake on its 137-acre tract. Other courses, outdoor driving ranges, and a complete pro shop allow the entire family to enjoy golf at any level.

The Lodge's Racquet Club was rated by *Tennis Magazine* as one of the "50 greatest tennis resorts." In addition to 16 indoor and outdoor courts, there is a tennis stadium. The Dennis Van der Meer Tennis University features instruction for all skill levels. The Racquet club also offers the Executive Health Education Laboratory which can evaluate your health status and recommend programs to prevent future problems.

The community also provides hundreds of acres of open space, wilderness hiking, skeet shooting, fishing, riding, 16 swimming pools, and aerobic classes.

The Communities of Four Seasons has a full-time social director who supervises organized trips, on-site entertainment, on-site crafts, activities for teens, newsletters, and even valet and concierge service. All property owners have privileges at the private golf, racquet, and health clubs; use may be on a daily, weekly, or annual basis. Current annual family memberships cost $1,000 for golf alone or $1,250 for golf, tennis, and health.

HOMEOWNER ASSESSMENTS, TAXES, AND UTILITIES

Racquet Club mid-rise condos range from $90,000 to $150,000 for full-time ownership; timeshares are from $5,000 to $15,000 per week. Garden condos are in the same $90,000 to $150,000 range; timeshares are $10,000 per week. The full-time units carry a $168 to $207 monthly community association assessment and the timeshares have $66 to $187 weekly assessments.

Townhouses in the Treetop village cost up to $275,000 with a monthly community association assessment up to $170 per month. The majority of homes are single-family residences with a price range of $90,000 to $1.5 million. The monthly community association assessment is $31 and the owner is responsible for exterior building and grounds maintenance. So far, 548 homes have been sold. Most of the condo and townhouse units have three bedrooms; there are a few two-bedroom and one-bedroom units.

Cable television is available for all units. The primary heat is provided by electricity and all wires are underground. The condo project has a central municipal sewer system. The single-family units have aerated waste treatment systems at each homesite. Well water is provided by a private water utility. There are extra storage facilities available within the community.

RESTRICTIONS IN THE COMMUNITY

All owners are members of the community association. A design review committee must approve any condo changes, and an architectical control committee meets twice monthly to consider single-family home designs, renovations, or landscaping plans.

There are no age, children, or visitor restrictions. No pets are allowed in the timeshare units, and all single-family homeowners' pets must be on a leash when outside. Timeshare units have stated occupancy limits. There are no restrictions on renting full-time units.

No businesses are permitted to be operated in the residences. Condo and timeshare units are only allotted two parking spaces per unit. The association provides a special parking area for recreational vehicles. There are right of first refusal restrictions on the resale of condo units. Guards at the perimeter entrances and frequent patrols in the community augment the local police and fire coverage. Four Seasons strictly enforces restrictions to protect property values.

LAKE SHERWOOD ESTATES

P.O. Box 1085
Lake Sherwood, Missouri
63357
314-828-5777

$40,000 to $160,000
225/1,300 Single-family
Homes and Lots
Mixed Architecture

2 outdoor pools
Boating, sailing, skiing
64 boat slips, marina
2 outdoor lighted tennis courts

190-acre lake with 7 miles of shore
Wooded island with sand beach
Hiking trails, picnic areas
On-site campground

INTRODUCTION

Lake Sherwood Estates is one of the most outstanding year-round residential lake developments in the Midwest. This 1,200-acre community is designed to be a weekend hideaway, a permanent home, or a special place to enjoy your retirement. When you purchase a homesite, you can begin to build now, or you can plan to build later and still make full use of the lakes, woods, and recreational facilities. This private master planned community was carefully planned to create a forest park environment that is wholly separate from the workaday world.

Located 35 minutes from Chesterfield and Mid-Rivers Mall and just 20 minutes from Washington and Wentzville, Lake Sherwood is close enough for commuting. St. Louis is just 40 miles away. Interstate 70, the nearest major highway, is eight miles from the development. Lambert Field, 30 miles from the site, provides air transportation.

Police protection is provided by the Warren County sheriff's department; there is also on-site security. The community has guarded gates and a 24-hour patrol. There is a volunteer fire department within Lake Sherwood. Washington Hospital, the nearest center with emergency care, is 12 miles from the site.

There are no services offered within the community, but all needed services are within ten miles. A grocery store and a liquor store are two miles away; a hair salon and a restaurant are within five miles. Ten miles from the site you will find a pharmacy, a medical clinic, a dry cleaners, retail shops, and a movie theater. Area attractions include the St. Louis Zoo, the Mississippi River, the Arch, art museums, breweries, and the Six Flags theme park.

RECREATION AND SOCIAL ACTIVITIES

Life at Lake Sherwood centers around water activities. The 190-acre deep-water lake, with its seven miles of scenic wooded shoreline, provides hours of boating, sailing, waterskiing, and fishing. There are also five smaller spring-fed, stocked lakes. Launching ramps, docks, 64 boat slips, and dry boat storage racks are located at the association's marina area. A unique feature of the main lake is the little wooded island with a sandy beach.

Within the development there is a campground with electrical hookups, showers, and restrooms. Lake Sherwood has several picnic areas and park facilities.

Two illuminated outdoor tennis courts, two swimming pools, and a clubhouse are also available.

The association's active social network sponsors many holiday events (Easter egg hunts, Christmas parties, and so on.) as well as organized activities for its youth, including baseball and teeball. The association also sponsors an adult softball team. Active committees in the community include youth, architectural review, parks and recreation, lakes and dam, clubhouse, security, and roads.

Homeownership at Lake Sherwood automatically entitles you to participate in all of the recreational facilities, but there are some user fees for some activities.

HOMEOWNER ASSESSMENTS, TAXES, AND UTILITIES

Lake Sherwood Estates consists of 2,300 wooded lots overlooking the lake, with far-ranging vistas of forest and countryside. To date, 1,300 lots have been sold. As of January 1991, 225 single-family homes had been built. These homes range in price from $40,000 to $160,000. Lots can cost up to $16,000. All lot owners pay yearly assessments of $360. Undeveloped lot owners pay from $40 to $60 per year in property taxes.

The association employs a full-time executive manager and office and maintenance staff. The 1991 total operating and capital budget is $742,089. Assessment income for 1991 is estimated at $600,000. Income from user fees, rentals, snack bar, and the like is estimated at $142,000 for 1991.

Owners may choose any builder they wish to construct their home. Although there is a mix of architecture within the community, there are also strict building guidelines enforced by the association.

The association owns the central water and sewer systems in the community. All lots have access to electrical and telephone hookups. Heat is provided by both gas and electric sources. Utilities are both above and below ground. There are no extra storage facilities within Lake Sherwood.

RESTRICTIONS IN THE COMMUNITY

Individual homeowners are responsible for their own building and grounds maintenance within this single-family community. The association handles all of the common area maintenance tasks. All building or renovating must have prior approval from the architectural control committee. All landscaping installations must be neatly maintained by the owner.

There are no restrictions on age or length-of-stay for visitors. Pets are allowed but must be leashed when off the owner's property. Lake Sherwood does not have any regulations limiting occupancy in a home, nor are there any rental restrictions. Businesses are not allowed to operate from a home. There are no restrictions on the resale of units. Vehicles may not be parked in one place longer than five days. The association provides a special area to park boats.

Index